CHILD DEVELOPMENT

Social Work Practice with Children and Families
Nancy Boyd Webb, Series Editor

Child Development

A PRACTITIONER'S GUIDE

DOUGLAS DAVIES

Foreword by Nancy Boyd Webb

THE GUILFORD PRESS
New York   London

©1999 The Guilford Press
A Division of Guilford Publications, Inc.
72 Spring Street, New York, NY 10012
http://www.guilford.com

Printed in the United States of America.

This book is printed on acid-free paper.

Last digit is print number: 9 8 7 6 5 4 3 2 1

Library of Congress Cataloging-in-Publication Data

Davies, Douglas, 1942–
   Child development : a practitioner's guide / Douglas Davies.
      p.   cm. — (Social work practice with children and families)
   Includes bibliographical references and index.
   ISBN 1-57230-429-4
   1. Social work with children. 2. Child development   I. Title.
II. Series.
   HV713 .D395   1999
   362.7—dc21

                                                    98-43264
                                                    CIP

For my family—Tobi,
Justin and Laurel,
Aaron, Elizabeth, Hannah, and Hayden

In memory of Ian

About the Author

DOUGLAS DAVIES, MSW, PHD, is Clinical/Practice Associate Professor at the School of Social Work and Lecturer in Psychiatry at the Medical School, The University of Michigan, Ann Arbor. He is an infant mental health specialist, and has published several articles on intervention with young children and their families. In his practice, he works with children and families, supervises clinicians, and offers consultation to mental health agencies and child care centers. He frequently presents professional workshops on practice with infants and toddlers, play therapy, treatment of child witnesses of domestic violence, and developmental approaches to child therapy.

Acknowledgments

There are many people to thank for their help on this project, and many others who have indirectly contributed to this book because of what I have learned from them. I am grateful to my child clients and their parents, who have taught me about the realities of child development during 20 years of practice. Nearly all the cases presented in this book are composites based on more than one client. To preserve confidentiality I have also altered all information which might identify individuals.

During my early years of practice I was fortunate to have many wise supervisors and mentors from the Child Development Project and the Child and Adolescent Psychiatry Service at The University of Michigan. They include John Bennett, Jr., Jeree Pawl, Rebecca Lohr, Morton Chethik, Elinor Rosenberg, Jack Novick, Tom Horner, and Peter Blos, Jr.

My students at The University of Michigan School of Social Work have enthusiastically supported teaching that integrates developmental knowledge and practice realities. Their positive response to my teaching during the last 10 years has encouraged the formation of the approach I have taken in this book. One former student, Jane Bornstein, read the chapter on practice with infants and raised several questions which helped me improve it.

Two of my colleagues at the School of Social Work, Sallie Foley and Laura Nitzberg, read the manuscript and offered helpful suggestions. Sallie used the manuscript as the basis for part of a course and provided a teacher's perspective on how to make the book useful in social work education. Laura and Sallie, my co-teachers in the Post Graduate Social Work Seminar at The University of Michigan Medical Center, have been wonderful colleagues and good friends.

The staff at The Guilford Press was uniformly professional and supportive of this project. I want to give special thanks to my editor at Guilford, Rochelle Serwator, who gave the completed manuscript an astute and sensitive reading. Rochelle has a gift for sympathetically understanding what a writer is saying and then helping him or her say it in a clearer and more complete way. Jeannie Tang, Senior Production Editor, and Bert Zelman, Copyeditor (of Publishers Workshop, Inc.), provided meticulous help in the final stages of production.

Nancy Boyd Webb, the Series Editor, asked me to write this book, conveyed her faith that I would be able to do it, and then provided valuable feedback on each chapter and on the book's organization. I thank her for her intellectual acumen and her personal kindness in shepherding this project to completion.

My wife Tobi found time in her intense work schedule to read every word, functioning as an in-home editor, as well as a base of loving support. Her suggestions helped make my writing clearer, and her frequent injunctions to "tell a story about this" encouraged me to include many examples of words and behavior of real children to illustrate developmental concepts. My son Justin, a preschool teacher, read the chapters on infants, toddlers, and preschoolers. I knew I was on track when he said my descriptions of young children matched the behavior of children he saw every day. My son Aaron and daughter-in-law Elizabeth helped keep me writing through their consistent interest and emotional support during our weekly dinners together.

A portion of Chapter 3 is adapted from Blos and Davies (1993) (copyright 1993 by Zero to Three/National Center for Clinical Infant Programs; adapted by permission). I am very grateful to Dr. Blos for granting us permission to adapt our collaborative work, for his helpful comments on the chapter, and for his valuable supervision and consultation on my clinical work. The case in Chapter 9 is substantially based on Davies (1992) (copyright 1992 by Plenum Publishing Corporation; adapted by permission). I am grateful for permission to quote in Chapter 6 two passages from Nelson (1989) (copyright 1989 by Harvard University Press; reprinted by permission of Harvard University Press), and to adapt in Chapter 2 a figure from Bowlby (1988) (copyright 1988 by Basic Books; adapted by permission).

Throughout this project I have had the loving encouragement of my family, and this book is dedicated to them with much love. I would like to make special mention of my grandchildren: Ian, who died shortly after birth last year, and Hayden and Hannah, born 3 weeks ago and doing well. I lovingly remember Ian for the brief time he was with us, and look forward to watching Hannah and Hayden grow and develop.

Foreword

In planning the series Social Work Practice with Children and Families, I wanted to include a book about child development to provide a foundation for practitioners who work with children. *Child Development: A Practitioner's Guide* by Douglas Davies has exceeded my hopes. It conveys complex theoretical information about children's growth and development through practice examples that illustrate how children's everyday experiences can help or hinder them. Not only does the book offer a solid portrayal of child development from birth until preadolescence, it also skillfully and wisely presents the influence of family and the wider world as vital contributors to the child's ever-changing adaptation.

Davies's many detailed case examples demonstrate the interdependence of nature and nurture in children's development. The chapters are organized to alternate between extensive reviews of normal development followed by in-depth practice illustrations with children whose development has veered off course. The book demonstrates the value of a transactional and ecological perspective through emphasis on the intricate balance between the child, the caretaker, and the wider environment.

Highlighting the preventive value of early intervention, this book clearly outlines what children need for their optimal development. Each case example takes the reader through the assessment and intervention process step by step. Beginning with the point of view that the child is poised for ongoing developmental change, Davies illustrates how to intervene in a way that recognizes the child's needs and facilitates the child's natural "self-righting tendencies." The book is an admirable example of the strengths perspective applied to children.

I am confident that students, faculty, and practitioners alike will welcome having a resource such as this book as a reference and a guide. We can consult the detailed appendices of expected developmental milestones and can balance our understanding of these with the equally valuable appendices of risk and resiliency factors in childhood. Readers of this book will learn about the many mediating influences on children in formulating an assessment, as well as about the numerous potential resources in the child's social environment in planning helping interventions.

NANCY BOYD WEBB, DSW
Distinguished Professor of Social Work,
Fordham University
New York, New York

Preface

This book describes child development and how it can be applied to practice with children. Beginning practitioners often feel intrigued and perplexed by the behavior of children and wonder what is "normal." Developmental knowledge provides a framework for assessing where a child falls within normal expectations and where she or he does not. Any given piece of behavior can be normal, mildly abnormal, or reflective of serious problems, depending on its developmental timing. It is normal and typical, for example, for a 4-year-old to believe in monsters and ghosts, at least at bedtime, while the same beliefs in a 10-year-old are often indicators of generalized or trauma-based anxiety and impairments in reality testing. By demonstrating the value of a developmental framework, I intend to make the book as useful as possible to practitioners working with children.

Knowledge of the abilities and developmental tasks that are typical of children of a given age can inform our clinical work and casework in powerful ways. Knowing what developmental tasks the child is currently struggling with helps us empathize with the child's sense of reality, allowing us to enter the child's world, as opposed to merely seeing him or her as a bundle of symptoms. Knowing where a child is functioning developmentally, especially in the area of the presenting symptoms, helps us define what skills and capacities to target in our treatment plans. Knowing what skills and capacities will soon be appearing as a result of development helps us plan interventions that utilize and support these emerging abilities. Knowing how children at a particular developmental level represent themselves—through behavior, play, or words—informs us about how to communicate with them and helps us plan treatment activities, using appropriate materials. Knowing what a child *cannot* do because she or he has not reached a particular developmental level creates realistic expectations about the goals of treatment, and allows us to communicate the child's developmental realities to parents. Finally, knowing the next steps in development helps us evaluate the effects of intervention, going beyond the goal of decreasing symptoms, and adding positive developmental progress as a normal measure of change.

Developmental knowledge also provides us with a lens for reviewing a child's history. To understand how earlier experiences have influenced the child's development and contributed to current problems we need to know the child's strengths and limitations for handling stress and trauma at a given age, and how, as a result, the child may have responded internally to past trauma and stress. For example, we interview the mother of a depressed 6-year-old boy and find out that his father abandoned the family when the child was 3. Drawing on our knowledge of development we recall that 3-year-olds are still egocentric and have magical views of cause and effect, which means that they see themselves as the center of the world and believe that their thoughts and behavior can cause things to happen. This leads to a question that can be pursued in the evaluation: to what extent does the child's depression reflect guilt and self-blame based on a belief that his father left because of something he did? A knowledge of development does not automatically provide answers, but it helps the practitioner decide what lines of inquiry will be most fruitful to understand the relationships between a child's past and present realities.

PLAN OF THE BOOK

Part I introduces the idea that the child's development is the outcome of transactions between innate maturational processes and the child's environment. I begin with a brief discussion of the transactional model of development. This is followed by chapters describing attachment and relationships with parents and risk and protective factors as contexts that influence the course of development. The application of these concepts is illustrated with examples from practice.

Part II presents information about the course of child development. Chapters 4, 6, and 10 cover infancy, toddlerhood, the preschool period, and middle childhood, respectively, including salient facts, tasks, and processes in development from birth to age 11. In addition to presenting information from the research literature, I will also provide frequent vignettes of observations of children in their "natural"

settings—home, child care center, school, playground, neighborhood—
as well as in practice settings.

Each of these informational chapters is followed by a practice
chapter (Chapters 5, 7, 9, and 11) which presents ways of applying theoretical and factual information about development. These chapters
illustrate how each period in development has special issues and characteristics that must shape our practice so that we can respond help-
fully to our child clients and their parents. Each period provides
opportunities and limitations that must guide our work. For example,
we will not get far by trying to *talk* about worries with a 4- year-old.
But the 4-year-old's imaginative play often provides us with a drama-
tized account of what worries her. Since the best way to make developmental concepts real is to observe children at different developmental
levels, I will suggest observational exercises at the end of each practice
chapter. My aim throughout will be to demonstrate how to think
developmentally in practice with children and their parents.

DOUGLAS DAVIES

Contents

❖ PART I ❖

Contexts of Development: A Transactional Approach

Introduction:
Perspectives on Development

Development is the outcome of transactions between the child and her environment. This simple-sounding idea encompasses a complex and dynamic reality. I will briefly introduce some perspectives that help us think about how transactions between the individual child and her multiple relationships and contexts influence development. In Part I, Chapters 1–3 will present in some depth the impact of attachment and risk and protective factors as transactional contexts of development.

THE MATURATIONAL PERSPECTIVE

Starting at the individual level, development is founded on the child's innate characteristics, unfolds according to maturational time tables, and moves forward through a series of tasks and challenges of increasing complexity which the child must master in order to extend her ability to function within herself and within her environment (A. Freud, 1963; Gesell & Armatruda, 1947; Kagan, 1984). From a maturational point of view, the course of development seems inevitable. As the result of the growth of the brain and body systems, new abilities and higher level capacities for organizing experience emerge across time (Greenspan, 1979; Kagan, 1984). For example, between ages $1\frac{1}{2}$ and $2\frac{1}{2}$, children become capable of rapid language learning as the result of brain maturation (Kagan, 1981). A 6-month-old cannot yet speak words, let alone sentences, because the cognitive systems underlying language are not yet fully developed. Similarly, even a 2-year-old who is very precocious in language does not "get" jokes or understand

3

metaphors because the cognitive abilities required to understand wordplay do not develop until the elementary school years. As the result of maturation, then, a child has very different capacities for action and for understanding the world at ages 2 and 8. Maturational factors determine that any 8-year-old will be much more like other 8-year-olds than like a 2-year-old. Nevertheless, within a group of 8-year-olds, there may be important differences among individual children. Some 8-year-olds will be able to use their social and cognitive abilities more adaptively than others. These differences result from how developmental capacities have been shaped in the history of the child's transactions with multiple environmental contexts.

THE TRANSACTIONAL MODEL OF DEVELOPMENT

From the beginning, the child's transactions with immediate and wider environments influence development. The transactional model suggests that development results from "the interplay between child and context across time, in which the state of one affects the next state of the other in a continuous dynamic process" (Sameroff, 1993, p. 6). Recent research, for example, has begun to map transactional processes influencing brain development during the first year of life, demonstrating that physical touching, social interaction, and sensory stimulation promote physical brain growth and increase brain functions (Diamond, 1991; Greenspan, 1997). Thus, even a process that seems a biological given turns out to be transactional. As development proceeds, quality of parenting, opportunities and stressors in the child's and parents' lives, social circumstances, social institutions, culture, and historical events are all part of a widening circle of influence on who the individual child becomes (Sameroff & Chandler, 1975). The younger the child, the more the child's transactions with the environment are mediated through the quality of parenting, which is influenced by the parents' relationship and their individual characteristics, circumstances, and histories. During the early years parents are the conduits through which cultural values shape the child's developmental possibilities.

The transactional model also recognizes that the child, from the beginning, works to organize her experience. Rather than being seen as a passive container into which experience is poured, "The child actively creates his or her own environment, increasingly so with advancing development" (Sroufe, 1990, p. 339). Interactions between caregiver and child are "bidirectional." Infants and young children respond to adult behavior that is directed toward them, and adult responses are shaped by the child's actions as well as by the child's particular characteristics. In turn, the parent's ability to respond adaptively to the child's unfolding development is influenced by immediate circumstantial and more distant social factors that support, or alternatively create stress on, the parent. Consistent with family systems theory, the transactional model points out that changes in either the child or the parent can change their relationship and thus influence the course of development (Sameroff & Chandler, 1975; Wachtel & Wachtel, 1986).

Even though the course of development can be described in a linear format of "ages and stages," the transactional perspective helps us understand that the "causes" of *specific developmental outcomes* are bidirectional and circular. A toddler whose mother has a miscarriage and becomes depressed senses the mother's change in affect and responsiveness. The child may respond to her mother's emotional distress in typical toddler fashion through outbursts of anger or clamoring for attention. The toddler's behavior may cause the parents to realize that she is feeling insecure. They take steps to help her feel loved. They empathize with her feelings and provide explanations and reassurances. Alternatively, a stressed, grieving parent becomes angry at the toddler's obnoxious and demanding behavior, punishing her by yelling and spanking. Clearly, these different responses by the parents will influence development and the ongoing transactional context of development in different ways. The parents who rally to the toddler's distressed behavior not only help restore feelings of security in the short run but also present an experiential message to the child that they can be relied upon when she is distressed. Such experiences increase the child's optimism that problems are solvable. By contrast, the interaction of an angry toddler and punitive parents may establish a transactional context characterized by ongoing mutual anger and failure to resolve problems. In this case, the toddler may adopt a pattern of oppositionalism and mistrustfulness that interferes with future developmental tasks of learning to play cooperatively with peers or negotiate to solve problems.

MUTUAL ADAPTATION AS A TRANSACTIONAL PROCESS

The constant unfolding of new developmental tasks requires continuing adaptation by both child and parents. Parents in particular must make adjustments in the ways they respond to the child. The child who is beginning to walk is challenged by frustration and anxiety when he falls constantly. These negative affects need to be mastered.

Parents may provide extra encouragement and emotional support during this period of physical and emotional challenge, which not only helps the child persist in developing motor skills but also creates a climate of support that engenders self-confidence. When the child has mastered walking, new adaptations are demanded of the parents, which include being more watchful of the child or setting up barriers that limit where he can go, since now, as a walker, he can cover more ground in a shorter time.

Mutual adaptation to developmental change is a normal process for children and parents throughout development. However, when other stressors are added to the normal stress of transitional periods in development, adaptation becomes more difficult. For example, if a parent suffers a serious illness requiring extended hospitalization, a 5-year-old child may have more trouble adapting to the demands of the new task of entering school and functioning more autonomously. The parent is less available to support the child's autonomous functioning, and the child may be too anxious about the parent's illness to concentrate on new challenges to development. When such stressful or traumatic events occur, the demands on parents become greater. When parents and child are stretched beyond their adaptive capacities, the child may develop symptoms, which over time lead to maladaptive outcomes that threaten development (Emde & Sameroff, 1989).

THE ECOLOGICAL MODEL OF DEVELOPMENT

As the child grows older and enters the wider world outside the family, she encounters peers, schools and other social institutions, and the mass media and other aspects of society, all of which influence her development. Her parents and other caregivers must increasingly mediate the child's interactions with the wider world. Bronfenbrenner's ecological perspective captures the increasing complexity of the child's transactions with the environment.

Bronfenbrenner (1979) conceptualizes the child's experience as widening circle of transactions that mutually influence each other. At the center is the child interacting with others in his immediate environments, such as home, child care center, or school. These direct interactions with parents, caregivers, teachers, and peers shape the child's subjective experience of himself and others, and define roles, possibilities, and values available in his culture. Throughout development, children move further out in the circle, into child care settings, schools, sports teams, and in some cases blended families following parental divorce or foster homes following removal for abuse or neglect. The quality of links between family and these wider environments influences development. Strong links support development by providing a sense of continuity for the child. For example, good communication between parents and day care providers helps both respond appropriately to the child's developmental needs. The child feels more secure because he senses that the adults in his life know each other and communicate about him. By contrast, the stress and disorientation a child experiences after being removed from his biological family and placed in foster care can be exacerbated if the foster care worker, foster parent and biological parents fail to communicate about the child's welfare.

Farther out in the circle are institutions and environments with which the child does not directly interact but influence her development indirectly. For example, the parent's work setting may influence quality of parenting. The mother who is paid well and likes her job feels successful, and her positive attitude influences her feelings about her child; by contrast, poor working conditions or extended unemployment lessen a parent's sense of self-esteem and competence and may lead to negative behavior toward her child (McLoyd, 1989). Community institutions, such as the school district administration or city government, make decisions that influence the child's and family's life. If the school administration successfully convinces voters to increase school funding, classroom size can be reduced and activities that enrich learning can be increased. On the other hand, developmental risk for some children may increase if the school board lays off teachers and increases class size dramatically.

The ecology of development also includes broader forces: social and economic conditions, national and state government policies or laws, and cultural practices and values. Changes at this broad level—new welfare laws, an economic recession or a reorganization of the global economy—may reverberate through the lives of families and influence children's development. For example, a father who loses his industrial job when his company relocates to Mexico takes two lower-paying temporary jobs to survive financially; consequently, he has less time to spend with his family and the stress of economic uncertainty makes him less psychologically available to his children.

Bronfenbrenner's ecological perspective helps us appreciate the complexity of the transactions that influence the development of the individual child. He points out that responses to stressors or life transitions by the child, his family, and his immediate environments constantly influence developmental outcomes.

For example, a father is concerned that his child, who is temperamentally shy and "slow to warm up," may be overwhelmed by entry
into school. So he talks to other parents and the school principal, and
observes in two kindergarten classes, in order to find the teacher
who will be a good match for his child. The child is enrolled in a
supportive teacher's classroom. During the early weeks, he shows
anxiety about separation from parents and about joining in group
activities, but the teacher is aware of this and helps him establish
relationships with other children. At the same time, she communicates with his parents about his progress in an encouraging way. This
reduces their anxiety and allows them to encourage their child to try
new activities at school, as opposed to undermining his confidence,
as could occur if they felt the teacher did not understand his particular characteristics. Over the course of the year, the child becomes
comfortable at school and begins to internalize a belief that he is a
competent student who is capable of finding his way in an environment outside home. This good experience contributes to a positive
attitude about school in the future, which in turn influences his ability to take advantage of learning opportunities that further the development of cognitive skills and positive sense of self.

DEVELOPMENTAL PATHWAYS

The preceding example of the interaction of child, parent, and school is
also an example of John Bowlby's (1973) useful concept of "developmental pathways." Bowlby stated that the individual's transactions
with the environment create alternative paths that development proceeds along. At critical points, determined by periods of developmental change or by external influences, such as trauma or increased
opportunity, junctions appear and the child may move off the path she
was traveling and onto a different path. At these junctures, the child
may proceed in adaptive or maladaptive directions. A 2-year-old
whose parent develops a severe substance abuse problem may suffer
neglect and as a result move to a maladaptive pathway characterized
by precocious self-reliance and mistrust of relationships. By contrast, a
7-year-old who transfers from an underfunded and poorly equipped
school to a school rich in resources—at a developmental point where
new cognitive advances increase her motivation to learn—may move
to a more adaptive pathway.

How and whether development may be affected by increased risk
or opportunity depends on the timing of external factors in relation to
current developmental tasks. Developmental capacities that are currently emerging or have very recently been achieved are most vulnera-

ble to disruption by stressors. Capacities that have long ago been consolidated are less susceptible to disruption, although under conditions of severe stress these may also be affected.

For example, the toddler mentioned earlier, who was unexpectedly separated from her mother when her mother was hospitalized because of a miscarriage, developed symptoms that reflected disturbances in the particular developmental tasks of toddlers, including language acquisition, developing autonomous control of body functions, and practicing independence and mastering separation (Lieberman, 1993). She was in a period of rapid language learning and practicing, and she stopped talking. Prior to her mother's miscarriage she had begun to be interested in toilet training. She stopped using the potty. She was attempting to master anxiety about separation as a normative developmental issue. In the face of a real separation overlaid by an atmosphere of emotional separation caused by her parents' grief, her behavior became preoccupied with strategies for controlling separation, including repetitive symbolic play on separation themes, waking and crying for her parents at night, alternately being demanding and rejecting of her mother, and trying to be self-reliant. A short-term intervention helped this child and her parents master these symptoms of developmental interference.

However, even without intervention it is possible for mutual adaptation to change the course of development in a positive direction. New capacities emerge in the child that create improved adaptations. For many possible reasons, parents may become more effective facilitators of development during a new phase of development than they were in a previous one. Stressors and risk factors may be reduced. In result, the child's development may move away from "disordered" and toward an adaptive pathway.

Although the direction of development can change—and be influenced to change—at each stage, change is nevertheless somewhat limited by the pathways already taken. There is less flexibility for change as development proceeds. A child who has already traversed a long series of adaptive paths is not likely to be easily shifted to a maladaptive path. But similarly, the more maladaptive paths a child has traveled, the more difficult it will be to shift to a more adaptive one if the opportunity arises. As Sroufe (1990) points out, "change . . . is constrained by prior adaptation" (p. 336). This model creates a strong argument for early intervention as a means of shifting development in positive directions before the path into potential psychopathology is set.

Especially when thinking about children it is important to recognize that many "diagnoses" or "syndromes" represent conditions that are malleable rather than fixed (Bowlby, 1988). It is certainly possible for reactive problems in the child, combined with maladaptive responses by the parents, to evolve into "pathology" via the establishment of maladaptive behaviors and defenses as fixed ways of initiating and processing experience. However, children are also flexible and responsive to positive environmental change. Practitioners who work with children frequently sense in their young clients a strong urge to master problems and to move ahead in development. This is consistent with Campbell's (1990) argument that "strong, biologically based self-righting tendencies are assumed to be present in all but the most severely damaged infants; that is, movement is inherently toward normal development" (p. 10). While tasks that are currently being mastered are most subject to disruption, it is nevertheless likely that "self-righting tendencies" will be strongly engaged with those tasks, since they are also most pressing for the child. Finding ways to support the "self-righting tendency" is a primary goal of intervention based on a transactional perspective.

DEVELOPMENTAL PERSPECTIVES AND SOCIAL WORK PRACTICE

Effective practice with children is best informed by a transactional–ecological perspective, which acknowledges that the path of development is regularly influenced by maturational changes within the child, by the parents' responses to those changes, by external circumstances, by institutional or cultural changes that indirectly affect child and family, and by the child's reactions to all these changes. Bowlby (1988) pointed out that a child proceeding down a maladaptive or "deviant" pathway could return to the main adaptive pathway if positive influences were strengthened: "the course of subsequent development is not fixed, [and] changes in the way a child is treated can shift his pathway in either a more favourable or less favourable one. . . . It is this persisting potential for change that gives opportunity for effective therapy" (p. 136).

"Empowerment" and "building on strengths" are tenets of contemporary intervention approaches, especially in social work (Meyer, 1993). Translated into developmental terms, this means devising intervention plans that take full advantage of the self-righting tendency and of the child's developmental accomplishments, capacities, and proclivities; at the same time, a transactional approach to assessment and intervention looks for ways to help parents respond adaptively to a child's difficulties, to reduce environmental risks, and to increase opportunities for adaptive development.

Chapters 1, 2, and 3 expand the discussion of transactional contexts of development. Chapter 1 describes how the attachment relationship between parent and child influences the child's adaptations as development proceeds. Chapter 2 amplifies the ecological perspective through a discussion of risk and protective factors that influence developmental outcomes, while Chapter 3 discusses the use of an analysis of risk and protective factors in practice.

❖ CHAPTER 1 ❖

Attachment as a Context of Development

This chapter describes how the early parent–child relationship mediates and influences the course of development. Although parenting is not the only influence on development, it is a critically important one. Attachment theory provides the most useful perspective on early parent–child interactions. John Bowlby formulated attachment theory, and other researchers, particularly Mary Ainsworth, have validated and refined it. Bowlby described attachment as a fundamental need that has a biological basis. The infant's attachment behavior has the goal of keeping close to a preferred person in order to maintain a sense of security. The motivation to stay close and to avoid separation from an attachment figure can be seen in an infant who wakes up from a nap and soon begins to fuss and cry, which alerts the parent to come and pick him up.

Bowlby pointed out that attachment serves as a protective device for the immature young of many species, including humans. Babies need the care of adults to survive, and they have many built-in behaviors, that attract adults to them, such as making strong eye contact, cooing and vocalizing, and smiling. Every baby with a normal neurological system develops a focal attachment to the mother or other primary caregiver. The beginnings of the attachment process can be observed in the early weeks of life, but attachment is clearly evident between 4 and 6 months of age. Although the behavioral expression of attachment varies across cultures, attachment is a universal phenomenon in humans (Bowlby, 1969; LeVine & Miller, 1990).

HOW ATTACHMENT DEVELOPS

Infants make attachments with specific people. Although a newborn infant may be comforted by anyone who picks her up, she very quickly differentiates her primary attachment figure(s) from others. During the early weeks of life she learns the particular qualities of her mother (assuming the mother is the primary caregiver). The baby, through repeated interactions, learns to recognize her mother—what her face looks like, what she smells like, what her touch feels like, how her voice sounds, etc. Through this process the infant's attachment becomes specific and preferential. Infants form attachments to particular people, and in an order of preference, usually to the mother, then the father, and then siblings, although infants who are in care full time with a single caregiver often develop an attachment to the caregiver that is second only to the mother.

FUNCTIONS OF ATTACHMENT

Attachment has four main functions: providing a sense of security; regulation of affect and arousal; promoting the expression of feelings and communication; and serving as a base for exploration.

Providing a Sense of Security

The implicit goal of attachment is to keep the infant feeling secure. When an infant becomes distressed both the parent and the infant take actions to restore the sense of security (Bowlby, 1969). For example, an infant becomes upset and communicates this to his mother by looking anxious, crying, or moving closer to the mother. The mother moves toward the baby, soothes him with her voice and picks him up. The baby continues to fuss briefly, then molds to the mother's body, stops crying, and soon begins to breathe more slowly and regularly, indicating a decrease in arousal and that the sense of security has been restored. In Bowlby's terms, the infant's distress signal, which is functionally an attachment-seeking behavior, activates the mother's side of the attachment system and the mother takes steps to calm the baby's distress.

Regulation of Affect and Arousal

A second primary function of attachment, as the above example suggests, is to regulate the infant's affective states. Over time, infants and parents develop transactional patterns of relieving the infant's states of disequilibrium. This interaction has been described as the dyadic regulation of arousal. "Arousal" here refers to the subjective feeling of being "on alert," with the accompanying physiological reactions of increased respiration and heartbeat as well as bodily tension. If arousal intensifies without relief, it begins to feel aversive and the infant becomes distressed. When this happens the infant sends out distress signals and moves toward the caregiver. In a secure attachment the infant is able to draw on the mother for help in regulating distress. The mother's capacity to read an infant's affects accurately and to provide soothing or stimulation helps the infant modulate arousal (Stern, 1985). Over time successful dyadic regulation of arousal helps the infant begin to develop the ability to regulate arousal through his own efforts. Through the experience of being soothed, the infant internalizes strategies for self-soothing. In contrast, "unresponsive or abusive parents may promote chronic hyperarousal that can have enduring effects on the child's ability to modulate strong emotions" (van der Kolk & Fisher, 1994, p. 150). Children who have not been helped to regulate arousal within the attachment relationship tend, as they get older, to feel at the mercy of strong impulses and emotions. They have more behavioral problems because they have not developed effective internal ways of controlling their reactions to stressful stimuli.

Expression of Feelings and Communication

As the attachment relationship develops during the first 6 months of life it also becomes the vehicle for expressing, experiencing, and sharing positive feelings and for learning to communicate and to play. For example, a 5-month-old infant initiates a game of peek-a-boo (which has been previously taught by her father) by pulling a diaper over her face. Her father responds by saying, "Oh, you want to play, huh?" and pulls the diaper off, saying, "Peek-a-boo!" and smiling and looking into the baby's eyes. The baby smiles and begins to wave her arms and kick her feet. The father says warmly, "Oh, you like to play peek-a-boo, don't you?" The baby vocalizes, then begins to pull the diaper over her face again in order to continue the game.

This example indicates how attachment is established and how it is perpetuated. Attachment develops out of transactions: the infant expresses a need—to be fed, to be played with, to be comforted—and the parent responds. Observations of these transactions when they are going well reveal important qualities of the attachment relationship: mutually reinforcing, synchronous behaviors on the part of the parent and infant, a high degree of mutual involvement, attunement to each other's affects, and attentiveness and empathy on the part of the parent (Stern, 1974, 1985).

However, even in the most secure attachment, synchrony is not always present. Parents are not always optimally responsive and attuned, nor do they need to be. Infant–parent transactions show moment-to-moment variability in the degree of synchrony, attunement, and mutual responsiveness (Tronick, Cohn, & Shea, 1986). Interactional mismatches between the baby and parent are commonplace, and they temporarily interfere with the infant's ability to regulate affects. An indicator of secure attachment is the ability of the parent and infant to use interactive coping skills to repair such mismatches when they occur, thus restoring equilibrium for the infant and for the attachment relationship (Tronick & Gianino, 1986b). For example, when a parent is preoccupied or even depressed, the infant watching her begins to feel out of touch, that is, a minor mismatch. The baby may whine, or alternatively smile and kick his feet, to attract the mother's attention. As the mother responds, the mismatch ends and the feeling of security is reestablished.

A Base for Exploration

Later in development, especially from age 1 year on, the attachment relationship becomes *a base for exploration*. Attachment theorists consider the motivation to explore and learn about the world and to develop new skills to be as intrinsic in infants as attachment motivation. Bowlby (1969) pointed out that the attachment and exploratory behavioral systems operate in tandem. The confidence with which the child ventures out depends a great deal on her confidence in her attachments. A child who is feeling secure while playing will not show attachment behavior. Since she is not concerned about attachment, exploratory behavior dominates (Bowlby, 1969). If a toddler has a secure base in her attachment relationship, she will feel free to explore her environment. On the other hand, a toddler who is anxious about whether her caregiver will be responsive and protective may be inhibited from exploring, because emotionally she remains focused on making sure her attachment figures are available (Lieberman, 1993).

PATTERNS OF ATTACHMENT

Beginning in the mid-1960s, Mary Ainsworth began to apply Bowlby's attachment theory in a series of studies that would lead to more a specific understanding of the dynamics of attachment and to the identification of three distinct patterns of attachment. First Ainsworth did an anthropological field study of mother–infant interaction patterns of the Ganda people of Uganda through intensive observation. She found that maternal responsiveness and sensitivity as well as infant reactions to separation were the most important indicators of quality of attachment behavior of Ganda mothers and infants (Ainsworth, 1967). Her initial observational studies of American mothers and infants confirmed the main findings of the Ganda study, providing strong support for the validity of attachment theory across cultures. However, Ainsworth also observed cultural differences between the Ganda and American infants' ability to handle stress. The American babies, when observed in the home, seemed less stressed by very brief separations from the mother or by the presence of strangers than had the Ganda infants. Ganda infants were much more likely to initiate attachment behavior (to cry, protest, or try to follow) when the mother left the room than were American babies.

Consequently, Ainsworth devised an experimental procedure called the "Strange Situation" to create a more stressful situation for American babies in order to elicit attachment behavior. This procedure aims to create mild but increasing stress on the attachment relationship in order to observe the infant's attachment strategies and the degree of security of attachment. In the Strange Situation, the mother and baby (12–18 months old) come into a room the infant has not seen before. After a brief period of play, while the mother sits and watches, a stranger enters the room. After the stranger talks with the mother, the mother briefly leaves the room and returns. The stranger leaves. Then the mother leaves the baby alone for a short time and returns. Ainsworth found that the infant's response to the mother's return was the most sensitive indicator of quality of attachment. Securely attached infants showed characteristic responses when reunited with the mother, and insecurely attached infants also reacted in distinctive ways. In Ainsworth's original study, infants between 9 and 12 months and their mothers were observed for a total of 72 hours in the home prior to the Strange Situation procedure. These independent ratings of the home observations correlated positively with ratings obtained from the Strange Situation procedure. Thus the validity of the strange situation as a research tool for the assessment of attachment in middle-class American samples was established via independent observations.

ATTACHMENT CLASSIFICATIONS

Ainsworth's observational and experimental studies have identified the characteristics of secure attachment and have delineated two types of anxious or insecure attachment (Ainsworth, Blehar, Waters, & Wall, 1978). A third type of insecure attachment has been described by Mary Main and colleagues (Main, Kaplan, & Cassidy, 1985; Main & Solomon, 1990). The attachment classifications are as follows:

- Group A: Insecure–Avoidant
- Group B: Secure
- Group C: Insecure–Ambivalent/Resistant
- Group D: Insecure–Disorganized/Disoriented

Infants in each attachment category present distinctly different reactions to the separation and reunion episodes of the Strange Situation procedure. These differences are seen not merely as reactions to the experimental situation but rather as outcomes of the history of attachment qualities and strategies that have developed over time (Zeanah, Anders, Seifer, & Stern, 1989).

Secure Attachment

The infants rated Secure (B) demonstrated confidence in the attachment relationship, even though they varied in how distressed they became in response to separation. When the mother returned they tended to greet her positively, to look relieved and happy and to move close to her. If distressed they wanted to be picked up, and they quickly calmed in response to the parent's attention and soothing. Ainsworth (1982) noted that in these securely attached infants, there was an expected pattern of exploratory versus attachment-seeking behavior: "When they were alone with their mothers, they explored actively, showing very little attachment behavior. Most of them were upset in the separation episodes and explored little. All of them responded strongly to the mother's return in the reunion episodes, the majority seeking close bodily contact with her, and all at least displaying keen interest in interacting with her" (p. 16). Ainsworth's prior, in-home studies of these infants and mothers showed that the mothers of the Secure infants were responsive, emotionally available, and loving. These babies could cope with the stress of a brief separation because they were confident of their parent's responsiveness. It has also been noted that Secure infants are able to communicate their feelings openly, including positive and negative affects, without the necessity of defending against negative feelings. They show confidence in their parent's ability to accept their full range of feelings and to help them regulate feelings that are distressing (Main & Hesse, 1990).

Secure attachments have a positive impact on later development.

Children with a history of secure attachment are more confident about exploring their environment and more open to learning. This is evident at first during the toddler phase when the child uses the mother as a base from which to explore, but it persists in later development. Good attachment relationships tend to be generalized to future relationships. Careful studies done by Sroufe and his colleagues at the University of Minnesota (Sroufe, 1983, 1989) have confirmed that general differences between secure and insecure attachment patterns persist from infancy through the preschool and elementary school years. Children judged as securely attached at 12 and 18 months were seen at 42 months as more flexible and resourceful. They had fewer behavior problems, sought attention from teachers in positive ways, and effectively elicited their teachers' support when distressed. They showed less negative affect and more age-expected control of impulses. They got along with other children well and showed a capacity for empathy (Sroufe, 1983). Studies of these children in later childhood showed similar associations between secure attachment history and social competence (Sroufe, Egeland, & Kreutzer, 1990). Overall, secure attachment is an important protective factor that promotes adaptive development throughout childhood. In contrast to the confidence shown by Secure infants, the infants in Ainsworth's other categories demonstrated anxiety and/or defenses against anxiety in their attachment behavior.

Avoidant Attachment

The infants classified as Insecure–Avoidant (A) showed very little attachment behavior during the entire Strange Situation procedure. They played independently, did not appear distressed when the mother left, and (strikingly) when she returned they ignored her, showed blank or restricted affect, paid attention to the toys, and actively avoided contact, even when the parent tried to get their attention. They gave the impression of self-reliance, conveying that the attachment was not important. Given the normal importance of attachment for an infant, attachment theorists have described the Avoidant pattern as a defensive strategy. The in-home study suggested why an avoidant defense might be needed: the Group A babies were frequently ignored and actively rejected by their mothers. Parents spoke of their infants in negative terms, often with inaccurate characterizations of the baby's behavior such as "He's just crying to spite me." The mothers were seen as angry, both in general and specifically at the infant. In particular they were intolerant of the infant's distress and tended to reject or punish the infant for being distressed. Out of these interactions, Avoidant babies develop precocious defenses against feelings of distress. Distress is split off from consciousness, and the defense mechanism of isolation of affect emerges. Avoidant infants tend not to show distress in situations that are distressing for most infants; rather they appear somber, expressionless, or self-contained. Evidence for these patterns of defensive suppression comes from a unique study that measured infants' heart rates during the Strange Situation. Both Secure and Avoidant infants had measurably similar physiological responses to stress during the separation episodes. However, the Secure infants expressed their distress, whereas the Avoidant infants appeared outwardly unconcerned (Spangler & Grossman, 1993). Note that the Avoidant pattern should not be equated with nonattachment. Rather, the defensive strategy of avoidance has been characterized as the baby's way of staying close to the parent while protecting herself from overt rejection: "The infant does not show positive attachment behaviors . . . upon reunion because she anticipates that a solicitation of attachment behaviors from the mother is likely to make her either pull back, reject the infant or get angry. In sum, the infant can maximize her proximity to the mother and optimize her felt security by doing nothing and showing nothing" (Stern, 1995, p. 427). Over time Avoidant infants have experienced the attachment as aversive rather than comforting. They have learned to expect to be rejected, and in response, in Bowlby's terms, their attachment behavior becomes "deactivated." They tend not to look to their mothers for help in regulating arousal and affects. Correspondingly, as toddlers, Avoidants infants tend to focus their attention away from the parent (and from their own internal states) and toward the outside world. Instead of striking a flexible balance between exploration and attachment as the need arises, they pursue action and exploration in a rigid and self-reliant way (Main et al., 1985).

In longitudinal studies, preschoolers judged Avoidant in infancy have higher levels of hostility and unprovoked aggression and negative interactions with other children. They generalize the defenses of avoidance and self-reliance to other relationships, tending to distance themselves from others and to maintain a self-reliant posture in distressing situations. Instead of expressing distress and asking for help with disappointment, they are likely to sulk or withdraw. Because they are emotionally distant and often behave in negative ways, Avoidant preschoolers tend to be viewed more negatively and subjected to more discipline by their teachers, thus reinforcing and confirming the child's untrusting assumptions about attachment (Sroufe, 1989).

DYNAMICS OF AVOIDANT ATTACHMENT: A BRIEF CASE EXAMPLE

The following observation describes interaction that has the qualities associated with Avoidant attachment. A teen mother, age 16, and her 7-month-old daughter were videotaped in a free play session. As Erica plays with a busy box, Ms. Jones leans back against the wall and says, "I'm not going to bother you." Erica picks up an inflated ball, which her mother peremptorily takes away from her. Then her mother points to colors on the ball, saying, "Can you say 'red'?" while Erica struggles to get the ball. As Erica crawls onto her mother's leg, she says, "Get offa me." The infant guidance worker suggests, "Maybe she's trying to get close to you." Her mother says, "No, she's trying to get over here without going around." Erica does not look at her mother and her face appears impassive throughout the session. Erica knocks over a toy telephone and her mother says, "No! You know better." The worker asks, "Do you think she knows better?"; Ms. Jones answers, "Yes." The worker persists, "What is she supposed to know better about?" "Lots of things, like crying for nothing, or beating on stuff." The worker says, "When 7-month-old babies beat on stuff they're just trying to make noise." Ms. Jones stands up and says, "Not this little girl. She's destructive." She moves to a corner of the room at a distance from her daughter. Erica does not react to her mother's leaving her side and continues to play with the telephone. Several times her mother calls her to come across the room. Erica looks at her without expression and continues to play. Ms. Jones says, "Bad baby," then goes back and tries to engage her by demonstrating how to press the levers on the busy box. Instead of imitating her mother, Erica puts her fingers in her mouth. Her mother roughly pulls them out. Erica begins to cry and turns away from her mother, who says, "Hey, what's your problem?" The worker asks, "Does she ever just like to be cuddled?" Erica's mother says, "No, not really, maybe when she's sleepy." "Do you hold her then?" "Nope, I give her a bottle and lay her down and shut out the light." The worker says, "You know it feels pretty good to be held." Ms. Jones responds with a dismissive laugh, and turns away from the worker and holds up a mirror to Erica, "Want to see the ugly baby?" Then she picks Erica up and puts her at the top of the play-room slide. She says, "Go down!" and laughs when Erica looks apprehensive. Then she helps her slide down. The worker says, "It looked like she was scared." Ms. Jones says, "It shouldn't have scared her."

The themes in Ms. Jones's view of Erica are dismissal of her needs for nurturance, ignoring her distress, attributing negative intentions to her and characterizing her in negative terms. Both mother and daughter seem more comfortable when they are not engaged with each other. During the brief times they are engaged, both of them are involved with the toys rather than one another. Ms. Jones puts physical and emotional distance between herself and her baby, as if denying the importance of attachment, and Erica in a complementary response, concentrates on the toys and ignores her mother. Observing their mutual avoidance makes the worker feel sad and anxious, and she focuses her interventions on encouraging closeness. In response, seeming to confirm the attachment pattern, Ms. Jones dismisses the worker's statements and turns away from her.

Ambivalent/Resistant Attachment

Infants classified as Insecure–Ambivalent/Resistant (C) showed behavior in the Strange Situation that conveyed a strong need for attachment but a lack of confidence in its availability. Consequently, they reacted intensely to the separation. Ainsworth describes their heightened affect and ambivalence: "These children were anxious even in the preseparation episodes. All were very upset by separation. In the reunion episodes they wanted close bodily contact with their mothers, but they also resisted contact and interaction with her, whereas Group B babies had shown little or no resistance of this sort" (Ainsworth, 1982, p. 16). The Group C babies were distressed and angry, and they could not be soothed by contact with their mothers. The in-home study described the mothers of the Ambivalent infants as inconsistently responsive to their infants' attachment-seeking behavior. Ainsworth notes, "The conflict of the C babies is a simple one— between wanting close bodily contact and being angry because their mothers do not consistently pick them up when they want to be held or hold them for as long as they want. Because their mothers are insensitive to their signals C babies lack confidence in their responsiveness" (Ainsworth, 1982, p. 18). The infants' heightened affect and ambivalent behavior reflects their anxious uncertainty about how their parent will respond: "C babies are doubly upset because they have learned to expect to be frustrated rather than comforted" (Ainsworth, 1982, p. 18).

The C pattern is associated with later disturbances in the infant's capacity for autonomous behavior. Because the child is uncertain of her parent's responsiveness, her attention tends to focus on the parent's behavior, moods, and degree of responsiveness, to the exclusion of other interests. Ambivalent toddlers remain focused on attachment issues at the expense of exploration (Main et al., 1985). Their concerns about separation tend to remain high into the preschool and school-age years, long after children with secure attachment histories have mastered normative separation fears. Longitudinal studies have linked the C category with behavioral inhibition and lack of assertiveness in preschool children and with social withdrawal and poor peer interaction skills in early school age children (M. F. Erikson, Sroufe, & Egeland, 1985; Renken, Egeland, Marvinney, Mangelsdorf, & Sroufe, 1989).

AMBIVALENT/RESISTANT ATTACHMENT
IN A PRESCHOOLER: A BRIEF CASE EXAMPLE

The potential interference of an Ambivalent attachment on development is illustrated by the behavior of a 4-year-old at a child care center. I observed Andrew in a scenario which his teachers said was occurring daily. While Andrew's mother talked with a teacher as she was dropping him off, he watched her alertly with a tight, tense expression. When his mother said good-bye, he grabbed her around the legs, beginning to cry angrily. She disengaged from his grasp and passed him to the teacher, who tried to comfort him by holding him. He cried louder as his mother left, then pushed the teacher away and lay on the floor, in a full-blown tantrum. After two minutes, he went to his cubby and sat morosely, sucking the hem of his security blanket. Ten minutes later he searched out his favorite teacher and then shadowed her, staying as close to her as possible throughout the morning. His behavior was also notable for what it did not include—active play and involvement with other children. In the preschool years, play and social interaction facilitate development. They provide the child with opportunities to learn about the self and to practice skills. This very insecure child remained caught up in attempts to maintain his attachments, which diminished his interest in normal 4-year-old activities that support development.

Disorganized/Disoriented Attachment

Mary Main and her colleagues have identified a third type of insecure attachment, which they label Insecure–Disorganized/Disoriented (Group D). Compared to the other insecure patterns, the D pattern represents a much less organized and consistent approach to dealing with an attachment relationship that the infant experiences as insecure. These infants show contradictory behavior when reunited with the mother after a separation. For example, the infant greets the mother happily and raises her arms to be picked up, then turns away, becomes motionless, and looks dazed. Or the infant shows simultaneous contradictory behavior: walking toward the parent with head averted; smiling at the parent while looking fearful. In this pattern, the behavior of the infant appears confused and disorganized, and her attempts to reestablish attachment are interrupted by conflicting behavior. Group D infants appear to lack an organized strategy for eliciting comforting when they are under stress. They do not seem able in a consistent way to signal the need for help from the parent in regulating affect. Lacking internal or dyadic strategies for regulating distressing feelings, they tend to remain aroused. This persistent distress, in turn, contributes to their internal sense of disorganization (Spangler & Grossman, 1993).

While Avoidant infants turn away from the parent and Ambivalent/Resistant infants come to the mother but are angry and do not feel comforted, D infants show elements of both patterns. Main believes that the contradictory behavior of D infants has been mirrored in the attachment behavior of their parents. A very high percentage of parents with Disorganized/Disoriented infants have histories of unresolved childhood trauma, such as the early loss of a parent, abuse, or witnessing of parental violence (Main & Hesse, 1990; Lyons-Ruth, 1996). They are anxious, fearful people who project trauma-based fears onto the present. Their infants have frequently been alarmed and frightened by the parent's intense expression of fearful emotions: "Frightening behavior on the part of the still-traumatized parent should lead to a disorganized/disoriented infant, since the infant is presented with an irresolvable paradox wherein the haven of safety is at once the source of alarm" (Main & Hesse, 1990, p. 180).

Other studies have found that very high percentages of physically abused infants are classified as Disorganized/Disoriented in the Strange Situation (V. Carlson, Barnett, Cicchetti, & Braunwald, 1989). The intense approach–avoidance conflict in the behavior of D infants has been linked to fear of the parent, uncertainty about how a parent will react, and a history of contradictory responses by the parent ranging from inviting closeness to angry rejection and physical or sexual abuse (Lyons-Ruth, Connell, Zoll, & Stahl, 1987; V. Carlson et al., 1989). Other parental factors associated with the D classification are bipolar depressive illness and active alcoholism, both conditions that tend to involve extreme and contradictory behavior (Main & Solomon, 1990). There is also evidence that Disorganized attachment is a symptom of the disintegrative effects that multiple interacting risk factors can have on families. Families characterized by poverty, parental psychiatric disturbance, parental substance abuse, and a history of abuse of the parent in childhood have much higher rates of D attachment. In Main's studies of infants in middle-class families not beset by multiple risk factors, the D classification rate was 14%. In high-risk samples, the rates are much higher, with 82% of a sample of abused infants classi-

fied as D (V. Carlson et al., 1989). This is consistent with general findings that when a family is overwhelmed by many risk factors, the likelihood of family disorganization and child maltreatment is greater.
Research on the impact of Disorganized attachment on later development is not as advanced as for the other attachment categories. However, there is a clear trend across studies linking D attachment with
high rates of aggressive, hostile, and coercive behavior in school-age
children (Lyons-Ruth, 1996).

ATTACHMENT, CLASS, AND CULTURE

A number of American studies, by Ainsworth and others, have demonstrated consistent rates of A, B, and C attachment patterns for
infants in both middle- and lower-class samples, including samples
that were racially and ethnically mixed, and samples that were either
primarily African-American or white (Ward & Carlson, 1995). However, longitudinal studies have shown that in the high-risk conditions
of poverty and other major stressors, attachment classifications may be
different at different points in time due to the impact of environmental
stressors on the parent's ability to maintain responsive attachment
behavior (Vaughn, Egeland, Sroufe, & Waters, 1979; M. F. Erickson et
al., 1985). As noted previously, the D category is associated with severe
psychosocial risk factors and is more prevalent in families affected by
multiple sources of risk (Lyons-Ruth, Repacholi, McCleod, & Silva,
1991).

Cross-cultural studies have yielded different percentages across
attachment categories, which have generally been explained in terms
of culturally based limitations of the Strange Situation procedure,
rather than in terms of large disparities in the percentages of securely
attached infants. Early studies of Japanese infants, for example,
assigned very high proportions of infants to the Anxious–Ambivalent/
Resistant category, based on their extreme reactions to the separation
episode and their inability to become calm when the mother returned.
Recall that the Strange Situation was created to induce mild stress in
American infants. American infants generally have many experiences
of separation from parents, and in general American culture encourages independence and self-reliance. Japanese culture has very different emphases, as Takahashi (1990) points out:

> Contrary to American culture, in which learning to cope with stress
> is seen as part of healthy development, the Japanese method of
> child-rearing strives to remove any kind of stress. . . . The Japanese

have long favored child-rearing methods in which a caregiver is always near the infant, such as co-sleeping, co-bathing and carrying the child on the mother's back.... Thus Japanese culture treats "being left alone" in striking contrast to American culture. In Japanese culture, it is therefore plausible that the extent of the strangeness of the "Strange Situation," and the accompanying stress go way beyond the bounds of "mild." Some infants, identified as type C babies by the procedure, even if securely attached to the mother, were too disturbed to be pleased at the reunion with her.... An objectively identical procedure does not necessarily guarantee applicability to other cultures. (pp. 27–29)

THE UNIVERSALITY OF ATTACHMENT

Although the aforementioned cross-cultural studies identify variation in the forms attachment behavior takes as well as differences in approaches to caregiving and expectations of infants, the universality of attachment is not in question. What factors seem to be universal? A baby needs to have an attachment to a primary caregiver (or, in many cultures, to a set of primary caregivers). Consistency, sensitivity, and contingent responsiveness on the part of the primary caregivers are essential to the baby's psychological development. When the attachment relationship is pervaded by the caregiver's inconsistency, insensitivity, lack of responsiveness, or negativism or rejection of the baby, the baby's psychological development is seriously at risk.

Research on the parent's side of the attachment has identified three major factors affecting the caregiver's capacity for responsiveness: (1) the caregiver's internal working models of caregiving, assumed to be derived from his or her own early experiences with being cared for (Main et al., 1985); (2) parental risk factors such as mental illness or substance abuse; and (3) whether the caregiver is receiving outside support from other adults. I will focus on the first issue here and will discuss the issues of parental risk factors and support for parents in Chapters 2 and 3.

ATTACHMENT AND FUTURE DEVELOPMENT

Sroufe (1989) points out that "the dyadic infant–caregiver organization precedes and gives rise to the organization that is the self. The self-organization, in turn, has significance for ongoing adaptation and experience, including later social behavior.... Each personality, whether healthy or disordered, is the product of the history of vital relationships" (p. 71). There have been many longitudinal studies that test this idea. Overall, they have found impressive links between quality of attachment in infancy and later development (Matas, Arend, & Sroufe, 1978; M. F. Erikson et al., 1985; Lyons-Ruth, 1996). Secure attachment in infancy and toddlerhood predicts social competence, good problem-solving abilities, and other personality qualities associated with successful adaptation in later childhood (Sroufe, 1989). Insecure attachment has been similarly linked to problematic behavior and social difficulties in school-age children. Although these links between insecure attachments and later characteristics are statistically strong, other factors such as infant temperament and environmental risk factors influence outcomes in the complex transactional causality described in the Introduction to Part I. Nevertheless, *the growing evidence of empirical studies points to quality of attachment as a fundamental mediator of development.*

Internalization of Working Models of Attachment

How are patterns of attachment carried forward as the child develops? To explain the continuing influence of attachment on development, Bowlby (1973) pointed out that the child gradually develops a working model of attachment based on how he has been cared for and responded to within the attachment relationship. Over the first few years of life, working models become stabilized as expectations of how relationships work and what one can expect of other people in terms of responsiveness and care. Correspondingly, models of the self in relationships also develop. The young child internalizes assumptions about how effective he is in using relationships, how valued he is, and how worthy of receiving care. The infant whose attachment initiatives have been responded to appropriately over time is likely to develop working models which say, in essence, "I can expect that people will respond to me with interest, concern, and empathy. My actions are effective in communicating my needs and maintaining my attachments." A central component of working models is a view of the self within relationships, which contributes strongly to the child's self-representation. The child with a history of secure attachment is likely to develop a positive sense of self, whereas the child with insecure attachments is more likely to develop disturbances in the view of self and in the capacity to maintain self-esteem (Bowlby, 1973). Working models also include a view of one's ability to regulate arousal and cope with stress. Infants who have been effectively helped with regulation of arousal through the soothing and contingent responding of their caregivers develop effective internal and social strategies for regulating affect and arousal and become more competent at coping with stress. By contrast, infants who have experienced high levels of arousal and intense affect without the help of dyadic regulation are likely to internalize a view of the self as ineffective and out of control and to develop maladaptive coping strategies, such as affective numbing or hyperreactivity leading to aggression and tantrums.

Attachment Theory and Family Systems Theory

There is significant overlap between the concept of working models and descriptions of family interactions in the family systems theory literature. In the clinical situation, a multigenerational approach to understanding current interactions in a family typically finds repetition of patterns of relationships, conflicts, and modes of coping with conflict or distress (Marvin & Stewart, 1990; Benjamin, 1993). The concept of working models suggests why these intergenerational repetitions occur. For example, family therapists have identified the common pattern of the "parental child," a child who is implicitly assigned the job of taking care of a parent, often a parent who is depressed. Bowlby (1978) has described this concept, using different terms, from the perspective of working models of attachment. When a parent inverts the parent–child relationship by requiring the child to take care of him or her, the child may learn that the only reliable way to receive love is to bestow care. Bowlby labeled the working model of attachment that develops out of this inversion as "compulsive caregiving" (Bowlby, 1978). When a person who has learned to be a compulsive caregiver becomes a parent, he or she may be possessive and protective of a child but also reenact the inversion of the parent–child relationship. The child is unconsciously viewed as the person who "should" at long last provide the parent with love. When there is more than one child, the parent may choose the child he or she most identifies with to become the caregiver.

Working Models as Organizers of Experience

Once established, working models tend to become unconscious. They become filters and organizers of the child's perceptions about relationships. They increasingly guide how the child appraises what is happening in relationships and how she behaves with others (Bowlby, 1980). By the third year, the working models developed through the child's primary attachment relationships have become relatively stable and are now applied to other relationships. The 3-

year-old with a history of secure attachment tends to expect that child care providers will be interested, supportive, and responsive. The child with a history of insecure attachment may mistrust the intentions and emotional responsiveness of other adults. In either case, the child unconsciously attempts to organize, shape, and perhaps control new relationships to make them fit her internal working models. Therefore, rather than being changed by single experiences, working models, once established, "will 'do' something to the event, or the individual's perception of the event, to bring it in line with the individual's conceptualization" (M. F. Erickson, Korfmacher, & Egeland, 1992, p. 499).

At the same time, assuming that parental behavior in relation to the child remains relatively constant, the child's working models are continually being reinforced through ongoing transactions with parents. Although working models can change through changes in parenting style and experiences in new relationships, this becomes increasingly harder after age 3–4 years, when models "become incorporated as stable interpersonal tendencies that endure over time" (Lyons-Ruth & Zeanah, 1993, p. 17). An obvious example is that many children who enter foster care following removal from the parents because of physical abuse behave in ways that seem intended to provoke abusive responses from foster parents.

PARENTAL MODELS OF ATTACHMENT

Bowlby (1988) argued that working models of attachment tend to persist throughout life and that they are particularly activated by parenthood, thus setting the stage for transmission of attachment patterns across generations. Main and her colleagues have explored the persistence of working models into adulthood and particularly parenthood, through a series of innovative research projects. Main did studies of attachment patterns of children at ages 1 and 6 years and found a high rate of consistency. That is, children assessed as securely or insecurely attached at age 1 were almost always classified the same way at age 6. The parents of these children were also interviewed using the Adult Attachment Interview, a protocol designed to elicit information about their working models of attachment through a discussion of memories of their attachment to their parents and past and current relationships with them. Finally, the results of the Adult Attachment Interview were matched with the attachment classifications of the children. The representations of attachment by the parents strongly correlated with the attachment classifications independently assigned to the children

(Main et al., 1985). Studies of the Adult Attachment Interview indicate that it is a valid and reliable instrument for studying working models of parents (van IJzendoorn, 1995). More recent prospective studies using the Adult Attachment Interview with pregnant women have found that the adult attachment classification prior to the baby's birth *predicts* the infant's attachment classification at 1 year of age in about 70% of infants (Benoit & Parker, 1994; Ward & Carlson, 1995). These studies present a striking demonstration of the power of parental working models in shaping attachments.

Characteristics of Secure Adults

The parents who were rated from the Adult Attachment Interview as having secure working models had five primary characteristics: (1) they valued attachment relationships; (2) they believed that their attachment relationships had a major influence on their personality; (3) they were objective and balanced in describing their relationships; (4) they showed a readiness of recall and ease in discussing attachment, which seemed to suggest that they had reflected on their experience; and (5) they took a realistic rather than an idealistic view of their parents and their attachment experiences (Main et al., 1985).

Many of the secure adults described good early experience and relationships with parents, but some described difficult histories that included trauma and loss. What distinguished the adults who were judged secure was not their actual experiences but rather how well they had remembered, understood, and integrated their early experience. The quality of their discourse distinguished them from the adults judged insecure. Their accounts of their attachment relationships tended to be fluent, coherent and organized, and they were easily able to include negative and positive feelings about their experiences. This matches Ainsworth's (1982) finding that securely attached infants are able to openly express a full range of emotions. Talking about their attachment experiences did not seem to make them overly anxious or cause them to resort to obvious defense mechanisms. This finding is consistent with findings about trauma. People who have experienced trauma but are able to recall and understand what happened are less likely to suffer from posttraumatic stress disorder or other trauma-related problems; by contrast, people who cope with trauma by repressing memories of it and dissociating their feelings about it are likely to show a variety of symptoms resulting from defensive maneuvers aimed at keeping the traumatic memories and affects out of consciousness (van der Kolk, 1987; Herman, 1992).

Characteristics of Insecure Adults

Adults whose working models reflected insecure attachments generally felt less positive about attachment relationships, tended to deny
the influence of attachment experiences on their personality, and did
not seem objective in their descriptions. Beyond these general considerations, the insecure parents fell into three main patterns, which
tended to match the Ainsworth attachment classifications of their
infants: (1) dismissive adults; (2) preoccupied adults; and (3) unresolved adults.

Dismissive Adults

Parents in this pattern "dismissed attachment relationships as being of
little concern, value or influence" (Main et al., 1985, p. 91). They did
not have vivid memories of attachment experiences and tended to
describe current relationships with their parents as distant or cut off.
The parents who dismissed the importance of attachment were likely
to have Avoidant infants (i.e., those who tend to turn away from parents and to depend on themselves rather than seeking attachment).

Preoccupied Adults

In the second insecure pattern, "the parents seemed preoccupied with
dependency on their own parents and actively struggled to please
them" (Main et al., 1985, p. 91). They tended to hold themselves
responsible for difficulties in their attachment relationships and to ide-
alize their parents. They showed anxiety about their current relationships and tended to worry about how others perceived them
(Bartholomew & Horowitz, 1991). The infants of these parents most
often were classified as Ambivalent (the pattern in which infants are
anxious about the availability of their caregivers).

Unresolved Adults

These parents had histories of unresolved trauma in childhood, including physical and sexual abuse. Many had experienced the death of a
parent during childhood and continued to show symptoms of disordered mourning. They continued to be fearful about loss and had irrational views, such as blaming themselves for being abused or for
"causing" the death of a parent (Main & Hesse, 1990). When they
described their attachment experiences, their accounts were disorganized and lacked coherence. The infants of these fearful parents were

most often classified as Disorganized/Disoriented (Main & Hesse, 1990).

Defensive Processes in Insecure Parents

The characteristics of the discourse of all three types of insecure parents also distinguished them from the secure parents: "Although . . . the parents of insecure infants gave us information regarding negative experiences and processes, . . . the information seemed to us unintegrated and perhaps not fully recognized as part of a coherent whole" (Main et al., 1985, p. 96). The discourse of many of the insecure parents was hard to follow, self-contradictory, apparently irrational, or shifted without clear transition from topic to topic. Many seemed unaware of contradictions and inconsistencies, particularly between the general and the specific. For example, a parent might state that her mother was "wonderful and understanding" but then go on to describe severe beatings or times she lied to avoid her mother's wrath, without noting the difference between the two representations of her parent. These stories suggested a defensive idealization of the parent(s) that was not integrated with the specific realities of the relationship.

Alternatively, many of the parents of insecurely attached children insisted they had almost no memory of their childhood and in particular claimed they could not recall much about attachment relationships, again suggesting that defensive processes were at work. Bowlby (1980) labeled such memory problems "defensive exclusion of information" (p. 45), which is motivated by the wish to avoid painful memories and stems from painful and negative experiences within the attachment relationship that led to "deactivation of attachment behavior" (p. 70). An aversive attachment leads to early emotional detachment, which in turn diminishes the salience of memories of the attachment relationship.

In summary, parents with secure relationships with their children give coherent descriptions of positive and negative elements of their childhood without strong defensiveness. Parents with insecure relationships with children either dismiss the importance of attachment or are preoccupied with attachment issues. They are unable to integrate particular memories with a general characterization of their early attachments (M. F. Erikson et al., 1992). Main emphasizes the influence of defensive processes on insecure working models and current attachment behavior: "Where the parent's own experiences and feelings are not integrated, restrictions of varying types are placed on attention and the flow of information with respect to attachment. These restrictions appear in speech in the form of incoherencies and in behavior as insensitivities" (Main et al., 1985, p. 100). These defense-based working models interfere with the parent's ability to perceive the child's attachment signals accurately, may cause them to ignore the child's attachment signals or may cause them to distort the child's signals to make them fit with their own attachment preoccupations.

THE ATTACHMENT PERSPECTIVE IN THE ASSESSMENT OF YOUNG CHILDREN

For practitioners the utility of the research findings that have validated attachment theory is that they orient us to observe interactional sequences and to look for congruency between parental working models of attachment and infant/child attachment patterns. Like family systems theory, attachment research teaches us that parent and child behavior tend to be complementary. Parents with working models derived from histories of secure attachment are responsive to their children, who in turn tend to develop secure attachments and positive working models. In contrast, parents who dismiss the importance of attachment are likely to dismiss their children's needs for comforting and nurturance. When these negative attitudes carry over into caretaking transactions, such children are likely to adopt the Avoidant pattern.

Although research contributes to our clinical understanding, it is important to distinguish between research instruments and clinical assessment. The Ainsworth Strange Situation and Main's Adult Attachment Interview reliably reveal attachment patterns when applied to individuals in a research setting. However, they are not directly transferable to practice. Research procedures require adherence to protocol, whereas social work practice requires the flexibility to adapt assessment strategies to the needs and manner of presentation of the client. Assessment depends on careful observation of interactions, usually across two or more interviews, as well as on a broad exploration of family history and psychosocial and ecological contexts. Nevertheless, knowledge of attachment patterns derived from research allows the social worker to observe for interactions and behavior that suggest a particular type of attachment. For example, on a home visit a worker notes that a mother treats her baby roughly while changing his diaper and seems frustrated over having to care for him. At the same time, the baby does not look at his mother, turning his head away when she comes near. These observations, which must be supported by future observations, suggest an Avoidant attachment. The following extended case example demonstrates the application of attachment concepts in an assessment.

KELLY AND HER MOTHER: A CASE EXAMPLE

Family Information

Child client	Kelly, female toddler, age 21 months at referral
Mother	Ms. Keeney, age 20, Irish-American; nursing student; socially isolated, depressed
Grandparents	Maternal: living in another state; grandmother unsupportive, grandfather supportive

Referral: Background Information

Kelly Keeney's mother referred her 21-month-old daughter for evaluation at the recommendation of the staff at an infant and toddler center, which cared for her full time while her mother attended a community college in a large city. Ms. Keeney was 20 and a single parent. They lived in a small apartment near the urban campus. Ms. Keeney's income was derived from Aid to Families with Dependent Children (AFDC) and student loans. She was a competent student and had plans to transfer to a 4-year college and get a degree in nursing. Kelly's father had broken off his relationship with Ms. Keeney during her pregnancy with Kelly. He had seen Kelly briefly two times but was not involved in her care and provided no financial support.

The center director had a sophisticated knowledge of infant development and attachment, which was reflected in the way she framed the staff's concerns about Kelly. Even though she had attended the center for nearly a year, Kelly was not demonstrating attachment to any single caregiver, and the staff reported feeling out of touch with her. She did not make eye contact, did not initiate many interactions with them, and often ignored their directions, even though she seemed to understand them. She did not interact much with other children, though it is important to note that she was one of only two children over 1 year of age attending the center. She seemed reckless and impulsive in her movements and often fell, but she usually did not cry or seek comfort when she hurt herself. One of the caregivers had been alarmed that Ms. Keeney did not raise her voice or intervene quickly when Kelly climbed up a bookshelf just after she arrived to pick her up. The director said that Ms. Keeney was a concerned parent but that she also seemed self-preoccupied, and speculated that she did not provide stimulation appropriate to a toddler.

Parent Interview

Ms. Keeney said she was worried about Kelly's development. She had recently taken a child development course and phrased her concerns in developmental terminology: Did Kelly's short attention span mean she was behind in cognitive development? She was not speaking very much, and did this signal a language delay? Ms. Keeney agreed that there might be an attachment problem. She said that Kelly had not been a cuddly baby and that she wouldn't hug or kiss her when she dropped her off or picked her up at the center. She explained that Kelly had been born prematurely and had to be hospitalized for 2 weeks after birth: "I was still in classes, and I couldn't spend a lot of time with her when she was in the hospital, so maybe she didn't bond to me." Ms. Keeney also wondered if Kelly was a lot like herself. Her mother had told her that she was never a cuddly or responsive baby, and she felt she had been an unhappy and withdrawn child. She did not want to have Kelly repeat her unhappy childhood but was worried that this was already beginning to happen. Ms. Keeney was eager to receive help and was open in reporting Kelly's history and her own childhood history.

Interacting Histories

Ms. Keeney reported the details of her pregnancy and Kelly's birth in an even, matter-of-fact manner that seemed incongruent with the emotionally difficult circumstances she was describing. During her first year in college she became involved in a relationship with a male student. Just before she learned she was pregnant, he broke up with her and dropped out of school. When she told him she was pregnant, he told her he did not want to resume the relationship and offered vague promises of financial support. Her mother was furious that she was pregnant and insisted that she get an abortion. However, Ms. Keeney realized in retrospect that she had delayed the abortion decision until it was too late because she had continued to hope that Kelly's father would come back to her. As the pregnancy progressed, her mother shifted to insisting she give the baby up for adoption at birth. When she said she intended to keep the baby, her mother threatened to cut off all contact and, once, threatened to kill herself. Ms. Keeney summarized this period in a bland tone, "Yeah, it was a hard time, but by the time Kelly was born, I wanted her."

The stress on Ms. Keeney caused by these losses and betrayals during pregnancy was intensified by the difficult circumstances of Kelly's premature birth. Ms. Keeney had enrolled in the winter term, hoping she would be able to complete the term. This was unrealistic and evidenced a denial of the impact of the coming baby on her life, since her due date was a full month before the end of the term. When Kelly was born 5 weeks prematurely, she felt totally unprepared. She had not bought a crib or taken childbirth classes. She had been concentrating on her schoolwork rather than thinking about the baby.

A Premature and Ill Infant and an Unprepared Parent

Although Kelly weighed nearly 5 pounds at birth, her lungs were immaturely developed. She was diagnosed with severe respiratory distress and placed in a neonatal intensive care unit (NICU). Shortly after birth her lungs collapsed and her condition became grave. She was placed on a respirator. Five days later her lung condition had improved sufficiently for the respirator to be removed. She made steady progress until she was discharged $2\frac{1}{2}$ weeks after birth.

Ms. Keeney recalled the period of Kelly's hospitalization as chaotic and painful, although when she reported the following events there was again a discrepancy between her bland affect and the painful content. Up to Kelly's premature birth, the pregnancy had been "easy." Ms. Keeney was alone during the birth. When she called her parents, her mother threatened suicide if she did not give the baby up for adoption. In contrast, her father was supportive and concerned about the baby's condition. When Kelly's lungs collapsed, Ms. Keeney was told that she might not survive. She called her mother again, who said that it "might be for the best if she died." She recalled feeling frightened and numb during the few days Kelly's condition was critical. Ms. Keeney's account of the period after she was discharged and Kelly remained in the NICU suggests loneliness and a sense of disorganization. She visited Kelly nearly every day but recalled that there were some days when "there was no one to take me." With the encouragement of the nursing staff, she began to nurse Kelly when she was about 2 weeks old. Her mother called her several times urging her to give the baby up. When she refused, her mother told her she was ruining her life and then cut off contact. When she called Kelly's father, he was neutral and unwilling to visit the hospital. Ms. Keeney recalled this conversation as extremely painful because she had fantasized that he would come back to her when the baby was born. She continued to attend classes and tried to prepare her apartment for Kelly's homecoming. She had ambitiously decided to paint the entire apartment but gave up, leaving the job half-completed, when she realized that Kelly would be discharged soon.

Ms. Keeney remembered Kelly's first year as increasingly stressful as she tried to manage full-time schooling and the care of an infant. In the early months, Kelly had been a quiet and undemanding infant who could be taken everywhere, including to class, and so hardly disrupted her life. But as she became more active and mobile, Ms. Keeney felt more and more intruded upon the baby's presence. She found a full-time sitter when Kelly was 6 months of age. Ms. Keeney began encouraging her daughter to play by herself and spent as much time as she could studying when they were at home. She was often frustrated by Kelly's increasingly demanding behavior. The pattern of expecting Kelly to play on her own persisted up to the time of the evaluation.

Parental Background

Ms. Keeney described her growing up primarily in terms of a difficult relationship with her mother and a supportive but somewhat distant relationship with her father. Her parents' marriage had been conflictual for as long as she could remember. Her mother had often threatened divorce and suicide as a means of controlling her father. Her father eventually stopped taking her mother's threats seriously and increasingly disengaged from the conflict. Ms. Keeney remembered that she had been very frightened by her mother's frequent threats to leave the family or to kill herself. Bowlby (1973) has described how parental threats of abandonment or suicide cause separation anxiety and a focus on the moods of the parent because the child is confronted with the possibility of losing a primary attachment figure.

Ms. Keeney's memories of her childhood overlapped with her concerns about Kelly. She said that she was worried that Kelly would grow up too distant from others, and noted she had been that kind of child. She herself had been a premature and ill infant. Her mother characterized her as a baby who had never liked being held; this attribution rang true for her because she remembered never wanting to be hugged or kissed when she was a child. She was withdrawn in school and did not remember having many friends. She said, "I was the kid no one liked because I was always whining and crying."

Observations of Attachment

I observed Kelly in three settings: my clinic office, the family's apartment, and the child care center. During the first part of the office visit

Ms. Keeney's mood was upbeat and she spoke and played with Kelly in an animated way. Kelly appeared happy about her mother's responsiveness. As they played together with a toy house, Ms. Keeney put a mother and baby in bed together and Kelly laughed happily. When Ms. Keeney suggested putting the baby in the play pen, Kelly's affect became solemn. Ms. Keeney put the baby in the play pen and said it was time for her nap. Kelly became distressed. She whined irritably and jerked away from her mother. She moved away from her and crawled behind a chair. A moment later, she began playing peek-a-boo and Ms. Keeney joined in. Then she asked Kelly if she was sleepy and went over to hug her, but she pulled away from her angrily.

After repeated observations of their interaction, I realized that this first observation had contained some important themes in their attachment. They could enjoy each other. Kelly was delighted when her mother was playing with her. However, when her mother introduced themes of disengagement into the play by suggesting the baby be put in the playpen and put down for a nap, Kelly withdrew from the joint play and became fussy. She reengaged her mother with peek-a-boo, but became angry and fussy again when Ms. Keeney suggested she might be sleepy. The pattern of their interactions suggested that Kelly wanted her mother's attention and that Ms. Keeney tended to set limits on how much she would respond to Kelly's bids for attention. Kelly became irritable but kept trying to engage her mother. The dominant theme was that she was both focused on the attachment and angry because she expected rejection or at least a lack of attunement. Their interactions seemed to approximate Ainsworth's C category, Insecure–Ambivalent/Resistant.

These attachment themes were more clearly presented during the home visit. Ms. Keeney seemed preoccupied and depressed. She told me that the evaluation had stimulated many sad feelings about her loss of Kelly's father and that she had been feeling down for the last 2 days. Kelly looked somber, and I was struck immediately that her affect mirrored her mother's. Kelly was pleased when I gave her my attention. However, her mother wanted to talk to me and suggested that she play in the bedroom, which was blocked from the living room where we sat by a wooden gate. I said that one reason for my visit was to see Kelly in her home and that I would like to be able to observe her. Ms. Keeney told her to play with her toys. As Ms. Keeney became engrossed in describing her own distress, Kelly became provocative and aggressive. She threw toys in her mother's direction and against the walls. Her behavior seemed angry, yet her expression was more blank than angry. Ms. Keeney seemed perplexed by her behavior. She asked Kelly if she was thirsty and got her some juice, which she accepted but did not drink. She continued to throw toys and her mother decided she must be tired. She took her into the bedroom and put her in her crib. She reappeared in a few minutes. I was struck that Ms. Keeney could not read her affects or perceive her wish for attention. Rather, her caretaking focused on controlling Kelly's intrusions into our conversation. She did not seem aware that what she was saying might be distressing to Kelly. Affectively, she seemed remote from her and preoccupied with her own memories. Over the two sessions I noticed how attuned and reactive Kelly was to her mother's moods: when Ms. Keeney was serious, Kelly was somber; when Ms. Keeney was depressed and preoccupied with her own worries, Kelly protested with aggressive behavior; when her mother was cheerful and animated, Kelly would mirror her positive affect and try to engage her.

At the child care center, I observed Ms. Keeney say good-bye to Kelly. She hugged her and Kelly returned the hug, but her face was blank and she looked away from her mother as she left. She seemed to withdraw emotionally. Yet I did not think this indicated, as suggested by the child care staff, that she was "unresponsive." Having previously observed Kelly's ambivalent behavior toward her mother, which seemed to express her need for more attention and more attunement from her, I believed her withdrawal was a defensive response to the distress of separation. Over the next 45 minutes I noticed that Kelly was acutely interested in the comings and goings of adults. She greeted each adult who came into the room and said good-bye when anyone left. The day I observed her, she was the only toddler at the center. She played by herself. Although there were caregivers present, they did not actively join in her play. In fact they were preoccupied with caring for the infants and tended to leave Kelly to her own devices. It appeared that the staff, like her mother, tended to expect Kelly to be independent and self-reliant. On Kelly's side, she made few approaches to the teachers. It appeared that she might be generalizing to other caregivers an expectation that she could not count on responsiveness if a caregiver was preoccupied.

Clinical Hypotheses Based on an Attachment Perspective

Prior to Kelly's birth Ms. Keeney experienced her pregnancy as the cause of significant losses. Both her boyfriend and her mother rejected her because she was pregnant. She went through the pregnancy without support and without the affirmation of anyone who could share her normal excitement and apprehensions. Understandably, her attitude toward pregnancy was ambivalent. On the one hand, she acknowledged the reality of the coming baby by seeking prenatal care and by imagining what the baby would be like. On the other, her positive attitude toward the pregnancy was primarily supported by the fantasy of getting back together with her boyfriend and forming a family. When he avoided her and refused her overtures, the fantasy could not be sustained and she increasingly felt intruded upon by the pregnancy. The pregnancy became subsumed under her grief. Her attempts to avoid grief by continuing in school influenced her denial of the impact of the pregnancy on her life. She registered for a full schedule of classes even though her due date was 1 month before the end of the term.

The crisis of Kelly's premature birth brought together forces that served to deepen Ms. Keeney's ambivalence. She faced the possibility of her infant's death. When it became clear that Kelly would survive, Ms. Keeney had to relate to her in a context, the NICU, where caregiving and decisions about the baby were controlled by medical personnel. Studies of ill and premature babies suggest that parents often feel like visitors and onlookers and find it difficult to feel close to their baby, with the result that their confidence as a parent is compromised (Minde & Stewart, 1988). Ms. Keeney had little opportunity to hold and care for Kelly until she was nearly 2 weeks old. This is not an unusual circumstance for the parents of ill, premature infants, but it added to Ms. Keeney's sense of distance from Kelly that had already been established by her preoccupation with grief and denial of grief during her pregnancy.

After Kelly was discharged, Ms. Keeney continued going to class, often taking the baby with her. Consonant with her own needs, she saw her as a quiet, undemanding baby who could be taken anywhere and who hardly disrupted her life at all. Her early caregiving, while well intentioned, was somewhat mechanical and attuned more to her needs than to Kelly's. Her lack of attunement was not merely the result of her attempts to go on with her life as it had been before Kelly's birth—she was also depressed. A longstanding dysthymia was made more severe by losses, rejection, and an internalization of her mother's blame for having and keeping Kelly. Ms. Keeney's depression led to inconsistent responsiveness to Kelly that continued to be evident at the time of the evaluation.

Parental Depression and Attachment

In attachment studies, psychological unavailability over time due to maternal depression is linked with insecure attachments, particularly Ainsworth's C classification, Insecure–Ambivalent/Resistant (Teti,

Gelfand, Messinger, & Isabella, 1995). If a parent is unavailable emotionally for long periods of time during infancy and early childhood, the child is likely to develop working models that are consistent with depressive symptoms. That is, the child's working model of attachment is that attachment figures are unavailable and uncaring, and the working model of the self is that I am unlovable and unworthy of love (Bowlby, 1988). By 3–6 months infants of depressed mothers look depressed themselves, showing less positive affect and lower activity level than normal infants. They mirror their mother's affects (Field, 1992). Kelly's "quietness" as an infant was strongly influenced by her mother's depression. Her masked expression, irritability, and limited range of affect as a toddler suggested she might be internalizing a depressive style. Toddlers of depressed mothers look more sad, speak less, and show less exploratory behavior (Radke-Yarrow et al., 1995).

Infants of depressed mothers are likely to develop difficulties in regulating feelings. Because the mother is preoccupied with depression, she frequently fails to respond to the infant's distress signals. In consequence, the infant does not receive her help in regulating affects and is likely to withdraw from the interaction (Tronick & Gianino, 1986a). Kelly's stoic, withdrawn appearance suggested she had adopted a defense of withdrawal, which was now being generalized to other relationships. However, another trend in Kelly's handling of affects was also evident—she could become very angry, particularly at her mother. Ms. Keeney acknowledged that she had felt intruded upon by Kelly as her mobility and activity level increased as she moved toward toddlerhood. She responded by developing new expectations for Kelly. Instead of expecting her to be quiet and adaptable, now Ms. Keeney required her to be more "independent," to play by herself. In response to these expectations, to her mother's attempts to limit their interaction, and to her mother's continuing depression, Kelly began to react with aggression. Unable to draw on her attachment relationship or on her own meager internal controls, Kelly tended to react to disappointment in her mother's responses to her with angry behavior.

Projections of Working Models

The quality of attachment was also influenced by Ms. Keeney's projections of her working models onto Kelly and her relationship with her. Although she wanted to see Kelly as a happy child, her perceptions of her were strongly influenced by her self-perception as a silent, withdrawn child who could not relate well to others. Her view of Kelly was further complicated by the merging of these negative self-images with her thoughts about Kelly. Kelly was associated with her rejection by her mother and boyfriend. Her mother's near-explicit message was, "Since you will not give Kelly up, I want nothing to do with you. If you had not had her, I would still love you." She also had fantasized that her boyfriend would have returned to her if she had not become pregnant. Thus her view of Kelly was linked to her model of herself as the unworthy child who "caused" others to reject her.

The parental side of her working models was also evident. Based on these models, it seemed "right" to think that Kelly should not make emotional demands on her and that she should push Kelly toward precocious autonomy and separation, as her mother had required of her. Further evidence of the carryover of her early working models was her difficulty in seeing Kelly's distress as attachment related. Instead, she tended to displace the distress away from the relationship by attributing it to hunger or sleepiness. Ms. Keeney was working very hard to avoid her loneliness and neediness, which were rooted in a childhood sense of deprivation in attachment relationships, her recent losses, and the current absence of supportive people in her life. Kelly's neediness threatened her defensive attempts to deny and avoid such feelings in herself. Instead of responding contingently and accurately to Kelly's signals of distress, she conveyed to her daughter that she should shut down her feelings as she herself had learned to do.

Research and Practice

The case of Kelly and Ms. Keeney illustrates both the uses and limitations of research knowledge in clinical work. By specifying which variables are relevant and which are excluded from examination, research approaches both clarify and simplify the lives of people being studied. Attachment research is remarkable in its exploration of the complexity of parent–infant interactions. Because of this, many practitioners find attachment research useful in their work (Cramer, 1986; Stern, 1995). Knowledge of infant and adult attachment patterns provides us with valuable lenses for viewing real behavior and understanding clients' histories. Nevertheless, when we evaluate individuals and families, we always find their lives are more complicated than research findings might indicate. For example, if we ask which attachment classifications fit Kelly and Ms. Keeney, we might argue that Kelly presents qualities of both Avoidant and Ambivalent attachment, while Ms. Keeney seems to embody aspects of Preoccupied and Unresolved adult attachment.

In practice, establishing the exact attachment pattern is far less important than understanding the specific dynamics of the attachment of a parent and child. Understanding these attachment dynamics both in the present and as a function of Ms. Keeney's working models pointed the way to an intervention plan, which combined individual therapy for Ms. Keeney and parent–child sessions. In the individual therapy Ms. Keeney explored the impact of her working models on her view of self and her view of Kelly in the context of a supportive relationship with the social worker. The parent–child work emphasized positive play activities that aimed to strengthen the parent–child relationship.

Although organizing the treatment using attachment concepts led to a successful intervention, there were clearly other factors to consider besides attachment in formulating the case and designing a treatment plan. Ms. Keeney demonstrated a number of strengths that are not obvious in an account that is sharply focused on attachment. She was bright, determined to complete her education, able to be warm and loving toward Kelly, and very anxious to receive help for her and for herself as a parent. Several other factors were affecting the quality of attachment. Ms. Keeney was poor, relatively isolated, and lacked the support of other adults for her parenting. She was still struggling with grief over several recent losses. It was necessary to view Kelly's attachment difficulties in the broader context of these parental and environmental risk factors in order for intervention to be successful.

CHAPTER 2

Risk and Protective Factors: The Child, Family, and Community Contexts

Development unfolds in individual, family and community contexts that influence its course. To understand a particular child's development we must attend to the transactions between that individual child and the layers of ecological context that surround him. In Chapter 1 we examined one critical context of development, the attachment relationship, and saw how variations in the organization of attachment contribute to the creation of different developmental pathways. In this chapter we will broaden the discussion of context to include individual qualities of the child, parental and familial factors other than attachment, and social/environmental factors, and discuss how these factors may protect and enhance the developmental process or, alternatively, may increase the risk of compromised or maladaptive developmental outcomes.

RESEARCH ON RISK AND RESILIENCE

During the 1960s clinicians and researchers studying psychosocial risk began to notice that children exposed to the same risk factors, such as growing up in chronic poverty, were affected differently. Some children developed serious disturbances, some seemed moderately or only mildly affected, and some even seemed to use the challenge of the stress to become stronger. Those children who had good outcomes in spite of exposure to risks to development were called "resilient." Resilience has been defined in a number of ways, including the following:

> The ability to function competently under threat or to recover from extreme stress or trauma quickly (Masten, Best, & Garmezy, 1990)
> "The capacity . . . to meet a challenge and use it for psychological growth" (A. L. Baldwin et al., 1993, p. 743)
> Good developmental outcomes and adaptive abilities in spite of growing up in high-risk situations (Rutter, 1987; Masten et al., 1990)

Each of these overlapping definitions captures important aspects of the concept. These definitions, however, imply that resilience exists primarily *in* the individual. Early studies emphasized the apparent constitutional "invulnerability" of children who seemed to succeed developmentally in the face of serious risks (Anthony, 1974; Anthony & Cohler, 1987). Recent conceptualizations recognize that the existence and development of children's resilience is a transactional process dependent on supportive factors in the environment, especially responsive, protective parenting. Resilient children tend to have had "environments that are supportive in critical ways [and] . . . the capacity for resilience develops over time in the context of environmental support" (Egeland, Carlson, & Sroufe, 1993, p. 518). Resilience is also now seen as a normative process rather than a special attribute that promotes adaptation only in high-risk conditions: "resilience is an integral part of development that every child must achieve" (A. L. Baldwin et al., 1993, p. 743). Of course it is harder to become resilient in adverse environments, and in such environments ongoing support is critical. Consequently, research has focused on intervening processes that serve to protect children's development in spite of their growing up under conditions of risk.

This research has practical applications consistent with the "person in environment" tradition of social work intervention (Karls & Wandrei, 1994). Social work focuses on promoting resiliency through ecological *and* individual interventions (Fraser, 1997). The identification of risk and protective factors and processes that impinge on the child and her family is a critical part of any assessment (see the appendix at the end of this chapter). From this assessment we are guided toward interventions that seek to increase protective factors and mitigate risk factors.

The following sections review findings on protective and risk factors. For the purpose of clarity, child, parental, and community/environmental factors are presented separately, though in reality all three levels of risk and protective factors interact to influence the development of the child. Even though they are presented separately, it is important to understand that risk and protective processes have a transactional relationship. Poor outcomes and resilience should be seen as a continuum of possibilities, based on the balance of risk and protective factors across development and on the timing of new stressors or opportunities in the course of a child's life (Egeland et al., 1993). Given this continuum of possible outcomes, it is important to examine the *balance* of risk and protective factors, since the presence of protective factors tends to offset risk (Dunst, 1993). It is also necessary to consider the *duration* and *timing* of risk and protective processes. At-risk children who are subject to protective processes over time are more likely to develop resilient traits and adaptive coping mechanisms.

PROTECTIVE FACTORS AND PROCESSES

Protective factors, either in the child or environment, mitigate risk by reducing stress, providing opportunities for growth, or strengthening coping capacities. Recent research on resilience has increasingly recognized the ongoing transactional process of development and protective factors. Children who are resilient tend to have experienced consistent, responsive parenting over time. While secure attachments in infancy and early childhood predict adaptive functioning in later childhood, most resilient children have actually had adequate parental support *throughout* their development (Egeland et al., 1993). It may be more appropriate to refer to protective factors as *protective processes*, since to be truly effective in promoting resilience they must be present across many years of the child's development (Rutter, 1990; Egeland et al., 1993).

Child Protective Factors

Factors "in" the child that influence vulnerability and resilience include biological conditions, genetic inheritance, and personality characteristics. "Inherent" protective factors noted in resilience studies have included good-natured temperament, good health, and above-average intelligence. Certain personality characteristics are associated with resilience, such as positive self-esteem, an active style of responding to stress, ability to elicit positive attention from parents and other adults, believing in one's ability to solve problems, and the ability to balance autonomous functioning with help seeking when necessary (Werner & Smith, 1992; Garmezy, 1985).

In long-term studies of high-risk children, Emmy Werner found characteristics associated with resilience at each developmental stage. In infancy, these resilient children were good-natured, active, and responsive, and did not have feeding or sleeping problems. As toddlers and preschoolers, they were somewhat advanced in the areas of "alertness and autonomy, their tendency to seek out novel experiences, and their positive social orientation" (Werner, 1993, p. 504). In middle childhood, they demonstrated the ability to get along with peers, good communication abilities, good cognitive and reading skills, effective use of academic skills independent of level of intelligence, many hobbies and interests, and the ability to find emotional support outside family and to use other adults as role models. They also demonstrated an ability to find niches that allowed them to utilize their talents and gain positive feedback (Werner, 1993).

Other studies have noted that an advanced developmental level is a protective factor, since the older the child, the better able he will be to appraise, interpret, and cope with distressing events (Rutter, 1985). Children who have a previous history of mastering the tasks of development are more resilient. The feedback that one has coped successfully with a difficult situation (coming from within as well as from others) serves to improve both appraisal and coping abilities and thus helps the child become more resilient in the face of future stressors (Rutter, 1987). Children who have coped successfully also tend to develop an "internal locus of control," which means that they believe they can take active steps to master difficult situations, as opposed to feeling that external events control them (Lazarus & Folkman, 1983; Rutter, 1987).

Parental Protective Factors

In general, the effectiveness of intrinsic protective factors is mediated by developmental level. The younger the child, the less effective qualities such as a positive attitude will be in mitigating risk and the more the child will need *external* protective factors that come from family support. Other internal protective factors, such as cognitively based coping skills or internal locus of control, are by definition not available to young children because they require developmental capacities the child has not yet attained. The very designation of child factors as "internal" or "intrinsic" is misleading because it obscures how they are influenced by the child's transactions with the environment from birth. As described in Chapter 1, resilient personality traits are linked to a history of secure attachment, responsive parenting, and positive working models of relationships and self (Garmezy & Rutter, 1983; Egeland et al., 1993).

In addition to secure attachment, other parental protective factors have been identified: parental warmth, good caregiving after the child has been through a stressful experience, modeling of competent behavior and coping skills, appropriate expectations of the child, household rules and structure, and monitoring of the child's behavior (Masten et al., 1990). Werner (1993) found that the expectation of prosocial behavior, such as taking care of siblings or helping relatives or neighbors, was associated with resilience: "At some point . . . the youngsters who grew into resilient adults were required to carry out some socially desirable task to prevent others from experiencing distress or discomfort. Such acts of *required helpfulness* can also become a crucial element of intervention programs that involve high-risk youth in community service" (p. 511; emphasis in original).

In turn, positive parenting abilities have been linked to the level of the parent's education and particularly to the quality of support the parent receives. A positive relationship between parents supports the parenting function. So does shared caregiving by parents and other relatives. The parents' involvement with kin and neighbors, family religious faith and participation, and access to health and social services also support parenting (Werner & Smith, 1992). Ongoing involvement with extended family is a particularly important protective factor for teen parents and their children. Children of single parents living in three-generational households have been found more likely to be rated securely attached (Wilson, 1989).

Protective Factors in the Broader Context

Although quality of parenting is the most important mediator of risk for children, other relationships can be protective. An ongoing positive relationship with a nonparental adult such as a grandparent, teacher, or friend's parent promotes resilience even when parenting ability is impaired (Rutter, 1987). For example, studies of children growing up with a severely mentally ill parent show that warm relationships with other adults, either in or outside the family, contribute to more adaptive functioning (Radke-Yarrow & Sherman, 1990). Positive experiences and feedback at school can also offset a stressful family environment (Werner, 1990). At a broader level, consistent parental employment, adequate housing, living in a safe neighborhood, and having adequate financial resources are all protective factors, which tends to become obvious only when these conditions are not present. In this context, social privilege, based on middle-class status and the absence of barriers such as racism, is at the root of many protective factors. Similarly, social inequality and disadvantage, based on structural lack of opportunity and racial or ethnic discrimination, is at the root of many risk factors.

RISK FACTORS

Research has identified many specific conditions that create developmental risk. In general, these factors include the following:

- Vulnerabilities in the child, such as mental retardation or chronic illness
- Impaired parenting
- Socioeconomic and institutional factors, such as lack of access to medical care or chronic exposure of the family to poverty and social disadvantage

Risks that are *chronic,* such as being reared by a schizophrenic parent, tend to have more far-reaching effects on development than do acute risks, such as the parent's experiencing a brief psychotic episode followed by recovery of normal functioning. Risk factors are increasingly dangerous as their number goes up because their effects interact with and potentiate one another, increasing the level of stress and making the child increasingly vulnerable. One or two risk factors can generally be coped with, but when there are three or more the child and parents are more likely to become overwhelmed, resulting in developmental or psychiatric disorder in the child. The most insidious and destructive scenario occurs when risk accumulates, both over time and in number of factors, and when there are few countervailing protective mechanisms (Garbarino, 1993).

Child-Based Vulnerabilities

Biological Factors

Children's development is put at risk by a range of biological conditions, including genetic syndromes, *in utero* exposure to teratogens (e.g., infectious diseases in the mother transferred to the fetus, or chemicals toxic to the fetus, such as alcohol or cocaine), prematurity and low birth weight, birth injury or anoxia, and chronic illnesses. Genetic risks range from specific medical syndromes such as fragile X and Prader–Willi syndromes (which cause mental retardation and severe developmental deviations) to more general risks for certain types of mental disorders. Psychiatric research has identified familial patterns, assumed to be based on genetic transmission, for a number of disorders, including autism, attention-deficit/hyperactivity disorder (ADHD), mood disorders, Tourette's and other tic disorders, and schizophrenia (American Psychiatric Association, 1994). For these disorders, no specific genes have been identified, but the frequency of first-degree relatives having these disorders, compared with prevalence rates in the general population, suggests a degree of genetic risk (American Psychiatric Association, 1994; Rende & Plomin, 1993).

Epidemiological studies have distinguished between the causes of severe versus mild developmental disorders that have a biological component. About 75% of severe disorders, including severe mental retardation, multiple physical anomalies, and severe neurological disorders, have biological causes related to damage to the fetus during the first 6 months of pregnancy. These include chromosomal anomalies, inadequate nutritional supply to the fetus *in utero*, adverse drug effects and prenatal infections (Kopp & Kaler, 1989). Less severe disorders—mild retardation, minor neurological and sensory difficulties—by contrast, have exclusively biological causes only about 20% of the time and instead "are linked to deleterious social and economic circumstances or to a combination of biological and social vulnerabilities" (Kopp & Kaler, 1989, p. 227).

Biological Conditions and Attachment. Biological vulnerabilities at birth have the potential to affect attachment (McFadyen, 1994). Infants born with biological damage are frequently harder to relate to. They may be less responsive than normal infants, or they may be irritable or constantly distressed. Parents may not know how to respond to an ill, premature infant and may at first resist investing emotionally in an infant who may die or be seriously compromised. Parenting risk factors, such as depression or a history of insecure attachment, may compound the parent's difficulties in relating to the infant. Finally, the environmental risk of being in a neonatal intensive care unit (NICU) for an extended period interacts with these child and parent factors (Minde, 1993). All of these risk factors were at play and affected quality of attachment in the example of Kelly and Ms. Keeney in Chapter 1.

Transactional Effects of Biological Conditions over Time. Biological conditions frequently compromise future development because they may have ongoing sequelae, such as mental retardation, neurological disorders such as cerebral palsy, congenital anomalies requiring surgical correction, behavioral and attentional disorders, and difficulties in the development of self-regulation (Rutter, 1989; Minde, 1993). These ongoing effects can also contribute to difficulties in attachment, or may, for understandable reasons, lead the parents to emphasize the child's "sick" or "delayed" qualities over areas in which her development is adequate. Often parents who have babies who are very ill in infancy or are diagnosed with chronic illnesses in early childhood have had to constantly monitor the child's physical states. Hyperattentiveness and protectiveness may persist as a generalized style of relating to the child they continue to perceive as fragile. Parents may constantly run interference for the child and limit her choices, limiting the acquisition of autonomous skills that are within her developmental abilities (Landry, Chapieski, Richardson, Palmer, & Hall, 1990). The child may internalize the parents' view of her and begin to restrict herself inappropriately. This may evolve into a form of "secondary gain," in which the child begins to use the illness or disability as a means of avoiding responsibilities and expectations (Feinstein & Berger, 1987; A. Freud, 1977). From the perspective of intervention, it is important to discuss with parents the need to develop appropriate expectations for what their child can accomplish and to encourage them to set limits on the child's using her disability to avoid doing things she is capable of.

The intensive and invasive medical treatment of chronic or serious illnesses such as cancer can also pose developmental risk, especially during early childhood when the child's coping mechanisms are not well developed. As an example, treatment of cancer may interact negatively with the young child's developmental immaturity and interfere with developmental tasks during the toddler and preschool years (Davies, 1992). The preschool child undergoing chemotherapy over long periods must be shielded from ordinary childhood illnesses because the drug treatment compromises his immune system. This means he must be kept away from other children during a period when play and interaction with peers facilitates developmental progress.

Secure Attachment as a Protective Factor against Biological Risk. Research on children with biological conditions suggests that secure attachment and responsive caregiving over time have more impact on developmental outcome than the particular biological deficit. This is not to say that the biological condition does not impact development, but rather that responsive parenting ameliorates the risks and helps the child develop adaptive coping mechanisms (Sameroff & Chandler, 1975). Summarizing research on this issue Lyons-Ruth, Zeanah, and Benoit (1996) note: "Most parents may be able to compensate even for severe deviations in the infant's behavior and development, although infants are not similarly able to compensate for parental disturbance" (p. 476).

Temperament

Temperamental factors constitute another child-based vulnerability. Temperament refers to constitutionally based personality traits that affect the child's orientation to the world. Thomas and Chess (1977), studying infants beginning at 3 months of age, identified three characteristic patterns of temperament, "easy," "difficult," and "behaviorally inhibited," also called "slow to warm up." Temperamentally easy children were found to have a positive mood, moderate activity level, adaptability to environmental change, regular biological patterns, good attention span and persistence, mild-to-moderate intensity and sensitivity, and positive responses to new situations. As described previously, resilience research has identified this type of temperament as a protective factor.

The other two patterns—"difficult" and "behaviorally inhibited"—have been implicated as potential risk factors. Children judged to possess a difficult temperament were the opposites of the easy children. Their mood tended to be negative, and they were very active, "negatively" persistent, overly sensitive, intensely reactive, and resistant to change. Their biological rhythms were irregular, and they tended to withdraw in new situations. Behaviorally, these traits translate into a restless, irritable, hard to soothe baby who wakes up many times at night. Children with difficult temperament are less rewarding for parents. Parents may quickly feel inadequate when they are unable to comfort an infant who is constantly fussy or, later, a preschooler who is negative and demanding.

Compared with both the easy and difficult temperaments, children described as "slow to warm up" tend to be less reactive, less overtly emotional or intense, and less active. They appear inhibited in new situations, although they may begin to participate actively if they have had enough time to size up a novel experience. However, strong behavioral inhibition has been associated with potential psychiatric risk. Kagan and his colleagues studied children who were very inhibited and found that, in contrast to less inhibited children, their reactivity to new situations was much higher and could be documented through physiological measures, including increased bodily tension, blood pressure, and heart rate (Kagan, Resnick, Clark, Snidman, & Garcia Coll, 1984). These physiological responses are characteristic of anxiety disorders, and later studies of these same children with high behavioral inhibition showed that they had higher rates of anxiety disorders in middle childhood (Hirshfield et al., 1992).

Temperament, Parental Factors, and Goodness of Fit. It appears that temperament is a risk factor primarily in combination with parentally based risk factors. Although it is widely believed, for example, that difficult temperament constitutes a risk factor for abuse, research studies show that parental personality characteristics and psychopathology, often exacerbated by external stressors, are the determinants of abuse, and that child factors, including temperament, are not significant factors (Wolfe, 1987; National Research Council, 1993). Similarly, studies of the family context of behaviorally inhibited children suggest that parents of these children have high levels of anxiety themselves and that they reinforce the child's inhibited behavior through overprotection and restriction of autonomy (Messer & Beidel, 1994).

Thomas and Chess (1977) proposed the bidirectional model of "goodness of fit" to explain the interaction between child temperament and parenting behavior. For example, a parent who tends toward self-reliance and prefers a "cool" interactional tone may feel frustrated and overwhelmed by an infant or toddler whose temperament inclines her toward high activity, intense emotions, and strong need for interaction. The fit here would not be a good one, whereas a parent with a more active, involved, and "warm" style would more easily adapt to the child's temperament and create a better interpersonal fit. The impact of temperament on development is best understood from a transactional perspective. When the parent of a "difficult" child is able to provide consistent empathy and limit setting while avoiding natural tendencies to overreact, withdraw from or take personally the child's behavior, the parent provides a "holding environment" for the child that encourages adaptive development.

Temperament as a Transactional Process. Recent research has raised questions as to whether what appears to be temperament is more the result of parental working models and early caregiving interactions (Lyons-Ruth & Zeanah, 1993). Given that temperament is assumed to be inherent, it was expected that it would be stable over time. However, in the original research of Thomas, Chess, and Birch (1968), difficult temperament in infancy *did not* increase risk for behavior problems, but difficult temperament at age 3 *did* predict later behavior problems. This suggests that there is a strong association between caregiving and temperament, since the link between difficult temperament and behavior problems was only evident after the child had been in a caregiving relationship for 3 years. Many studies have found correlations between the way parents describe themselves and the way they characterize their infants' temperaments. Highly emotional parents describe their infants as like themselves, and parents who characterize themselves in negative terms or who have significant depression or anxiety are likely to see their children as "difficult" (J. E. Bates, 1987). Lyons-Ruth and Zeanah (1993) point out that in infancy "adverse temperamental attributes have weak links with subsequent maladaptation unless contextual influences [the caregiving relationship] support the link" (p. 19). Other studies suggest that infants' characteristics are significantly influenced by the parents' working models of attachment. Several studies using the Adult Attachment Interview found that the mother's adult attachment classification during pregnancy predicted the child's attachment classification at 1 year of age in 70% of cases (Lyons-Ruth et al., 1996). The infants' behaviors were consistent with their mothers' expectations before birth.

These studies raise questions about the utility of thinking about temperament in isolation from the transactional context of the attachment relationship. What is perceived as temperament may also be determined by the parent's working models or the degree of stress a parent experiences. Parents under stress may have difficulty helping a child feel secure. The child may react with fussiness or aggression, which increases the parent's stress and leads him or her to perceive the child as "difficult." In clinical evaluation, however, it is very useful to explore the parent's perceptions of the child's temperament and to assess goodness of fit (Stern, 1985; Chess & Thomas, 1986).

Parental Risk Factors

The functions of parents are to protect the child, promote adaptive development and self-esteem, model and support the child's movement toward self-regulation, provide encouragement and opportunity for growth, and convey cultural values to the child. These functions begin in the attachment relationship and persist throughout development, both in the form of direct parental influence and through the child's internalization of working models. Winnicott (1965) pointed out that parents do not need to be perfect but rather "good enough." Although "good enough" parents make mistakes and may at times be inconsistent, overall they are able to carry out the normal functions of parenthood. "Good enough" parents are able to see their children realistically, have expectations of the child that are consistent with her actual developmental level and have the capacity to empathize with the child's point of view.

Parenting that heightens developmental risk involves relative failure or inability to carry out the normal functions of parenthood. Galdston (1979) suggests that "the parenting process can be described as dysfunctional when the welfare of the child is sacrificed to the needs of the parent" and when the parent acts on a distorted, unrealistic view of the child (p. 582). Parental risk factors derive from direct behavior toward the child, such as maltreatment, and from parental difficulties, such as substance abuse or psychopathology, which impair parenting ability. Other factors related to familial or parental status may increase parenting vulnerability. These include single parenthood and father absence, paternal unemployment, family disruption or divorce, large family size (four or more children), and low level of education for mothers (Rutter, 1987; McLoyd, 1989).

Positive parenting behavior serves to buffer stress in childhood. The presence of parental risk factors reduces the parent's ability to mediate stressors, making the child more vulnerable to intrinsic and environmental risk factors (Hammen, 1992). In general, the lack of parental support and mediation of stressors leaves children to cope on their own. The younger the child the less he will be able to cope on his own and the more likely he will develop maladaptive patterns of coping in response to stress. For example, the child who has been traumatized at age 3 or 4 by witnessing domestic violence frequently faces an impossible task at this level of development. He must master the trauma without the support of his mother, who has herself been traumatized by being beaten and consequently is unable to provide emotional support and explanations to her child. In this and analogous situations, the child may develop emergency-based coping strategies, such as hyperaggression and emotional numbing, which are understandable responses to the trauma but which, if they persist, become inappropriate and maladaptive coping mechanisms that impede development (Davies, 1991; Webb, 1991a). When parents help their children cope with stressful experiences, both directly and by modeling adaptive coping, the child's coping ability and stress resistance are augmented. When parents, because of their own difficulties, are not able to buffer children from stress, children do not learn adaptive coping and are more vulnerable to future stressors and psychopathology (Hammen, Burge, & Adrian, 1991).

The following discussion of parental risk factors provides brief descriptions of parent–child dynamics and developmental impacts associated with each risk factor. Although each factor is described separately for clarity's sake, it should be noted that parental risk factors often occur in clusters. Two substance-abusing parents may neglect and abuse their children, and expose them to intense conflict and domestic violence. In such a situation it is not possible to sort out the impacts of the separate risk factors.

High Parental Conflict, Family Disruption, and Divorce

Ongoing parental conflict is associated with a higher degree of developmental risk (Werner & Smith, 1992). Marital relationships that are full of anger and conflict, and (to a lesser degree) distancing, create insecure environments for the child. Young children exposed to chronic anger between parents show behavioral and affective disorganization and increased aggression. Some children exposed to frequent parental fighting take on a caregiver role to the parent with whom they are aligned (Cummings, Iannotti, & Zahn-Waxler, 1985). Parental conflict is especially difficult for the child when the parents triangulate the child into the conflict, by arguing about her or requiring her to take sides in the conflict. Many research studies have shown that children do better in adequately functioning single-parent families or stepfamilies than in high-conflict two-parent families (Long & Forehand, 1987). Even children who are distressed by their parents' divorce often answer the question "Is there anything good about divorce?" by saying, "Yes! Because they're not fighting all the time!"

Parental separation and divorce spawn a number of stressors that have an impact on children: disruption associated with the period before and after parents separate; frequently, the sense of loss of one parent; changes in residence and school, resulting in loss of prior friends and support systems; downward economic mobility; the mother's return to work or increase in work; depression and self-absorption in one or both parents; and later, parental dating, remarriage, and stepfamily relationships. In spite of these expected stressors, many children within a 2-year period seem to cope with their parents' divorce. After a period of shock, disorganization, and sadness or depression, many children seem to resume their normal developmental progress. Factors that have been found to buffer the child's reactions to divorce include the following: ongoing emotional availability and consistency in parenting; an ongoing relationship with the noncustodial parent; minimizing disruption of the child's home/school environment; the custodial parent's ability to establish a healthy postdivorce adjustment; and, particularly, the parents' ability to move beyond previous conflicts and to shift into the new role of cooperating to support the child's needs and development (Wallerstein, 1985; Kalter, 1987; Ahrons & Rodgers, 1987).

Research on custody arrangements suggests that children benefit from joint custody when parental conflict is low, when parents can communicate and cooperate on behalf of the child and when the parents prefer, or at least accept, joint custody as a means of each parent's maintaining a significant relationship with the children (Steinman, 1981; Hetherington, Stanley-Hagan, & Anderson, 1989). By contrast, joint custody in situations where the parents continue to fight—both in front of the children and through the legal system—tends to keep the child in the middle of the conflict and is associated with higher rates of psychiatric symptoms and ongoing enmeshment in the parents' conflicts (Camara & Resnick, 1988; Johnston, Kline, & Tschann, 1989). When parental conflict remains intense, sole custody buffers the child from ongoing conflict, because one parent is the child's primary caretaker and is in charge of decisions about the child. Some research shows that school-age children do better in the custody of the same-sex parent (Camara & Resnick, 1988, 1989). This is consistent with psychoanalytic theory, which asserts that during middle childhood children's development is promoted by identification with the same-sex parent.

Two parental factors after divorce present the most risk for children. The first is when the parent the child lives with suffers a decline in parental functioning after the divorce, often because the stress of divorce precipitates a serious depression, which lasts for several years. When parenting is impaired over a long period of time, the child has to struggle with divorce and loss issues on his own, without parental buffering, and is likely to develop ongoing symptoms (Kalter, Kloner, Schreier, & Okla, 1989). The second factor is ongoing hostility, fighting, and recrimination between parents. At times, only one parent actively tries to keep the conflict going, often through legal maneuvers, threats, and provocations such as keeping the children longer than the visitation agreement stipulates. Sometimes both parents are fully engaged in the struggle. In either case the effects on the child may be profound, because he is continually exposed to parental fighting, to put-downs of one parent by another, and to implicit or explicit requirements that he ally with one parent against the other. Children exposed to such conflicts often present with disturbed behavior, particularly aggression (Hetherington et al., 1989; Amato, 1993).

Harsh Parenting and Coercive Family Process

Harsh, punitive, and inconsistent parenting influences the child's working models, so that the child comes to expect interactions with parents to be negative and aversive. A child's difficult temperament may create the conditions for harsh parenting, but research suggests that ineffective parenting behavior, often based on the parent's working models, plays the major role in creating a pattern of negative interactions (Dishion, Patterson, & Kavanagh, 1992). Especially when the child is exposed to harsh and inconsistent discipline in infancy and toddlerhood, she is likely to model her behavior after the parent's. Patterns of mutually angry and coercive interactions develop. These patterns have been associated with the development of oppositional behavior and conduct disorder (Vuchinich, Bank, & Patterson, 1992; Grizenko & Pawliuk, 1994).

Patterson and colleagues have summarized the literature on family variables related to antisocial behavior as follows: "Families of antisocial children are characterized by harsh and inconsistent discipline, little positive parental involvement with the child, and poor monitoring and supervision of the child's activities" (Patterson, DeBaryshe, & Ramsey, 1989, p. 329). Patterson (1982) has described how demanding, negative behavior is reinforced in some families because parents pay much more attention to it than to prosocial behavior. In particular, interactions between parents and children come to be dominated by coercion and threat. Through systematic in-home observations of several hundred families, Patterson delineated a typical chain of events that tended to reinforce antisocial behavior. The first step was that the parent either ignored or "attacked" the child through teasing, physical punishment, or harsh, peremptory orders. Then the child counterattacked, with angry or aggressive actions. In response, the parent stopped attacking and shifted to a more "understanding" or placating stance. Finally the child returned to positive behavior. In this sequence, the child's negative behavior gets the positive response, and thus is reinforced (Patterson, 1982). As this chain of interactions is repeated, the child begins to internalize the notion that aggression is a means of escaping or exerting control over aversive events (Reiss, 1989). Over time the characteristics of the interactions—coercive behavior, escalation of anger, reactivity, negative affect—shape the child's working models of relationships. The parent's expectations of the child are also shaped. The expectation of conflict and coercion becomes solidified and both parent and child become perpetually "ready for trouble."

Children with disruptive behavior tend to internalize negative views of self that are based on how they are viewed by their parents. The child who has been treated negatively begins to see himself negatively. His expectations of relationships involve punishment, conflict, and rejection. He projects these working models and meets the world with mistrust, expecting to be aggressed against. As the child generalizes aggressive behavior and coercive strategies to relationships outside the family, he is likely to be rejected by peers and identified by teachers as having behavior problems. Their negative reactions, however, will seem to him consistent with his working models, and therefore, rather than being able to use their feedback to change his behavior, he is likely to become more coercive or oppositional because this is the strategy that has worked at home. The child's aggression often does provoke counteraggression or punishment, which tends to confirm his working models.

Children with disruptive behavior often view themselves as victims and blame others for "causing" them to be aggressive. Because they feel victimized, they believe that their aggressive behavior is justified, and this short-circuits feelings of guilt or remorse. Their self-image, as a victim who is hurt or treated unfairly and therefore has to be tough, contrasts with the ways others perceive them. For many children with disruptive behavior disorders, the self-image as a victim is accurate, because many have been abused or subjected to cruel punishments or been exposed to violence. The working model of self and others that develops out of coercive family processes interferes with moral development, distorts peer relationships, and—because of the child's aggressive stance—tends to foreclose opportunities to receive positive feedback.

Child Maltreatment

Maltreatment by parents, including neglect and physical, sexual, or psychological abuse, has serious and ongoing effects on children's development. Although it is useful to separate the different types of maltreatment for purposes of definition and study, in reality neglect and the separate forms of abuse often overlap. The child who is being sexually abused is often psychologically abused through threats of retribution or catastrophe if she discloses the sexual abuse. It is very common to read in case reports of children removed from their parents that they were often left without supervision and that they bear scars and bruises indicating physical abuse. Research also suggests that there is considerable overlap—as well as some differences—in the developmental effects of the different types of maltreatment. Psychological abuse is a common denominator across all types of maltreatment, and this may account for the common developmental effects (McGee & Wolfe, 1991). Another factor that may explain similar effects is that maltreatment is frequently traumatizing, so that a child's immediate and long-term responses to repeated maltreatment reflect posttraumatic symptoms and adaptations (Briere, 1992). Because this discussion of maltreatment must be brief, I will concentrate on commonalities in parenting behavior, interactional dynamics, and developmental effects across the different types of maltreatment.

In general the parenting style of maltreating parents has been described as less flexible, more punitive, and characterized by unrealistic expectations of the child's abilities. Maltreating parents deny or undervalue the child's needs and abuse the power they have over the child (Wolfe, 1987). The majority of neglected and physically abused children develop insecure attachments, ranging from 70% to 100%

across studies (Cicchetti, Toth, & Bush, 1988; Crittendon, 1992b). Many sexually abused children develop insecure attachments, though it is not clear whether this is primarily based on early caregiving patterns or on the traumatic disruption of attachment and shift in working models caused by exploitation of the child by an attachment figure (Alexander, 1992; Briere, 1992). Many sexually abused children, rather than having experienced chronically poor parenting, face in sexual abuse a trauma of betrayal, which compromises their ability to trust others and to perceive their intentions accurately (Finkelhor & Browne, 1985; Freyd, 1996). Neglectful parents tend to ignore or simply "not see" the child's needs. They provide little stimulation, do not monitor the child's behavior, and do not establish routines for the child (Egeland, Sroufe, & Erikson, 1983).

Trauma and Maltreatment

Many children who have been physically or sexually abused show symptoms and adaptations consistent with posttraumatic stress disorder (PTSD) (Briere, 1992). The essence of trauma is an overwhelming feeling of helplessness, often accompanied by physical or psychic pain, terror, and horror. In response to a traumatic stimulus, such as being severely beaten by a parent, the child experiences the physiological and affective arousal of the fight-or-flight response and finds that no action is possible and no help from outside is available. In the midst of the traumatic event, the child feels powerless and alone. From a cognitive point of view, in trauma horrified affect overcomes thinking. Being unable to get help, to act or to use cognitive strategies to avoid the horror, the child falls back on a more primitive defense, affective shutting down or numbing. The severity of trauma increases when the perpetrator is a parent or other close person on whom the child must depend. This is damaging because the individual's trust is betrayed. His expectations are reversed—a person who is supposed to protect becomes the victimizer (Finkelhor & Browne, 1985; Finkelhor, 1995).

Child Abuse Trauma and Developmental Interference. Once a maltreated child has been traumatized, and especially if the traumatization has been repeated, defensive adaptations occur that interfere with later development. The abilities to appraise reality accurately and to regulate arousal are compromised. Instead of being able to attend realistically to what is happening, the hyperaroused and hypervigilant traumatized child begins to view most events through the lens of trauma in an effort to avoid a repetition of the maltreatment. Essentially, because of generalization of the traumatic experience to new experiences, and because of accompanying hyperarousal, the child often is not able to differentiate between threatening and nonthreatening situations (Ornitz & Pynoos, 1989). Traumatized children show both generalized arousal—they tend to be "on alert" much of the time—and specific reactivity to triggers reminiscent of an aspect of the trauma (van der Kolk & Fisher, 1994).

Chronic traumatization tends to create rigid defenses. The child acts in an all-or-nothing fashion, either with acts of aggression, frantic attempts at escape, or intense psychological withdrawal and affective constriction. Dissociative and numbing defenses are particularly likely to develop in response to chronic physical or sexual abuse, although the child may also become enraged and aggressive when she feels under threat (Terr, 1991; Pynoos, Steinberg, & Goenjian, 1996). These defensive behaviors become established as coping devices and begin to function below the level of thought. Defensive behavior becomes automatic in situations that evoke memories or affective reminders of the trauma. Eventually, coping strategies such as affective constriction may become so generalized that the child's opportunities for cognitive and affective development are compromised (Terr, 1990, 1991).

Chronic traumatization interferes with the development of a young child's reality testing and even ability to symbolize. Abused toddlers who are in the early phase of language development may show delayed or impoverished language (Cicchetti & Beeghley, 1987). The toddler who does not yet have language as a reliable vehicle for encoding his experiences is hampered in processing trauma. The younger the child, the more likely the trauma will be registered nonverbally as affectively charged, fragmented imagery, which makes the child more reactive to similar affects and imagery. The ability to think about and understand an experience is a potent defense against traumatization (van der Kolk, 1987). Older school-age children and adolescents may fare better following trauma because they can use their cognitive abilities to master the stress. Younger children have more difficulty cognitively processing trauma because their ability to understand reality is not yet mature. The preschool child is likely to become confused about what happened and to egocentrically blame himself for the traumatizing acts of others. Studies of abused young children indicate that "maltreated children, like traumatized adults, have difficulty expressing specific and differentiated emotions. These deficits have been held responsible for the impaired impulse control seen in these youngsters. They have difficulty putting their feelings into words and instead act out their feelings without being able to resort to intervening symbolic representations that would allow for flexible response strategies" (van der Kolk & Fisher, 1994, p. 157).

Developmental Effects of Maltreatment. Maltreatment interferes with many areas of development, both as a result of the adaptations to trauma described above and the insecure attachments that maltreated children have experienced over time. Maltreated children are at risk for a wide range of psychopathology, including behavior disorders, PTSD, dissociative disorders, and depression (Cicchetti, Rogosch, Lynch, & Holt, 1993; Friedrich, Jaworski, Huxsahl, & Bengston, 1997). The developmental effects of abuse show up in infancy in the form of depression, poor affect regulation, high arousal, and anger. Severely abused infants show retardation in all spheres of development (Gaensbauer & Mrazek, 1981). Maltreated toddlers show high levels of aggression and anger, and are hostile in situations that do not seem to call for hostility (George & Main, 1979; Crittenden, 1992a). In school-age children chronic maltreatment has been linked to maladaptive problem-solving abilities, cognitive disorganization, poorer language development, and lowered academic performance (M. F. Erickson, Egeland, & Pianta, 1989; Eckenrode, Laird, & Doris, 1993; Beeghly & Cicchetti, 1994; Kurtz, Gaudin, Woodarski, & Howing, 1993).

Maltreated children tend to have histories of insecure attachment. The absence of a secure base in attachment has in turn been related to less exploratory behavior and less behavior oriented toward developing competence. A study of maltreated school-age children showed that their insecure attachments rendered them mistrustful and less ready to learn from new adults (Aber & Allen, 1987). Working models based on mistrust of adults and defensive emphasis on self-protection interfered with these children's ability to engage in learning. Both physically abused and neglected children have been found to develop a more self-centered orientation and have less capacity for empathy than normal children. They show disturbances in the development of the self. For example, a study of self-conceptions of maltreated children showed that early school-age children tended to exaggerate their abilities and aggrandize themselves, in a fantasy mode that is more typical of 4-year-olds. By third or fourth grade, this defensive view of self had been given up and replaced with negative, depressive views of self that reflected a sense of inadequacy and self-blame (Vondra, Barnett, & Cicchetti, 1989, 1990).

Socially, maltreated children have more difficulty appraising what others intend and what is happening in interactions (Finkelhor, 1995). Because they anticipate aggression and rejection, they may misread the behavior of others and take defensive actions that are not appropriate to the situation (Weiss, Dodge, Bates, & Pettit, 1992). These problems, combined with impairments in ability to trust others, lead to ineffective relationships with peers. Peers tend to reject and isolate them because they are more aggressive and negative in interactions (Mueller & Silverman, 1989; Salzinger, Feldman, Hammer, & Rosario, 1993; Dodge, Pettit, & Bates, 1994).

Foster Care as a Secondary Risk Factor

As an outcome of maltreatment, placement in foster care is associated with serious risk. Most children placed in care have been maltreated and therefore must cope with the effects of abuse on their development. When they enter care, however, they suffer a loss of parent, family, and a familiar environment. Once in care they face problems of adaptation. Finally, given the inadequacies of the foster care system, they frequently must cope with disruptions of new relationships and environments, as they are moved from one foster home to another. The child welfare system often does not provide treatment for at-risk foster children and typically responds to problems of adaptation by moving the child to another foster home (Molin, 1988; Folman, 1995).

The number of children entering foster care has been rapidly increasing since 1980, with an even faster increase in recent years because of the crack cocaine epidemic (Folman, 1995; Children's Defense Fund, 1998). Because of the disorganizing effect of substance abuse on parenting, children's preplacement experiences have been chaotic and they enter care with serious developmental problems (Klee, Kronstadt, & Zlotnick, 1997). They often have been severely neglected, show disorganized attachment, are used to fending for themselves, may have "disorderly" habits, such as eating whenever they are hungry or hoarding food, and will tend not to look to others for help, guidance, or structure. When these precociously self-reliant and undersocialized children enter a foster family in which the adults hold authority and take responsibility for family functioning, they may resist the new structure, in part because their sense of control and autonomy has been usurped, and in part because their early experiences of abuse and neglect have made them terrified of being dependent (Fanshel, Finch, & Grundy, 1990). These characteristics in turn make it difficult for foster parents to engage with them.

Disrupted Attachment and Foster Care. Disruption and loss of attachments are central to the experience of the foster child. Even if the child's attachment to the biological parent fits one of the insecure categories, removal to foster care represents a disruption of attachment and a loss of an attachment figure. Children coming into foster care should be seen as grieving children, even when they are relieved to have been removed from the abuse (Fanshel & Shin, 1978). The child welfare system tends to keep only minimal information about children's preplacement histories (Fein, 1991). Caseworker turnover and multiple placements reinforce the foster child's feeling that "nobody really knows me." This is a particularly difficult issue for children in foster care because frequently their preplacement experience has been traumatic. The subjective experience of trauma involves feeling helpless and alone, and having no one to turn to for support. When traumatized children enter care with people who do not know about the traumas they have experienced, the sense of being alone may be intensified.

Not knowing about the child's earlier traumas leaves the foster parent without any context for interpreting or empathizing with the child's ongoing symptomatic behavior (Folman, 1995). Some foster parents who unrealistically expect a child to make a rapid adjustment to foster care may pathologize behavior that is obnoxious but normal under the circumstances (Molin, 1988). Taking behavior problems at face value, rather than as symptoms of trauma or the stress of entering care, may cause foster parents to become rejecting or punitive. In clinical evaluation, it is important to consider that a foster parent's impressions of a child may represent only a current snapshot. Especially if a child has recently come into care, the "symptoms" reported by the foster parent may reflect the child's crisis (Folman, 1995). A social worker assigned to a child's case may well learn more about the child's history from the child, and then can convey information to the foster parent that contextualizes and makes sense of the child's symptomatic behavior.

Threats to Continuity for Children in Foster Care. Studies of foster care indicate that foster children must cope with many changes and secondary stressors over which they have no control: replacement (change of foster home); caseworker turnover; conflicts between workers and foster parents; conflicts between foster parents and biological parents; inconsistency in parental visiting; return home, followed by reentry into foster care; and failed adoptions (Proch & Taber, 1985; Folman, 1995). Consequently, many foster children live with an uncertain sense of the future. They do not know if or when they will be returned to parents or shifted to another foster home. If the biological parent is inconsistent about visiting, does not visit at all, or is not complying with requirements for return of the child—such as getting substance abuse treatment—the child's uncertainty is intensified. Uncertainty about whether the child will be returning home may limit the foster family's ability to invest in the child, which further conveys to the child how tenuous his status is.

Many children who move through multiple placements, or are returned home only to be removed to foster care again, adapt to these discontinuities in relationships and environment by detaching and becoming self-reliant (Kates, Johnson, Rader, & Strieder, 1991). Repeated placement "failures" may predispose children to expect to be removed from whatever family they are placed with, and consequently they resist attachment and may act out negative interactions from previous negative relationships. This is particularly likely to occur when a child's working models of attachment involve the expectation of neglect or maltreatment (Littner, 1960). However, these working models may have been confirmed for the child in foster care, especially if foster parents become punitive or even abusive in response to acting out (Rosenthal, Motz, Edmonson, & Groze, 1991).

Risk in Foster Care as a Function of Early Experience. Although this review of research on risk in foster care has highlighted risk factors of the foster care system and the discontinuities between the child preplacement and placement experiences, it is important to state that the few longitudinal studies show that children's functioning in foster care is predicted by their preplacement experiences in their families of origin (Fanshel & Shinn, 1978; Folman, 1995). Many children with histories of insecure attachment, severe maltreatment, and early trauma and loss, along with a corresponding absence of protective factors, may enter foster care already on a seriously maladaptive pathway that shapes the child's behavior in care regardless of the quality of care.

Witnessing Family Violence

Recent research demonstrates that children who witness their mothers being attacked by fathers or male partners are at risk for traumatization and impediments to development (McClosky, Figueredo, & Koss, 1995; Gleason, 1995). Studies of child witnesses of domestic violence report profiles similar to those of abused children, showing clinically significant problems at rates two to four times higher than those in children in the general population (Fantuzzo & Lindquist, 1989; Jaffe, Wolfe, Wilson, & Zak, 1986). There is a significant overlap between domestic violence and maltreatment, particularly physical abuse. Straus found that 50% of male batterers also abuse their children (compared with 7% of control group males) and that 24% of battered women are also abusive (compared with 10% of control group women) (Straus, 1983).

Like physical abuse, witnessing violence tends to be traumatic. Hyperarousal, fearfulness, reactivity to posttraumatic reminders, and posttraumatic play and defenses are common in children exposed to chronic domestic violence (Kilpatrick, Litt, & Williams, 1997; Lehmann, 1997). It is not surprising that witnessing violence should be traumatic, given that the child, at close range and in the midst of intense emotions, sees her mother being brutalized. The impact of seeing the primary caregiver attacked heightens the impact of trauma (Fick, Osofsky, & Lewis, 1996). Clinical reports document increased risk to child witnesses because of the chronic traumatization of their mothers (Davies, 1991; Gaensbauer, 1996). An aspect of trauma, which is often also explicitly enforced by the batterer, is social isolation. Battered women may not have access to social support, and this has a negative impact on their ability to provide the support and understanding the young child needs to cope with reactions to witnessing violence. The mother may not be able to make connections between the child's symptomatic behavior and the experience of witnessing violence. This is particularly likely when the child is under age 6 and has difficulty articulating her worries, or when the mother defends against recognizing the child's posttraumatic symptoms because they remind her of her own traumatization. The mother may become more punitive rather than understanding. The child may experience this as a failure of attachment and become even more symptomatic. Boys may be more at risk for the combined effects of traumatization and attachment failure because the mother may interpret the boy's symptomatic aggression as indicating that "He's just like his father" (Davies, 1991).

Living with a violent parent may also affect moral development. Not only does the child see violence as a means of controlling relationships and responding to stress, he may also learn that violence is "justified." Studies of male batterers reveal a value system founded on the egocentric view that their needs are primary and that the needs of others are unimportant. Operating from this perspective, the violent man tends to rationalize his violence as being the fault of his spouse (Gondolf, 1987). Children, particularly boys who identify with their fathers, may internalize this moral logic.

Children who have witnessed violence show higher rates of aggression toward peers. This behavior has been explained in terms of the posttraumatic defense of identification with the aggressor and as the result of imitation of and identification with a parent who models violence as a means of domination or tension reduction (Davies, 1991; Webb, 1991a). Because of same-sex identification and cultural sanctions of male aggression, boy witnesses are particularly likely to behave aggressively. School-age girls, for similar reasons of identification and socialization, show higher rates of depression (Davis & Carlson, 1987; Henning, Leitenberg, Coffey, Turner, & Bennett, 1996). Children of both

sexes exposed to chronic violence may adopt numbing and dissociative defenses and develop a sense of powerlessness, because they cannot stop the violence (B. E. Carlson, 1990).

The risks of exposure to domestic violence may be moderated if
the mother is able, in spite of being victimized herself, to maintain a
positive and supportive relationship with the child. Other supports for
the mother, such as extended family or domestic violence shelters, may
serve as protective factors, since their presence may allow the mother
to leave the violent relationship (Osofsky, 1996a).

Death of a Parent

The death of a parent in childhood may create developmental risk,
depending on a number of circumstances. Earlier research suggested
that parental loss during childhood heightened the risk for psychiatric
disorder, particularly depression (Bowlby, 1980). Recent formulations,
while acknowledging that parental death is a severe stressor, have
focused on transactional factors that may heighten or decrease risk.
Important factors to consider include the quality of the child's attachment relationship with the parent before death, whether the death was
unexpected or traumatic, the surviving parent's or caretaker's ability
to provide emotional support and facilitate the child's mourning, and
the degree of overall disruption in the child's life (E. R. Shapiro, 1994;
Worden, 1996).

Heightened Risk: Stigmatized and Traumatic Deaths. Deaths from suicide or murder carry more risk because of their traumatic nature. Similarly, when the nature of death carries a stigma, as in murder or suicide, in crime-related circumstances, or from AIDS, the child's risk
increases because the family's shame, guilt, and need for secrecy may
prevent open mourning and lead to distorted understandings about
the death and the child's relationship with the deceased (Webb, 1993a).
Children confront a more complicated grieving situation and severe
developmental risk when the circumstances of death are violent and
especially if the child witnessed the death, including the extreme of
witnessing one parent murder the other. In these circumstances the
child will experience the loss as traumatic and will show symptoms of
posttraumatic stress, including hyperarousal, emotional numbing, frequent intrusive thoughts about the way the parent died, memories of
hearing the shots or seeing the blood, and fears about personal safety
and dying that lead particularly to sleep problems and nightmares (Eth
& Pynoos, 1985; Malmquist, 1986; Bevin, 1993). This has implications
for intervention planning. When the loss has led to posttraumatic

stress, the trauma work must precede the grief work. A person who is caught up in the horror of what has happened must be helped to understand and cope with posttraumatic symptoms *before* moving on to exploring the loss (E. R. Shapiro, 1994).

Variables Influencing Ongoing Responses to Parental Death. A child's internal reactions to loss are influenced by familial and cultural contexts. A child whose parent dies usually is being cared for by an adult who is also grieving, whether it is the spouse, partner, or parent or other relative of the person who has died. It is not easy for an adult to grieve his or her own loss and remain a responsive caregiver. Children may feel a double loss, because their remaining parent is emotionally less available and may have trouble maintaining security and predictability in day-to-day experience. Adults who receive support while they are grieving are better able to respond to children's grief (E. R. Shapiro, 1994). The critical variables that decrease risk following the death of a parent are responsive caregiving, the surviving caregiver's maintenance of consistent routines and a stable home life, the caregiver's ability to facilitate the child's mourning by talking and reminiscing about the dead parent, and cultural practices that support mourning (Silverman & Worden, 1992; Reese, 1982; E. R. Shapiro, 1994).

Permission to mourn and open discussion about the deceased parent help the child maintain an internalized image of the parent, even as the intensity of grief diminishes. E. R. Shapiro (1994) explains why this is important: "Because so much of a young child's development is yet to be completed, the image of a dead family member, especially a parent, remains a crucial source of support for the child's ongoing development. As a child's cognitive capacities mature, he or she continues to review and transform the internal working model of the deceased parent with new cognitive tools to meet new developmental needs" (p. 74). Positive identifications with a deceased parent contribute to the child's sense of personal identity, promote internalization of values, and provide an image of the attachment relationship that the child can draw on when under stress (Silverman, Nickman, & Worden, 1992).

Parental Psychopathology

Studies of children of severely mentally ill parents show high rates of exposure to abuse, neglect, and bizarre behavior. Parents suffering from schizophrenia and manic depression often behave inconsistently and lack emotional attunement (Grunbaum & Gammeltoft, 1993;

B. Dunn, 1993). The risk for being the object of inappropriate parental behavior is especially great when the child is viewed as a fantasy object or has been incorporated into the parent's delusional system. For example, a schizophrenic father wanted his infant son to become an opera singer and played loud opera music 24 hours a day in the baby's room. At an extreme the child may be terrorized, injured, or even killed by a parent who has delusionally turned the child into a persecutor or identified him with the parent's wish to die (Anthony, 1986). Children of severely disturbed parents may grow up feeling isolated from peers and community because of the parent's illness. They may develop a confused sense of reality, as a result of the parent's bizarre behavior. Sometimes the parent's strange actions and psychotic episodes have not been explained or discussed within the family, creating a sense of their "normality," which, as the child grows older, becomes increasingly dissonant with the larger social reality (B. Dunn, 1993). Children often become caretakers for their parents and siblings. They may develop strong feelings of guilt and disloyalty about differentiating themselves from the psychotic parent, as well as about their "failure" to change the parent (Rutter & Quinton, 1984; B. Dunn, 1993).

Studies of Maternal Depression. Maternal depression may have serious impacts on attachment and later development. Mothers with severe and chronic depression are likely to have children who are insecurely attached, in the range of 55–87% across studies (Teti et al., 1995). Compared with nondepressed controls, depressed parents show less physical affection, play less with their infants, and provide less stimulation. Children experience frequent and long periods of disengagement from the parent preoccupied with depression (Field, 1992). Infants of depressed mothers are likely to develop difficulties in regulating feelings. Because the mother is depressed, she frequently fails to respond to the infant's distress signals. In consequence, the infant does not receive her help in regulating affects and is likely to withdraw from the interaction (Tronick & Gianino, 1986a). Depressed parents are more critical and more likely to characterize the child negatively. Children exposed repeatedly to such negative attributions tend to internalize them as a way of viewing themselves, creating self-representations that are critical, self-deprecating, and self-blaming. This creates vulnerability to depression in themselves (Jaenicke et al., 1987; Hammen, 1992).

Some depressed parents, rather than ignoring or rejecting their children, require their children to take care of them, establishing an enmeshed relationship that restricts the development of autonomy (Radke-Yarrow et al., 1995). I evaluated the child of a severely depressed mother who literally hovered over her 5-year-old son. While he played, she sat within inches of him with her arms above him in an enclosing and protective gesture. He in turn appeared lethargic, waiting for his mother to take the lead in play, and spoke in baby talk during the entire interview. The presenting concern, from her point of view, was that he wanted to spend time watching television or playing alone in his room. She was not able to tolerate these signs of emotional autonomy. Depressed mothers who behave in this way foster the seemingly paradoxical combination of children who are securely attached yet function poorly outside the attachment relationship (Radke-Yarrow et al., 1995). Because of their strong identification with a severely depressed mother who lovingly demands that they remain totally involved with her, their movement toward autonomy, independent competence, and ability to relate to peers is compromised.

Although secure attachment is almost always seen as a protective mechanism, in the special circumstances described above a more distant relationship with the depressed parent can be deemed protective (Radke-Yarrow et al., 1995). This is also likely to be true of children of psychotic parents—lack of identification and distancing become protective factors. The most salient protective factor for children of mentally ill parents is an ongoing positive and developmentally appropriate relationship with another adult (Werner, 1993).

Parental Substance Abuse

Most substance-abusing parents have multiple risk factors, including child maltreatment, psychiatric disorders, marital conflict, or domestic violence (Sheridan, 1994). Consequently, it is difficult to specify the particular effects of parental substance abuse on development. Nevertheless, it is clear that parental substance abuse and addiction create serious risks, primarily because parenting ability is often severely affected.

The most common effects of prenatal drug exposure are intrauterine growth retardation, which causes low birth weight, and regulatory problems, such as decreased responsiveness or irritability after birth. Studies of prenatal exposure to cocaine, heroin, methadone, or marijuana do not demonstrate long-term developmental effects that are clearly attributable to drug exposure (Zuckerman & Brown, 1993). The clear exception is fetal alcohol syndrome, resulting from prenatal exposure to extremely heavy drinking by the mother, which has long-term developmental sequelae, including cognitive delays and possible mental retardation, hyperactivity, and delays in motor development (Institute of Medicine, 1996).

Although drug-exposed newborns may have lower birth weights, smaller head circumference, difficulties with self-regulation and symptoms of drug withdrawal, the consensus of studies seems to be that quality of caregiving after birth is a better predictor of developmental outcome (Zuckerman & Bresnahan, 1991). If caregiving is adequate, the effects seen soon after birth tend to gradually disappear. However, a parent who remains drug addicted after the child's birth is unlikely to be a good caregiver. Such a parent tends to be neglectful of physical and nutritional needs and emotionally uninvolved with the infant (Black et al., 1997). Poor caregiving increases the negative effects of prenatal exposure (Zuckerman & Brown, 1993).

Widespread use of crack cocaine by parents has caused them to neglect or abandon children because for crack users the addiction tends to take priority over the needs of the children. As noted previously, the crack cocaine epidemic has led to a large increase in foster placements of young children (Besharov, 1990). A study of children raised by mothers addicted to crack cocaine during the first 3–4 years of their lives had much higher rates of emotional and behavioral disturbance compared with a group of children reared by drug-free mothers. Problems with aggression, emotional regulation—as marked by frequent long crying spells—and poor peer relationships characterized these children as preschoolers (Hawley, Halle, Drasin, & Thomas, 1995).

Studies of alcoholic families have demonstrated that interactions between parents and children are characterized by inconsistency in the parent and uncertainty in the child, lack of parental warmth, and coercive parent–child dynamics, which other research has linked to behavior disorders in children (Steinglass, 1987; Campo & Rohner, 1992). School-age children who have grown up in families where one parent is an alcoholic have poorer social skills, peer relations, and academic performance (Sher, Walitzer, Wood, & Brent, 1991).

Community and Socioeconomic Risk Factors

The protective mechanism of responsive parenting is itself vulnerable to risk factors based on socioeconomic status, social disadvantage, racism, dangerous physical environments, and the generalized failure of a society to support families. Parents facing several contextual risk factors may not be able to provide adequate parenting, especially when these external stressors interact with parental and child risk factors. As children get older they may be exposed to community risk factors directly, with less parental mediation than during early childhood. A child walking to school each day in a dangerous neighborhood, for example, may be exposed to frequent violence, illegal drug activity, and intimidation by gang members. If the child is aware that his parents cannot shield him from these dangers, his vulnerability to influence by antisocial peers may increase because he perceives them as more powerful than the adults who cannot protect him (Garbarino, 1993).

Social Policy and Risk

Compared with other industrialized nations, social policy in the United States increases risk for children, especially working-class and poor children. The United States provides far less programmatic support to children and families than do western European countries with comparable economic strength. Over the last 20 years, there has been a decline in the condition of American children on a number of indicators: there have been increases in child poverty, births to single teens, children in single-parent families, children in homeless families, and child deaths and injuries by firearms. Rates of child immunizations and children with medical insurance decreased during the 1980s and early 1990s, but have begun to rebound in response to federal child health programs established since 1993 (Children's Defense Fund, 1995, 1998).

Child poverty, an overarching risk factor, has increased dramatically. The poverty rate for children under 6 years of age is a critical indicator of risk, since the early period of development is more vulnerable to disruption (Duncan, Brooks-Gunn, & Klebanov, 1994). The poverty rate for children from birth to age 6 has increased from the low point of 15.3% in 1969 to 22.7% in 1996, which represents 5 million children (Li & Bennett, 1994; Children's Defense Fund, 1998). Nearly half of these children are deeply impoverished, living in families making less than 50% of the federal poverty level. African-American and Hispanic children are more likely to be growing up in poverty (54% and 44%, respectively), yet poverty cuts across all ethnic groups and is nearly as prevalent in rural as in urban areas (Knitzer & Aber, 1995). However, since African-American and Hispanic children have higher rates of poverty than white children, they are disproportionately harmed by these societal risk factors. This deterioration of societal protection for children and families has been fueled by state and federal policy decisions, as well as by economic forces and the acquiescence of employers to a free-market ideology. In the political climate of the 1990s, in which punitive attitudes in Congress lead to cuts in child and family support programs, the number of children affected by the devastating risk factor of poverty will increase (Edelman, 1997). Private sector supports for families are also declining. For example, employers increasingly do not provide health insurance. Between 1987 and 1993, even though employment rates remained constant, the percentage of children with health insurance provided by their parents' employers dropped from 64.1% to 57.3%; if this trend holds, less than 50% of children will be employer insured in the year 2000 (Children's Defense Fund, 1995).

Poverty and Parenting

Poverty creates or intensifies many other risk factors that directly influence the child. McLoyd (1990) points out that "chronic poverty is not a unitary variable or a distinct event, such as job or income loss, but a conglomerate of stressful conditions and events" (p. 314). The impact of poverty on young children is largely mediated through its impact on their parents. The daily stresses of chronic poverty tend to undermine a parent's sense of competence, engendering feelings of helplessness and frustration. Poor parents have little control over their lives. Economic constraints limit choices about where they will live and where their children will go to school. The urban poor have no choice but to live in dangerous areas with high crime rates, where their children may see violence or become victims of it. External factors often force families to move; poor children face destabilizing moves and school changes much more frequently than do middle-class children (McLoyd & Wilson, 1991). Poor families on welfare also have crucial decisions about their lives made by caseworkers or constrained by the rules and procedures of the welfare bureaucracy, and more recently by the cost-cutting drive of "welfare reform."

Chronic poverty is dehumanizing and tends to damage parents' capacities for maintaining self-esteem and hope. These feelings tend to make parents become less responsive and more negative toward their children. Feelings of hopelessness, an external locus of control and chronic distress are associated with higher rates of maternal depression and substance abuse, factors which further compromise parenting ability (Halpern, 1993; McLoyd & Wilson, 1991; Garrett, Ng'andu, & Ferron, 1994). Studies of men who become unemployed show that they tend to become more angry, negative, and punitive toward their children (McLoyd, 1989).

Parents in chronic poverty tend to monitor their children's behavior less, with significant negative effects: "Low parental monitoring of children's peer activities has been associated with externalizing behavior problems in childhood ... and with lower child competence in classroom peer activities" (Bolger, Patterson, Thompson, & Kupersmidt, 1995, p. 1109). Parents who are poor have higher rates of single parenthood, divorce, harsh parenting, and child abuse and neglect (Hernandez, 1988; McLoyd, 1990; Herrenkohl, Herrenkohl, & Egolf, 1983). These grim aggregate findings, however, should not be taken to mean that there are inevitable links between persistent poverty and poor outcomes for individual children. Parents who resist the stressors of poverty, provide support and adequate monitoring, and stay involved with their children's schooling provide some buffering for their children (Bolger et al., 1995). But such parents must be highly resilient themselves and must make extraordinary efforts on behalf of their children.

Other Risks Associated with Poverty

Poverty and disadvantage spawn other risk factors, including inadequate nutrition, inadequate housing and homelessness, inadequate child care, higher exposure to environmental toxins such as lead-based paint, exposure to the danger of community violence, and lack of access to health care. These risks potentiate others. For example, a consequence of poor or inaccessible prenatal care is a higher rate of preterm infants born to poor families. Prematurity and neonatal health problems make the attachment process more difficult, setting the stage for the development of insecure attachments. In the current situation of governmental withdrawal of support for poor parents, Halpern (1993) notes that "the paradigmatic example of highest-risk infancy—a constitutionally vulnerable infant, a vulnerable and overwhelmed caregiver, and an unsupportive social and community context—is rapidly becoming the norm for poor infants" (p. 83).

As children reach school age, poverty becomes associated with underfunded and therefore poorer schools (Kozol, 1991). The child who has grown up in poverty for 6 years enters school at a disadvantage because of the developmental effects of early poverty (Dubow & Ippolito, 1994). A longitudinal study found that "children who experienced persistent family economic hardship started out behind other children on every measure of school-based competence . . . and generally stayed behind throughout all the years of the study" (Bolger et al., 1995, p. 1122).

Racism and Minority Status

Minority status is a risk factor created from historical and structural racism. Because of its historical roots, racism has been established as a value of the majority culture, now more often held covertly or even unknowingly than expressed overtly. In its institutional forms, including residential and educational segregation and many forms of employment and economic discrimination, racism has limited opportunities for people of color, both historically and continuing into the present. In these structural forms, racism has led to economic disadvantage and disproportionate poverty rates for African-Americans and Hispanics. However, it is important to differentiate between racism and race as risk factors, because calling race a risk factor subtly shifts the source of risk to something that is inherent in the individual. Race is not a cause of poverty, while racism and poverty *are* historically and structurally connected (Hirschfeld, 1996).

Racism as an attitude spans a range of beliefs, from negative stereotyping to fears of difference to "color blindness," which denies cultural differences. Both minority and white children begin early to learn American values about race, and experimental studies have demonstrated that they already know by age 3–4 that it is more desirable to be white (Spencer & Horowitz, 1973). Many minority children are able to resist applying negative racial or ethnic stereotypes to themselves, either because they have positive parental or other role models or because they use members of their own group as reference points for assessing themselves (Canino & Spurlock, 1994). Nevertheless, racial learning continues throughout childhood for minority and majority children not only through direct experiences with disadvantage or privilege but also through the imagery presented on television. Hirschfeld (1996) notes:

> For every episode of *The Cosby Show* a kid watches, he sees dozens of athletic shoe ads. These ads depict blacks as animal-like and dangerous, engaged in "violent" games of basketball played on inner-city courts and viewed through chain-link fences. When the child sees whites in these ads, they tend to be portrayed as disciplined, focused and controlled, running in parks or working out on sparkling exercise machines. What message do we expect children to take away from this? (p. 3)

Not only are ideas of white power and privilege and negative stereotypes of African-Americans emphasized in such imagery, but also the images the minority child receives of himself are highly stylized and simplistic. The minority child who does not identify with the negative imagery may feel "invisible," because members of his group are not portrayed positively or with complexity (Spencer, 1990).

Some minority children may internalize negative images based on racism, although this is not a typical response (Spencer, 1985). Those who do, however, often because their parents have internalized and transmit negative racial messages, are particularly at risk for poor self-esteem and depression. In response to this risk and the general need to help children cope with racism, minority parents face added parenting stresses that white parents do not have to deal with (Greene, 1992). In a racist context, where children will face prejudice and discrimination, it is adaptive to prepare them for encounters with racism in the same sense that it is helpful to prepare a child in advance for any stressful situation such as a medical procedure.

Minority families may utilize other culturally based protective mechanisms that reduce risk. African-American parents, for example, may gain support from membership in churches that have a strong communal orientation or from close ties to their extended family (Wilson, 1989). Hispanic family structure is also characterized by support from extended family networks and extraparental support of children through the system of godparents, or *compadres* (Mindel, 1980; Garcia-Preto, 1982). These supportive mechanisms are cultural traditions. Although social support is seen as a protective factor in general, the ability to marshal support is critical for families living in poverty, because social isolation intensifies the effects of poverty. Studies of poor minority mothers found that ongoing social support increased their self-esteem, which was linked to more acceptance and warmth toward their children (McLoyd, 1990; Taylor & Roberts, 1995).

Whether exposure to racism becomes a significant risk factor depends on the balance of other risk and protective factors. Spencer (1990) has characterized minority status as "an at-risk *context* that is exacerbated by economic disadvantage" (p. 268; emphasis in original). In practice situations the actual impact of racism must be assessed in the context of the individual child and her family. For some children, exposure to racism may be a clear risk because it contributes to feelings of hopelessness, negative images of the self, and depression. Other children, with the support of their parents and extended family, may regard racism as a challenge to master, in which case it does not pose the same degree of risk.

Exposure to Community Violence

In poor urban areas, children are exposed to high rates of community violence, which includes observing street fighting between gang members, seeing at close range wounded or dead victims of drive-by shootings, or becoming victims themselves. The most vulnerable children, as measured by the accumulation of other risk factors related to poverty, have the highest rate of exposure to community violence (Garbarino,

1993). As crimes involving firearms have increased in inner cities in the last 25 years, the chances of poor urban children witnessing lethal violence have increased. Garbarino (1995) has tracked this trend in Chicago. Between 1973 and 1993, the city's overall homicide rate increased by 400%, with rates in the poorest areas of the city going much higher. In three of Chicago's high-risk neighborhoods, 31% of elementary school children had witnessed a person being shot and 84% had witnessed a physical assault (Garbarino, 1995). Studies of similar areas in Washington, DC, New Haven, CT, and New Orleans, LA, yielded similar rates of children's exposure to street violence (Osofsky, 1996b). Garbarino (1995) argues that gang warfare linked to drug trafficking in these violent neighborhoods creates an atmosphere of actual violence and imminent threat akin to a war zone. In such an atmosphere, children are aware of the violence and danger of their neighborhood even though they may not have directly witnessed a murder or assault (Richters & Martinez, 1993).

Psychological Consequences of Exposure to Community Violence. Children exposed to chronic violence, whether at home or in the community, may develop symptoms of PTSD and make adaptations to trauma that interfere with development. Risk of trauma increases if the violence is intense, as in shooting, when the child is close to the event and when the child knows the victim or the perpetrator (Fick et al., 1996). When exposure to violence is repeated, or when the threat of violence remains high, the child may show a progression from symptoms of PTSD to defensive adaptations that stress toughness, emotional constriction, aggression, and uncaring behavior toward others. Children may both identify with the aggressor and the victim, developing a model of the self that requires aggressive behavior for self-protection yet also contains a fatalistic view that the child will die before adulthood (Williams, Singh, & Singh, 1994). Children who witness gun violence especially learn prematurely how vulnerable the human body is. They also learn that the adults in their families and community are not able to prevent the violence from occurring. Adults trapped in poverty in violent neighborhoods may also become resigned and fatalistic, conveying to their children that violence cannot be prevented. In response to chronic trauma in the context of the failure of adult protectiveness, children may either become depressed and withdrawn or may adopt a violent stance themselves as a means of self-protection (Bell & Jenkins, 1993). Older school-age children may join gangs, model the behavior of violent older peers, and view possession of a gun as a sign of social status and safety (Garbarino, Dubrow, Kostelny, & Pardo, 1992).

Countervailing Protective Factors against Exposure to Violence. Embracing a violent lifestyle or depressive withdrawal, however, are not inevitable outcomes of living in a violent neighborhood. Consistent with general trends in resiliency research, Richters and Martinez (1993) found that a stable family and a safe (nonviolent) home environment significantly buffered children from the effects of violence occurring outside the home, as measured by their successful academic performance and relative freedom from behavioral symptoms.

Transactional–Developmental Variables That Increase Risk

Risk that the child's ability to cope with stress will be compromised or overwhelmed increases under the following conditions:

1. *When the child is unable to mobilize coping strategies that are adequate to cope with a stressor.* This is especially likely when the child is under 6 years of age and has not proceeded far enough in cognitive development to have established adequate appraisal strategies. The younger the child, the fewer internal adaptive coping mechanisms she will possess and the more vulnerable she will be to acute or enduring environmental stressors. Studies of children's reactions to natural disasters such as floods or hurricanes consistently show that children under 5 years of age have more severe symptoms than do older children, which reflects their immature coping mechanisms (Farver & Frosch, 1996).

2. *When caregivers are not able or not available to reduce the child's stress.* Parenting is the critical mediator of risk. If parents are unable to buffer the child, he may be overwhelmed by environmental risk factors. Development is a variable here as well. The effectiveness of protective factors related to internal characteristics of the child is mediated by developmental level. In general, the younger the child, the less effective qualities such as a positive attitude or above-average intelligence will be in mitigating risk, and the more the child needs external protective factors that come from family support.

3. *When acute stressors interact with multiple ongoing risk factors, tipping the balance between coping and vulnerability.* For example, a child who appears resilient because of supportive parenting in spite of living in poverty in a neighborhood where violence is commonplace is traumatized by the murder of a classmate and becomes depressed and apathetic.

4. *When failures in active coping have become part of the child's expectations.* The child, through exposure to chronic stress, has learned there is nothing she can do to avoid the stress and thus takes the passive

stance of "learned helplessness" (Seligman, 1975). This is a common pattern in children who have been sexually or physically abused chronically from an early age. Such children do develop defenses to help them cope with the repeated abuse, but frequently the defenses are based on passive rather than active coping. The child begins to depend on defenses that split off emotion from experience, such as dissociation and isolation of affect.

5. *When early maladaptive coping mechanisms and defenses have become rigidly established, and then are mobilized in indiscriminate fashion in response to even minor stress.* For example, the young child who has been abused or has witnessed frequent domestic violence may become hypervigilant and easily aroused at any hint of aggression. Even in an inappropriate situation, as when another child speaks to him in a loud voice, he may attack the other child because his fear has become generalized. Reliance on early, rigid defenses interferes with development because it limits the child's flexibility in appraising and responding to experience and prevents learning of more adaptive coping mechanisms.

6. *When the child is exposed to multiple risk factors over time, resilience diminishes.* The child's coping abilities are worn down and overwhelmed (see Figure 2.1, which presents a hypothetical example of the effects of accumulating risk factors on an individual child's development). Sameroff (1993) found that children whose environmental circumstances presented a high number of risk factors over time tended to do poorly. Summarizing a follow-up on children first studied at age 4, Sameroff states:

> We were disappointed to find little evidence of . . . resilient or invulnerable children. . . . At age 13 we found the same powerful relationship between environmental adversity and child behavior. Those children with the most environmental risk factors had the lowest competence ratings. . . . Whatever the child's ability for achieving high levels of competence, it was severely undermined by the continuing paucity of environmental support. Whatever the capabilities provided to a child by individual factors, it is the environment that limits the opportunities for development. (1993, p. 8)

CONCLUSION

It is important to conclude this extended discussion of risk factors and their potential impacts with a reminder that protective factors within the community, family, or child may be marshaled to ameliorate risk.

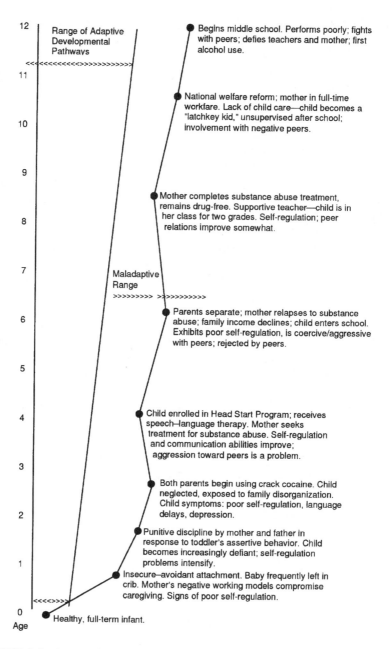

FIGURE 2.1. Accumulation of risk and maladaptive developmental pathways. Adapted from Bowlby (1988). Copyright 1988 by Richard P. J. Bowlby, Robert J. M. Bowlby, and Anthony Gatlin. Adapted by permission of Basic Books, a member of Perseus Books, L. L. C.

Risk factors are not fate. Risk and protective processes are on a continuum and constantly interact. When protective processes are present across time, even in high-risk situations, children's development is guarded and resilience grows (Egeland et al., 1993).

Awareness of the presence of risk factors calls attention to the need for intervention, including preventive intervention if the effects of risk are not yet manifest. Sameroff's (1993) findings on the power of chronic and multiple risk factors suggest that the provision of protective factors should also be conceptualized from a long-term perspective. Programs aimed at decreasing risk through early intervention should not be thought of as inoculation against future risk. The protective internal characteristics of the child that are strengthened through early intervention will not stand up against multiple environmental risk factors. If early interventions work, they should be continued across the course of childhood and adolescence. Knowledge of risk and protective factors is an essential aspect of the social work practitioner's knowledge base. I will illustrate the practical uses of a risk and protective factors analysis in evaluating children and their families in the next chapter.

APPENDIX: SUMMARY OF RISK AND PROTECTIVE FACTORS

Child Risk Factors

- Prematurity, birth anomalies
- Exposure to toxins *in utero*
- Chronic or serious illness
- Temperament: difficult or slow to warm up
- Mental retardation/low intelligence
- Childhood trauma
- Antisocial peer group

Parental/Family Risk Factors

- Insecure attachment
- Parent: insecure adult attachment pattern
- Single parenthood (with lack of support)
- Harsh parenting, maltreatment
- Family disorganization; low parental monitoring
- Social isolation, lack of support
- Domestic violence
- High parental conflict

- Separation/divorce, especially high-conflict divorce
- Parental psychopathology
- Parental substance abuse
- Parental illness
- Death of a parent or sibling
- Foster care placement

Social/Environmental Risk Factors

- Poverty
- Lack of access to medical care, health insurance, and social services
- Parental unemployment
- Homelessness
- Inadequate child care
- Exposure to racism, discrimination
- Poor schools
- Frequent change of residence and schools
- Exposure to environmental toxins
- Dangerous neighborhood
- Community violence

Child Protective Factors

- Good health
- Personality factors: easy temperament; positive disposition; active coping style; positive self-esteem, good social skills; internal locus of control; balance between help seeking and autonomy
- Above-average intelligence
- History of adequate development
- Hobbies and interests
- Good peer relationships

Parental/Family Protective Factors

- Secure attachment; positive and warm parent–child relationship
- Parent: secure adult attachment pattern
- Parents support child in times of stress
- Household rules and structure; parental monitoring of child
- Support/involvement of extended family, including help with caregiving
- Stable relationship between parents
- Parents model competence and good coping skills
- Family expectations of prosocial behavior
- High parental education

Social/Environmental Protective Factors

- Middle-class or above socioeconomic status
- Access to health care and social services
- Consistent parental employment
- Adequate housing
- Family religious faith and participation
- Good schools
- Supportive adults outside family who serve as role models/mentors to child

❖ CHAPTER 3 ❖

Analysis of Risk and Protective Factors: Practice Applications

This chapter presents practice applications of the analysis of risk and protective factors. Risk and protective factors should be viewed from a developmental perspective. Infants and young children depend on external protective mechanisms—a secure attachment, protective parents, a predictable environment. As development proceeds, the child gradually becomes more capable of responding to stress using her own internal resources. For example, the school age child can usually cope successfully with a separation from parents lasting several days, whereas a toddler, because of her cognitive limitations and the particular developmental tasks she is working on, may become symptomatic after a separation of less than a week.

HOW TO USE RISK FACTOR ANALYSIS

Risk factor analysis can be used in evaluation both predictively and retrospectively. If we identify a cluster of present risk factors, we can predict that unless some are eliminated, or protective factors are added, there may be a negative outcome for the client. Such an analysis helps us prioritize intervention goals so that we address first those issues that create the most immediate risk. We can also use an analysis of risk factors retrospectively to understand a child's current difficulties. Often we find, by asking careful questions during an evaluation, that the child's difficulties began during a period when there were several interacting risk factors. Identifying this cluster of risk factors and linking them to the current symptoms becomes our first step in understanding the child's problems. In this chapter I will present two cases that illustrate these two applications of an analysis of risk and protective factors.

PREDICTION OF RISK: ASSESSING CURRENT RISK AND PROTECTIVE FACTORS

The following case presentation describes a family that was thrown into crisis by the birth of a gravely ill baby. The parents' immediate adaptation to this crisis created significant stress for their older children, ages 2 and 5, and the crisis reverberated throughout the family. The case provides an illustration of how the analysis of current risk and protective factors can inform and guide evaluation and treatment.

Alan: A Case Example

Presenting Problems

Alan Emery was delivered by emergency cesarean section following a diagnosis of intrauterine fetal distress, at 2 weeks past his mother's due date. He was in extreme respiratory distress due to asphyxia caused by meconium aspiration. Meconium is fecal matter that in normal circumstances constitutes the infant's first bowel movement after birth. Alan's distress *in utero* (cause undetermined) caused his bowels to release the meconium into the amniotic fluid in the womb. Infants "breathe" the amniotic fluid as their lungs develop. Alan's lungs had taken in the meconium in the amniotic fluid, causing severe damage to them. Because of his extremely grave condition he was rushed to a neonatal intensive care unit (NICU) at a major medical center. He was placed on a heart–lung machine for 3 days and remained in intensive care for 3 weeks before being transferred to the moderate care nursery.

Alan made a spectacular recovery with the aid of skilled medical care and cutting-edge technology. After he was out of danger, his mother, Mrs. Emery, remained very anxious and agitated, because she had been told that Alan's birth asphyxia had caused brain damage that would result in an undetermined degree of mental retardation. She asked, "How retarded will he be? Can we take care of him at home? Will he be able to go to school? Will he have to be put in an institution?" The medical staff had been concerned about Mrs. Emery throughout Alan's hospitalization because she had asked ceaseless questions about his condition but had not been able to take in the answers because her anxiety was so intense. Mrs. Emery's questions about Alan's potential retardation were, of course, impossible to answer, and the only accurate answer, that it was too early to know, seemed to increase her distress. Because of Mrs. Emery's increasing agitation, the NICU staff began to question her ability to care for Alan after discharge and referred the family to the Infant Mental Health Unit. The evaluation request also raised concerns about Mr. Emery's ability to provide support for his wife and baby because he had a disabling diabetic condition.

Assessment

I met with Mr. and Mrs. Emery about 4 weeks after Alan's birth, after his medical condition was stable. Even though Alan was no longer in danger, the assessment was carried out in an atmosphere of relative crisis, which waxed and waned as stress increased and subsided. Because of the crisis atmosphere, and because of emerging stressors that increased risk for the mother, infant, and other family members, it became necessary to constantly assess the balance of risk and protective factors. In order to help the reader appreciate the fluidity of a crisis situation that bred further crisis, I will first present the events as they emerged and then discuss how the analysis of risk and protective factors contributed to the intervention plan.

I was introduced to Mr. and Mrs. Emery as a social worker with the Infant Mental Health Unit at a predischarge planning meeting with the medical staff. Mr. Emery was a 46-year-old African-American, while Mrs. Emery was Latina and 40 years of age. During the meeting the parents were told that tests had confirmed that Alan had sustained brain damage and severe hearing loss in both ears. The medical team also recommended a number of services and evaluations for Alan following discharge. After the meeting I talked with them in the hall. Mrs. Emery was clearly very anxious as she tried to sort through the potential meanings of brain damage and hearing loss for Alan's subsequent development. Mr. Emery was more concerned about how they would follow through on the many services that had been recommended. I offered to help them prioritize and sequence the recommendations so that they would not feel so intimidating. I also told them that I was familiar with infant development and could provide ongoing assessment of Alan's progress. They accepted these offers, and we made an appointment for 2 days later.

During this brief interview, I also asked about the family and learned that the Emerys had two other young children, Jimmy, age 2, and Paul, age 5. They had been staying with a family friend for nearly 3 weeks while both parents were preoccupied with Alan's condition and spending long hours at the hospital. Mrs. Emery's 15-year-old son and 19-year-old daughter from a previous marriage also lived at home. Mr. Emery told me that he was permanently disabled from working because of a serious diabetic condition. He was concerned about the cost of the follow-up services for Alan because their sole income was his Social Security disability benefits, which were currently just adequate to support the family. Mrs. Emery referred to her "nerves" and asked if I could prescribe medication. I offered to arrange for her to see a psychiatrist with our program. At this early point in the assessment I was concerned about potential risk factors associated with life-threatening illness at birth. Although my concern focused on Alan and Mrs. Emery, as individuals and as a dyad, there were other immediate family risks to consider. Risk factors that were either potential or present and contributing to stress at this point are summarized below:

Child risk factors: Alan

- Health status: residuals from heart–lung machine treatment; seizure disorder(?)
- Medical trauma as possible interference with attachment(?)
- Virtual separation from parents while in intensive care for 17 days a further interference with attachment(?)

Maternal risk factors: Mrs. Emery

- Traumatic delivery experience; traumatic reactions to child's near death?
- Health status: recovering from major surgery
- Psychiatric status: Intense anxiety/confusion an interference with attachment and caregiving ability(?)

Family risk factors

- Father's health status: disabling diabetic condition
- Reactions of younger children (especially 2-year-old Jimmy) to month-long separation from parents, older siblings
- Overall disruption of family routines
- Family overwhelmed by need to arrange many postdischarge services for baby
- Financial stress: marginal fixed income

Observations of Parents and Infant

Two days later I met with Mr. and Mrs. Emery as they visited Alan in the moderate care nursery. Because of the medical reports, I had prepared myself to see an unresponsive baby. I had also wondered if Mrs. Emery's anxiety would compromise her ability to respond to him. Alan, now 5 weeks old, was a large, placid-looking infant who was focusing on his mother's face as I entered the room. She was smiling and talking to him, and he watched her alertly. As she held Alan, Mrs. Emery told me how much progress he had made. He had been comatose at birth, and she had believed he "would not make it." She smiled at Alan and said in a bright, singsong tone, "Yes, you were lying so still, we thought you'd never wake up. But you did, and look at you now!"

While she held Alan, she told me the story of his birth. She had known something was wrong because the baby had stopped moving. She called her doctor, who reassured her that often there was less movement as delivery approached. But the next day she was certain that something was wrong and went to the emergency room. Immediately after she had been examined, she was taken to the operating room. She was awake during the cesarian-section surgery. She realized something was wrong with her baby when she saw the doctors frantically trying to resuscitate him. Later she would expand the story, adding that she had been convinced that Alan was dead and that the doctors were lying to her because they wanted to cover up their mistakes. However, just before Alan was rushed to the NICU, the surgeon had her touch his chest. She could feel his heart beating. Mr. Emery described running between home, the NICU, and the other hospital where Mrs. Emery was recovering from surgery. He said it was easier after he had placed Jimmy and Paul with a family friend. Mrs. Emery commented that after being discharged following surgery, she had been shocked when she saw Alan in the NICU. He was unmoving and unresponsive.

At the end of this visit, both parents voiced optimism about Alan's future. They said that if he was retarded, they would make sure he got special education help. Mrs. Emery expressed apprehension about Alan's coming home, but I was struck by how much calmer and organized she seemed while holding Alan, compared to the reports of her distress and agitation. Being in physical and affective contact with her baby seemed to calm her. We arranged to meet at least one more time before Alan's discharge, which was expected in the next 5–10 days. After this interview and observation I felt more optimistic because I had a clearer picture of the family's strengths that would likely serve as protective factors. Mrs. Emery's responsive caregiving and Alan's alertness diminished my concern about the risk of poor attachment and inadequate caretaking. Some of the potential risk factors were discounted and those that remained seemed balanced by several protective factors:

Protective factors, observed in hospital before Alan's discharge

- Mother–infant attachment is proceeding well; mother is invested in baby and comfortable caring for him.
- Baby is alert and responsive in spite of health problems.
- Relationship between parents appears cohesive: they are in agreement about the baby's needs.
- Father is invested in baby and appropriately concerned about how to organize and manage his care.
- Availability of supportive friends (the family that cared for Jimmy and Paul) is an important backup.

In the treatment plan that was emerging in my mind, I expected to provide ongoing support for the development of attachment, monitor Alan's developmental progress, and possibly advocate for early intervention services. Our program allowed for home visits, and I expected to see the family at home once a week. I reviewed these ideas with Mr. and Mrs. Emery and they agreed. Mrs. Emery again requested medication, and I arranged a psychiatric appointment for her for 2 days later. I also set an individual appointment with me for 3 days later. My perception of Mrs. Emery had begun to change. Although she was still anxious, her calmness when she was with Alan challenged my previous belief that she was in crisis. I was also aware that I had not yet taken the parents' histories and that I did not know what Mrs. Emery was like when she was not under severe stress. Nevertheless, the good quality of her interaction with Alan seemed reassuring.

An Emerging Crisis

However, in retrospect, the case was moving into a critical phase. I will describe the events of a tumultuous week. Mrs. Emery canceled her psychiatric appointment and missed her Friday meeting with me. I could not reach her by phone. In retrospect it was clear that these missed appointments were symptomatic of Mrs. Emery's intensifying anxiety and disorganization as Alan's discharge approached. I learned later that the next day, Saturday, she had been brought to the Medical Center emergency room by ambulance because of a possible heart attack. However, she had been cleared medically, given an antianxiety medication, and referred to the Adult Psychiatry Service. On Sunday Alan's physicians ordered his discharge for the following day.

The discharge decision was made on the basis of Alan's medical stabilization, the medical staff's perception that Mrs. Emery was a competent though anxious mother, and their assumption that the

Infant program was providing support for Mrs. Emery. I did not know that discharge was imminent, and the medical staff did not know that she had not kept her Friday appointment with me. Nor did Mrs. Emery inform Alan's doctors about her emergency room visit. When I read the emergency room summary a week later, it was also clear that Mrs. Emery did not provide the physician there with a link between her somatizing anxiety symptoms and her awareness that Alan would be discharged soon. Structural factors in a complex institution contributed to a lack of communication between professionals, and Mrs. Emery also presented a different set of concerns and different parts of her story to different professionals. *No one had the whole picture,* and in retrospect it appeared that Mrs. Emery had unconsciously disrupted professional coordination because of her deepening distress. To the list of risk factors, we now need to add some institutional ones:

Institutional risk factors
- Family relating to large, decentralized medical institution
- Inadequate or slow communication among hospital departments

Social workers who work in large institutions or coordinate clients' care across agencies must always be the alert for structural factors that may increase risk for clients.

On Tuesday, when I learned that Alan had been discharged, I called Mrs. Emery. She said that Alan was doing well but that she was feeling terrible because she had not been able to sleep for 3 nights. She again asked me to arrange an appointment with a psychiatrist. I scheduled an appointment for the next day. At this point I did not know and she did not tell me about her emergency room visit or their referral of her to the Adult Psychiatry Service. When I was informed that Mrs. Emery had canceled her psychiatric appointment on Wednesday, I called her again. She asked me many questions with intense and pressured affect. Repeatedly she tried to establish my role: "Will you talk with me about the baby's development?" and "Isn't it the psychiatrist's job to talk to me if I want to talk about my problems?" Recognizing that she was frightened by a focus on herself, I restated our original agreement—that I would monitor Alan's development. She said, "So you'll be the baby's therapist, and if I need someone to talk to I can see the psychiatrist." I agreed. Because of her agitated and disorganized presentation, I suggested a home visit that evening.

When I arrived, Mr. Emery greeted me and showed me that Alan was sleeping in a bassinet. He said that Alan was doing fine, but that his wife was upset. Mrs. Emery appeared severely depressed and anxious. She talked in an agitated manner, and at times her thinking became tangential with some loosening of associations. She showed me a letter from her mother, which mentioned the funeral of a distant relative. She said, "It's so depressing. How could she write a letter about death at a time like this? Is she trying to drive me crazy?" Then she retold the story of the cesarean, focusing on how she thought the baby was dead. I said that I thought she was tremendously upset by what had happened to her and her baby and that she was worried about her baby now that he was home. She agreed and again asked for medication. Because of the psychotic features in her presentation, I suggested an evaluation by the Adult Psychiatry Service, which she agreed to.

When she was seen at the Adult Psychiatric Clinic the next day, she appeared only anxious, not psychotic. When I came for the next home visit a day later, on Friday, Mrs. Emery was clearly psychotic. She had constructed a paranoid delusional system involving being damaged by doctors. She complained that she and Alan had been guinea pigs for the hospital, and that doctors had been monitoring her movements and taking pictures of her, so that everyone would know who she was. She said that a newscaster had spoken directly to her from the TV set, saying, "We know what you did." The psychosis, with its externalization of blame, persecutory delusions, and fantasies of malevolent damage could be understood as a desperate defense against overwhelming guilt that she was responsible for her baby's damage, as well as unacceptable rage at the physician who at first did not take her concerns about the baby seriously. Given her unconscious sense of having "caused" her baby to nearly die, she was terrified of damaging him further. Her acute psychosis had been precipitated by Alan's discharge. Mr. Emery confirmed that she had never expressed delusional ideas in the past, which supported the diagnostic impression of a brief reactive psychosis precipitated by severe stress.

Reassessment: The Crisis of Mrs. Emery's Psychosis

Changes in the lives of clients often require reassessment from the perspective of the new circumstances. A case that had begun in a medical crisis had now evolved into a psychiatric crisis. Mrs. Emery had met with the Adult Clinic psychiatrist a second time, and antipsychotic medication and hospitalization had been recommended. She had refused both. She angrily told me, "That psychiatrist wanted to take me away from my baby. I told her to forget it!" (It was interesting to learn from the psychiatrist that Mrs. Emery had brought Alan to the appointment and had cared for him appropriately during the interview.) Mrs. Emery's psychosis and her refusal of treatment that focused on her as an individual forced me to reconsider the original treatment plan of supporting the family and providing ongoing assessment of Alan's development. It was uncertain that this treatment plan would be adequate, given Mrs. Emery's inner disorganization and uncertain contact with reality. Other questions had to be evaluated before deciding to continue with the original treatment plan or institute a new one. The most pressing questions were whether Mrs. Emery's psychosis put Alan and her other children at risk, and whether other family members would be able to moderate that risk.

The emphasis of this crisis reassessment was on *the analysis of family risk and protective factors.* While ongoing assessment in the context of intervention sometimes reveals new problems, it may also reveal new resources that were not evident in the original assessment. During the second home visit and two home visits the following week, it was evident that even though Mrs. Emery was manifestly psychotic, she was affectively in touch with Alan, responsive to his signs and able to hold and feed him. She was also able to speak for him, telling Mr. Emery to change his diaper or her teenage son to quiet the younger children while Alan was sleeping. These warm, concerned, and appropriate responses to Alan alternated with delusional outbursts against the doctors. Even though Mrs. Emery was psychotic, Alan was not being drawn into her delusional system. On the contrary, her relationship with him seemed to be an island of reality and calm for her. Mr. Emery competently cared for Alan and kept the household going, insisting that Mrs. Emery rest. His inability to work outside the home, conventionally a risk factor, was in this case a protective factor because it allowed Mr. Emery to be consistently available to his wife and children.

At the fourth home visit, I met Mrs. Emery's 19-year-old daughter, Bettina. When I arrived she was diapering Alan. While I talked with Mrs. Emery, Bettina rocked Alan and sometimes joined in the conversation. Mrs. Emery seemed at ease with her daughter's caretaking. I had known Bettina lived at home and that she was working and attending a community college. I observed that she looked very comfortable with Alan. I commented on this, and she said she liked to take care of him. I said that it was good she was able to help her mother while she was recovering. I felt relieved that here was another competent family member who was sanctioned by Mrs. Emery as a caregiver for Alan. During this same visit I met the public health nurse who had begun visiting to monitor Alan's physical status. With Mr. and Mrs. Emery's assent, we agreed that we would each visit twice a week on alternating days in order to maximize professional assessment of Alan's development. Ongoing assessment thus revealed new protective factors that balanced the acute risk of Mrs. Emery's psychosis:

Emergent risk factors, postdischarge

- Mother's acute reactive psychosis is precipitated by baby's discharge.
- Mother's refusal of psychiatric intervention appears to escalate risk.

Protective factors, observed during home visits

- Father is competent to care for baby *and* available.
- Teen children are part of family and able to help out.
- Baby is separated from mother's psychosis.
- Infant mental health worker (social worker) is making frequent home visits.
- Public health nurse is making home visits on other days.
- Parents have access to health care system and other supportive services.

In spite of Mrs. Emery's reactive psychosis, the presence of these additional protective factors made it possible to maintain the outlines of the original treatment plan. This was a difficult decision because of the risk posed by Mrs. Emery's psychosis. The public health nurse's impressions agreed with mine that Alan was receiving adequate care and that Mrs. Emery was highly invested in him. It was very helpful to have another professional confirm my perceptions of a situation that was so anxiety provoking. The revised intervention plan maintained the goal of monitoring Alan's developmental status but added an objective that specifically supported Mrs. Emery's reconstitution from psychosis. This objective was based on the observation that Mrs. Emery was not delusional in her caretaking of Alan. Rather, when she was engaged with him, she appeared neither psychotic nor anxious. She implicitly used Alan as an organizer of her experience. Hypothesizing that the trauma of Alan's near death and Mrs. Emery's irrational belief that she had damaged him had precipitated her psychosis, I believed that as Mrs. Emery saw Alan as developing and viable she would be reassured by the "real baby" and be able to give up her overwhelming guilt and rage and the psychotic defense against these feelings.

This assumption was also based on an understanding of the usual course of reactive psychosis (American Psychiatric Association, 1994; Horowitz, 1986). The features of brief reactive psychosis are psychotic symptoms such as delusions, behavioral disorganization, disorganized speech, and hallucinations. In nearly all cases there is a major stressor that precipitates the psychotic episode. By definition, it is time limited, lasting from a day up to a month. The psychotic symptoms diminish as the stress decreases, and gradually the person returns to his or her previous level of functioning. Brief reactive psychosis is not related to schizophrenia. It is more common in people with personality disorders (American Psychiatric Association, 1994). Horowitz (1986) sees reactive psychosis on a continuum with other stress response disorders as an extreme expression of posttraumatic stress disorder (PTSD). An additional—and crucial—consideration in this case was that Mrs. Emery had many people who were supporting her, most prominently her husband, but also her adolescent children, the public health nurse, and myself.

A Realistic View of the Baby Decreases Stress

Within a month following Alan's discharge, Mrs. Emery showed only occasional flashes of psychotic symptoms. As she invested more and more in Alan, she became increasingly oriented to reality. Our collaborative work during this period focused on a weekly assessment of Alan's development. At each home visit, we watched Alan together. Mrs. Emery would tell me her observations of Alan's behavior and raise questions about its meanings. For example, she had noticed that his left eyelid drooped slightly. She was convinced that he responded to sounds by turning his head, which led her to question the diagnosis of severe hearing loss. I suggested that she explore these questions with Alan's pediatrician. It was obvious to both of us, however, that Alan was developing within normal limits affectively and socially. At $2\frac{1}{2}$ months, he was smiling, responding with pleasure when he was cuddled, and crying when he was uncomfortable. To Mrs. Emery, who had already cared for four babies, these were heartening signs that Alan, in spite of his traumatic early history, was a normal baby in many ways.

Gradually, we were putting together a coherent picture of Alan that included his strengths and limitations. Increasingly, I felt that this accurate view of the real baby in front of her was replacing the terrifying first image of Alan as unmoving and lifeless. As this occurred, her psychosis disappeared. Her ability to maintain a positive and realistic view of Alan was tested when he was diagnosed with cerebral palsy at age 13 weeks, after he had been home for 6 weeks. Hints of psychotic thinking in Mrs. Emery returned briefly, but with Mr. Emery's support, this time she used her anxiety to take steps to further Alan's development by putting him in a physical therapy program and by applying for social security disability benefits for him.

Who Is at Risk?: A Family Perspective

Parallel with this assessment and intervention on Alan's behalf, another story of family stress was unfolding: Jimmy's and Paul's reactions to the separation from both parents and to Mrs. Emery's reactive psychosis. Their behavior made clear that it was essential to extend the assessment of risk beyond the identified client. Each child expressed his distress in behavior characteristic of his level of development.

Jimmy, at 25 months, was extremely needy following the month-long separation from his mother. He tried to follow her everywhere, made constant demands for snacks, and had tantrums if he was refused anything. Such behavior represents normal responses of a toddler to stress. However, his mother, given her intense preoccupation with Alan, could not tolerate having another child with difficulties. Instead of being able to read Jimmy's behavior as the anxious reactions of a young child whose attachment has been disrupted, she saw his actions as "bad" and "mean." The unhappy combination of Jimmy's 2-year-old oppositionalism and his serious anxiety regarding attachment was leading to behavior that brought punitive responses from his parents. It also appeared that Jimmy's behavior represented for Mrs. Emery an acting out of the "craziness" she was trying so hard to suppress in herself.

Paul was dealing with his own separation distress by trying to win his parents' approval by being the good boy. This too was consistent with his developmental level. At age 5 he was in the process of internalizing a conscience and was thus eager to suppress negative or hostile impulses in himself. He was using Jimmy as a scapegoat, displacing his own angry feelings onto Jimmy and at times goading him into misbehavior. Then, when Jimmy misbehaved, Paul would seek his mother's attention by telling on Jimmy. In a particularly poignant example of this dynamic, Jimmy went to his mother's room and smeared his face with Mrs. Emery's cosmetics and Paul rushed to tell his mother. Mrs. Emery punished Jimmy. She was still caught up in the blunted and concrete thinking of an individual recovering from psychosis and was unable to see that Jimmy's behavior might represent an attempt to get close to her by putting on the cosmetics he associated with her smell and touch.

Jimmy's and Paul's problems were at first difficult to incorporate into the treatment plan because Mrs. Emery was so exclusively concerned about Alan. Further, given her guilt-ridden psychosis and anxiety, it was not possible to link Jimmy's behavior to the separation or to suggest she change her reactions toward him. In the short run, I addressed their issues by suggesting to Mr. Emery that he give them more attention and I also employed emergency "sidewalk counseling." I would talk to the boys outside and put into words the upset and worry they had experienced during the separation and their confusion about how different their mother had become since returning home. After 2 months of home visits, when Alan was about 4 months of age and Mrs. Emery had begun to feel more confident about his development, she was able to turn to Jimmy and Paul and tell them she understood their upset. With her returning capacity for empathy, she was more able to respond warmly to them as she had before the crisis of Alan's illness.

The analysis of risk should be applied to all family members, not just the identified client (Blos & Davies, 1993). The Emery case provides a good example of how a growing accumulation of risk factors can put other family members at risk. Clearly, Mrs. Emery's separation from Jimmy and her angry punitiveness toward him were putting his development at risk. The risk was intensified by his developmental status as a toddler. While Paul was less obviously at risk, his excessive tattling on Jimmy suggested that he was also struggling with reactions to the separation and loss of his mother's emotional responsiveness.

Lessons from the Analysis of Risk and Protective Factors

Especially in emergent crises it is important to do a careful analysis of risk and protective factors and try to figure out how to augment the protective factors as a means of reducing the risk factors. For the purposes of intervention planning, it is necessary to distinguish between immediate and potential long-term risk factors. For example, preliminary assessments suggested that Alan would be mentally retarded. However, that risk factor was not of immediate importance. By contrast, Mrs. Emery's intense anxiety was of more immediate concern. The medical staff was concerned that she was too confused to follow up on the services Alan would need. Further, new and unexpected risk factors emerged when stress on the family increased. Mrs. Emery's acute psychosis and, later, Alan's diagnosis of cerebral palsy required ongoing assessment of the balance of risk and protective factors.

Such an assessment was critical because of the potential impact of the mother's acute psychosis on her caregiving capacity. Was Alan at risk for neglect? For abuse? Would a Protective Services report need to be filed? Should Mrs. Emery be hospitalized? Since she refused hospitalization, should she be committed? The answers to these questions had a bearing not just on treatment goals but on *serious case management decisions* that had the potential to change this family's life.

When she was psychotic, Mrs. Emery established a clear split between, on the one hand, the physicians she delusionally believed had damaged Alan and, on the other, those helpers, including myself, the public health nurse, and Alan's pediatrician, whom she saw as helping her with her baby. Mrs. Emery implicitly realized that I accepted her requirement that I focus on the baby, not her, and that I take a positive approach that avoided any hints of blame that would reverberate with the overwhelming self-blame the psychosis was defending against. I was very reluctant to raise any issue that she would perceive as criticism. Essentially, I felt that if Protective Services and/or the legal system became involved, the Emerys would shift from being voluntary to involuntary clients and that their view of me would shift from helper to harmer. I believed that Mrs. Emery, given her delusional state, would only be able to see a Protective Services report as cruel and punitive toward her, and so my alliance with her would be destroyed. I also believed that such an "insult" would help perpetuate her psychosis because she would see it as another example of persecution by a professional. Yet, if abuse or neglect is suspected, social workers are required by law to report it. The ability to do home visits and the careful analysis of risk and protective factors enabled me to see the particular strengths of this family and the particular quality of Mrs. Emery's psychosis. This analysis yielded the conclusion that Alan was not at risk for abuse or neglect, in spite of being exposed to the typically high-risk situation of a parental psychosis.

RETROSPECTIVE ANALYSIS OF RISK AND PROTECTIVE FACTORS

The retrospective analysis of past impacts of risk factors must be based on a detailed knowledge of development. In evaluating an older child, the practitioner tries to learn what stressors the child has been exposed to throughout her development and what protective mechanisms may have moderated those stressors. The timing of these events can be matched with the child's developmental level. Often such an analysis illuminates connections between the child's current symptoms and past risk factors, leading to an understanding of how the child adapted to past stressors and how those adaptations carry over into her current behavior.

Assessment of External and Internal Adaptations to Risk

Children may adapt to harsh parenting, abuse, or witnessing domestic violence in early childhood by developing behavior problems, which may show up as defiance of adults and aggression toward peers. These children are likely to come to our attention when they reach school age because their behavior is so problematic. However, in assessing the potential impacts of early risk factors, it is important also to look at developmental progress, adaptation, and current symptoms in terms of the child's internal life. Some resiliency literature inappropriately tends to equate behavioral adaptation with mental health (Luthar & Zigler, 1991). But a school-age child may appear to be functioning well superficially, in that he does his work and does not get into trouble, yet may be beset with anxiety that interferes with peer relationships and the development of autonomy. Indeed, although disruptive behavior problems are more likely to lead to a referral of a child, anxiety disorders are the most common type of childhood psychiatric problem (Anderson, Williams, McGee, & Silva, 1987). Children may be functioning adaptively judged by behavioral measures yet score high on measures of internalizing symptoms such as anxiety and depression (Luthar & Zigler, 1991). A study of abused children judged resilient because they had been able to function well behaviorally indicated that they struggled with continuing inner pain and feelings of being unable to enjoy life (Egeland & Farber, 1987). These findings suggest that resilience is not a unitary phenomenon. Rather it is often a mixed picture— a child is resilient in some areas but vulnerable or rigidly defended in others. Resilience developed in response to severe stress and risk conditions often has costs.

Assessing the Evolution of Early Risk Factors

In retrospective analysis of the impact of stressors on young children, it is particularly important to try to understand the quality of attachment during the period of risk and to determine whether the attachment has been a significant protective factor over time. As described in Chapter 1, during the first 2 years of life coping is primarily a transactional process, with the infant signaling distress and the caregiver responding with soothing or stimulation, which restores the infant's affective equilibrium. Only gradually does the child develop effective internalized coping mechanisms. During the preschool years, the child's ability to regulate affect and behavior and to organize experience cognitively continues to depend in a large degree on parental responsiveness and on transactional patterns of affect and behavior regulation. Toddlers and preschoolers, because of normative limitations in level of cognitive development, are prone to interpret experience in concrete, egocentric, and magical ways that confuse cause and effect and fail to distinguish between thought and action (Piaget, 1952a). These cognitive limitations, as well as immature internalized mechanisms for dealing with stress, leave the young child vulnerable to stressful or traumatic experiences. The younger the child, the more likely that she will become behaviorally disorganized and traumatized when stress is extreme because she lacks skills for mastering stress through cognition or action.

Parents play a critical role in supporting and developing the young child's capacity for affect regulation by providing comfort, by modeling coping strategies, and by explaining and clarifying their experiences, particularly those that are stressful for the child (Matas et al., 1978; Schafer, 1979). If the parent is unable to help the young child modulate his reactions to serious stress, the child has the frightening internal experience of having to confront the anxiety-producing stressor alone. In this emergency, the young child is likely to develop an array of defenses that may include dissociation and other forms of affective inhibition, as well as tendencies toward being controlling and relying on fantasies of omnipotence and more action-oriented defenses such as acting out, restlessness, and identification with the aggressor (Pynoos et al., 1996). These defenses are reinforced by the child's affective reactivity to current stimuli reminiscent of the stressful situation and, for some children, conscious ongoing fantasies that the stressful or traumatic events will be repeated. This interplay of fantasy and defense then may be carried along through time, shaping the child's emotional life and orientation to the world. However, what adults usually see, and often misread, are the behavioral manifestations of the child's defenses. They are less likely to be aware of the child's fantasies and fear of repetition of stressful or traumatic events.

When the parent is unable to help the child modulate her reactions to stress, a problem that began in a linear process of cause and effect is often transformed into an transactional problem that is best thought of as bidirectional and circular. The child's symptoms are unfortunately reinforced and maintained by parental responses. For example, in the previous clinical illustration, Jimmy Emery's attachment with both parents was disrupted by the month-long separation following his brother's birth. Jimmy reacted with anger and despair. When he came home he expressed these feelings in the nonverbal behavior typical of toddlers. He was defiant, insistent on getting his way, and apparently intentionally destructive, as when he made a mess of his mother's cosmetics. His mother, especially during her brief psychosis, responded with frustration and anger, punishing him for actions she was only able to read as misbehavior. Her reactions increased his sense of her emotional distance and led to increased anger and misbehavior. The adaptive task for Jimmy and his mother was to find a way to reestablish a secure attachment before these symptom-based transactions evolved into a characteristic style of interaction between them. Fortunately, the resolution of her psychosis and the lessening of her anxiety about the baby allowed her to see Jimmy more sympathetically and to respond to him in more nurturant ways, which, also in circular fashion, helped him feel more connected to her and led to less symptomatic behavior. In cases where symptoms have persisted for a long time, it is necessary to identify in the risk factor analysis transactional patterns that perpetuate the symptoms.

Alex: A Case Example

Presenting Problems and Assessment

Alex Carty was an 8-year-old boy whose presenting problems included aggression toward his mother and sometimes toward peers at school, restlessness and disruptiveness in class, and difficulty concentrating on schoolwork. Shortly before referral he had hit a girl in the head with a rock and injured her. The school social worker described him as "impulsive, aggressive, and possibly on his way to a conduct disorder." Both his mother and teacher saw him as an anxious, "jumpy" child, who always seemed to be on alert. His parents had divorced 3 years previously. Alex's father had been abusive to his mother and to Alex. Alex had witnessed many physical fights and arguments between his parents. Beginning at age 2 he also became the object of his father's impulsive verbal and physical attacks. His mother, who had been victimized herself, had been unable to protect Alex. The attachment relationship could not mediate the experience for Alex because his mother was depressed, overwhelmed, and traumatized herself. The parental separation occurred when Alex was nearly 5. His father left the state and cut off contact, so Alex had not seen his father for more than 3 years. At the time of the evaluation, Ms. Carty alternated between angrily rejecting Alex for his aggressive behavior toward her and children at school and feeling guilty that she had not stopped his father from hurting him. Her view of him was similarly inconsistent, alternating between seeing him as being very much like his father versus thinking of him as a vulnerable child who had been abused. In the retrospective examination of risk and protective factors, several issues seemed salient:

Risk factors: Age 2– 4½

- Frequent witnessing of father's physical attacks and emotional cruelty toward his mother
- Frequent verbal abuse by father
- Several incidents of physical abuse by father
- Mother's traumatization and depression interrupted interactive coping that might have mitigated Alex's stress
- Identification with father as an aggressive male model, followed by loss of father
- Alex's cognitive immaturity and lack of internal coping mechanisms at time of abuse

Protective factors: Past

- Responsive parenting by mother, first 2 years(?)
- Cessation of violence and abuse due to parental divorce

The transactional patterns between Alex and his mother that had developed in response to their difficult history were helping maintain Alex's symptoms. At the same time, Mrs. Carty's present concern about Alex suggested that transactional protective mechanisms could be utilized to help resolve Alex's difficulties:

Risk factors: Current

- Mother negatively identifies Alex with his father and is frequently critical of him.
- Mother does not set effective limits on Alex's aggression toward herself, which reinforces his use of aggression as a coping mechanism.

Protective factors: Current

- Mother's current concern about Alex is indicated by her dissatisfaction over her negative attitudes toward him.
- Involvement of both Alex and Mrs. Carty in treatment.

Alex's presenting symptoms of aggression, impulsivity, anxiety, and hyperalertness were consistent with research on the outcomes of early physical abuse and witnessing violence (Dodge et al., 1994; Fantuzzo & Lindquist, 1989). It seemed likely that his symptoms represented posttraumatic dynamics associated with early experiences of witnessing violence and being abused. As treatment proceeded and increasing evidence of PTSD accumulated, this hypothesis was confirmed. Significantly, the interpretation of Alex's current symptoms as rooted in past trauma helped Ms. Carty see Alex more empathically and provided her with a rationale for working to change her parenting style by establishing firmer limits, which provided Alex with a greater sense of safety.

Comment on Diagnosis

During the assessment, Alex did not meet the full DSM-IV criteria (American Psychiatric Association, 1994) for PTSD, although several symptoms of the disorder were present and were likely related to trauma. As the therapeutic relationship developed, Alex made clear links via play and words between his current symptoms and his traumatic abuse. But we should note that his symptoms could be conceptualized in other ways. If we looked at his current symptoms without reference to the history and did not give sufficient weight to the anxiety in his presentation, the school social worker's suggestion that he was on his way to a conduct disorder might seem plausible. From the perspective of knowing that Alex had been abused and had witnessed a great deal of violence, the symptoms of impulsive aggression and fighting more likely represented trauma-based defenses. But what had started as desperate coping devices expressed via the behavioral repertoire available to a 2-year-old were now disconnected from their experiential sources. They had taken on a life of their own, had become generalized ways of relating to the world, and in the eyes of others had become pure behavior, or just the way Alex was. The long time between the trauma and the present, and the long time during which Alex's symptoms seemed to have a life of their own, had thoroughly masked the connections between trauma and later symptoms. The assessment of past risk factors helped me stay alert for posttraumatic play and other indicators of memories of abuse as treatment unfolded.

Intervention: The Exploration of Trauma

The account of my work with Alex will be selective, focusing on how the hypotheses regarding early trauma as a risk factor were confirmed by Alex's play material. I will briefly summarize the main themes of our work and then describe in detail a dramatic session in which the connections between the father's past abuse and Alex's current thoughts and behavior could be addressed directly.

I saw Alex in a nondirective play therapy that at first emphasized the development of our relationship. Given his abuse by his father, I was concerned that he would be anxious about working with a male therapist. However, it soon became clear that he was more ambivalent than fearful of me, as the themes of wishes for a male to identify with and mistrust of males emerged in his play. Though it was clear he was very interested in me, in his play with soldiers he repeatedly defeated my army men while saying that his were invulnerable. A prominent theme in this play was trickery. For example, he told me that one of his tanks had been abandoned and that my soldiers could take it over. He gave me instructions about what my soldier was supposed to do, saying, "You go inside the tank. You're looking around, but it's too dark to see. You light a match. You say, 'Hey, what's all that liquid?' It's gasoline! BOOM!" Variations on this theme of trickery and complete dominance continued across many sessions, taking on the quality of posttraumatic play with its repetitive, unvarying, and driven quality. Alex's mother had told me that his father had sometimes been kind and engaged with Alex and other times became abusive abruptly. I understood his play as a reversal of his experience: he became the sadistic trickster, and I became the confused victim. He had coped with ongoing fears of being hurt by identifying with the aggressor. He had also responded to the anxiety associated with being abused by adopting a defense or coping mechanism organized around a fantasy of being in omnipotent control. Alex's play presented both the fears (his play was full of violence) and the defense (he was in total control, his soldiers never lost). This coping mechanism was helpful to him as a fearful and vulnerable 3- and 4-year-old. However, ongoing fearfulness and reliance on omnipotent fantasy as a defense interferes with the developmental tasks of the school-age child and with the growth of more adaptive coping mechanisms such as reasoning about problems.

I commented on Alex's play by saying that kids did not like being tricked and hurt. I felt it was helpful to Alex to feel that I understood his fears. Out of this, he began to identify with me more. This showed up in his initiating play projects like building with Legos that we worked on together and asking me "masculine" questions like "How old were you when you started shaving?" Gradually, he became more trusting of me, which allowed him to use our sessions to work through some internal dilemmas that had seemed unsolvable at an earlier developmental stage. The therapeutic relationship in work with children has many of the characteristics of an attachment relationship, including the function of transactional affect regulation. Specifically, the child comes to rely on the therapist to provide empathy and a background of security as he represents dangerous, frightening situations in play. Affects and fantasies that would overwhelm the child if they were discussed directly can be explored in displacement, via play and indirect interpretations, in the safety of the therapeutic relationship.

A Detailed Play Therapy Session

I will present the process of an hour in which Alex clarified what his father's abuse had meant to him and how it had shaped his current concerns and behavior. This session followed many hours of relationship building and many hours of symbolic play representing traumatic themes. Alex built a long car out of several green Lego squares. He said, "Let's drive it," and we carefully lowered it to the floor. As he pushed it, it broke it in two and he said, "Now you've got one too." We drove our cars a bit and he said, "You know we're in space. We're on the planet Pluto. Is Pluto close to the sun?" I said, "No, it's the farthest in our solar system." He put an orange Nerf (foam) ball on top of the file cabinet and said, "That's the sun." He instructed me to drive my car under a chair, which he called a cave, and then told me to drive it out. He became a giant Plutonian monster tromping toward my car, and I quickly scooted it back into the cave. Then he told me to be the monster. I moved with giant steps toward his car, but he said, "You can't see. My car's got reflectors, and the sun's blinding you." He held the foam ball sun close to my face and said, "You can't stand the heat," and I retreated. Then he became the monster again and nothing I did could stop him. To prevent him from smashing my car, I tried the strategies he had previously used. I held up the sun and he said, "I can freeze the sun." Then he stepped on my car and smashed it. I said, "It doesn't matter if you're driving your car or being the giant, you're the one who's got the power and you're the one who wins! This play makes me think maybe there was a time when you were little when you didn't have any power and that scared you a lot. Maybe somebody did something that made you feel that way."

Alex said, "Yeah, my dad."

"What happened?"

"When I was 3 years old I was wrestling with my dad and I scratched him and bit him and he just picked me up and threw me in my room." (He goes through the motions of picking someone up by the back of the neck and flinging him through the air.) "I just hit the wall. Do you know I got a dead tooth?" (He opens his mouth to show me.)

"I can't see which one it is. How did it happen?"

"My dad. I hit the wall with my face and now my tooth is dead."

"Is this something your mom told you or something you remember?"

"I remember it."

"Do you still worry about your dad sometimes?"

"Wouldn't you worry if you thought he was going to come and take the kids?"

"Where did you get the idea that your dad might do that?"

"I heard him tell my mom. He said if she ever divorced him he'd come and take the kids."

"Now I can understand why you like to be in control and have all the power, because you really worry what might happen if your dad would come and you couldn't stop him from taking you."

Alex was looking worried and agitated. He said, "I know I'd still recognize him." Then he looked uncertain. I said, "Maybe you're worried you wouldn't recognize him."

"Even if he wore a mask, I'd know him as soon as he spoke. I'd say, 'I know it's you.' I know what I'd do then, too, I'd run down the hall by the office ... "

"Oh, you're imagining he'd come to school."

"Yeah. I couldn't stay in the classroom because there aren't any doors that lock. I'd get in the bathroom by the office because it's got a deadbolt and he couldn't get in, and once I got the door locked, I'd say, 'Ha, ha, you can't get me.' "

Discussion

Alex's fully imagined fantasy of his father's coming to kidnap him was one he had lived with alone. The fantasy had some adaptive elements, in that he had developed a careful plan for getting away. Yet the fantasy was also stuck in a 3-year-old's perspective. In the fantasy, as in his subjective experience of the abuse episodes, he imagines himself alone with his father. There is no one to help him, and he must find a way to take control of the situation on his own. So his fantasy represents his aloneness in the traumatic situation and his solution has an omnipotent quality—he heroically saves himself. This hidden fantasy is a vivid example of the "fate of the stressor" once it is internalized as a fearful expectation. Alex's aggression toward other kids at school suggested that he had generalized this fear to situations unrelated to the original trauma. His reliance on identification with the aggressor, a coping mechanism held over from an earlier developmental period, was interfering with current developmental tasks of moving into the world of peers and establishing higher-level coping devices.

My interventions in subsequent sessions focused first on specifying the omnipotent coping device as represented in play and describing how it had originated in response to his father's violence. I said, "I understand why your guys always have to win. In your inside feelings, it's very scary if they get beaten. If they would get hurt, even in pretend, I think it would remind you of how you felt when your dad hurt you when you were 3." Then I helped him think through more adaptive coping devices. For example, I introduced a developmental perspective on his fantasy of being kidnapped at school, saying, "When you were 3, you didn't know how to get help. Maybe you didn't even know some of the words to get help yet. And your mom couldn't help you because she was so upset herself, so I can understand that you felt like you had to do everything yourself. But now you're older and you know a lot more about getting help." I suggested some ideas and strategies he had not imagined, saying, "If you saw your dad at school, you could tell your teacher or you could tell the principal. They would try and stop him. If necessary they would call the police to come and protect you. You and I can talk your worries over with your mom, and she can talk to the principal to let him know not to let anyone take you from school." One aim of these interventions was to help Alex see, from the perspective of his more advanced developmental level, that he had resources to deal with potentially traumatic situations that he did not have when he was younger. A second aim was to suggest and help him apply a concrete, cognitive perspective on solving the problem that worried him. A third aim was to modify his internal coping mechanisms so that he relied less on omnipotent fantasy and more on rational, intellectualized ways of regulating anxiety that were more consistent with his current level of development.

In summary, the identification of early risk factors, whose potential impact is assessed in terms of the child's developmental level when they occurred, helps the practitioner generate hypotheses about the sources of the child's current symptoms. In Alex's case, the linkages between past trauma and current symptoms, defenses, and conscious fantasies were vividly revealed as he learned to trust the therapeutic relationship. For Alex, trauma was not yet a past experience relegated to memory but a daily source of fear. One of the features of PTSD is intrusive memories of the event. It appeared that Alex was thinking frequently of his father's abuse and that he had carried the memory forward in time, transforming it into a fear that his father would hurt him in the future. From the perspective of his fears, his symptomatic behavior, inappropriate and generalized as it was, made sense. The analysis of past risk factors allowed me to understand how early trauma influenced this child's current behavior.

❖

EXERCISE

Using the form below, analyze the balance of risk and protective factors for one or more of your clients. Include past and current factors.

ASSESSMENT OF RISK AND PROTECTIVE FACTORS

Child risk factors   Child protective factors

_____   _____

_____   _____

_____   _____

_____   _____

_____   _____

Family risk factors   Family protective factors

_____   _____

_____   _____

_____   _____

_____   _____

Social/environmental   Social/environmental
risk factors   protective factors

_____   _____

_____   _____

_____   _____

_____   _____

_____   _____

The Course
of Child Development

Introduction:
A Developmental
Lens on Childhood

In Part II, Chapters 4–11 present an overview of child development for use in mental health practice. When we meet a child we are confronted with the need to form an objective view of her development. This involves assessing how well she is responding to current challenges of development in several areas, including relational and social, self-regulatory, cognitive, moral, and expressive domains. We also need to develop an empathic understanding of the child's current situation and past experience. We must appreciate her external experience—environmental circumstances, caregiving, significant events—as well as her internal responses—how she how reacted to her experience, how she understood it, what defenses and views of herself she formed in response to the experience, all in the larger contexts of her family, community, and culture.

BARRIERS TO UNDERSTANDING THE CHILD'S PERSPECTIVE

To the beginning practitioner, children's ways of thinking and responding to the world can seem mysterious. It feels harder to reach an empathic understanding of a child's experience than an adult's. We can more readily understand adults because they communicate and think in ways similar to our own. Adults express themselves primarily in words, whereas children tend to express themselves through behavior and play characteristic of their particular level of development. Most adults have

111

at least some capacity for logical thinking, reflection on their experience, and integrative modes of thinking, such as being able to move back and forth between the abstract and the concrete, the general and the specific, the past and the present. In the course of normal development, these cognitive abilities are not well established until adolescence. Children think differently from adults, and the younger the child the more divergence in cognitive characteristics we see. Children live in the present and tend not to make links between past and present experiences. They have little interest in reflecting on their experience. They tend to think in very concrete and specific terms. It is also more difficult for adults to empathize with the child's experience of the world because they have forgotten much of their early experience. Further, as their capacities for understanding and thinking about experience have developed, they have evolved beyond the more primitive thinking characteristic of young children, and this makes it difficult for adults to understand the young child's view of reality.

Another barrier to empathy is adult reactions to the ways children sometimes express their distress. Children's symptomatic behavior—aggression, oppositionalism, throwing tantrums, refusal to follow rules, behaving "irrationally" in myriad ways—can be perplexing and disturbing to adults. This can lead to attempts to simply get rid of the behavior instead of trying to understand what it expresses. The adult's understandable impulse to control the child short-circuits empathy. A related problem is the difficulty in conceptualizing the symptomatic behavior of children. Often the reasons for children's symptomatic behavior are obscure. Diagnosis of children seems harder than adult diagnosis because children often do not readily fit into available diagnostic categories; instead, they may present with a variety of symptoms—behavior disturbances, anxiety, social withdrawal—that are consistent with several diagnoses. Further, it is often hard to differentiate children's difficulties from the transactional context of family interactions. In adults, symptomatic behavior can often be understood in the context of regularities in personality. That is, the adult's symptoms as well as strengths may seem more consistent and predictable because they reflect an established personality. The same cannot be said of children, who to a much greater degree are changing as development proceeds and are more reactive to changes in their family circumstances.

USES OF DEVELOPMENTAL UNDERSTANDING

The best way to overcome the obstacles to understanding children is to gain a working knowledge of development. This includes knowing salient tasks and abilities, and ways of thinking, communicating, and behaving that characterize a given age. Anna Freud (1963, 1965) created the very useful concept of "developmental lines," suggesting that development can be seen as a number of specific domains that unfold parallel to one another. The advantage of the developmental lines concept is that it allows us to focus on different aspects of development independently, so that we can identify a child's areas of relative developmental strength and difficulty. For example, a school-age child may have good relationships with peers and parents, indicating adequate attachments and social development, and at the same time have difficulties in academic tasks, suggesting possible problems in cognitive development related to learning disorders.

DEVELOPMENTAL "STAGES" AND DISCONTINUITY

While it is useful to consider the child's progress in each developmental line or domain, it is equally important to recognize that change comes in "packages" (Sroufe, 1989), meaning that development transforms multiple domains simultaneously. Development is not simply additive. Emerging capacities transform capacities that developed earlier, so that the child, across developmental lines, appears to be a different kind of person: "Existing capacities and levels of organization are subordinated and integrated into new, more complex levels of organization" (Sroufe, 1989, p. 71). For example, as changes in the school-age child's cognitive abilities create firm distinctions between fantasy and reality, the role of fantasy undergoes a reorganization. The school-age child still utilizes a great deal of fantasy, but unlike a 4-year-old, he has clear ideas about what is pretend and what is real, and he is less inclined to impose fantasy onto reality. This more accurate reality orientation, in turn, influences perception, views of self, social behavior, and play. This new organization of the self in middle childhood can be used as a yardstick to differentiate a 9-year-old functioning age-appropriately from another 9-year-old who is still relying on a fantasy approach to reality, which in turn prevents him from integrating and using his new cognitive capacities in age-expected ways. The interaction of different domains in creating increasing complexity means that a school-age child is not simply a more advanced preschooler but fundamentally thinks, communicates, behaves, and sees the world *differently* from a preschooler.

Therefore, even though development in the abstract seems to be continuous and gradually unfolding, most parents are aware that development also appears discontinuous at times. The child who almost suddenly begins to read fluently in third grade, after struggling in the first and second grades, has probably not attained this competence through practice, though practice and instruction have helped. Rather, it is more likely that this jump in ability is based on brain maturation—on the emergence of new cognitive abilities that were not yet present in the first and second grades. Maturation of the brain (and body) makes new capacities available (such as memory or language) at predictable times for all children. How these capacities are shaped depends on the environment, but *when* they emerge is determined by maturation. A 1-year-old cannot learn to talk in sentences, no matter how much she is talked to and how much she "practices" talking by babbling, because her brain has not matured sufficiently.

INTERACTIONS BETWEEN MATURATION AND ENVIRONMENT

At the same time, new environmental demands, if not grossly mistimed in relation to the child's existing capacities, stimulate and shape development (Kagan, 1984). For example, children entering elementary school face major adaptive tasks determined by their new environment. They must learn to sit still, to work quietly, to listen for and follow directions, and to concentrate on structured academic tasks. They must learn to inhibit impulses to play or impose fantasy on their current experience, because those impulses, so typical of the preschool child, are not adaptive in a second grade classroom. Finally, development that is emerging may be enhanced or slowed by concurrent events in the family's life. The birth of a sibling may create enough stress to temporarily compromise a 3-year-old child's emerging sense of independence from his mother and his growing interest in play with peers. But the direction of change in response to environmental stress is not always predictable. "Resilient" children have been described as responding to stress by becoming more effective. For example, a 10-year-old boy responded to his parents' separation by becoming more conscientious and competent in school.

THINKING DEVELOPMENTALLY IN ASSESSMENT AND INTERVENTION

To assess children accurately the practitioner must be aware of steps and timing in the evolution of developmental lines, transformations that distinguish one developmental stage from another, tasks the environment poses at each stage, and circumstantial challenges that may affect the course of development. It is less helpful to put too much emphasis on overarching descriptions if they tend to codify a particular stage into a dominant image that may obscure its complexity. For example, descriptions of the toddler phase, such as "anal stage" (Sigmund Freud), "autonomy vs. shame and doubt" (Erik H. Erikson), or "preoperational stage" (Jean Piaget), each focus on important aspects of toddler development. Yet thinking of a particular phase of development with such labels tends to limit appreciation of the *multiple changes* that are occurring across many areas of functioning. Further, once one examines a particular domain of development such as cognition, it becomes nearly impossible not to observe how complexly cognitive development interacts with other domains of development. For example, in a 6- to 7-year-old the emerging cognitive ability to think about another person's perspective becomes a foundation for the development of morality, empathy, and give-and-take in relationships.

In each stage of development, new capacities emerge that can be drawn upon to help children. The developmentally sophisticated practitioner knows how to use the "tailwinds of development" to push forward the aims of treatment. For example, the young school-age child, because of her increasing internalization of right and wrong, ability to understand sequences and cause and effect, and wishes for tangible signs of accomplishment, can join with her parents and clinician in devising a behavioral plan that makes connections between compliant behavior and positive reinforcers. An 8-year-old can conceptualize the idea that if she gets ready for school on time each morning, she will gain credits that add up to a reward at the end of the week. Becoming involved in the planning helps the child invest in the plan and increases her motivation for change. On the other hand, at each stage in development there are skills and capacities that have not yet emerged. Correspondingly, what is not yet present in the child cannot be used to advantage in intervention. A 3½-year-old, for example, is much less able to participate in behavioral treatment planning, because her ability to understand cause and effect is still quite limited.

ORGANIZATION OF DEVELOPMENTAL CHAPTERS

In each of the chapters on development (Chapter 4, 6, 8, and 10) I will provide details of progress in the different domains of development and will also present summaries of the most salient issues for each phase. I will try to maintain a balance between the details of the "ages and stages" approach and summary snapshots that characterize the essential issues of a particular developmental period. Each developmental chapter presents the major adaptive tasks of each stage of development, as well as the characteristic expressions of the following eight developmental lines:

- Physical development
- Relational and social development
- Cognitive development
- Language and communication
- Expressive development, including play and fantasy
- Regulation of affect and behavior, including defense and coping strategies
- Moral development
- Sense of self, self-organization, and relation to reality

Each developmental chapter will be followed by a practice chapter illustrating applications of developmental knowledge to the realities of practice. The practice chapters (5, 7, 9, and 11) briefly describe how the level of development influences a child's behavior, play, and capacity to relate and discuss developmentally appropriate assessment and intervention approaches for each stage of development. Finally, each practice chapter presents one or more detailed case narratives, which illustrate salient issues and the ways a developmental perspective can be utilized for each stage. These case studies will also present a range of developmental themes, including transactional issues, developmental delays, developmental interferences, and the influences of psychosocial stressors, trauma, and intrinsic strengths and deficits on development.

❖ CHAPTER 4 ❖

Infant Development

This chapter examines the infant's developmental tasks and the inter-actions that support them within the attachment relationship, describing what the infant brings to these tasks and how parents and other caregivers facilitate the infant's adaptation. It also presents an account of infant's gradual development of a sense of self and how this is promoted through the relationship with the caregivers. Cognitive, affective, and social development are woven together and are facilitated by the parent's interactions with the infant. The rapid rate of development and how it unfolds within the caregiving matrix will be highlighted. In contrast to subsequent developmental chapters, this chapter presents an integrated narrative of infant development as the outcome of trans-actions between maturation and caregiving. Later chapters will focus more on domains of individual development and somewhat less on caregiving, since in the phases following infancy the child increasingly becomes more of an autonomous and separate self.

THE INTERACTION BETWEEN MATURATION
AND CAREGIVING

Infant development is inseparable from the progression of the infant's relationship with caregivers. The best overall answer to "Which is more important, nature or nurture?" is "Both." The infant's cognitive, emotional, and physical capacities unfold steadily, but simple matura-tion is not sufficient to cause adequate development. Contemporary accounts of infancy all emphasize the role of parents and other care-givers in supporting the infant's gradual development of competence and a distinct sense of self (Lyons-Ruth & Zeanah, 1993). The infant needs adult partners who can help her negotiate the developmental tasks and opportunities that maturation opens up. Infants have built in capacities that allow them to organize and find patterns in their experience, while the caregiving and interactional activities shape what their experience will be. The experiences caregivers present to the baby reflect the values and emphases of the parents' particular culture (Reed, 1995). As described in Chapter 1, attachment relationships provide the context for interactions that promote development. For this reason, *the quality of attachment is a crucial variable.*

BRAIN DEVELOPMENT: THE IMPORTANCE OF EARLY EXPERIENCE

Brain development is most rapid during the first 2 years of life. During the last 2 months of gestation and throughout the first year after birth, the brain grows rapidly through the production of synapses, dendrites, and nerve fiber bundles. The dense branching and outreach of dendritic fibers links billions of individual neurons and, on a broader scale, the different regions of the brain (Johnson, 1997). This integration of the circuitry of the brain makes possible the development of sensory, perceptual, emotional, regulatory, motor, and cognitive functions (Shatz, 1992). After birth, brain growth and the particular ways brain functions are organized are subject to the influence of the infant's environment. Experience influences which neural pathways will be strengthened, which will remain available, and which will atrophy.

Recent research has begun to show that appropriate caregiving and stimulation enhance brain development, whereas understimulation and poor or traumatizing caregiving retard or shape brain functioning in maladaptive ways. For example, at an extreme, an infant who is abused adapts through hyperalertness, hyperarousal, and numbing. Out of necessity, the neural pathways controlling these extreme forms of self-regulation are strengthened and become overused. The infant who constantly expects danger and frequently shuts down affectively may be so constrained by this adaptation that cognitive development is impaired (Perry, 1994). From the perspective of brain growth and its effects on subsequent development, the transactions between infants and caregivers take on critical importance.

METAPHORS OF INFANT–PARENT TRANSACTIONS

Kenneth Kaye (1982) proposes a useful metaphor to describe how the parent facilitates infant's developmental progression; he suggests that the infant is like "an apprentice in the shop of a master craftsman. The apprentice learns the trade because the master provides protected opportunities to practice selected subtasks, monitors the growth of the apprentice's skills, and gradually presents more difficult tasks" (p. 55).

A second useful metaphor for the caregiver's function in promoting development is "scaffolding" (Bruner, 1985). In its dictionary definition, a scaffold is a temporary framework that supports workers and materials while a building is being erected. As applied to development, the parent provides support—a "scaffold"—for the infant's cognitive, emotional, and motor development until the infant has accomplished a particular developmental skill and can use it autonomously. An early and quite literal example of scaffolding is that in the first few months the caregiver compensates for the infant's inability to reliably control his head movements. A young infant's neck muscles are not strong enough to prevent his chin from slumping to his chest, which limits his ability to scan the environment visually. However, if a caregiver provides support for the baby's head by holding him at the proper angle, this allows him to look out at the world and see what is going on, opening up a wider visual horizon.

A later example of scaffolding, common in interactions between parents and 6- to 7-month-olds, is that the infant repeatedly drops a toy and the parent picks it up and hands it back to her each time. This infant is experimenting with control of her hands, control of an object, with a rudimentary concept of disappearance and reappearance, as well as engaging in a fun game with her parent. But if the parent does not support the infant's actions by retrieving the toy each time, she cannot exercise her abilities. Scaffolding makes possible actions the baby could not do on her own. Parental scaffolding clearly continues throughout childhood, but it is most evident during the first 3 years.

CAREGIVERS' ADAPTATIONS
TO DEVELOPMENTAL CHANGE

A task of parenting is to know when to raise the scaffold in response to the infant's changing abilities. Sander (1975) describes the developmental process as requiring frequent adaptation by the parent:

> With one component, the infant, rapidly growing and consequently rapidly changing, new qualities and quantities of infant behavior are constantly introduced into the content of interaction. The regulation of infant functions, based on behaviors that have become harmoniously coordinated between mother and infant, will become perturbed with the advent of each new, and usually more specifically

focused and intentionally initiated, activity of the growing infant. Thus adaptation or mutual modification on a new level is required. (p. 135)

The overall direction of these adaptations is toward the infant's "progressive assumption of control of situations as part of the widening of his scope of self-regulation vis-à-vis the environment" (Sander, 1975, p. 135) and toward the parent's gradual relinquishing of control.

In this model, phases of coordinated interaction, in which the parent has adapted to infant's developmental status alternate with periods of "perturbation," when the parent must change his or her behavior in response to new developments in the infant. A good example occurs between 7 and 9 months, when the infant begins to crawl. This is a momentous change for the baby because now she can cover ground on her own. She does not need the parent to carry her from place to place. She has much greater control over her movements and can explore her immediate world more easily. Because the crawling baby is more autonomous, the parents must adapt by "baby-proofing" the house. A speedily crawling infant can get into all sorts of trouble. Parents have to redesign the environment to keep the baby safe. At the same time, parents must adjust to new attachment demands of a mobile baby who can come to them when she wants contact.

THE NEONATAL PERIOD: BIRTH TO 4 WEEKS

Infancy research has changed the once-dominant view that infants have few abilities at birth, and now we recognize that infants do not have to learn to perceive the world. Instead, "perception is prestructured" and learning processes "build upon these predesigned or emergent structures" (Stern, 1977, p. 57). Infants are born with a number of abilities that become the bases of future development. In full-term infants these abilities are either present at birth or become evident during the neonatal period, the first 4 weeks of life. The senses of sight, hearing, smell, touch, sensitivity to pain and responsiveness to changes in the position of the body are all present at birth (Kagan, 1984). Newborns can see close objects 8–10 inches away with fairly good acuity and can visually track slow-moving objects. By age 6 months, an infant's visual acuity will be close to an adult's (Rose & Ruff, 1987). Infants show a preference for looking at the human face over other objects. They can hear well. Experimental studies show that they respond particularly to the sound range and intonation patterns of the human voice. They show the ability to orient to sights and sounds, to remain alert for short periods, to modulate affective and physiological states (such as turning away, withdrawing in the face of over-stimulation), and to use the comforting of a caregiver to decrease arousal (Brazelton, 1990).

During the first year of life the infant's capacity to discriminate between sounds, colors, objects, characteristics of persons, and other differences develops rapidly. From birth onward, and with increasing acuity, infants notice differences and similarities and remember them. This early ability to discriminate at the level of the senses later becomes the basis of categorical thinking and generalization. An example of very early recognition and discrimination of smells came from MacFarlane's (1975) classic study of nursing newborns. By 3 days of age they had already learned the smell of their mother's milk. Nursing pads soaked with their mother's milk and milk from another woman were placed on either side of the baby's head; invariably, she turned toward the pad with her mother's milk on it.

One of the most surprising human abilities that is innate and observable in earliest infancy is cross-modal perception, which involves the ability to translate and generalize from one perceptual mode to another. For example, if I put my hand into a bag filled with stones of different shapes and sizes and choose one without seeing it, I can later see the stone without touching it and know it was the one I chose. I have been able to "take information received in one sensory modality and . . . translate it into another sensory modality" (Stern, 1985, p. 51). Experimental studies have shown that newborns can make such cross-modal transfers of information. Three-week-old infants with their eyes covered were given differently shaped pacifiers. After they had sucked on them, they were shown the two different pacifiers. The infants looked much more at the pacifier they had sucked on, indicating they recognized the object across sensory modalities (Meltzoff & Borton, 1979). Integration of the senses is not something that is learned but rather is innate.

Neonates also have a number of physical reflexes. Some reflexes, including rooting toward and sucking at the breast and grasping with their hands, become the basis for early social interactions with caregivers. Newborns also show pleasure through smiling and calm alertness, on the one hand, and distress through fussiness or crying, on the other, "teaching" their caregivers what they like and do not like. The parent's observation of what pleases or distresses the newborn leads to efforts to extend pleasurable states or to end distress. Through this, the infant begins to understand contingent responding and to develop expectations of how caregivers will respond to his signals. The infant learns very early that when he cries, he will be picked up.

The newborn's "innate" capacities have genetic components but have also been shaped by prenatal influences and by the birth experience. Brazelton (1996) points out that "prenatal experiences have been incorporated into the developing brain and have been fueling the development of this brain. We now know that nutrition, infection, drugs and psychological experiences of the mother are indeed transmitted to her fetus and affect both the current behavior and developmental potential of the child" (p. 131). The idea that the mother's psychological state can impact the fetus *in utero* may seem surprising; however, a number of studies have linked high levels of anxiety and stress in pregnant women with higher levels of fetal activity and higher levels of irritability after birth (Grossman, Eichler, & Winickoff, 1980). Infants whose births have been physically difficult or who have been affected by anesthesia during delivery or medical procedures after birth often are less responsive and alert during the days following birth. They need time to recover (Field, 1989).

In the first week after birth, infants begin to show the capacity for "state modulation," exemplified, on the one hand, by the ability to remain alert and attentive and, on the other, by the ability to shut out or habituate to stimuli in order to remain asleep (Brazelton, 1990). For example, one episode of the Neonatal Behavioral Assessment procedure involves shining a light 10 times above the eyelids of a sleeping newborn. The baby reacts to the light at first by jerking her body; however, by the fourth time the light is shined, she does not move and remains asleep, indicating that she has quickly habituated to a familiar stimulus (Brazelton, 1992). The ability to habituate supports the development of self-regulation. She does not have to respond to familiar things, which lessens the frequency of arousal and allows her to remain more calm and alert during the brief periods when she is awake. The baby's ability to maintain an alert and calm state for increasing periods of time supports her orientation to the external world, which in turn allows her to begin to take in information. The clearest evidence for very early learning ability comes from studies demonstrating that newborns can discriminate their mother's voice from a stranger's after only 3 days of contact with the mother (DeCasper & Fifer, 1980). Infants also quickly learn to notice novel stimuli, to habituate to familiar stimuli, and to discriminate between the novel and the familiar (Kagan, 1984).

During the neonatal period infants vary in their abilities to regulate internal states, to habituate to stimuli, and to maintain states of alertness. At the ends of the continuum, some infants may be lethargic and withdrawn whereas others are hypersensitive, crying frequently, and unable to calm themselves. Hypersensitive infants have more trouble developing smooth patterns of self-regulation. They are more reactive and less able to habituate, which means they are more frequently responding to external stressors by becoming physiologically aroused. Consequently, they startle more easily and cry more. The frequent crying of hypersensitive infants reflects not only distress but an attempt to block out intruding stimuli. However, crying is an "expensive" defense because it keeps the infant in a state of distressed arousal and can have an impact on the early relationship with parents. *In the early weeks, therefore, parents and infants face a task of mutual adaptation initiated by the parents.* Parents must learn to "stimulate lethargic babies and contain overreactive infants" (Brazelton, Nugent, & Lester, 1987, p. 800).

AGE 1 TO 3 MONTHS

During the first 2–3 months of life, the infant has two basic developmental tasks: (1) to develop a basic capacity for self-regulation, and (2) to become oriented to the external world, particularly the human world represented by caregivers (Greenspan & Greenspan, 1985). Between 1 and 3 months, the baby is becoming more alert and more settled. Compared to the neonatal period, when he slept most of the time, he is awake for longer periods and is getting more interested in his environment. He is also learning how to regulate internal states.

Self-Regulation and Dyadic Regulation

"Regulation" refers to processes that maintain feelings of well-being, control the amount of stimulation coming in, and modulate the degree of arousal. During infancy, caregivers provide an external structure of regulation by responding appropriately to the infant. Slowly, the infant expands her strategies for self-regulation. Self-regulation and dyadic regulation proceed together in infancy. It is difficult to separate the two. However, the infant who has been responded to contingently develops the capacity for self-regulation (Emde, Gaensbauer, & Harmon, 1976). During the first 3 months, regulation has two components: regulation of body rhythms and regulation of arousal.

Regulation of Body Rhythms

Infants at birth do not have regular patterns of sleep, eating, and elimination. Gradually, with the parent's help, they develop regular patterns, which gives a beginning sense of predictability to their experience. For example, a newborn sleeps about 16 hours a day, with the same proportion of sleep and wakefulness during the day and night. By about 6 weeks, the circadian rhythms are becoming established and the infant is sleeping primarily at night, with well-defined nap periods during the day (Coons & Guilleminault, 1982). Although this is primarily a biologically and maturationally based change, it is encouraged by the parents' own sleep and wake cycles. Concurrent with the development of relatively regular sleep patterns, the infant, with the parents' encouragement, begins to eat primarily during the day. By responding to the infant's signs of hunger and at the same time establishing a general schedule of feeding times, the parent helps shape the infant's experience of hunger, feeding, and satiation into a regular pattern. By 3–4 weeks, following a period of weight loss while feeding patterns were being established, the infant has regained his birthweight, which helps parents feel they are succeeding. As caregivers respond to the baby's needs as well as shape his experience in accordance with their own needs and routines, the baby feels a sense of regularity and predictability.

As the baby's rhythms of sleep and wakefulness, feeding and elimination, become more regular, she feels more predictable to the parents. Parents describe that infants become more "settled" in this way between 1 and 2 months. The parents' perception that the baby is more settled at this point is also based on the fact that the parents have spent enough time caring for the baby to get to know her characteristics and behavioral patterns (Leach, 1978). For example, they have learned to distinguish between types of crying due to hunger, discomfort or pain, alarm, and fretfulness related to tiredness or lack of regulation. Parents of 1- to 2-month-olds say they "know" their baby and begin to ascribe personality characteristics to her.

Regulation of Arousal

The second component of self-regulation is called *regulation of arousal.* At first this is primarily a dyadic process, with the infant signaling discomfort and the caregiver moving in to reduce the baby's distress and arousal. During the early months infants depend on parents to feed them when they are hungry and pick them up when they are distressed. If the caregiver is responsive and predictable, the baby develops expectations that he will be fed or comforted, within a certain time frame. Out of this awareness, the infant develops a beginning ability to wait. His parent's responsiveness helps him manage his anxiety, because he learns that his needs will be met (Lieberman, 1993). Good experiences with dyadic regulation lay the groundwork for self-regulation and in the long run promote autonomous coping and resiliency. Nevertheless, internal regulatory capacities develop slowly, and the baby's reliance on the caregiver for help in regulation of arousal and affect will continue to be a primary coping mechanism for the next several years.

However, the young infant is also learning to regulate arousal by depending on the self. By 3–6 weeks, when the infant is coordinated enough to reliably get her hand to her mouth, she discovers that if she sucks on her hand or thumb, she feels calmer. She discovers that she can calm herself by looking at her parent's face or by watching the mobile above the crib. Another means of self-regulation under the infant's control is called gaze aversion. If a parent is behaving in a manner that is too stimulating, the infant looks away. The infant shifts her attention away when she is becoming aroused to the point of distress (Stern, 1974).

The maturation of the central nervous system during the first month of life also contributes to the capacity for self-regulation by making the infant's reactions to stimuli more predictable and organized. He can delay reactions to hunger. He is less fussy and reactive, which means his states of calm alertness last longer. When he is awake his attention span is greater and his awareness focuses more on observing and exploring people and objects (Emde, 1989). While maturation of the nervous system helps smooth out the 1-month-old's degree of reactivity, it is important to note that a baby born prematurely will take longer to appear more settled and capable of regulating arousal. The premature infant's central nervous system development is "behind" by the number of weeks of prematurity. Illness, intrusive medical procedures, and a period of time in the neonatal intensive care unit (NICU) are frequently associated with prematurity and also contribute to slower early development. Consequently, it is normal for a premature infant to be more easily overstimulated, more reactive, and unsettled for a longer period (Minde, 1993).

Temperament and Self-Regulation

As the infant becomes more regulated and more social, the amount of fussy crying and "colicky" discomfort diminishes. Newborns tend to cry easily and to have a low threshold for distress; in normal infants by 3–4 months, however, crying has become much less frequent, because of improved self-regulation. However, some infants remain fussier, harder to comfort, and more irritable. Researchers on genetically transmitted temperament have described these babies as "difficult" (J. E. Bates, 1983). While difficult temperament in infancy has not been found to be a stable characteristic across childhood (Hubert, Wachs, Peters-Martin, & Gandour, 1982), it can persist if caregivers are unable to help calm and contain the baby or if their responses actually reinforce the baby's lack of regulation. Fussy, irritable behavior that persists after the first 2–3 months due to temperamental factors (or due to prematurity, illness, or prenatal drug exposure) creates an adaptive hurdle for the infant and her parents.

Parental Responses to "Difficult" Infants

Many parents with "difficult" infants find ways to reduce their irritability. Some find that containing techniques, such as holding the baby a great deal or swaddling him tightly in blankets, reduces irritability and increases security. Others discover that their "difficult" infant is hypersensitive to stimuli and in response take steps to reduce new stimuli or slow the pace of events in the infant's environment. Or they interact with him using only one sensory modality at a time; instead of overstimulating him by talking to him and jiggling him simultaneously, they talk to him while holding him still (Brazelton, 1992). These are examples of the concept of "goodness of fit" in the sense that the parent responds adaptively to the infant's difficultness (Chess & Thomas, 1986).

Some parents with difficult infants, on the other hand, respond with frustration, irritation, or anxiety to the infant's constant fussiness and disregulation. They experience their baby as impossible to console and may blame themselves or the baby. These parents may not respond adaptively, and instead express anger, handle the baby roughly or abruptly, or emotionally withdraw and leave the baby to "cry it out." In such cases, the parent's behavior reinforces the infant's temperamental tendencies toward irritability, hypersensitivity, and disregulation (Seifer & Sameroff, 1986). A cycle of mutually negative feedback can be established, which in turn interferes with secure attachment.

Orientation to the World: Beginnings of Interaction

During periods of calm, we also see the baby becoming increasingly attuned to the external world and particularly to her mother or primary caregiver. In the first 2 months the baby's sensory modalities become more organized and acute. As early as 2–3 weeks we can observe an infant staring intently at her mother's face or looking at her fist or listening to voices. Over the next month she begins to expect certain events will occur when she feels certain things. For example, when she is hungry she expects to be fed. She has taken in and remembers the rhythms and routines her caregivers have organized for her. The 2-month-old orients to sight and sounds, and is also becoming more interested in objects. She can visually track objects that are moving. Her body registers excitement when she sees a bright-colored toy, and she will try to grasp it, though usually without success since the aim of her reach is not yet accurate.

By 6–8 weeks infants show a preference for face-to-face interactions and are very responsive to their caregivers' facial expressions, movements, and voice tones (Reed, 1995). They study their caregivers' faces and begin to establish eye-to-eye contact and to smile at about 4–6 weeks. They are beginning to express a range of emotions, as shown through facial expressions, and by 3 months they can recognize and respond to the emotions of their caregivers (Haviland & Lelwica, 1987). They can share affects and already are aware of violations of affective expectations. For example, in an experimental procedure, if a parent shifts from interacting with a 3-month-old infant to a "still face"—a silent, blank expression—the baby will become worried, distressed, and more active. This experiment clarifies that 2- to 3-month-olds discriminate between different types of emotions, have begun to internalize expectations about the affective components of their relationships with parents, and are very sensitive to interruptions in the flow of affective exchange (Tronick, Als, Adamson, Wise, & Brazelton, 1978). While the still-face experiment imposes only a brief disruption of affective exchange, it points to the more difficult situation of infants whose caregivers are inconsistent in their emotional responsiveness. Parents who are depressed, subject to radical swings of mood, or preoccupied and anxious due to stress may present an affectively disturbing image to the infant, which may cause him to withdrawal emotionally and leave him without a model for sharing and organizing affects.

The Development of Interaction Patterns

In normal interactions between parents and 3-month-old infants, the behavior of caregivers tends to mimic the give-and-take of conversation. The baby makes a gurgling sound, and the parent responds with a happy "Oh, you're trying so hard to talk, aren't you?" The baby smiles in response, and the parent smiles back and says, "You keep makin' those big noises and pretty soon you will talk!" The parent structures the interaction into the turn taking that characterizes conversation by waiting for the baby's responses and then commenting on them. The parent carries the load in these early interchanges by initiating speech, imitating the baby's facial expressions, and affectively underlining the baby's affects (Stern, 1985). But the baby is learning about the structure and the pleasures of human interaction, and in a few months will be initiating "conversations" and taking an active role in perpetuating them.

By 3 months infants are regularly smiling and cooing during face-to-face interactions. As the infant's interest in face-to-face interaction increases, caregivers begin to talk to them more. Observational studies across cultures show that parents' "infant-directed speech," or "parentese," has some universal features, including a gentle, high-pitched tone, and short, repeated utterances that sound exaggerated (Kaye & Fogel, 1980; Reed, 1995). Infants respond by laughing and cooing and making other sounds. Infants and parents begin to "talk" to each other, with the parent using simple phrases and the infant making cooing sounds. These vocalizations are not random, but rather represent the infant's first clearly communicative behavior. Laughing is a response to feelings of pleasure in an interaction. Cooing has a communicative intent, as is known by any parent whose 3-month-old infant has stared into his or her eyes while cooing repeatedly. It is clear that the attachment relationship is beginning to develop.

AGE 3 TO 6 MONTHS

The continuing development of attention, perception, sensory acuity, and memory between 2 and 3 months, along with repeated experiences with caregivers, allows the infant to make clear distinctions between caregivers. This makes possible and leads to the development of attachment. That is, the baby learns to recognize his mother—her face, voice, odor, gestures, touch, characteristic affective tone, how she handles him, and even what kinds of interactions she prefers. Already at this age, the baby knows his mother (assuming that she is the primary caregiver) and prefers her to others, although he will also have a strong preference for others, such as his father, grandparent, or child care provider, who regularly care for him.

Attachment

There are several hallmarks of the infant's behavior during the attachment phase, many of which demonstrate that infants make preferential attachments to the particular people who are their primary caregivers:

- An increase in social smiling occurs, with special smiles for parents.
- The infant shows a strong interest in face-to-face, eye-to-eye contact with caregivers.
- The infant increasingly attempts to engage the parent through looking, smiling, cooing, babbling, and motor activity.
- Primary caregivers now can comfort the baby by means other than holding: with voice, looks, or the presentation of a toy.
- The infant responds differently and preferentially to her mother, father, and others, reserving the brightest smiles for her primary caregiver, or beginning to show distress if, for example, her mother hands her to a babysitter. Infants who are in day care often reflect their preferential attachment by "storing up" reactions to the absence of the parent and then going through a fussy and sometimes passionate crying episode when their parents pick them up (Brazelton, 1992).
- The infant demonstrates that she has developed different expectations of different people. For example, she may attempt to engage her mother or father in play but not her grandmother; though she enjoys playing with her father, she may want comforting only from her mother.

As attachment develops, the particular characteristics of the caregivers begin to shape the infant's view of himself and relationships. The infant learns the parent's expectations, preferences, facial expressions, and affective tone and mirrors them. If the infant has multiple caretakers, by 6 months he will register his awareness of their differences by interacting with them in different ways (Stern, 1995).

Play

The development of relationships, cognitive abilities, and the infant's growing interest in the external world can be clearly seen by observing babies while they are playing. As the infant becomes more coordinated and able to see at a distance as well as close up, there is a general spurt in her interest in the external world. She wants to look at everything, and explore everything with her fingers and mouth. She is particularly attracted to her caregivers and to new objects in her environment. She can be observed scanning her surroundings and listening to sounds intently. Between 3 and 6 months, the infant's interest in the world and in her caregivers leads to the development of play. Play in infancy is primarily exploratory and interactive. Although infants show pleasure in play and actively seek stimulation, at first they do not initiate play interactions. In the early period of play development, the parent takes the lead in play, socializing the infant in the "baby games," such as peek-a-boo, that are traditional in the parents' culture. Parents facilitate the infant's interest in play interactions through exaggeration. They speak, gesture, and make facial expressions that are much more dramatic than they would use with an older child or an adult. Stern (1974) suggests that the parent's more dramatic animation helps the infant reach "an optimal level of arousal" to engage in play interactions (p. 410). He suggests that there is an optimal range of stimulation for helping the infant to become engaged and continue to play. Understimulated infants are not drawn in to sustained interactive play; overstimulated infants turn away or withdraw, short-circuiting engagement. Parents usually are able to discover the optimal level of stimulation for their particular baby unless factors like parental emotional disturbance, psychosocial stressors, or serious deficits in the infant interfere.

Types of Infant Play

Several forms of play predominate during the first year, including the following:

Vocal Play. Infants enjoy listening to themselves. By 4 months, they have a repertoire of sounds, including grunts, squeals, trills, and vowel sounds such as "ah," "ooh," and "oh." Babies can be overheard "talking" in their cribs. This playful vocalizing has a self-sufficient quality. The baby is not trying to communicate, but rather is experimenting with and enjoying the sounds he can make. At about 6 months, this vocalizing becomes babbling, which combines consonant and vowel sounds ("ba-ba," "um-um") and reproduces inflection tones and speech rhythms he has heard from his caregivers (Locke, 1993).

Exploratory Play with Objects. Infants explore objects with their eyes, hands, and mouth. They are interested in shape, color, and texture, as well as in the movements and sounds objects make. Joan Piaget (1962) labeled this type of play "sensorimotor play," describing it as the infant's way of learning about the properties of objects by looking at, touching, and manipulating them. While exploratory play does serve this cognitive function, it also provides the baby with feelings of pleasure, which is a central element of all forms of play. Parents facilitate exploratory play.

For example, a father shakes a rattle to attract his 4-month-old daughter's attention to it. She looks at it with interest and reaches for it. He brings it close enough to her hand for her to grasp it. As she looks at it and then brings it to her mouth, he says, "How does it taste? Like plastic, I bet!" Then, if she has not yet made it rattle herself, he shakes her hand to demonstrate its sound. She looks strongly interested, pauses as if she is figuring out what to do, and then begins to bang the rattle. Her father says, "You did it!" When the infant's interest wanes, she drops the rattle. The father notices that she has disengaged and hands her something new, and the play continues a bit longer. Although this play focuses on the rattle, it has a strong interactive quality and sense of shared pleasure. The interaction also has a strong element of scaffolding. The parent, out of his knowledge of his baby, sets up a situation and process through which the infant enjoys the toy and learns about it. His observation of her disinterest causes him to give her a new object. This too is based on his knowledge of her—that, as is typical of 3- to 6-month-old infants, she hungers for novelty and often becomes bored by familiar toys.

Interactive Play. Between 4 and 5 months, the infant begins to initiate interactions on his own, often by vocalizing or smiling at the parent. It is now clear that the attachment relationship is being used for something else besides getting comforted and feeling secure. It is being used by the baby as a vehicle for communication and for developing a sense that he can be a force in the world. The baby joins in interactions and works to keep them going. The exchanges between parent and baby begin to last longer and to become increasingly complicated. At this point, the baby is remembering the kinds of interactions that are pleasurable and tries to get the parent to repeat them. Behaviorally, the infant is expressing what the toddler or preschooler will later say in words, "That was fun, let's do it again—over and over."

The baby is also more aware of the environment, scanning it visually and reaching out for objects. Parents, by watching what interests the baby, are now following the baby's lead. For example, a parent becomes aware that the infant is looking at a toy and then brings the toy within the baby's reach. Or, after the baby has learned from repetitions of this experience that looking and reaching are signals of wishes, she reaches for the toy with the expectation that her father will bring it close enough for her to grasp. At the same time, especially during the 5th month, the baby is becoming more competent in using her hands, as well as her eyes and hands in coordination. She can shake a rattle that has been placed in her hand, shift it from one hand to the other, and reach for objects with good aim. The baby's increasing effectiveness in signaling, in taking initiative and in grasping, holding, and manipulating objects, all of which is "scaffolded" by the parent's actions, leads to a sense of "competence and voluntary control over . . . her environment" (Brazelton & Yogman, 1986, p. 7).

Baby Games. Parents also play ritualized, repetitive games with their infants. The mother teaches the baby a game, sometimes of her own spontaneous creation, and more often one traditional in her culture. In the American culture, for example, parents often play peek-a-boo, "I'm gonna get ya," and "tickle" games with their babies. These games operate on the principle of repeat and vary.

> For example, a mother changes her 5-month-old's diaper and then lightly tickles her stomach. The baby becomes excited. The mother pauses, to allow the suspense to build, then says, "I'm gonna get ya," and tickles the baby more forcefully. The baby laughs. The mother pauses and looks at the baby. The baby, anticipating the next tickle, kicks her legs and begins to squeal. The mother says again, with more drama, "Ah-m-m-m gon-na get ya!" The baby shrieks and laughs. But after the next tickle, the baby not only laughs, somewhat hysterically, but also looks away. Then the mother, sensing that the baby is at the edge of being overaroused, lowers the intensity of her behavior or perhaps shifts to another game, so that the infant's arousal decreases to a comfortable level.

This is an example of what infancy researchers call "a mutually regulating dyadic system" (Stern, 1977, p. 122), in which both partners attend to one another's behavior and affects in order to keep an exchange going at a pleasurable level. The mother is gearing her actions and monitoring the baby's responses with the implicit goal of keeping the level of stimulation within an optimal range. The infant signals, through her responses, when the parent's play behavior is at the right level of stimulation, as well as when it is too much or not enough. The parent uses this feedback to either maintain or modify her play behavior.

Winnicott (1971) suggested that if the parent adjusts her behavior by following the baby's cues, the baby experiences the pleasure and excitement of feeling in control of the play. In peek-a-boo, for example, the mother controls her disappearance and appearance, but the infant feels that he is making things happen. And, in the sense that his responses encourage his parent to disappear and appear over and over, he is in control. By 8–9 months, the baby actually will control the game by covering his own face. Before 6 months, parents almost always initiate games, but by 8 months infants can clearly signal that they want to play a game. An 8-month-old, for example, will clap his hands to show his parent that he wants to play patty-cake.

Baby games contain humor, suspense, and excitement, which both players share. Infants will not play with any adult, however. They experience a range of positive affects and humor when they are playing with people they know and trust (Trevarthen, Murray, & Hubley, 1981; Winnicott, 1971). This is an essential idea, since the parent's behavior in baby games—tickling, poking, presenting toys and taking them away, hiding from the baby—has strong elements of teasing. The crucial difference between hostile teasing and baby games occurring in the context of a secure attachment is that the parent does not push the infant's arousal to the point where anxiety and helplessness supplant pleasurable excitement. The parent gives in—by showing him- or herself or giving the toy back—before the baby feels helpless, and the baby has the exhilarating feeling of making the parent come out of hiding.

Baby Games as Indicators of Difficulty

Parent–infant games can also reveal parental difficulties that may put the infant at risk. Fraiberg's (1974) clinical studies show that the observation of baby games may provide a sensitive index of how the parent–infant relationship is developing. Fraiberg describes teasing that gives a parent pleasure even as the baby becomes distressed and disorganized—repeatedly pulling a bottle from a baby's mouth during a feeding, or "rough-house" play at the border of abuse that becomes frightening or painful to the infant. One father, who had been physically abused in childhood, played aggressively with his son, as Fraiberg reports: "Father briskly pats Timothy's bottom and says, 'You're bad . . . again.' He then holds Timothy's arms and moves them in a mock boxing motion. He says, 'Bet you like to be beat up, you like to fight. I could break you right in half' " (Fraiberg, 1974, p. 214).

> In an example I observed, a mother put a ball in her 7-month-old son's hand and swung his arm hard in a throwing motion and said "Throw the ball at daddy." The baby laughed at first, but as his mother kept manipulating his arm he became somber and looked frightened. Then he began to whimper. She was oblivious to this because she appeared caught up in expressing hostility toward her partner. This was registered by her aggressive facial expression as well as her behavior. As the "game" continued, the mother kept repeating, "Throw it at Daddy! Boom!" The ball had turned into a bomb! She was using her infant, in the context of playing a game, to act out anger.

These examples have in common the parent's insensitivity to the baby's needs and feelings, the baby's becoming overaroused to the point of distress, and the parent's exploitation of the baby to satisfy or act out his or her own needs. Baby games with these qualities, in contrast to mutually pleasurable games, suggest risk for the infant and point to the need for a careful evaluation of the parent's difficulties.

A NORMAL INFANT AND
A COMPETENT PARENT: A CASE EXAMPLE

The following observation of an infant and parent interacting with a toy illustrates some themes of the account of infant development so far. This description highlights the following:

- The developing competencies of the infant
- The infant's intense involvement with the external world
- A smoothly functioning infant–parent partnership in action
- Sharing of pleasurable affects that characterizes play during the attachment period
- Parental scaffolding of the infant's experience

Four-month-old Rashid and his 19-year-old mother are participating in a developmental guidance program at a teen health center. In this program, a social worker engages the parent in discussions of infant development and parenting through viewing of videotaped play sessions with her baby. The intervention attempts to support existing strengths and to increase the parent's ability to observe and understand her baby (Share, Givens, Davies, Eley, & Chesler, 1992; McDonough, 1993).

Ms. Jamison is an African-American single mother. She and Rashid live with her mother and father and siblings. She receives solid emotional and concrete support from her family. Rashid is cared for primarily by his mother, but also has warm attachments with his grandmother and his mother's sister. Rashid appears to be developing well and his mother is warmly engaged with him. As she talks to the social worker who is videotaping them, Ms. Jamison speaks easily about Rashid, raising questions about him and conveying that she knows him well. Rashid is drooling. His mother wipes his chin and says, "I wonder if he's cutting a tooth. Babies aren't supposed to be slobbin' this much when they're 4 months old." The worker asks Ms. Jamison what calms Rashid if he gets upset. She says proudly, "If I pick him up! If I pick him up he calms right down." She adds, "If my sister picks him up and he's real fussy, he won't like it. He always wants me." The worker says, "He knows you and likes you best." She replies, "Yep! He'll settle right down with me."

The worker suggests that Rashid might be interested in some of the toys. His mother gently places Rashid on his back on a blanket on the floor, then puts a "gym" with *Sesame Street* characters suspended from a bar above him. She positions it above his chest so that he can both see and reach the figures. She says, "Look at them," and swings them gently. Rashid is already looking raptly. As he takes in the brightly colored, slowly swinging figures, his legs and arms begin to move rhythmically in excitement. His mother laughs at his excitement, and he turns toward her, catches her eye, and smiles. She says, "You like it! You want them!" Rashid smiles and kicks his legs. Then he calms momentarily as he stares at the figures. His mother says, "See Big Bird," and turns the figure so he can see its face. Rashid continues to alternate between attending to the toy and responding to his mother's voice with smiles. His mother points to the different characters, saying, "Here's Bert, here's Ernie, here's Big Bird." After she does this, Rashid vocalizes and touches the figure with his feet. He reaches for them with his hands but is not able to grasp them. His mother suddenly realizes that she has placed the gym so that the characters face away from Rashid. She turns it around and, speaking for Rashid, says, "I can't see their faces, mom. There you go. Now I see 'em." She discovers that Big Bird makes a squeaking sound, and she squeezes it while Rashid watches. Rashid reaches for it but is not yet coordinated enough to grasp it. She says, "I'll squeeze it for you," and he kicks his legs in excitement. After a minute, Rashid's attention wanes and his mother says, "OK, you're getting tired of this—you're just looking at your shoes now." She props him up to a sitting position, so he can see the toy from a different perspective. He looks for several seconds, then shifts his gaze away from the toy. She says, "OK," and picks him up, and he smiles at her.

From this brief observation, which lasts only 5 minutes, we can identify two fundamental forces that interact to shape infant development. The first is Rashid's motivation to take in and master his environment. Rashid shows interest in the world that is characteristic of his age. He uses his already well-developed attentional skills in a sustained engagement with a new and interesting toy. Even though he does not yet have the physical skills to accurately reach out and grasp the toy, he is highly motivated to do so and he keeps trying despite his lack of success. He "grasps" the figures with his eyes, however, and registers pleasure by smiling, gurgling, and kicking his legs. He shares his excitement and interest with his mother. Overall, he takes an active role in shaping his own experience. While this view of the infant as active may seem a truism, it serves to correct an older view of the infant as a passive recipient of what the environment presents (Stern, 1974). This view of the infant as actively initiating behavior and striving to become more competent becomes even clearer during the second half of the first year, when, for example, the infant will crawl energetically to reach a toy at the other end of a room.

The second shaping force illustrated in this vignette is how adult behavior provides structure and direction to the infant's experience. Rashid's mother does a number of things that facilitate his experience with the toy. She helps focus his attention by pointing to the figures and swinging them. She affirms his pleasure in looking at Big Bird by commenting in warm tones and by smiling back when he smiles at her. She reinforces his interest in the toy by mirroring it and focusing her attention on the toy at the same time he does. She is able to take his perspective when she realizes that the figures are not facing him; she acts on this perception by turning the toy around, which changes and extends his experience of it. She explores the toy herself and discovers that it makes a noise; she shows this to Rashid and squeezes it several times, realizing that he is interested. He reaches toward it. She imagines he would like to make the noise himself and squeezes it because she knows he is not yet able to do it himself. Finally, she is attentive to his decrease in attention and gives him a chance to look at the figures from a new angle. This temporarily increases his attention. When his interest wanes, she realizes it and picks him up.

This is an ordinary example of a parent interacting with an infant in response to his interest in an object, but when the actions of the parent are listed *it becomes clear how much she facilitates and shapes the infant's experience.* The parent knows more, sees things in a broader perspective, and is more organized than the infant. She uses her skills in perspective taking, her ability to recognize Rashid's affective and motoric signals of interest (and waning interest), and her advanced ability to explore the object. She demonstrates actions that are beyond his ability, and he seems to imitate her. It is as if she is thinking, "I know you cannot squeeze this toy now, but I will show you how to do it, so that you will begin to get the idea and so you'll know what to do when you're physically ready." Her behavior does not merely affirm the status quo but points the way to higher developmental levels. At the same time, her approach is facilitative rather than intrusive. She encourages him to engage with the toy in his own way and then tries to add to his experience.

In the case example, we can see Rashid's mother's behavior in terms of both metaphors introduced at the beginning of this chapter.

He is her young apprentice, and her actions provide scaffolding for his development. She provides him with experiences that promote his developing physical and cognitive skills, and at the same time she supports him physically and affectively as he exercises his abilities.

AGE 6 TO 12 MONTHS

During the second half of the first year, the infant advances rapidly in cognitive, motor, and social development. The baby's understanding of the world becomes more sophisticated, as she begins to understand cause and effect and intentionality, and realizes that other people have minds of their own. During this half-year the infant's interests all seem to intensify. She becomes more interested in exploring the world, more compelled to develop physical and cognitive skills, *and* more involved in her attachment relationships.

At about 6 months the infant's interests begin to shift away from an exclusive focus on interactions with attachment figures to an increasing interest in objects and the external environment generally. Stern sees this as evidence that the infant's confidence in the attachment is established and also hypothesizes that the infant is developing internal "schemas" or representations of the parents and the attachment relationships that allow him to "keep the parent in mind" even when he is not interacting with her (Stern, 1983). Parents describe their 6- to 7-month-old infants as more self-reliant. For example, when the baby wakes in the morning, he may not cry for the parent to come but instead will play—with objects in his crib or with his own voice—for up to half an hour before becoming fussy and alerting the parent to come. The baby at this age is not less interested in his relationships with parents. Rather, his interest in the external world, spurred by cognitive and motor development, becomes nearly as compelling as his involvement with caregivers. In spite of this increased capacity for autonomy and self-regulation, however, parents also describe the 7-month-old as intensely involved with them. Preferential attachment reaches its height between 7 and 9 months. This is demonstrated by the baby's pleasure in extended play with the parent, as well as by the emergence of stranger and separation anxiety.

The emphasis of the 6-month-old's play and social interactions also changes. In the first 5 or 6 months, interactive play in which infant and parent take turns is at the center of the infant–parent relationship. As the infant's interest in objects increases, the relationship gradually focuses more on "joint attention activities" in which the parent and infant share experiences of objects or events. This particularly involves sharing affects and the parent's communicating an understanding of the baby's feelings. Strikingly, after 6 months, the infant becomes more of a leader in interactions with parents. Instead of primarily following the parent's lead, the baby initiates interactions more frequently. This behavior is intentional, in the sense that the infant tries to elicit particular responses from parents. The infant's behavior is becoming goal directed, reflecting cognitive advances in the understanding of cause and effect. For example, the baby who was a happy participant in peek-a-boo when the parent put a diaper over his face now begins the game by trying to pull the diaper over his face himself.

Physical Advances

One of the primary thrusts of infant development is toward increasingly full control of the body. As the infant's muscles strengthen and as she works to master control of bodily movements, she becomes more capable and independent. Infants take pleasure in mastery and are strongly motivated to establish control of their bodies. Physical abilities develop in a progression "from top to bottom." This progression follows the maturation of the central nervous system and muscular system. Between birth and 6 months, babies develop control of head and neck movements, then hand movements and hand–eye coordination, and then initial control of the upper body. During the second 6 months of life, there are dramatic developments in physical abilities and control involving the trunk, arms, and legs, including sitting, crawling, standing, cruising (walking while holding onto furniture), and walking.

These new abilities support the growth not only of new actions but also of new perspectives. Sitting is a good example. By about 8–9 months, the baby's back muscles are strong enough to allow him to sit erectly without support for long periods. From the erect sitting position, he can see more. He is higher and can turn his head and twist his trunk to see in all directions. His hands are free for use in grasping objects and bringing them close for examination. At 4 months, he could only sit supported and had more limited control of head and neck movements. He was far more passive and dependent, in the sense that what he looked at was determined by the position his caregiver had placed him in. Now he scans his environment following his own interests. His physical control affords him more autonomy in choosing what he will pay attention to. Similarly, by 8–9 months the infant's adeptness at crawling allows him to be more independent in realizing his wishes.

Motor Skill Development and Infant Stress

Between 8 and 12 months infants practice motor skills with particular intensity. All of the skills they are working on add up to a big spurt in motor development. As in other periods of rapid development, infants typically experience emotional disequilibrium and anxiety, which shows up now as lower tolerance for frustration, poorer affect regulation, increased attachment behavior, difficulty falling asleep, and waking in the middle of the night, apparently from frightening dreams. These reactions derive not only from the driven effort toward mastering physical skills but also because the new skills themselves create new experiences of anxiety. Mobility is not only exciting but causes uncertainty and fear when the infant finds she has crawled too far away from her parent, into an unfamiliar room, or to the bottom of a stairway. The infant who is practicing standing, cruising while holding onto furniture, and walking will often fall and will frequently be aware of the discrepancy between what she wants to do and her body's ability to do it. Gradually, the baby does master these skills and again becomes more confident and settled. The acquisition of physical control in sitting, crawling, and walking gradually permits the infant to take those abilities for granted, freeing her to become more curious and interested in her environment. By 1 year of age the infant, while continuing to work on mastery of motor skills, is increasingly concentrating on cognitive explorations.

Cognitive Advances

Memory

The development of memory and other cognitive functions follows the maturation of the brain. Between 8 and 12 months, the infant's memory abilities show rapid development (Rovee-Collier, 1990). Kagan (1984) describes three components of memory that can be demonstrated between 8 and 12 months but not earlier: (1) remembering something from the past; (2) being aware of connections between past and present; and (3) being able to predict a future event based on past experiences. An example that provides evidence for maturation of memory functions is "stranger anxiety," which shows up in infants across cultures at about 9 months. The infant begins to react with frightened expressions, withdrawal, or distress when an unfamiliar person comes near. Kagan (1984) explains stranger anxiety in terms of the infant's new ability to compare the face of the stranger with images of familiar faces he holds in his memory. This new ability to make comparisons based on memory leads to feelings of uncertainty when the infant does not recognize the stranger, and so the infant becomes anxious.

Similarly, the separation anxiety that also becomes prominent at 8–9 months can be seen as related to memory and anticipation. The baby is able to remember previous separations and recognizes the immediate signs that the parent is planning to leave. She also remembers feelings of distress associated with previous separations and anticipates feeling them again. As this awareness becomes clearer, reactions to separation intensify (Kagan, Kearsley, & Solano, 1978). Separation protests—crying, clinging to the parent, attempting to crawl after the parent—also represent a new level of coping behavior. The baby becomes aware of an impending loss of proximity to her parent and takes active steps to change the situation. While memory gives rise to separation distress, memory gradually helps the infant learn to regulate affects in response to separation. The baby learns that the parent who leaves also comes back. This remembered awareness makes brief separation understandable and bearable. The infant's distress lessens as reunion following separation becomes established in consciousness as a predictable experience.

Memory and Mental Representation

The infant's memory now includes generalized and specific images of objects and people. Infants under 7 months treat objects that disappear as "out of sight, out of mind." If an object is hidden from them, they will not look for it, even though they watched the parent hide it. At around 8 months, they will search for an object that is hidden (Rosser, 1994). For example, if a parent hides a toy under a diaper, the baby will pull the diaper off to find it. This ability is called *object permanence,* which means that the infant has a mental representation of the toy and not only can remember how it was hidden but also imagine where it is without being able to see it (Piaget, 1952b).

The infant also forms representations of caregivers, which is thought to lead to a concept of *person permanence.* This is a difficult concept to grasp because it seems so obvious that a person can recognize another person he or she is familiar with, even when that person's behavior and moods are somewhat different. However, this ability to internally represent another person develops gradually in infancy through repeated interactions with attachment figures. Internal representation involves being able to hold the person in mind when he or she is not present. It is not clear exactly when this ability develops. Stern (1983) argues that infants probably can evoke memories of the parent during the first 6 months. Nevertheless, separation anxiety at 8 months does suggest that infants have the ability to think about their parents when they are not there and to miss them. Stranger anxiety at about the same time suggests that infants have clear representations of their caregivers and other familiar people, and find it confusing and jarring when a person who does not match any of these representations comes close to them.

Awareness of Other Minds

A shift in cognitive awareness of others occurs near the end of the first year, which is consistent with the development of internal representations. Infants becomes aware that others have their own point of view and intentions. They also realize that "their subjective experiences, their attention, intentions and affective states can be shared with another" (Bretherton, 1987, p. 1079). This leads to a new perspective on the behavior of others. Infants observe the actions of their caregivers and begin to learn from them. New behaviors that illustrate this shift in awareness include the following:

Joint Attention. Older infants begin to look at a caregiver to see where she is looking and then look in that direction or at that object. If an infant follows the gaze of an adult and then cannot tell what is drawing her attention, he checks back with the adult, trying to discern what she is looking at (Scaife & Bruner, 1975).

Social Referencing. The infant looks at a caregiver to see her attitude toward a new person or situation. By 1 year of age, when infants meet a new person or encounter a new event or object, they often look back at their parent for help in assessing the new situation. If the parent's affect is approving or positive, they will approach the new person or situation, but they will not approach if the parent registers concern or disapproval. The need for social referencing develops in connection with the infant's developmental progress. As the infant becomes more perceptive of reality, she feels uncertain more often (Emde, 1992). For example, uncertainty increases when her developing motor skills put her in potentially dangerous situations. A 10-month-old may crawl to the top of a flight of stairs, look down, and then look back at the parent for help in assessing the danger she senses. A look of alarm or a sharp "No!" from the parent will stop the baby from going down the stairs.

Social referencing has also been demonstrated experimentally. Researchers created an ambiguous situation that caused uncertainty in infants over 6 months of age. The infant was placed on a table that was extended by a piece of Plexiglas. The see-through extension created a "visual cliff" where the wooden part of the table no longer existed. The infant's mother was standing at the end of the Plexiglas extension, that is, on the other side of the "cliff." When infants approached the visual cliff, they looked at their mothers with uncertainty. If the mother registered fear, the infant would not cross the Plexiglas panel; if she expressed encouragement and smiled, he would crawl across the cliff (Sorce, Emde, Campos, & Klinnert, 1985).

Following (and Giving) Directions. At about 9–10 months infants begin do simple things their parents ask them to do. Soon after this development, infants begin to consciously direct their caregivers to do things for them. This represents a new level of intentionality. At 6 months, for example, parents had to intuit their infant's wishes. During the second half of the first year the baby learns to intentionally signal a wish to the parent. For example, a 1-year-old can point to a toy, then look at her mother, signaling that she wants her mother to get it for her, or she can lift her arms toward her father while whining or vocalizing "uh-uh," which conveys the command, "Pick me up."

Imitative Learning. Infants begin to watch their caregivers with the aim of understanding how they are doing something. They can be seen trying to do the same thing that the caregiver is doing with an object (Tomasello, 1995). Imitative behavior also provides evidence for improving memory. Piaget (1952b) coined the term "deferred imitation," which refers to imitation of something that happened in the recent past. This type of imitation, as opposed to immediate imitation, requires that the infant remember what she observed. By age 11 months, infants can remember and imitate actions that were demonstrated to them 24 hours previously. By 14 months, they demonstrate increasing power of memory by being able to imitate actions which occurred up to a week earlier (Meltzoff, 1988)

These cognitive developments reflect the infant's awareness that the behavior of others and their own has meaning. Over the next year, this awareness that others have a point of view leads to a direct awareness that they also have reactions to the child's behavior. A parent who says about a 6-month-old infant, "He's crying because he's trying to upset me," is suggesting something that is developmentally impossible, because a 6-month-old is not yet aware the parent has a perspective. By contrast, one can observe a 2-year-old beginning to cry while obviously checking to see what impact his crying is having on an adult. But even by 1 year of age, the new awareness that others have a point of view that may be influenced creates a new understanding of communication and its utility. The 9- to 12-month-old realizes that he can influence others through his signals and actions. This realization increases his motivation to communicate and express himself in understandable ways. This sets the stage for language learning in the second year of life.

Language and Communication

When the infant speaks her first few words between 9 and 12 months, language development has clearly begun. However, a look back shows that the infant has been preparing to speak since birth. During the early weeks of life infants can discriminate between speech sounds as their parents talk to them. In the first few months the infant develops a repertoire of sounds—grunts, cries, and single syllable vocalizations. The infant vocalizes experimentally, repeating sounds in varying patterns, clearly listening to herself and enjoying the different sounds she makes. After age 6 months, brain maturation makes possible the more complex consonant–vowel combinations heard in babbling (Locke, 1993). The increase in vocal abilities has a self-reinforcing quality. Babies, like older people, enjoy hearing themselves "talk." Parents also respond to these language-like sounds by talking more and more to the infant. Thus the ability to "speak" derived from maturation becomes reinforced by the parent's enthusiastic responses to babbling (Locke, 1993). In turn, the infant's babbling increasingly mimics the parents' speech sounds and patterns.

While early babbling cannot be considered language, it is a precursor of language, as demonstrated by the observation that between 6 and 10 months babbling focuses imitatively on the sounds used in the parents' native language (E. Bates, O'Connell, & Shore, 1987). Although all infants are capable of producing the range of sounds used in all human languages, by 10–12 months the infant has learned the favored sounds of his caregivers' language and less frequently uses sounds that are not included in that language. Parents often actively shape this process of sound learning by "translating" the baby's babbled sounds into the closest equivalent words (Locke, 1993). Playing with sounds also becomes integrated into interactions with caregivers. As noted previously, 3-month-olds "talk" to their parents by cooing, and when this occurs parents begin to reinforce the infant's vocalizing by talking to them more. Vocal play is an important aspect of infant–parent interaction that develops between 4 and 6 months.

By 9 months, gestural forms of prelanguage communication also develop. Some examples include (1) the infant looks at something she wants—a toy or food—then looks at the parent for help in getting it; (2) to get help from an adult, the 9-month-old repeats "requests" by fussing and looking at the object, then back at the adult; and (3) the infant shows or hands objects to the adult (E. Bates, Camaioni, & Volterra, 1975). By 1 year of age, the infant communicates actively by pointing at objects.

At about 10 months, the infant becomes capable of imitating parents' gestures in ritualized games like patty-cake. This ability to imitate behavior coincides with evidence that the baby is beginning to comprehend the parents' words. Shortly after this the baby shows the beginnings of true language when he says words intentionally. As has been true for previous development, the infant's relationship with parents provides the context for the development of communication based on *words*—sound combinations that mean the same thing to the speaker and listener. Through repeated labeling of objects and actions, caregivers teach the infant his first words (Baldwin & Markman, 1989). At this early stage, the infant can say only a few words, although experimental studies have shown that already the infant's receptive vocabulary exceeds his speaking vocabulary (E. Bates et al., 1987). The parent and baby, through attachment behavior and social play, and with joint attention activities as the infant matures, have been practicing communicative exchanges for many months. When the child's cognitive development reaches the point of comprehending and speaking words as intentional communication between 9 and 13 months, the continuing exchange between parent and infant becomes the scaffolding for actual language learning (E. Bates et al., 1987).

A Developing Sense of Self

As the infant passes the age of 6 months, her increasing social competence and intentionality can be taken as signs that she is aware of her needs and how to express them. These qualities have been described as signs of the emergence of a subjective sense of self (Stern, 1985). This view contrasts with that of Margaret Mahler and associates, who described the infant's early relationship with the mother as symbiotic and hypothesized that the infant did not begin to experience herself as a separate self with separate intentions from the mother until the second year of life (Mahler, Pine, & Bergman, 1975). While it is true that toddlers show a more dramatic awareness of their separateness and insist strongly on realizing their intentions, research since the study of Mahler et al. has demonstrated that the infant's development of a separate sense of self begins early in the first year (Bretherton, 1987). Earlier formulations that presented the infant as "fused" with the mother and unable to differentiate the self from the other (Mahler et al., 1975) leaned heavily on another older concept—that infants' perceptual abilities develop slowly during the first year. More recent research on the young infant's perceptual abilities, however, has demonstrated that infants are making all sorts of distinctions from the first month of life, including distinctions between objects, people and the self and other (Stern, 1983; Rosser, 1994).

During the first year, the sense of self derives particularly from the infant's feeling an increasing sense of control. In the early months of life, the caregiver provides the structure that helps the infant organize expectations. The caregiver provides "more" at the outset but gradually creates room for participation by the infant. The infant, in turn, gradually has more capacity for participation. If parents are sensitive to the infant's signals and initiatives in the early months, the infant begins to feel effective and in control, even though the parent is making this possible.

> For example, a responsive mother watches her 4-month-old while feeding him and delivers the applesauce each time he opens his mouth. At first, she feeds the baby rapidly because he shows that he is hungry by eagerly taking the food, swallowing it, and opening his mouth again. Over the course of the feeding, the parent slows the pace in response to the baby's signs of satiation. While the parent is orchestrating the feeding, the baby feels in charge because the parent is responding contingently. Over time this has an impact on his view of himself: "An infant whose mother's responsiveness helps him to achieve his ends develops confidence in his own ability to control what happens to him" (Bell & Ainsworth, 1972, p. 1188). By contrast, an infant whose parent pushes food at him too rapidly is likely to choke, spit up, or turn his head. Feeding becomes not just an unpleasant struggle but also an experience where the infant feels that he lacks influence to control what happens (Bretherton, 1987).

Self-Esteem and Self-Efficacy

Infancy researchers have been particularly interested in the emergence of the self and how the infant's view of self is shaped in interactions with caregivers. Two aspects of the sense of self have been particularly studied: self-esteem and self-efficacy. Self-esteem involves feeling good about oneself. Self-efficacy involves feeling effective and competent in one's actions and interactions. Many studies have found links between the quality of the infant's sense of self and the quality of attachment relationships. When parents are responsive and sensitive to the infant's behavioral cues and to her experiences of distress, the infant's self-esteem increases because the parent's responses are contingent and empathic. The infant feels valued and understood. When the infant experiences the parents' responsiveness as "evidence" that her efforts to communicate, share affects, gain attention, or express distress are effective, her sense of competence increases.

The infant's sense of self-efficacy is more likely to develop strongly "when a caregiver's behaviors are contingent upon the affective and behavioral cues coming from the infant, rather than geared to a schedule or to the caregiver's convenience" (Demos, 1986, p. 59). At the same time, as noted in Chapter 1, sensitive parents are not always optimally responsive and therefore the infant at times has negative feelings because the parent is preoccupied, unresponsive, or simply misunderstands the infant's signals. These "mismatches" present the infant with chances to act to restore a positive or attuned interaction. The sense of competence is increased when the infant and parent are able to overcome these periods of dyssynchrony (Tronick et al., 1986). Researchers studying self-efficacy have found that it is self-reinforcing. The infant who has many experiences of success feels more and more effective.

Parental Support and the Infant's Experience of Mastery

The infant's experience of success depends a great deal on the quality of parental scaffolding. This issue has been illuminated by studies of "mastery motivation" of 6- to 12-month-old infants. The desire for mastery is an intrinsic motivation reflected in the infant's push to explore the environment, to solve problems, to learn, to exert control, to develop competence, and to succeed in developmental tasks (Harter, 1978). Mastery motivation is perhaps most obvious in the infant's persistent work on developing physical skills. Dramatic examples are the precrawling baby who exerts tremendous effort as she pulls herself across a room with her elbows, or the 9-month-old repeatedly trying to pull herself to a standing position. However, older infants also shows the same degree of interest and work just as hard to influence their parents to interact with them. They will smile, make noises, and touch or pull on the parent to get his or her attention.

Mastery motivation can increase or decrease depending on whether the infant feels successful in her efforts toward mastery. Parental support for the infant's efforts at mastery and competence allows her to feel more successful and contributes to self-esteem. Support includes not only hands-on help or structuring the infant's activities but also the parent's emotional encouragement and expression of pleasure when the baby succeeds at a task. A number of studies have demonstrated that support has effects on later attitudes and abilities: "Caregivers who are emotionally available and who promote ... exploratory behaviors have infants who demonstrate greater task persistence, greater pleasure in goal-directed behavior, and greater subsequent social and cognitive competence" (Lyons-Ruth & Zeanah, 1993, p. 27). A consistent lack of support, as occurs in neglect, may result in feelings of incompetence, lowering the infant's self-esteem and perhaps over time creating an internal model of "learned helplessness," where the child believes that she cannot succeed by her own efforts (Aber & Allen, 1987). In social interactions, the infant whose behavior succeeds in eliciting a positive and sensitive response from the parent feels encouraged to continue the behavior. Such infants learn to expect to be successful in their actions. During the first year, interaction patterns, coping experiences, and resulting views of self are the building blocks of the child's working models of self and relationships.

APPENDIX: SUMMARY OF INFANT DEVELOPMENT, BIRTH TO 12 MONTHS OF AGE

This chart on infant development follows a chronological sequence, rather than developmental lines. Since development in infancy unfolds more rapidly than in later stages this organization provides a clearer view of how an infant develops. Since there are individual differences in rate of development in children, I have indicated time ranges encompassing normal development.

Overall Tasks

- To develop attachments and dyadic strategies for maintaining them
- To gradually gain control over motor skills
- To develop a beginning ability to regulate arousal and affect

Neonatal Period: 0 to 4 Weeks

- Perceptual abilities are present at birth
- Orientation to sounds and sights within range of visual acuity (1 week +)
- Orientation to human face and voice (1 week +)
- Recognition of primary caregiver (1–4 weeks)
- State modulation begins: alternating states of alertness and habituation to stimuli (1–2 weeks)
- Discrimination between novel and familiar stimuli (2–3 weeks)
- Cross-modal perception and integration of senses (3 weeks)

Age 1 to 3 Months

- Developing capacity for self-regulation of body rhythms (with help of care-givers): regulation of sleep/wake and feeding/elimination cycles (1–2 months)
- Beginning capacity for regulation of arousal, including dyadic strategies and self-soothing (1–3 months +)
- Orientation to external world: using the senses to take in impressions of the environment (2 weeks–3 months +)
- Interactions with caregivers: beginnings of preferential attachments; focusing attention on caregivers for longer periods; social smiling; cooing (1–3 months)

Age 3 to 6 Months

- Development of attachment: consistent recognition of primary caregiver(s); clear preferences for interacting with them; responsiveness to parents' playful behavior; ability to use attachment relationship to regulate arousal and affect (3 months +)
- Play develops: within the attachment, relationship (interactive play and baby games); exploratory play, utilizing the senses; both forms of play gradually become more elaborate and complex (3–4 months +)
- Memory develops, as indicated by the infant's preference for certain types of pleasurable interactions and play sequences (3 months +)
- Motor skills: gradual development of control over upper body functions, including head and neck control (3 months +), reaching for objects (4 months +), grasping objects (4–5 months +), eye–hand coordination 4–5 months +), coordinating hand movements by bringing the hands together (4–5 months +)

Age 6 to 12 Months

- Initiates play interactions, rather than depending on parent to initiate them; this is evidence for the beginnings of intentionality, goal-directed action, and awareness of cause and effect (6–7 months)
- Intensification of interest in relationships, own body, and the physical world (6 months +)
- Ability to "entertain" self for brief periods, due to interest in the physical world and own body (6 months +)
- Beginning ability for mental representation: the infant apparently can keep the image of the parent in mind for longer periods by remembering him or her (6–7 months +)
- Language and communication: vocalizing and babbling (4–6 months); gestural communication expressed via looking and pointing (8–9 months); understands first words (8–9 months); speaks first words (9–12 months)

- Persistent motivation to develop physical skills, especially locomotion, in a progression of creeping, crawling, cruising, and walking (7–14 months)
- Feelings of autonomy and pleasure based on the development of physical skills; also feelings of frustration and anxiety while the infant is working to master physical skills (6–12 months +)
- Memory: beginning awareness of connections between past and present, and predictability of repeated events, as indicated by reactions to separation from parents; awareness of differences between familiar and unfamiliar events and people, as indicated by stranger anxiety (8–10 months)
- Object permanence: looking for a hidden object shows the infant can keep an object she has seen in mind, even though it is not longer in sight (8–9 months)
- Beginning awareness of others' point of view: joint attention and social referencing (9–12 months +)
- Following simple directions: responding to parents' words and gestures (9–10 months)
- Imitative learning: watching caregivers to learn how to do things (9–12 months)
- Sense of self begins to develop, based on feelings of self-efficacy (a beginning sense of feeling control over action and communication with caregivers), and self-esteem, when the infant feels successful at accomplishing a goal. The development of a positive sense of self is strongly related to responsive caregiving (6–12 months +).

❖ CHAPTER 5 ❖

Practice with Infants

Infant mental health is an approach that derives from the rich knowledge generated from observational research on parent–infant interaction presented Chapters 1 and 4. Essentially, this research demonstrates that when parents are attuned to the infant's signals and feelings, encourage and take pleasure in communicating with the infant, and respond to the baby's needs in a timely way, the baby's development as an individual self and social person is supported and enhanced.

Infant mental health practice applies this perspective to situations where quality of interaction is compromised or at risk. In infant mental health practice both the parents and the baby are seen as clients. Intervention aims to promote strengths and resolve difficulties in their interaction. The baby is present when the parents meet with the infant mental health worker, and "baby watching"—the collaborative observation and interpretation of the baby's behavior—is a primary focus. The infant mental health worker often "speaks for the baby" in order to help the parents understand the infant's nonverbal behavior. The worker also puts the observations he or she and the parents make about the baby's behavior into a developmental context, which becomes the basis for forecasting future developmental steps. In cases where negative interactions have developed between parents and baby, the worker attempts to help the parents reflect on how their working models may contribute the problem (Fraiberg, Adelson, & Shapiro, 1975). Through this focus on the baby and on the evolution of the interaction, the baby becomes comprehensible to the parents. Developing the capacity to understand the baby in turn supports the parents' sense of competence and allows solutions to the problems to be generated (Fraiberg, 1980; Barnard et al., 1988).

When there are concerns about the infant's developmental status, a number of standardized assessment instruments can be utilized, including the Bayley Scales of Infant Development, the Infant Mullen Scales of Early Learning and the Connecticut Infant–Toddler Developmental Assessment. The Bayley is the most widely used assessment tool. Although the Bayley is not predictive except in cases of serious developmental delays, it provides a useful snapshot of an infant's current strengths and weaknesses in the cognitive and motor areas, identifying areas that may require intervention (Clark, Paulson, & Conlin, 1993).

Specialized tests should never be the sole evaluation procedure. Testing, when indicated, should be part of a comprehensive evaluation that includes observation of the infant–parent relationship, since quality of attachment and the infant's social abilities are better predictors of developmental outcome than are specific aspects of infant development (Bernstein, Hans, & Percansky, 1991). The following case example of infant mental health practice illustrates the use of observation in the assessment of transactional issues between an infant and her parents.

ASSESSMENT AND BRIEF INTERVENTION WITH AN INFANT AND HER FAMILY: A CASE EXAMPLE

The case of 1-year-old Julie and her parents illustrates an infant mental health assessment conducted by a social worker with training in this specialized area. My account focuses particularly on the transactional context of infant development, showing how an infant's early, probably normative difficulties in self-regulation stimulated a negative pattern of caregiving that compromised her attachments and threatened her affective and social development. The case also illustrates a brief intervention that was incorporated into an assessment. I will present the process of the assessment in detail so that the reader will be able to reflect on the material as it unfolds.

Family Information

Child client	Julie Bryan, age 12 months
Mother	Mrs. Bryan, European-American, age 28, homemaker
Father	Mr. Bryan, European-American, age 30, auto worker
Sibling	Erica, age 3

Referral

Julie Bryan's pediatrician referred her a few days after her first birthday. Since she was a few weeks old, Julie had cried for 6–12 hours every day. During her first year four different medical specialists had evaluated her, finding no physical causes for her crying. Julie's mother had twice rejected the pediatrician's suggestion for an infant mental health referral, but she accepted it this time because the baby's problems had not abated.

Initial Telephone Contact

Mrs. Bryan said immediately that Julie had been screaming many hours every day since she was 2 weeks old. The problem had waxed and waned but had recently worsened. Currently, Julie cried whenever she was taken out of the house and even when her mother left the room. Julie seemed very anxious with strangers and even avoided her father. Mrs. Bryan said, "I know they're supposed to be scared of strangers at this age, but this is just too much. Sometimes I have to be rough with her. I just put her in the crib and let her scream, because I can't take it anymore. How can I stop her from crying? She's got to shape up." She described times during the summer when she had put Julie in her crib and gone outside, to get away from her crying. I empathized with how hard it was to have a baby who cried constantly. I said that I had no immediate answer to stopping Julie's crying but hoped that a careful evaluation would provide some answers.

Mrs. Bryan's tone was anxious and exasperated. However, it was important to avoid answering her urgent questions with quick, formulaic answers based on general knowledge of infant development. By saying that I wanted to understand the problems thoroughly, I was conveying that I would think about Julie as an individual. This stance helps parents view the worker as someone who will try to provide thoughtful information about their baby. As it turned out, it was especially important that I did not try to answer Mrs. Bryan's pressing questions, because I learned later that she had already received many prescriptive but unsatisfactory answers from physicians, parenting books, and neighbors.

I asked if there had been any difficulties or medical complications with the pregnancy and birth. The pregnancy had been without problems and full term. Julie had been a healthy child whose developmental milestones of the first year had emerged at normal times. For the first 2 weeks, Julie had been "a good baby." Then the screaming began. As I listened I wondered what had originally caused Julie's crying—

perhaps an irritable temperament, perhaps early difficulties in self-regulation; but it seemed likely, given the duration of the problem, that the original difficulty had shaped parent–infant interactions in a way that perpetuated Julie's screaming. Mrs. Bryan noted, reflectively, that after the pediatrician had suggested counseling, when Julie was 8 months old, she had done a lot of reading about infants and that Julie had cried much less. I asked how she accounted for that change. She said, "I really don't know, but I must have done something. But then it started up again after about a month." This was a hopeful statement, suggesting that Mrs. Bryan could still imagine doing something to change the interaction.

I said that I could understand Julie best by seeing her in her home environment with her family and asked if there was a time when Mr. Bryan could be home. Mrs. Bryan was hesitant, saying that her husband worked every day from 7 to 7 but that he could get off if it was really necessary. I said I felt it *was* necessary because I wanted to get Mr. Bryan's views of the problem and to observe Julie as she related to all family members.

Commentary: Including the Father

Mrs. Bryan's uncertainty about her husband's participation and her comment about Julie's avoidance of her father raised questions about the degree of his involvement with her. In assessing children in two-parent families, it is critical to include both parents. Research on resilience consistently finds that family stability and mutual support between parents are protective factors for children's development. The father's emotional support of the mother influences the quality of caregiving she provides to the infant (Crockenberg, 1988). In families where traditional sex role divisions prevail (whether the mother works outside the home or not) and fathers are not highly involved in caregiving, the father's influence is indirect, through support for the mother. When fathers are highly involved caregivers, their influence is more direct and infants establish strong preferential attachments and mutually regulating patterns of interaction and play with fathers (Yogman, 1982; Belsky & Rovine, 1988). Mrs. Bryan's hesitancy to involve her husband in the evaluation might have a number of different meanings. However, I would not be able to learn about his influence on his wife's caregiving or his relationship with Julie without seeing him directly. This point may seem obvious, but too often in practice fathers are excluded, at times by their own preference, but also sometimes by their partners with the acquiescence of practitioners.

THE FIRST TWO HOME VISITS:
LEARNING ABOUT THE FAMILY

Mr. and Mrs. Bryan voiced many complaints about Julie's constant crying. She would cry whenever Mrs. Bryan left the house, or even the
room. Mr. Bryan said Julie avoided him, though he amended this to
say that she had been more willing to play with him recently. I asked if
there were times when Julie did not cry, and Mrs. Bryan said with
exasperation, "Oh, yes, as long as I'm right there every minute, she
doesn't have any trouble. She's stuck on me, and I can't seem to break
her of it." She said that physicians and neighbors had told her to let
Julie "cry it out" and eventually she'd "outgrow it." However, when
she tried to follow that advice, Julie would cry in her crib for at least
an hour and Mrs. Bryan would feel a failure as a mother. Nevertheless,
leaving Julie alone had been Mrs. Bryan's primary strategy ever since
the crying began at age 2 weeks. I asked how she had explained the
crying to herself. She responded, "Well, I just call it her getting mad at
me for not being with her every minute." She said that Erica had been
such an easy baby that she wasn't prepared for Julie. I said, "I don't
know yet why Julie cries, but I do know from seeing babies with similar problems that letting them cry it out usually doesn't work." Mrs.
Bryan said, "It relieves me to hear that."

Observations of Julie

Julie struck me as a pretty and appealing baby. She had brown curls
around her ears and was still nearly bald on top. I could see her two
new lower teeth but noted that her most frequent expression was more
a strained grimace than a smile. When I said hello to her, she looked at
me warily and curiously, but did not cry, as her mother had said she
would. Later she approached me several times without anxiety. Julie
was just beginning to walk and still felt more comfortable cruising
along the furniture. She could climb up on the couch and get down on
her own. She was adept at crawling. These observations told me that
her motor skills were appropriate for age. Her language development
appeared behind. At 1 year, one expects an infant to be babbling
expressively using a wide range of sounds, using pointing and other
gestures, and beginning to use a few real words. Julie's language was
limited to grunting noises during this visit.

    Erica was playing at her mother's feet. When Julie crawled near,
Erica pushed her away, then crawled up on to her mother's lap.
Julie pulled herself up next to her mother, who extended her arm.
Julie wanted to climb onto her lap. Mrs. Bryan did not move to
accommodate her, and Erica, in response to Julie's advance, molded

herself closer to her mother's body. Julie tried to climb up, and Erica spread her body out to cover Mrs. Bryan's lap and thighs. Julie whined and grimaced and continued to stand as close to her mother as she could. Mrs. Bryan did not remark on the rivalry going on between the children. In observing this scene I remember thinking that there's not room for two babies in this family. It appeared that Erica was the favored child and Julie was the outsider. I also felt sad that Mr. Bryan did not offer to take Julie but left his wife to cope with two needy children. I asked Mrs. Bryan how it felt to have two young children wanting her attention at the same time. Mrs. Bryan laughed and said that Erica was pretty independent, so that it was not much of a problem. This led to a discussion by both parents of what an easy child Erica had been, how little rivalry Erica had shown, and how much more difficult Julie was. That response seemed incongruous with the scene I had just observed, and also felt defensive, in that a question about Mrs. Bryan's feelings was deflected into a positive description of Erica. The parents seemed to be saying that Erica is not needy or rivalrous—she is our good child. Neither of them remarked on Julie's whining bid for attention. This observed interaction raised questions about whether Mr. and Mrs. Bryan had been able to "make room" for Julie. However, since this was our first meeting and my question had brought a seemingly defensive response, I decided to continue to observe rather than ask more questions about this issue.

History Taking

I asked Mrs. Bryan how she had felt during the pregnancy. She sighed and said she was worn out and felt cooped up. Her husband was working long hours, and she was home alone with Erica. She said that she had not had a postpartum depression after Julie's birth. This led to a description by both parents of her depression after Erica's birth. Mr. Bryan said, "It lasted for about 8 months. She wouldn't talk to me about it. I thought we were going to get a divorce." Mrs. Bryan sounded wistful as she said the depression had been caused by having to give up her job: "After I had Erica, all of a sudden I didn't have anything to do and I felt cooped up and lonely." By contrast, she had not been depressed after Julie's birth. She recalled feeling happy and energetic for the first few weeks, before Julie's crying bouts began. She described how she tried to stop Julie's crying by changing her environment, moving her from room to room in the house. She said," She wouldn't have cried if I'd held her all the time, but I couldn't do that 24 hours a day. After a while, I had to get a little rough with her." This was the second time she had used this phrase, and I asked her to clarify. Again she said, "Just put her in the crib and leave her there. . . . You know, I've never cuddled her much. She hasn't been the kind of baby that you just want to come up and cuddle, and that may have had some effect."

A Demonstration of the Problem

As I was leaving, Mrs. Bryan said, "She's made a liar out of me. She hasn't screamed once since you've been here!" I said that sometimes a baby does not behave in her usual way when a new person is present. She said, "Maybe I can show you." She got up and left the room. Julie saw her mother leave and immediately crawled after her. As she passed her father's chair, he reached out to her, but she crawled past him and began to cry in a fearful tone. Mrs. Bryan reappeared smiling and said, "That's the scream." She picked Julie up and Julie stopped crying. Mrs. Bryan said, "If I hadn't come back, or if I'd put her in her crib, she'd really be screaming now."

Mrs. Bryan's Story

Mrs. Bryan asked to schedule the next home visit in the early afternoon because Julie's screaming was worst then. Mr. Bryan had said that he didn't need to be there because the problem was primarily between Julie and her mother. I agreed to meet at the earlier time but told them that Mr. Bryan's point of view and his relationship with Julie were important to understanding the problem and that I would want him to be included in future visits.

During the second home visit 2 weeks later, Julie did not cry at all. Mrs. Bryan commented that she was coping with separations more easily and was going to her father more often. Julie had also been waking up crying at night, but Mrs. Bryan said she just needed to pat her a few times and she would go back to sleep. This was a different image of Julie, as a more manageable child. It is not unusual for such progress to occur during an assessment. This is not a "miracle cure," but rather reflects that the parents, with the worker's support, are paying attention to the child's problems in a different way. A conscious focus on the problem often subtly changes the interactions that have grown up around the problem. For example, in response to a new development, Julie's crying in the middle of the night, Mrs. Bryan was comforting her immediately, rather than leaving her to cry it out, and Julie was going back to sleep. Mrs. Bryan's reporting of progress in only the second interview also made me feel that she was investing in the assessment as a vehicle for change.

The family had been on a week's vacation, and Mrs. Bryan said that they all had enjoyed the time together. This break in the family's routine also contributed to Mrs. Bryan's more hopeful attitude. She said the children really liked it when her husband had time off. This led to a discussion of Mr. Bryan's work schedule. He was away from home for 12 hours each day, and his schedule required him to work for 21 days at a stretch, followed by 2-week periods when he had weekends off. She presented this information with clear ambivalence: her tone was matter of fact, but her facial expression was strained and unhappy. He had always worked this intense schedule, but before the children were born she had also worked long hours and had arranged her work schedule to match her husband's, so they had spent more time together. He had been present at Erica's birth, but a day later had gone into a 21-day work period. She came home from the hospital with her first baby and had received little help from her husband. They had no relatives in the area. I commented that it sounded difficult. She said, "There was nobody to help me out. I was depressed for about 6 months. It's a lot of work to take care of a baby." I agreed and said, "And even more work to take care of two." Mrs. Bryan felt she adapted to the new role of parent, especially as Erica got older and became more social and fun to play with. Erica had been an even-tempered infant who was happy going places outside the home. After Julie came home from the hospital, Mr. Bryan again had to work 3 weeks straight. Mrs. Bryan began to feel trapped again. Two children were not as portable as one. She had felt increasingly trapped after Julie's crying began. She also complained that Julie's crying had made it hard to feel comfortable about leaving her and hard to get babysitters, so that since Julie's birth she and her husband had rarely gone out and were spending even less time together.

As we talked, Erica and Julie played together near Mrs. Bryan. Julie climbed onto the couch next to me and pointed out the window. She babbled expressively. When I asked if she was showing me the pretty blue sky, she smiled broadly and babbled more. (This small incident points to the importance of making multiple observations of infants and young children. During the first home visit I had been concerned that Julie's language development was behind. However, her expressive babbling and pointing at the sky made me revise this first impression and see that her language ability was developing normally.) In response to Julie's insistent babbling, Erica called out to Julie and they played with their voices, one shouting and the other shouting in response. Mrs. Bryan asked Erica to play with some blocks, and the shouting stopped. Later the children frolicked on the floor, rolling on top on one another and laughing. But when Julie was on top momentarily, Erica became angry and began hitting her. Julie grimaced but did not cry. Mrs. Bryan allowed the hitting to continue for a long time—by my subjective response—before she asked Erica to stop.

At the end of this meeting, I made a few comments. First, I suggested that we focus on how difficult it was to feel trapped again after Julie's birth and on how Julie's problems had affected their marital relationship. I said that stress can circulate within a family—that the stress she felt over being trapped and less involved with her husband could have spilled over to Julie and made her more anxious. Mrs. Bryan was unsurprised by this interpretation and said, "You could be right." Second, I said that it would be important for Mr. Bryan to be involved in subsequent meetings, since the problem involved interactions in the family rather than just interactions between her and Julie. Mrs. Bryan was skeptical but looked pleased and relieved by this suggestion.

Impressions

Julie was developing adequately in the motor and cognitive areas, but her social development, as reflected in her ambivalent attachment, anxious demeanor, and intense reactions to separation, was compromised. Although separation anxiety is common between 8 and 12 months, Julie's seemed atypically intense and also part of a pattern of anxiety about her attachments that dated back to the early months of life. It was not clear what had caused Julie's crying originally. According to Brazelton (1992), between 3 and 12 weeks about 85% of infants go through a period of fussy crying at the end of the day. In the past, this fussing and irritability was called "colic" and was attributed to gastric distress. Although some babies do cry because of gastrointestinal pain, the irritable fussing of most young infants does not have obvious causes.

Brazelton (1992) recasts this phenomenon in developmental and maturational terms:

> Whenever a certain behavior is so predictable and widespread, we assume that it is adaptive and look for the purpose it serves. This fussing began to look like an organizing process. An immature nervous system can take in and utilize stimuli throughout the day, but there is always a little bit of overload. . . . Finally, it blows off steam in the form of an active, fussy period. After this is over, the nervous system can reorganize for another twenty-four hours. (p. 63)

Brazelton suggests that if parents can strike a balance between providing comfort and allowing the baby to cry for brief periods (5–10 minutes), babies will gradually become better organized and the fussy periods will become less frequent and disappear within a few months. Some infants with difficult temperament are more sensitive to internal and external stimuli and take longer to outgrow the fussy times.

Julie, however, did not seem to fit the profile of a child with a difficult temperament. At present she did not appear to be a globally hypersensitive infant. Her ability to accept the falls and bumps of learning to walk and to tolerate Erica's aggressive play without becoming seriously distressed suggested adequate internal affect regulation. Her one area of hypersensitivity focused on the presence or absence of her mother. Julie's crying for a long time had been a transactional response. When her mother left her alone, she would cry. Hearing her cry caused Mrs. Bryan to avoid her for longer periods, increasing Julie's anxiety and insecurity. It seemed that Mrs. Bryan did not want Julie to depend on her at a time when dependency is normal. In this negative spiral, Julie felt less and less secure in her family and Mrs. Bryan became resentful and more distanced from her.

I wondered whether Mrs. Bryan had brought negative expectations to Julie's infancy based on her painful memories of her loneliness and depression during Erica's early months. Perhaps Julie's crying at 2 weeks had felt like a confirmation of those expectations. Had Mrs. Bryan felt helpless and defeated? It was clear that her early attempts to cope with Julie's crying minimized her own potential power to change things. Instead of offering more comforting, she hit on the idea of moving Julie from room to room, hoping that the change in environment would calm her. I wondered if Mrs. Bryan had been angry with Julie when she did not stop crying, and if her strategy of leaving Julie alone might represent an attempt to protect Julie from her anger and to defend against her own guilt about being angry. Her repeated statement, "Sometimes I have to get a little rough with her," seemed to reflect her anxiety that she might hurt Julie and her guilt over hostile impulses toward her.

In these first two sessions I had observed and learned enough to hypothesize that Julie's crying represented a transactional issue that involved the whole family. I decided to focus this issue by exploring Mr. and Mrs. Bryan's memories and understandings about how the crying originated and what perpetuated it.

THE NEXT TWO HOME VISITS

I was very pleased that Mr. Bryan was not only present but very active during these sessions. Mr. Bryan reported that Julie was coming to him more since they had been on vacation. I said that he had been able to spend more time with her then and perhaps that made it easier for her to come to him. He agreed. When Julie saw me she began babbling exuberantly as she had when she was looking out the window during the previous visit. I said, "I remember you showed me the sky last week. You're really trying to tell me something." Then I explained to Mr. Bryan how impressed I had been when Julie pointed at the blue sky and babbled so expressively, as if it was the most exciting thing she had ever seen. He said wryly, "Well, it's a rare thing around Cleveland in the winter." He said he too had noticed that she was babbling more and getting ready to talk. As we talked Julie came up to him and he took her on his knee. He said, "See, she never used to do this." When I said that it must feel good, he agreed but emphasized that this was a recent development. I said, "It must have been frustrating to have a daughter who wouldn't come to you." Mr. Bryan did not respond, and Mrs. Bryan said ironically, "Oh, but she would come to me!"

As Julie bounced happily on her father's knee, I asked them to think back to when Julie's crying started. Mr. Bryan said, "I think she had a bad colic at the beginning." I said that a very fussy baby who cries a lot is really stressful for parents. I added that something had happened that kept Julie's crying going long after infants outgrow colic. Addressing both parents, I said, "I've wondered if a pattern started out of your responses to her early crying. She was not an easy baby and her crying really got to you, so much so that it was hard to be with her. I remember you told me you didn't know what to do and that you decided leaving her alone to cry it out would help. I wonder if her crying for long periods with no one to comfort her made her feel anxious and insecure. And then, after the colic was past, she would get anxious if she was away from you and begin to cry. I'm not blaming you for feeling like getting away from her when she cried, but when you weren't there I imagine she became more worried and cried more." Mr. Bryan was thoughtful about this idea and said, "I think that's possible." Mrs. Bryan also agreed but looked anxious. She said, "Maybe Julie wanted me all the time then, because that's the way she is now." She described her frustration when Julie's crying had persisted: "I'd thought, if I could just get through the first 6 months, when you've got to pay attention to the baby all the time, I'd have it made. But Julie's crying threw a monkey wrench into that plan." I empathized with how difficult that had been for her.

Instead of continuing this discussion, she shifted her focus to Julie, whom she had taken on her lap. For the first time I had seen, Mrs. Bryan began to play a game with her. Julie tossed her empty bottle onto the coffee table. Erica, sitting on Mr. Bryan's lap, laughed at

Julie's performance. Mrs. Bryan retrieved the bottle and handed it to Julie, who tried to push it off the table repeatedly. Each time, Mrs. Bryan, prevented the bottle from falling. As the game proceeded, both children were laughing excitedly and both parents were enjoying the game. I enjoyed it too, because it showed the family's ability to have fun together. Although this was a typical "baby game," I was struck by the latent content of the scenario: Mrs. Bryan was actively preventing the bottle from disappearing from sight, much to Julie's pleasure.

At the end of this visit, I pointed out that Julie seemed to be doing better. She was allowing her father to hold and play with her, was becoming more expressive, and was tolerating separations better. I asked them to think about what they had done to make things go better. I asked them to pay attention to what they were doing and what Julie was doing when things were going well, suggesting that would help us figure out what would help during difficult times.

I felt encouraged after this session, particularly because Mr. and Mrs. Bryan had given thoughtful and undefensive responses to my formulation of Julie's crying, even though it must have been difficult to hear. I was also encouraged by Mrs. Bryan's acknowledgment that Julie's problems involved wanting her mother, by Mr. Bryan's deepening engagement in the assessment process, and by the family's shared pleasure during the game with the bottle. Seeing the strengths in these parents gave me confidence that they could do the painful work of looking at their early feelings about Julie.

In the next session, I asked Mr. and Mrs. Bryan to describe their feelings when Julie's problems first began. Mr. Bryan said he had tried to comfort her, but when she continued to cry, "I just gave up." I asked what he did after he gave up, and he described putting Julie in her crib and then going down to the basement so he wouldn't hear her cry. He said he tried not to worry about her, yet felt bad about giving up on her. I was impressed with his honesty. I commented, "It didn't sit well with you to give up. It must feel better now that Julie is improving and she's coming to you."

Mrs. Bryan answered the question with a story I had not heard before. She had decided not to nurse Julie, and Julie had thrown up her formula feedings while she was still in the hospital after birth. Mrs. Bryan said, "She threw up all over me. It was all over my hands. I wondered if she had an allergy, and I asked her doctor if it would have been better if I'd nursed her, but he said it wouldn't have made any difference." She described taking Julie to several specialists, and how each simply told her that she would grow out of her crying. She said, "We kept trying, but when she got to be 6 months old and was still crying, I stopped taking her to them and tried to figure things out myself. I kept telling myself, it's got to get better." I said, "You've been concerned parents and it's all the more frustrating that you tried so hard to solve the problem but weren't able to." After I said this Mrs. Bryan took Julie on her lap and held her. (This response was encouraging. It is fairly common in infant work to see that when a parent feels understood and supported, she can turn to her infant.)

I also said that "It's got to get better" sounded like a hopeful feeling, but I wondered if she had other feelings that were more negative. Mrs. Bryan smiled anxiously and did not reply. I said, "I'm trying to put myself in your place and think how I might feel if I had a baby who cried all the time and I couldn't comfort her. I think I would get angry at a baby like that." Mrs. Bryan replied, "Oh, I've been angry with her a lot. Sometimes I just put her in her crib, because I was afraid I was going to hurt her." I said that her anger was understandable, but that it is very hard on a parent to feel angry at a little baby—it can make a parent feel terribly guilty. Mr. Bryan said that his feeling was not so much anger as giving up. He said, "If I can't solve a problem, I try to ignore it." I said that their feelings seemed justified, given how hard it was to comfort Julie, but that feeling either angry or resigned could complicate a parent's relationship with a baby. I suggested that each of them had reasons based on their own feelings for drawing back from Julie, and that even though Julie was improving, those feelings continued to influence how they saw her. I added that Julie had her own feelings as well, that she seemed mad at her mother and distant from her father. Mr. Bryan said, "Her cry does sound mad now." Mrs. Bryan had previously expressed frustration that Julie had demanded her attention when she was trying to write a letter earlier that day. I referred back to that and said, "It seems like you and Julie are mad at each other a lot because you can't seem to please each other. This is the feeling that's grown up between you, and it's kept going, even though her feeding problems and colic are long past." Mrs. Bryan agreed that she and Julie were mad at each other. She said, "I really wasn't attached to Julie, not for the first 6 months. I could have given her away at any time."

This was an important session. The assessment process was gradually creating a story that made sense of Julie's crying and their reactions to it. Both Mr. and Mrs. Bryan had described their negative feelings toward Julie, and we had begun to link their feelings to their behavior toward her. Julie's crying was being redefined from her own internal problem to a transactional issue with a long history in the interplay between her behavior, her parents' difficult feelings, and their defenses against negative feelings toward Julie, which had taken the form of trying to distance themselves from her. The formulation of

Julie's problems had been a shared endeavor between the parents and myself. Although an experienced practitioner might be able to understand the dynamics of the problem and interpret them very quickly to the family, it is better to engage the parents in a shared process of discovery. Parents who have reflected on the evolution of a problem are more likely to accept the worker's formulation and intervention recommendations.

OFFICE SESSIONS: VIDEOTAPING AND INTERPRETIVE SESSIONS

The family came to our agency for a videotaped session. I had told Mr. and Mrs. Bryan that I wanted to make a videotape of Julie for use in consulting with colleagues. I also told them we could watch the tape together at our next meeting. Julie and Erica enjoyed the toys in the playroom, while Mr. and Mrs. Bryan watched from the couch. Julie crawled rapidly, taking pleasure in moving around the room. She also took a number of steps without holding on. She and Erica played independently of their parents. Julie's affect was curious and good natured. A critical incident occurred midway through the session. Julie climbed onto a child's chair and sat for a moment, proud of her accomplishment. However, as she started to get down, she lost her balance and fell off. She began to cry and crawled over to her mother. Mrs. Bryan visibly shrank back from her and then stood up and crossed the room to get Julie a bottle. Julie crawled after her, whining. Even though Julie accepted the bottle, she pulled up by holding onto her mother's pant leg and raised her arms to signal she wanted to be picked up. Mrs. Bryan stood there for a few moments, then put the bottle in Julie's mouth and returned to the couch. Julie sucked on the bottle for a minute, then resumed playing. Later she climbed up on the couch between her parents, and again Mrs. Bryan folded her arms and leaned away from Julie.

Mr. and Mrs. Bryan came without the children the following week, and we viewed the tape together. Videotape has been widely used in infant mental health practice (Osofsky & Eberhart-Wright, 1988; McDonough, 1993). Video is a nonthreatening medium that offers concrete visual data that can become the basis for an individualized guidance process directly relevant to the parents' concerns and to the child's particular developmental stage. The practitioner can use the tapes to point out the infant's current tasks, celebrate recent accomplishments, and forecast upcoming steps in development. Viewing videotaped sessions allows parents to see strengths and vulnerabilities in their infant and in their parenting abilities that they might not otherwise see.

Mr. and Mrs. Bryan were pleased with the image of Julie on the tape. They noted her interest in the new toys and her independence. Mr. Bryan said, "She looks like a normal 1-year-old." As we watched her work to get up on the chair, I commented on her persistence. When she sat on the chair, Mrs. Bryan said, "Yay, you did it!" When she fell off the chair, Mr. Bryan said, "Oh, now she's going to want some sympathy." As Mrs. Bryan saw herself shrink away from Julie on the tape, her expression became somber. When she watched Julie reaching to be picked up and herself standing above her unmoving, Mrs. Bryan spoke for Julie, saying, "Pick me up, you idiot!" Mrs. Bryan's reactions to observing her own behavior and her ability to speak for Julie were encouraging. She acknowledged the validity of Julie's request for comfort. She saw her own refusal to provide comfort clearly, without resorting to defensive distortions.

Afterward I suggested that the tape showed Julie's strengths and age-appropriate development, as well as the problem that had prompted them to request an assessment. I said that after meeting with the family several times I had seen a lot of progress in a short amount of time. Julie was crying less and was coping with separations better. She was becoming more playful and more involved with Mr. Bryan. I said that although I had made some suggestions about handling separations, I thought that Julie's improvement was due to her becoming aware of their concern about her. Their concern and determination to help Julie had made the biggest difference so far. I was optimistic, I said, that their concern would allow them to change their ways of responding to Julie before her problems became worse. There was a problem—one we had just seen on the tape—that would require more work to resolve. I pointed out that neither of them had been able to comfort Julie when she fell, but said I was very impressed by Mrs. Bryan's ability to speak for Julie and say what she needed. In order to understand how the problem evolved, I said, it had been very helpful to learn the early history of Julie's crying. When Julie could not be comforted, they found that very hard to cope with and put distance between themselves and her by leaving her to cry it out. This made Julie anxious and fearful that they didn't care, which made her cling and cry all the more. A problem that began as colic became a problem in their relationship. On their side, because Julie was such a difficult baby, they felt she could never be satisfied and that she was making them feel like bad parents, which made it harder to reach out and comfort her. Mrs. Bryan looked sad and said, "I could disagree with you . . . ," then began to cry. She said, "It was so hard when she was little. I don't want it to be this way. I was always more attached to Erica than I was to Julie. But Julie's my girl too." I said, "That's right, and I know you want to get this worked out. I know what I've said was painful to hear. But I wanted to tell you as clearly as I could, because it's not too late to do something about it. I am worried that if you don't make some changes in your relationship with Julie now there will be problems later on. Already by age 1 it's become like a battle between you and Julie, and there's a danger that could get worse as she gets older and that you'll always be fighting with her. But it really doesn't need to be that way if we can get the problems worked out now."

Mr. Bryan said that he had been worried about how Erica would react to a new baby and so he had concentrated on paying attention to her. He remembered that when Julie's crying started he had turned even more toward Erica when he was home. I said that both of them had helped Erica cope with the intrusion of a new baby, but I suspected that Erica had gotten a lot of love before Julie came along and so she already had a secure place with them. Mrs. Bryan said, "And Julie just got rebuffed."

Mrs. Bryan opened the next session by saying, "After last time, I really wanted to disagree with you. But I thought about it a lot. I decided to watch myself when I was with Julie. I did catch myself getting mad at her when she was fussing and wanting to come to me. I caught myself sort of flinching away like I did on the tape. So I tried something different. I opened my arms, and Julie came and wriggled up against me and she was so happy." I told her she had been courageous to look at the problem in their relationship and that it was great to hear that welcoming Julie had made her so happy.

Mrs. Bryan's ability to observe herself and change her behavior was very encouraging. However, when a relationship problem has persisted for a long time, it is not sufficient to focus on behavioral change alone. Both Mr. and Mrs. Bryan had acknowledged during the assessment that their attitudes toward Julie had been shaped by their inability to console her. They had begun to examine their anger toward her and to reflect on the defensive strategies they had adopted. Just as Julie had begun to internalize a working model of her parents as inconsistently available and at times rejecting, her parents had built up images of her as a demanding, never-satisfied baby. The ongoing power of these images and defensive behaviors could potentially undermine the parents' sincere attempts to respond differently to Julie. Consequently, I suggested that our work focus in part on their memories of how they felt when Julie was inconsolable in early infancy. I said, "Though those times are behind you now, they still influence how both of you feel about Julie, especially when she's clingy or crying." Mrs. Bryan responded by saying that she remembered wanting to get away from Julie because she was afraid she would lose control and hurt her. Mr. Bryan said he was so frustrated and angry that he wanted to throw her against the wall. I said, "That helps me understand why both of you would walk away from her. Really, you didn't want to hurt her, but it was hard not to stay angry at her. I think it would help to remember and talk about how you felt, about your understandable anger and how it has influenced your relationship with Julie." I believed that their attitudes toward Julie would change if they could reflect on their "unacceptable" anger and how it caused them to distance themselves from Julie. Exploration and validation of their anger could be a pathway to diminishing their defenses against getting close to her, which in turn could lead into a more consistent responsiveness to Julie.

DISCUSSION

The assessment of Julie and her family was informed by a knowledge of infant development in its transactional context. Julie's difficulties probably started in the young infant's typical fussiness at the end of the day. However, her parents were not able to tolerate her crying and responded in ways that decreased rather than increased her ability to regulate arousal. When an infant has to wait too long for relief of distress repeatedly, she begins to feel fearful and anxious in the face of mild distress, which increases the distress. It was likely that for Julie as a young infant the experience of anxiety was constantly reinforced by her parents' solution of letting her "cry it out." Her anxiety and disregulation, expressed in frequent bouts of crying, alienated her parents from her, so that the dyadic regulation of arousal so helpful to young infants was not available to her. This affected her confidence in her attachments and probably kept her focused on keeping her mother close. However, this preoccupation with her mother's proximity, combined with both parents' tendency to avoid her when she was crying, prevented the full development of the pleasurable activities that emerge in a secure attachment between 3 and 6 months. Julie and her parents did not learn to play together or to find mutual pleasure in interaction that is characteristic of this age. (It was encouraging that both parents were beginning to play with her more at age 1.) Although she could play independently and showed normal interest in the world when her mother was present, these capacities seemed to disappear when her mother was not present.

"Goodness of fit" was poor between Julie and her parents in the first month of life. This set the stage for difficulties in Julie's ability to cope with stress. From the parents' side, there were several factors influencing their difficulties in helping Julie regulate arousal. It seemed that Mrs. Bryan was under stress from having become a parent for the second time. In a parent who is already stressed, having another child is a risk factor for further stress. It was likely that Mrs. Bryan's experience of loneliness and depression during her first child's infancy promoted negative expectations of how she would feel during Julie's infancy. She felt unsupported by her husband, who also felt alienated from Julie. They were unable, until the period of the assessment, to come together to support each other. Prior to that Mr. Bryan had resigned himself to Julie's problems and had implicitly withdrawn support for his wife's attempts to cope with those problems.

Julie had come to be seen by her parents as a demanding, impossible-to-please baby. Their view of her, colored by their anger and anxiety, made it difficult to see what was normal about her. For example, they could not see her stranger anxiety, separation anxiety and increased fussiness in response to working to master motor skills, all characteristic of 9- to 12-month-old infants, as aspects of normal development. Rather, they could only see these responses as continuing evidence of her earlier problems. Fortunately, over the course of the assessment, they began to see Julie's behavior in more normative terms. Throughout the assessment I supported this changing view by pointing out Julie's normal behavior and underscoring their descriptions of how Julie was improving.

The assessment prepared the family for more extensive work, yet it was an intervention in its own right. The assessment served to do the following:

- Define the original problem of crying in developmental terms
- Frame Julie's difficulties in a transactional context
- Focus the parents' memories and observations of their current feelings and behavior on *interactions* rather than on Julie as an individual
- Help the parents distinguish between their images of Julie and her current actual behavior
- Lead the parents, through a gradually deepening examination of their behaviors, feelings and defenses in relation to Julie's problems, to a more empathic understanding of themselves and Julie
- Bring Mr. Bryan into a more supportive role and a fuller partnership with Mrs. Bryan on behalf of their children

The assessment also constituted a prognostically hopeful beginning, in that the Bryans showed determination to cope with Julie's difficulties, were responsive to initial interpretations (as shown by observation of Julie and their behavior between sessions), and demonstrated a capacity to work on understanding themselves in relation to their infant.

OBSERVATION EXERCISES

1. Spend 20 minutes observing a 5- to 6-month-old infant with one of his primary caregivers—either mother or father. Focus your observation on the following issues:

   a. Affective tone of parent and infant.
   b. Parent's physical handling of the infant.
   c. How well does she or he know the baby?
   d. Attunement and responsiveness to each other: eye contact, smiling, sharing perceptions, and attention.
   e. Parent's responsiveness to the baby: ability to see baby's needs, read his signals and cues, take his perspective, see him "as he is."
   f. Dyadic regulation: if mismatches or distress occur (e.g., the infant becomes fussy, or the infant reacts to the parent's attention shifting away from him), how do they restore a sense of synchrony?
   g. Play: If the observation includes play between the parent and infant, what is the content and process of the play? What do they do together, and how do they keep the play going?

2. Spend 20 minutes observing a 10- to 13-month-old infant who is on the verge of being able to walk, preferably in her home. Focus your observation on the following issues:

   a. Interaction—What is the balance of independent and attachment behavior? What does the infant do to gain the parent's attention? Does she use babbling, gestures, smiles or glances? Does she approach the parent? Does she share experience/objects with the parent by showing and pointing? How does the parent respond?
   b. Motivation—How intently does the infant practice physical skills such as crawling, pulling up, and cruising by holding on to furniture?
   c. Affective style/temperament—What affects and attitudes does the baby show as she practices physical skills? Descriptive terms might include exuberant, pleased with herself, determined, excited, reckless, self-contained, calm, irritable, easily frustrated, and the like.

d. Dyadic and self-regulation—Observe how the infant responds to frustration. For example, how does she react when she falls repeatedly? Does she become affectively disorganized? Does she remain task focused? Does she turn to a caregiver for emotional support?

e. Reflect back to your observation of a 5- to 6-month-old. What differences do you see between that baby and the 10- to 13-month-old?

❖ CHAPTER 6 ❖

Toddler Development

As the infant enters the second year of life, she becomes a toddler. The name of this developmental period, which covers 12–36 months of age, comes from the verb "toddle," to walk with short and wobbly steps. The image of the transition into toddlerhood is an infant pulling herself up, standing, looking around expectantly, taking several steps, falling down, and then repeating the process over and over, with gradually less wobbling and uncertainty. Toddlerhood is marked by the child's increasing ability to do things on her own and with gradually improving skill. The upright posture presents her with a new and wider view of the world. Walking permits her to move more easily and to cover greater distances. The toddler's increasingly effective motor skills make possible all sorts of new actions. Cognitive advances, combined with curiosity and will, intensify her desire to experience and understand everything she sees. Before she can use words to ask about the world, she uses actions to explore her environment and to raise questions about what she is experiencing. The new theme of the toddler is exploration.

The toddler moves into the world, but she is not ready to move out of the attachment system that has provided security during infancy. The need for secure attachment is carried along and transformed as the infant evolves into a toddler. *Toddlers have a dual orientation: toward maintaining attachment and toward exploring the world and the self* (Bowlby, 1969). The direction of toddler development, however, is toward individuation, toward a sense of the self as differentiated from others and capable of autonomous thought and action.

170

There is corresponding shift in the toddler's motivation and goals. During the first year, the infant generally wants to interact with her parent. This is a major goal of her behavior. In the second year, the toddler increasingly wants to realize her own inner goals (Sander, 1975). By about age 2½, the toddler has begun to be self-aware, as indicated by correct use of the pronoun "I," to think of herself as able to take action and to evaluate how well she has done something. The toddler's growing self-awareness and knowledge is paralleled by growing awareness of how the world—her family, immediate environment and, implicitly, her culture—is organized. The toddler period marks the child's gradual internalization of parental standards and expectations, as well as the construction of internal understandings of how the world works. The 2-year-old works very hard to make sense of her experience. Increasingly, she thinks her own thoughts and expresses her own ideas, using her developing capacity for symbolization, through play and language.

PHYSICAL DEVELOPMENT

Toddlers continue to grow at a rapid rate, though not nearly as fast as during the first year. Between ages 1 and 3, American toddlers, on average, increase in height from 29 to 38 inches and in weight from 20 to 33 pounds (Cole & Cole, 1989). Motor abilities, most dramatically symbolized by walking, increase considerably. Control of hands and eye–hand coordination improve so that, for example, a 2-year-old can stack three blocks and use a spoon, fork and cup efficiently. Between 1½ and 3 the toddler develops sufficient voluntary control of bladder and bowel muscles to be toilet trained.

Even though toddlers are gaining motor skills rapidly, they often must concentrate intently to maintain control of their bodies, especially between 1 and 2 years of age. The gap between what a toddler wants to do and what he *can* do physically is a frequent source of frustration. However, by age 3 the toddler walks with ease, runs, climbs stairs, and can peddle a tricycle.

Brain development continues rapidly up to age 2, then slows, since by that time length and branching of neurons has nearly reached adult levels (Cole & Cole, 1989). The theme of brain development during the toddler period is integration of functions. As myelination establishes connections between the brain stem, cerebral cortex (and different parts of the cerebral cortex), and frontal lobes, integration of perceptual and cognitive functions increases and self-awareness begins to develop (Fischer, 1987).

ATTACHMENT AND SECURE BASE BEHAVIOR

During the second and third years, the toddler's ability to regulate affect and behavior and to organize experience continues to depend to a large degree on parental responsiveness and on transactional patterns of regulation. A secure attachment during the first year predicts the child's continuing ability to use the parent's help to regulate affect and behavior in the face of frustration or stress (Matas, Arend, & Sroufe, 1978). This capacity to utilize the attachment relationship on a continuing basis promotes mastery, social competence and the development of autonomy (Sroufe & Waters, 1977; Frodi, Bridges, & Grolnick, 1985). Working models of attachment develop. Although the toddler continues to depend on the actual relationship with the parent, she is also constructing representations of the caregiving relationship that allow her to gain comfort by thinking about the parent or by symbolizing the attachment through play (Lieberman & Pawl, 1990). When the parent has been consistent in helping the child cope with situations that arouse anxiety, helping the child appraise situations that may be dangerous, and helping the child feel secure, the child internalizes these capacities as part of her working models: "Reliable protection by the mother allows the child to become self-protective" (Lieberman & Pawl, 1990, p. 379). Toddlers who have secure attachments with both parents show more positive affects, better frustration tolerance, and better problem-solving abilities than do insecurely attached toddlers (Easterbrooks & Goldberg, 1984).

Transitional Objects

Transitional objects (or comfort objects) exemplify the toddler's ability to symbolize the attachment relationship (Winnicott, 1958). Toddlers use transitional objects such as blankets, teddy bears or other stuffed animals, or dolls to help them cope with separations from parents and other potentially stressful situations, and with their growing sense of separateness. A transitional object is a single, preferred object that the toddler takes to bed. After the parent leaves, the child may suck on it, snuggle with it, or talk to it. A toddler often takes his comfort object when he is going away from home or is going to be separated from his parents. The transitional object symbolizes the relationship with the mother, but also the toddler imbues it "with magical powers to soothe, protect, and empower the toddler to continue to explore the world" (Gemelli, 1996, p. 238). The transitional object, like the toddler's internal representations of the parents, is under the child's control, and he can use it to play out comforting aspects of the attachment when the parent is not present.

Secure Base and Exploration

The attachment relationship forms a context for the exploratory behavior that is so characteristic of the toddler period. A secure attachment creates a secure base from which to explore (Bowlby, 1969). Toddlers with secure attachment may spend relatively long periods playing by themselves without demonstrating an attachment behavior. Young toddlers are so interested in learning about the world, exploring the properties and functions of objects and toys, and experimenting with and practicing physical skills that they often appear surprisingly independent and self-absorbed. A parent, watching her 14-month-old examine all the toys in a play room, said, "It's like this at home, too—I can't get him to pay attention to me." Yet when the box with a crank on the side that he was turning exploded a doll into his face (a jack-in-the-box), he looked shocked and ran to his mother. She cuddled him for no more than a few seconds. They looked at the jack-in-the-box together, and she demonstrated how it worked while he watched. Then, although he was still wary of the jack-in-the-box, he continued to play with the toys, with little interaction with his mother. This brief example illustrates the interaction between the attachment and exploratory systems in the early toddler period. If the toddler is feeling comfortable and secure, his interest in exploring his immediate world dominates. However, if he becomes distressed, this activates the attachment system and he "returns to base" and receives comfort or explanation from his parent until his sense of security is restored (Bowlby, 1973). The toddler's ability to walk toward or away from his parent often indicates how he is feeling. When he moves away in exploration he shows his confidence in doing something on his own; when he moves back toward the parent, he is expressing a wish to feel secure and protected (Lieberman, 1993).

The secure base phenomenon so prominent in the behavior of toddlers as they move away to explore and then return to the caregiver is actually established in the attachment period during the first year. Although attachment behavior, dyadic play, and mutual regulation between infant and parent were stressed in the account of infancy, it is important to note that infants spend a lot of time *not* interacting with their parents. They play with objects or with their own bodies and look around curiously, studying their immediate world. In this sense they are already exploring "away" from their caregivers. In the first year, they have also learned how to return to base, or more precisely have learned how to bring the base back to themselves (Stern, 1977). They have practiced disengaging and reengaging. If infants and parents have been able to work out effective ways of restoring attachment security after the infant has been focused on other things or after a separation, the infant develops a sense of having a secure base, which will be put to use more obviously when she is a toddler.

Additional Functions of Attachment during the Toddler Period

In addition to providing a secure base, the attachment relationship takes on some other new functions in supporting the child's development during the second and third years, including the following:

• *Providing modeling for behavior.* Toddlers watch their parents carefully and imitate their behavior, mannerisms, and words.

• *Social referencing.* As toddlers encounter new situations, objects and people, they turn to the parent for help in evaluation. If a stranger kneels down to talk to the toddler, he is likely to reach for his parent's hand and catch her eye in order to learn whether this is a safe person. The toddler relies on the parent to mediate between himself and new experiences and people.

• *Helping the toddler construct an understanding of the world.* The parent increasingly is an explainer and clarifier for the child—putting things into words in order to help the toddler understand her experience and feelings. Parental explanations often include preparing the child in advance for unfamiliar or stressful experiences, describing in words what is going to happen. Everyone, including toddlers, appreciates advance preparation. But toddlers in particular benefit, because they encounter so many things that seem new and confusing. Providing information and clarification can be seen as a cognitive and affective dimension of providing a secure base. This function of attachment has implications for the treatment of toddlers (and older children) who have had stressful or traumatic experiences. Parents can help the child master a difficult experience by putting it into words, locating it in the past, and providing reassurance (Bennett & Davies, 1981).

• *Encouraging and scaffolding the toddler's language and communication skills.* The parent helps the toddler learn language and construct images of the world by "filling in" connections, asking questions, and adding elements to help the child create narratives. Dialogues between parents and toddlers have similar formal qualities to infant–parent play at 4–6 months in that the parent tends to take the lead and structure the language situation so that the child can participate. When toddlers begin to speak, parents talk to them using simplified grammar, frequent repetition, and a slow pace in the service of making language accessible to the toddler. Recordings of ordinary conversation between toddlers and parents reveal that they are "co-constructing" accounts of recent events (Engel, 1995). Greenspan and Greenspan point out the special role of parental encouragement and admiration at this age: "Admiration invites the child to feel pride and investment in his new activities. A toddler needs this pride and interest in his new physical, psychological and thinking abilities. . . . When the admiration is there, the toddler feels support for his new capacities. If parents are repeatedly indifferent, the toddler may suffer by feeling disappointed and not learning to appreciate his abilities" (Greenspan & Greenspan, 1985, p. 107).

• *Continuing dyadic regulation of affect.* The parent, through comforting, setting limits, and putting things into words, helps the child learn to regulate feelings, especially helping the child cope with powerful feelings, such as anger in tantrums, or frustration over not being able to accomplish a task. The attachment relationship "expands" to contain a wider range of affects, including negative feelings that arise in conflicts between the parent and toddler. The toddler's need to assert himself and to be in control poses a challenge for the parent, who may find herself struggling with her own anger as she tries to help the toddler cope with his strong feelings. However, toddlers particularly need the support of parents in regulating affects because their internal controls are not well developed.

RELATIONSHIPS AND SOCIAL DEVELOPMENT

Both within the family and in interactions outside the family such as in day care, the toddler begins to learn about social tasks and expectations, as they are defined by his culture. Mastering skill and understanding in the following tasks will continue to dominate social development throughout childhood:

• Sharing and reciprocity
• Controlling impulses for social reasons
• Status, roles (including gender roles) and social rituals

Increasingly learning how to be a social person will be negotiated in interaction with peers, not just parents. By age 2, toddlers have begun to engage in social play with peers, especially if they are in day care. Toddlers alternate between solitary play, parallel play (playing side by side, without direct interaction), and social play. Early social play lacks the imaginative role taking of 4-year-olds. It revolves around imitation of each other's behavior, shared interest in toys, and simple games like chasing each other (Brownell & Brown, 1992). Older toddlers show the beginnings of cooperative pretend play by taking on different roles, for example, with one child playing the parent and pretending to feed another child (Howes, 1988). Through these interactions toddlers begin to learn social skills of engaging another person, coordinating actions with another child's, and sharing feelings. These beginning social skills reflect the 2-year-old's dawning awareness that others have their own ideas. This awareness allows the toddler to choose to coordinate her play with another child's (Brownell & Carringer, 1990).

Although toddlers' play with peers displays a motivation to be social, this motivation competes with the toddler's wish to be autonomous and in control. Between 2 and 3 years of age, the toddler's awareness of being an autonomous self develops. This is signaled in language by the emerging use of "I," "me," "my," and "mine," and in behavior by increasing insistence on having things his way. These normal developmental steps mean that toddlers have much less ability than older children do to subordinate their own wishes in order to maintain reciprocity and harmony in play. Consequently, their play together is often not sustained and is conflictual, as when two toddlers shift from sharing a toy to competing for it. Toddlers often become possessive of toys. They apply the word "mine" to whatever toy they happen to have. To a toddler "mine" means "I have it." They regard objects they possess as extensions of themselves (Elkind, 1994), regardless of who the actual "owner" is. Parents and caregivers sometimes fail to understand the importance of the toddler's developing an autonomous sense of self, as manifested in possessive behavior, and scold or punish toddlers for "not sharing."

COGNITIVE DEVELOPMENT

Toddlers' rapid cognitive development is interwoven with other areas, such as development of language and the sense of self. Details about cognitive advances will be highlighted in the context of other areas of development throughout this chapter. The following brief discussion presents some of the major themes of cognitive development.

Toddlers show an intense interest in learning to understand their own bodies, the physical world, and the social world. They seem to notice everything. By age 18 months they want to know how things work and how to use objects, such as a comb or washcloth, "correctly." They have begun to internalize the standards of their parents. They have learned to notice if a toy is broken and have constructed an internal map of their home environment, so that they notice and may even become distressed if something is dirty, missing, or out of place. They become aware of gender differences and around the age of 2½, for the first time identify themselves as female or male.

As toddlers become capable of observing patterns and regularities in their lives, they develop conscious cognitive expectations. For example, a toddler who has regularly been comforted when she has been hurt is likely to come to her caregiver and ask her to kiss the hurt to make it well. The toddler develops a sense of sequence and rudimentary ideas of cause and effect. She becomes capable of thinking ahead, wondering about what will happen in the near future, imagining possible outcomes. This cognitive advance allows the toddler to predict and anticipate what is going to happen, but it can also be a source of uncertainty and anxiety, when a toddler correctly understands that *something* is going to happen but does not know what. For these reasons, toddlers sometimes show fear in novel situations and distress over transitions from one activity to another.

The toddler's improving cognitive abilities are demonstrated by his capacity for observation and imitation. Toddlers watch their parents and others carefully and are capable of imitating sequences of behavior. When a parent is cooking, they enjoy stirring with a spoon in an empty pot. If a toddler sees his parents dancing, he will try to dance like them. Most parents have at least a few disconcerting experiences when their toddler imitates them too well. A toddler riding in a grocery cart, for example, said, "Shit!" when his father made a loud noise by dropping a can into the cart. This little boy was not trying to embarrass his father, but rather was saying what his father had said earlier that morning when he dropped and broke a cup.

The toddler's persistence and determination, which can be very frustrating for parents, is also a sign of cognitive development. Specifically, by about age 20 months, toddlers persist at activities, whether playing with a toy or repeatedly climbing up to forbidden places, because they can now formulate a conscious goal *and* keep the goal in mind. They now have "the ability to sustain ideas and action plans" because they can hold ideas in memory for longer periods (Kagan, 1981, p. 139). Consequently, they are no longer as distractible as they were earlier. A 1-year-old can be distracted from pushing the buttons on the TV set if a parent shows him an interesting toy. He evidently stops thinking about the TV buttons. But a 2-year-old keeps the TV buttons in mind and keeps pushing them until *he* is satisfied or until a parent stops him. Kagan (1981) argues that the 2-year-old's increases in memory, goal-directedness, and self-awareness are made possible by the rapid growth of the brain's cerebral cortex between 15 and 24 months.

LANGUAGE AND COMMUNICATION

From the first birthday to 18 months, the toddler's language acquisition proceeds gradually. Then, at about 18 months, the child's wish to communicate in language takes on new urgency. Language development seems to be driven by an inherent "urge to convey" one's thoughts (Locke, 1993), as well as by the toddler's awareness that language is a social tool (Rice, 1989). Understanding of words precedes the ability to speak them, and therefore receptive vocabulary accumulates ahead of speaking vocabulary. Toddlers can understand about 50 words between 13 and 15 months, but they are not able to speak 50 words until 18–22 months (Locke, 1993). At about 18 months, there is a burst of language learning marked by the toddler's wanting to know the names for everything. By 20 months, toddlers are beginning to combine two words, using verbs and adjectives in addition to nouns ("play ball," "dirty bugs"), and to string contextually related nouns together ("daddy . . . ball . . . grass") in rudimentary sentences. During the third year of life, vocabulary continues to develop rapidly, as do grammar, syntax, intonations, and pronunciation accents that are particular to the parents' culture. By age 3, the child has a large vocabulary and command of present, past, and future tenses, enabling her to follow conversations and understand narratives. She has come to rely on words—as opposed to gestures and actions—as her main way of communicating (Bruner, 1983).

This increasingly complex use of language is paralleled by other developments, including the emergence of symbolic play, improving memory, improving cognitive organization, and verbally mediated thinking—thinking in words (Case, 1985). The acquisition of language should be seen not simply in terms of increases in the number of words or complexity of grammatical structure but rather as a fundamental shift in the child's ability to process and organize experience. Language allows the child to construct representations of his experience and to locate them in a narrative or time sequence (Bruner & Lucriello, 1989).

Language, combined with a beginning understanding of how narratives are organized, provides the child with a way of sharing her inner life in an active way. Older toddlers begin to tell stories about their everyday life. Storytelling, symbolic play, and combinations of the two become a way of organizing experience through the use of narrative. The stories of 2½- and 3-year-olds begin to show the quality of all narratives, in that they have characters (often the child herself), a beginning, a sequence of happenings, and an ending, as well as some element of tension, excitement, or humor (Engel, 1996). When older toddlers tell stories about their experience and receive interested responses from adults, their sense of power increases. Rather than having to depend on parents to intuit what has happened to them, they can now convey directly what happened and how they felt about it. Engel (1996) points out that "children tell stories as a way of solving emotional, cognitive and social puzzles and to sort out problems and concerns" (p. 8). Like symbolic play, storytelling allows the child to comment on stressful experiences "at a distance," using a medium that is under the child's control. When a child becomes capable of symbolic play and storytelling, these abilities can be utilized in play therapy to help her process and master stress and trauma.

Language and the Construction of Meaning

Toddlers also begin to think in words and to use thinking as means of constructing a view of the self and the world. Studies of narratives told by very young children demonstrate that they are often trying to "talk through" something they do not understand or find troubling. The stories of 2-year-olds go beyond merely trying to objectively describe the world in language; rather, they use narrative language to bring a personal sense of order and understanding to their experience. It is useful to think of toddlers' brief narratives, which are usually expressed in declarative sentences, as often reflecting questions about experience (Engel, 1995). What is the ocean? Is it dangerous? Why did Mommy yell when I went near the edge of the dock? Was I bad? For the toddler, there is a great deal to understand.

Many toddlers (though not all) demonstrate thinking in words by talking to themselves when they are alone, especially at nap or bed time. This is an extension of vocal play of infants when they are in their cribs. Crib talk gives the toddler practice with words and linguistic structures, just as vocal play represents the infant's practice with sounds. But toddlers' monologues before they go to sleep demonstrate a new dimension: they are thinking about and processing the events of the day. Katherine Nelson and her colleagues have analyzed the crib speech between the ages of 21 and 36 months of Emily, a child whose parents audiotaped what she said after they had tucked her in and left the room. Emily's monologues were often organized around questions of memory and anticipation: What happened? What is going to happen? The content frequently focused on variations in routine and novel situations—in other words, on events that Emily was trying to understand and put in perspective. The raw transcripts of Emily's monologues provide a fascinating window on a young child's attempts to make sense of the world. Here is an example from age 28 months. As he was tucking her in, Emily's father told her about a trip to the beach they would be taking the next day. Emily later talked to herself about the trip, clearly trying to anticipate what it would be like:

> "We are gonna at the ocean. Ocean is a little far away . . . I think it's a couple blocks away. Maybe it's . . . down downtown and across the ocean and down the river . . . The hot dogs will be in a fridge. And the fridge would be in the water over by a shore. And then we could go in and get a hot dog and bring it out to the river, and then the sharks go in the river and bite me, in the ocean. And ocean be over by . . . I think a couple blocks away . . . we could find any hot dogs, um the hot dogs gonna be for the beach. Then the bridge is gonna, we'll have to go in the green car, 'cause that's where the car seats are." (Nelson, 1989, pp. 66–67)

The parents' notes indicate that Emily had never seen the ocean, nor had she ever eaten a hot dog. Not surprisingly, she keeps going back to these two elements of her father's description trying to make sense of them. In her statements about the ocean and hot dogs, many questions are implied: Where is the ocean? Is it far away? Is it like a river? Will we drive across a bridge? Where will the hot dogs be? Since hot dogs are food, will they be in a refrigerator? Will the fridge be in the water? (Perhaps this reflects a previous experience with a cooler submerged in water.) Will sharks be in the water? Emily is trying to prepare herself for a new experience by constructing some pictures of it in advance. She combines her father's statements with her general knowledge, attempting to assimilate unknowns into what she already knows. For example, it is plausible to think there will be a fridge at the beach because that is where food is kept at home.

Emily's out-loud monologues demonstrate several functions: practicing language skills, recounting memories, anticipating experiences, processing emotionally difficult events, solving problems and questions, and reflecting on interactions between herself and others (Nelson, 1989). The young child's nighttime monologues have the same function Jean Piaget (1951) ascribes to symbolic play, to sort out and contain experiences that have been stressful or hard to understand. Emily's overriding aim, according to Nelson (1989) is to construct "an understandable world within which she can begin to take her place . . . [and that is] a coherent representation of her experience" (pp. 27, 34). Crib talk tends to disappear around age 3. The child continues to think in words, but speaking out loud is replaced by inner speech, or silent thinking in words (Bruner & Lucariello, 1989).

Language and Self-Regulation

Toddlerhood marks the beginning of the child's ability to substitute words for action. Language allows the 2-year-old to say what she wants instead of merely acting. To understand this development, contrast a 14- to 18-month-old with a 2½- to 3-year-old. The 14-month-old is attracted by a doll another toddler is playing with and simply grabs it. In response, the other child bites the first child. In this exchange neither child announces her intentions in words. Each one acts immediately following an impulse. An older toddler, however, may say, "I want the doll." She not only communicates a wish, which the other child may or may not respond to, but she also uses words to delay action on her impulse. Containing an impulse in language, "I want that," inserts a thought between impulse and action that may allow the child to think about the consequences of the action. Bruner and Lucariello point out that representing thoughts and feelings in language has a "cooling function." That is, putting an idea or feeling into words, whether out loud or in thought, "helps to 'cool' or reduce some of the uncertainty and emotionality in the child's world just by its displaced mode of representing that world in memory and thought" (Bruner & Lucariello, 1989, p. 76).

Even though this ability is developing, toddlers do not use it consistently. They still want to fulfill their wishes and express their emotions immediately, and frequently they act on impulse. It is important to recall that although a 2½-year-old can understand a great deal of what is said to him and may be speaking in sentences, representation in language is *only beginning* to help him delay impulses.

Language as Communication

Toddlers are nevertheless excited about their new ability to communicate about their experience in words. The child begins to discover that language is a much more precise and predictable means of communication than gesture or action. Language allows children and parents to share awareness on a new level, because they are communicating through words that mean approximately the same thing to each of them. The parent's verbal confirmation of the toddler's perceptions and feelings validates them and contributes to the development of a sense of self. To express one's thoughts in words and then have them confirmed in words gives the child the feeling that her thoughts are real and valuable. This awareness provides the toddler with a powerful motivation for learning language. The power of this motivation is evident in the toddler's attempts to get her thoughts across to others. She will use a few words, fill in the blanks with sounds, use a variety of gestures such as pointing, and frequently convey an emotional urgency to be understood.

Limits of Toddlers' Language Abilities

In spite of toddlers' dramatic progress in language development, they have important limitations in their language and cognitive abilities. Because the wish to communicate is very strong, toddlers can become very frustrated when they cannot express themselves clearly. This can occur because they are unable to pronounce the words clearly or because they do not yet know the words. The frustration is also a product of growing self-awareness. The toddler is more frustrated because he *knows* that others are not understanding him. Frustration over not being able to communicate is a common source of angry or aggressive behavior in normal toddlers. Even when a toddler has a good command of words, limitations in cognitive and affective development often cause the words to mean different things to the toddler and the parent. For example, an older toddler may use words that denote complex ideas and relationships, such as "truth," "share," and "promise," yet not fully understand their meanings (Leach, 1978).

Toddlers' use of language, especially when they are under stress, is frequently less a vehicle for describing "objective" reality than a way of conveying thoughts influenced by wishes and magical thinking. If a toddler is accused of doing something wrong, she is likely to "lie." These lies by adult standards are, from the toddler's point of view, attempts at self-protection. The toddler who expediently says, "I telling the truth!" may not be and further does not understand the meaning of "truth." She is not yet motivated by an internalized belief in the importance of truth telling. Rather, she shapes what she says to try to gain the parents' approval and avoid their disapproval. Wishes easily overcome logic and "truth" in the thinking of toddlers.

SYMBOLIC COMMUNICATION AND PLAY

During the early part of the toddler period, the child's play with objects is consistent with play in infancy. The younger toddler is interested in the properties and functions of objects. He plays with toys by learning what they feel like, what noises they make, how they look, what they can do. Piaget (1951) labeled such use of toys and objects *sensorimotor play.* Play in the kitchen—banging pots and pans, fitting them together, or pouring water between them—is typical sensori-motor play for a toddler.

Between 1 and 2 years of age, sensorimotor play is increasingly associated with figuring out how things work and learning about cause and effect. Toddlers watch parents to see the correct way to use objects and try to imitate them. They learn through observation and then experimentation that knobs and buttons turn on the TV set or radio. Similarly, they act out the rituals of caregiving—patting, hug-ging, combing hair, feeding. Sometime between 12 and 18 months, tod-dlers' imitations of caregiving or eating behavior take on a pretend quality. For example, a 16-month-old takes an empty cup, looks at her father to signal he should pay attention, lifts the cup and "drinks" from it, says "ummm," and then laughs. In this sequence, the child has carried out an ordinary behavior, drinking, but since she has done it knowing there is nothing in the cup, she has transformed the behavior into play. Imitation has evolved into pretend play (Piaget, 1951).

Midway through the second year *imaginative play* begins to alter-nate with sensorimotor play. The toddler begins to use toys symboli-cally and to integrate them into play scenarios. One of the earliest types of symbolic play occurs when the toddler substitutes one object for another. For example, as a 16-month-old boy was playing with pots and pans, he stepped into two pots and said, "Shoes." Then he tried to shuffle across the kitchen and laughed. Between age 2 and 2½, toddlers make a more dramatic substitution by pretending they are someone else. *Pretend play* in normal toddlers often revolves around imitations of adult behavior, with the toddler in the adult's role. A 2½-year-old may pretend to feed his teddy bear, brush its teeth, and put it to bed, a sequence that demonstrates an organized view of his caretaker's behavior. Toddlers enjoy pretending to be animals. Piaget (1951) described his 26-month-old daughter's pleasure in walking on all fours and saying, "Meow."

Gradually toddlers' play becomes more complex and comes to represent the child's commentary on her experience. Play takes on a psychological function for the 2-year-old by giving her the freedom to explore experience through pretend. Piaget and Inhelder (1969) de-scribe the new function play fulfills. The toddler is

> obliged to adapt himself constantly to a social world of elders whose interests and rules remain external to him, and to a physical world which he understands only slightly. . . . It is indispensable to his

affective and intellectual equilibrium ... that he have available to him an area of activity whose motivation is not adaptation to reality but, on the contrary, assimilation of reality to the self, without coercions or sanctions. Such an area is play, which transforms reality by assimilation to the needs of the self. (pp. 57–58)

Play becomes a vehicle for expressing strong feelings, a way of raising and answering questions about stressful and confusing aspects of reality, a mode of solving problems through "trial action," and even, within limits, a space where normal social rules do not apply. As noted earlier, one of the developmental tasks of the toddler is to establish a compromise between his own wishes and the rules and expectations of his parents. The need to shape one's behavior to meet social demands is not easy for toddlers, who, as part of establishing a sense of self, want to follow their own desires. Toddler negativism and willfulness reflects this conflict. Symbolic play provides the toddler with relief from the demands of reality.

Play as Coping Strategy

Play provides the toddler with a nonverbal means of coping with confusion or stress. It is noteworthy that pretend play emerges at the same time as language, suggesting that a more general symbolizing function underlies both. However, Bowlby (1980) noted that "because a child's use of language lags far behind his non-verbal modes of representation, there is a persistent tendency for adults to underestimate a young child's cognitive capacities" (p. 429). Piaget (1951) noted that symbolic play offers the young child a vehicle for reliving and assimilating the stressful aspects of reality, at a distance, through fantasy that is under the child's control. Piaget underscored this aspect of play when he said that a young child's doll play in the evening would reflect all the child's pleasurable and difficult experiences of the day.

It is important for practitioners to realize that the play and behavior of very young children is a representation of cognitive and affective processes and that observation of such play provides us with a window on experiences and feelings that the toddler cannot yet represent in language.

Play as Representation of Experience

Symbolic play is referential: it refers back to the child's experience. It has a narrative quality and a point of view which conveys the child's perspective on her experience. This type of play begins at about age 2 and continues to develop into the complex, rich, and sometimes fantastic imaginative play of the preschool child. The symbolic play of toddlers often appears as fragments of narrative elements strung together. As in the crib narratives of Emily, described previously, the elements that are emphasized often represent aspects of the child's experience that have been perplexing or stressful. The following example illustrates the analysis of symbolic play in a 2½-year-old who was showing behavioral reactions to a history of witnessing domestic violence.

JARED: A BRIEF CASE EXAMPLE

Child client	Jared, age 2½
Mother	Ms. Taylor, age 23, Anglo-American, separated from Jared's father, working as a retail clerk
Father	Mr. Taylor, age 28, Anglo-American; substance abuse problems, no contact with Jared and Ms. Taylor

Jared had been referred because of aggressive behavior at his family day care home. He hit and bit other children and often hurt himself intentionally, running his head into the wall and then laughing. For a 6-month period, when Jared was between 10 and 16 months old, he had witnessed many episodes of his father's aggression toward his mother. The parents separated when he was 16 months old, but he witnessed more such episodes until the father moved out of state when he was 20 months old. Jared's mother was also concerned that his father had played "very roughly" with Jared when he was a young toddler.

I wanted to assess possible links between family violence and Jared's symptoms. As the first interview began I told Jared that my job was to help boys with their worries and explained to Mrs. Taylor that by observing Jared's play together we could learn what worried him. Then we could begin to respond in a reassuring way to his concerns. Jared repetitively pushed a car fast until it crashed and each time said, "It's broken." I asked Mrs. Taylor about this play, and she immediately associated to his father's pleasure in driving fast. Then she told a story of how the father, while hitting her in the car, accidentally hit Jared. She said he was only 5 months old then, so she doubted he would remember it.

As she told this story, Jared had found a small baby doll and put it in a little crib. I asked Mrs. Taylor if there were experiences he might remember. She described an incident after the separation, when Jared was 18 months old. She had closed the door in her husband's face. He kicked out the glass in the door, and it sprayed over Mrs. Taylor and Jared, whom she was holding. Jared screamed and began hitting her, which she understood as his anger toward her for having refused to let his father in. As Mrs. Taylor described this event, Jared lowered a roaring plastic dinosaur into the baby's crib, saying, "Monster bite baby." I called her attention to this play as Jared continued to repeat it, noting that the monster appeared while she was telling the frightening story about the father's violence. In the second session Jared elaborated the symptomatic play, this time having the dinosaur repeatedly break down a Lego door and bite the baby inside. Mrs. Taylor said, "This is obviously about the night Al broke the door." I commented that Jared was showing us that he experienced his father as a frightening monster, and suggested that we were learning very specifically what Jared worried about—that something like that incident could happen again and he could be terrified and hurt. Mrs. Taylor said, "Every night he goes to the front and back doors to make sure they're locked." She had not previously connected this ritual with the door-breaking incident.

Jared's symptomatic play conveyed his anxiety that the violence he had seen might occur again. When the issue of his father's violence was raised in his presence he quickly moved from diffuse crashing play to a stark and exquisite representation of his frightening experience when his father broke the door and he and his mother were showered with glass. From this clearer vantage point afforded by observation of Jared's play, it was possible to read his presenting symptoms of aggressiveness, fearlessness, reversal of affect, and self-hurting behavior as attempts to cope with tremendous anxiety about being hurt. He was hyperalert to danger and, like so many young children who have witnessed violence, was quick to attack in order to ward off imagined aggression. Play became a vehicle for expressing concerns Jared could not yet express in words. The observation of his play clarified for his mother and the therapist that he was preoccupied with fears of repetitions of violence, and allowed them to collaborate on a treatment plan that would directly address his fears and traumatic memories (Davies, 1991).

REGULATION OF AFFECT AND BEHAVIOR

The toddler gradually develops capacities for self-regulation. During infancy, regulation of arousal was a dyadic process. Although we can see many elements of self-regulation in infancy and many examples of the toddler's need for the parent's help in regulating arousal and behavior, in toddlerhood there is a general shift toward more autonomous self-regulation that is part of the toddler's overall movement toward an autonomous self. It is typical for a toddler to try first to cope with a challenge by using her internal resources. If the toddler feels successful in this, her ability to recover from upset or stress increases. When internal coping devices do not work, the toddler quickly turns to external supports, particularly her attachment relationships with caregivers. The toddler's cognitive characteristics present challenges to effective self-regulation. Her egocentric perspective prevents her from viewing reality objectively. Her difficulty in understanding the causes of events may lead her to confuse cause and effect. The urgency of her wishes and affects may lead her to believe that feelings and thoughts can cause things to happen. So the toddler, because of normative limitations in level of cognitive development, is prone to interpret experience in concrete, egocentric, and magical ways that confuse cause and effect and fail to distinguish between thought and action (Piaget, 1952a). These cognitive limitations, as well as immature mechanisms for dealing with stress, leave the toddler vulnerable to stressful or traumatic experiences. Parents play a critical role in supporting and developing toddlers' capacity for affect regulation by explaining and clarifying their experiences, particularly those that are stressful for the child (Matas et al., 1978; Schafer, 1979). For toddlers, and for older children as well, adaptive coping has two dimensions: (1) the ability to cope with stress using internal means; (2) the ability to signal and engage caregivers, who can take steps to assist the child in coping with a stressor that overwhelms the child's internal coping strategies.

Sources of Anxiety for Toddlers

Although the toddler wants very much to be in control of his own affects and impulses, the reality is that his capacity for self-regulation is not well established. Consequently, toddlers need parental limits and support for help in controlling impulses and allaying anxiety. Table 6.1 presents typical sources of distress and anxiety for toddlers.

The "Terrible 2's" from a Developmental Perspective

The toddler's many sources of potential distress, difficulties in autonomous regulation, and determination in asserting herself often lead to behavior that appears willful and negative, as implied in the phrase, "the terrible 2's." Toddler behavior is often distressing to parents and other adults because it appears irrational and out of control, both affectively and behaviorally. A 20-month-old boy, Patrick, demonstrates typical behaviors during this phase:

> Patrick had an active and intense temperament. He loved movement and activity. He had to be watched carefully because he seemed fearless and would try to run into the street. He expressed his feelings

TABLE 6.1. Sources of Anxiety for Toddlers

- *Difficulty understanding what is happening,* based on lack of knowledge and unclear ideas of cause and effect. Egocentrism and magical thinking can cause misconceptions which create anxiety.

- *Difficulty communicating.* Toddlers can think better than they can speak. There are questions they want to ask and statements they want to make, but their language has not developed to the point that they can find the words. Lieberman (1993) points to the frustration this engenders: "Often what passes for negativism is really the toddler's desperate effort to make herself understood" (p. 38).

- *Frustration over not being able to do what they can imagine.* For example, a 2-year-old boy watched his 5-year-old sister put on her jeans and then tried to imitate her. He tried to lift one leg up as his sister had done and lost his balance and fell down. He tried a few more times and became angry, kicked at his pants, and then went whining to his father for help.

- *Conflicts between wanting to be on their own versus wanting parent's help.*

- *Separation or threat of separation from caregivers.* This is connected with a more fundamental source of anxiety—"that the parent will not be reliably available at times of need" (Lieberman, 1992, p. 563).

- *Fears of losing the parent's approval and of being unloved, rejected, or abandoned.* This is particularly common during the toddler period because the child's wishes and behavior frequently clash with the parent's expectations. "Toddlers' anxiety over losing the parent's love is fueled by their experience that they no longer love the parent when they are angry at her. Because of their cognitive limitations, young children find it difficult to understand that others may feel differently than they do in a given situation" (Lieberman, 1993, pp. 130–131).

- *Reactions to losing self-control.* Although toddlers often appear to lose control of their impulses, they do not like to. It feels frightening to dissolve into a temper tantrum, or to hit or bite a peer and see the distress of the other child.

- *Body anxieties.* Fear of body damage, anxiety about parental demands for toilet training, concern about observations of differences in the genitals of boys and girls.

intensely and at this age was having frequent tantrums, especially when he was frustrated or told "No." He was quick to anger and would sometimes hit his parents if they prevented him from doing what he wanted to do. He was speaking very little, which made him rely on action to express himself. Patrick was sitting in a high chair at a restaurant, with his extended family, who were on vacation together. He was eating while adults around him talked. When he finished eating he picked up a fork and threw it the length of the table. It bounced along and landed on his grandmother's plate. His parents were shocked and scolded him. Perhaps Patrick had felt excluded from the adult conversation. Perhaps this active child felt confined in the high chair and throwing the fork was a signal of his displeasure. Acts like this are often intentional, not merely impulsive, and may represent the toddler's assertion of will, dissatisfaction, anger, or his sense of being affectively out of contact.

After lunch, at the beach, Patrick splashed in the waves with his uncle. He was delighted. Later, Patrick's uncle was lying on the sand, dozing. Patrick threw a handful of sand in his face. Perhaps Patrick felt ignored and became angry, as had apparently happened at the restaurant. Perhaps his misguided aggression was an attempt to get his uncle to play with him again, a request he could not yet make in words. Such behavior angers adults and may provoke punitive behavior. Patrick's uncle did speak angrily, saying, "I don't like it when you throw sand in my face!"

Such intentional aggressive acts perturb the equilibrium of the toddler–caregiver relationship. The adult's challenge is to reach out to the child and promote or acknowledge the toddler's attempts to restore the equilibrium following aggressive behavior (Sander, 1975). Patrick's uncle pointed to a pail and shovel and suggested they dig a hole and fill the pail. Patrick picked up the pail. His uncle said, "Let's go over there, away from the people, so we don't throw sand on them." Sander suggests that restoring the positive relationship after it has been violated by the toddler's destructive actions helps restore the toddler's inner equilibrium. By contrast, "should the caretaker . . . fail to aid in restoring the facilitating self as the toddler had previously experienced it, the toddler's own familiar 'good self' as a constant frame of reference would be impaired" (Sander, 1975, p. 199).

Sources of Aggression in Toddlers

A more sympathetic view of toddler negativism, implied by Sander's analysis as well as Patrick's uncle's behavior, recognizes that toddlers face difficult developmental challenges that lead to frequent frustration, internal conflict, and conflicts with their parents. One of the possible responses to these conflicts is aggression. Lieberman (1993) lists three factors that may lead to aggression in the toddler or to expressions of anger, frustration, and anxiety that parents may perceive as aggression: (1) disagreements about what is safe; (2) the toddler's desire to have it all; and (3) opposition and negativism that go with wanting to have things their way. When a toddler's will is thwarted, he may become quickly frustrated and may have a temper tantrum, hit, or throw things. Aggression may also show up in disputes with other children over toys.

Toddlers may also react strongly when parents or other caregivers expect them to function above their developmental level. For example, children can be ready for toilet training from age 15 months to 3 years. They signal their readiness by letting their parent know when they are urinating or defecating. Toddlers whose parents begin toilet training too early are often more angry and aggressive because they face the frustrating situation of the parent's exerting control over an internal bodily function. When toddlers are pushed to do something they are not yet ready or able to do, such as using the toilet, or picking up their toys, or happily sharing their toys with other children, they react with refusal, protest, and tantrums.

Strategies for Self-Regulation and Coping

Although the toddler faces a wider range of normal stressors than an infant, her range of strategies for coping with stress and self-regulation is also increasing. These include the following:

Dyadic Regulation

Dyadic regulation between parent and child continues, but in a new form, with the parent explaining and clarifying the toddler's fears of unknown or stressful events, setting limits that help the child contain her impulses, and remaining a secure base, available to comfort the child. The toddler can more easily elicit a parent's support by going to the parent and, during the third year, telling the parent what is wrong (Kopp, 1982).

Self-Stimulation as an Outlet for Tension

Toddlers may suck their thumbs, masturbate, or rub themselves and cuddle with transitional objects during times of fatigue or distress. These behaviors are normal responses to internal or external stress, and occur particularly at the end of the day. They should not be seen as problematic unless they occur constantly. Caregivers should examine the child's life for sources of stress if self-stimulation is constant (Brazelton, 1992).

Play

Play—both interactive and with toys—becomes available during the toddler period as a vehicle for mastering stress and anxiety. For example, a 2½-year-old who has a secure attachment can actively master separation distress by playing out a caretaking role with a doll.

Language

Language becomes available as a means of organizing experiences and feelings. The older toddler's capacity for thinking and expressing himself in words helps him delay actions. Between the ages of 2 and 3, the toddler begins to learn the names of feelings, including "negative" emotions such as anger, fear, and sadness, which allows him to convey feeling states more precisely (Michalson & Lewis, 1985). The toddler who can say, "I am mad," is likely to get a more empathic and focused response from a caregiver than one who expresses anger through aggression or a temper tantrum.

Internalized Standards of Behavior

Internalized standards of behavior develop in response to parental demands and modeling. As the child internalizes ideas about behavior that is acceptable and not acceptable, she begins to regulate those behaviors, at least when a parent is present. She also learns the value placed on different emotions by her culture, and learns to inhibit "inappropriate" affects and emphasize "appropriate" ones (Malatesta & Haviland, 1985). By the third year, the child begins to use these internal standards to self-monitor affects, impulses, and behavior. When the older toddler can prevent herself from acting on the impulse to do something that is prohibited, her anxiety diminishes and self-esteem increases (Kagan, 1981).

Familiarity

Familiarity decreases stress. As previously unknown events, such as going to a child care center, are repeated, the child's anxiety diminishes simply because he knows what to expect.

Sources of Difficulties with Self-Regulation in Toddlers

Anxiety is signaled by physiological arousal. Variations in young children's arousability can be due to temperamental factors or previous experiences. For example, a child who is temperamentally more reactive may become more quickly and highly aroused in an unfamiliar situation, and consequently may need more external help to regulate arousal. A less reactive child in the same situation may not become aroused to the point of becoming distressed. Children who have had repeated stressful or traumatic experiences, or who have not been helped to regulate arousal by parents during infancy, may also become highly reactive because they quickly feel helpless and anxious in response to stressors. In Chapter 5, I noted that Julie did not seem to be a globally hyperreactive infant; however, out of repeated experiences of overarousal because she was left to cry, she became highly reactive in situations when her mother left her. Toddlers with histories of insecure attachment demonstrate problems in self-regulation by showing more anger and physical aggression; at the same time, because the attachment relationship has not adequately helped them regulate arousal as infants, they tend not to rely on the parent for dyadic regulation (Matas, Arend, & Sroufe, 1978).

Similarly, toddlers who have had traumatic experiences, such as witnessing domestic violence, are often highly anxious and reactive in situations (e.g., competitive play with other toddlers) that contain mild elements of threat. Such toddlers often have difficulty regulating arousal and anxiety in new, ambiguous, or mildly stressful situations, because the experience of arousal itself has become associated with the previous trauma (Drell, Siegel, & Gaensbauer, 1993). Toddlers exposed to harsh and coercive discipline, maltreatment, or high levels of parental conflict also show more difficulties with self-regulation and aggression than do other toddlers (Londerville & Main, 1981; Rieder & Cicchetti, 1989).

MORAL DEVELOPMENT

During the second year, as the toddler becomes more mobile, he begins to have conflicts with his parents. His climbing on to the kitchen counter, for example, brings a quick and possibly sharp rebuke from his parent. At this point the conflict is external, between the child's wishes and the parent's prohibitions. However, through experiences of parental disapproval and approval, and through a new cognitive awareness that others have expectations and standards, the child's moral development begins.

As the second year proceeds, toddlers gradually internalize ideas of standards and deviations from expected norms, based on what they have learned from their caretakers (Kagan, 1981). For example, a 1-year-old boy may notice a tear or hole in his T-shirt, consider it interesting, and stick his finger through it. The same child at age 18–24 months, on discovering a hole, looks worried and says, "Oh, oh," points out the hole to his parent, and may even ask to change the shirt.

The infant notices the hole as a discrepancy, whereas the toddler sees it as problematic or incorrect (Kagan, 1981). The toddler's behavior reflects important shifts in cognitive development. Toddlers are working very hard to "construct" or make sense of the world. They are beginning to perceive and expect regularities in their experience. They are generalizing from one experience to another, looking for common elements. They have begun to internalize parental standards. Consequently, by about 18 months they become more acute in noticing deviations from what is expected, particularly when the norm violated is associated with their parent's disapproval. The toddler's concern with deviation and damage is reflected by common words in his vocabulary—"dirty," "messy," "missing," "yucky," "boo-boo," "broken." Kagan (1981) attributes this concern to the toddler's new awareness of cause and effect: "When the child sees a crack in a toy, he infers that the crack was caused by someone's action. Because that class of actions is associated with adult disapproval, he responds affectively" (p. 124). It should be added that the toddler's affective reaction of concern or worry is linked to his egocentric view that if he sees the broken toy he is somehow involved in its breaking.

Development of Evaluative Abilities and Standards

By 18 months and with increasing frequency up to about age 26 months, toddlers focus intently on evaluating their environment. Evaluative words such as "good," "bad," "hard," "easy," "nice," and "mean," reflecting standards of behavior and performance learned from adults, appear in their speech (Bretherton, McNew, & Beeghly-Smith, 1981). By age 20–24 months, toddlers begin to evaluate their own behavior, as indicated by their pleasure in mastery and by their frustration when they cannot accomplish a task. A toddler who has worked to stack five or six blocks smiles broadly, looks to her parent for approval and recognition, and says, "I did it!" This toddler has developed the ability to make judgments about her behavior and to feel pride when she succeeds. The toddler is particularly likely to feel pride and self-approval when a parent notices her success (Emde, Johnson, & Easterbrooks, 1987). The same toddler may cry in frustration when she is unable to put on her socks. In both cases she has an internal representation of a goal and of the behavior required to realize it, a model of "correctness" or "success."

Two-year-olds *know* when they have done something well; they also know when their actions have not been successful. In a series of experimental, observational, and cross-cultural studies, Kagan (1981) and his colleagues demonstrated that toddlers become distressed when they are confronted with a task they believe they cannot do. If an adult modeled a series of actions with a toy that the toddler could not understand or seemed too hard, the toddler was likely to become upset. At 14 months, younger toddlers did not become distressed when a "difficult" action was modeled. But by 23 months a significant majority became upset. Kagan (1981) interpreted the toddlers' distress as reflecting a self-evaluative awareness of their level of competence, as if the 23-month-old was thinking, "I feel I should do what this grown-up is showing me, but I know I can't and it is upsetting to realize that I am confronted with a standard that I can't meet."

The Parents' Point of View and Internalization

Added to these cognitive elements, toddlers are learning from their parents concepts of correct and incorrect, proper and improper, permitted and prohibited (Kagan, 1984). The older toddler reflects this development when he looks up at the kitchen counter and says, "No! No!" This may not be enough to stop him from climbing up again, but it shows that he has begun to incorporate the parent's point of view. In a rudimentary form, he experiences a conflict between his wish to climb up and his wish to please his parent. Another indication that the toddler remembers his parent's prohibition is that he looks to his parent and checks her reaction when he has the impulse to do something forbidden (Lieberman, 1993). The toddler's developing capacity for representational thought means he can now recall and think about what kinds of behavior the parent approves or disapproves (Kopp, 1982).

The development of a clearer understanding that others have intentions also supports early rule learning. For example, the toddler who has learned from the parent's strong reaction that she is not to wander across the street inhibits that particular action in the future. In inhibiting a forbidden action, the toddler implicitly acknowledges her parent's point of view, as if she is thinking, "I want to do this, but my father does not want me to." Internalization supports moral development especially through the child's imitation of parental behavior. Through observing parents' behavior, including how a parent copes with stress, sets limits on herself, acts consistently or inconsistently, the toddler learns, imitates, and begins to internalize the "rules" of acceptable and unacceptable behavior. By age 2, this process is also supported by the toddler's understanding of language. Her understanding of words and tones that set limits—"No," "I don't want you to do that," or "Get down right now!"—helps make internalization possible. Her understanding of language also allows parents to increasingly set the limits through words alone. When the child is motivated to please her parent, verbal limit setting becomes increasingly successful.

The crib monologues of Emily provide some wonderful examples of a toddler in the process of internalizing parental rules and prohibitions. At 29 months, on a day when she and a friend were scolded for waking up her baby brother, Stephen, Emily produced the following monologue:

> "And we don't do it that much. But sometimes you go rinky-dinky all over the house. And do *that.* And go running away. And Stephen says I don't like *it.* Why do you do *that* says Pooh-Bear. And my mom says you look like a ... Why why why why. Why did you do *that?* [repeated five times]. Why did you go flying about getting out of bed. Why do you do *that?* I think maybe you wanna do *that.* But you can't. Over and over you can't ... Why were you running around in Stephen's room and the other room and another room. Children what are you doing? Why did you two do *that?* You can't do that. You can't. . . . "(Nelson, 1989, pp. 164–165)

Emily's intense tone conveys distress over being scolded. She is processing a stressful experience in words as a means of coping with it. However, this remarkable monologue clearly demonstrates how a child works to take in parental injunctions. The form Emily imposes on her experience reflects her mother's affects and point of view. It sounds as if she is repeating exactly what her mother said. Implicitly, she is identifying with her mother's prohibitions and attempting to internalize them. It is noteworthy that her mother's affects—apparently exasperation and anger—made a powerful impression on Emily. In the learning of rules and prohibitions, strong parental affects—anger, disgust, irritation, shock—play an important role in signaling to the toddler what is important (J. Dunn, 1987). Emily does not like her mother's disapproval, and it appears that she is working extra hard to take in the content of the rule "Don't make noise and wake Stephen up" in order to avoid disapproval in the future. Such experiences are the building blocks of later conscience development. Phrases like "You can't" and "Why did you do that?" become enshrined in "inner speech" as prohibitions that older children (as well as adults) use to criticize themselves when they have violated their internalized expectations and rules.

Prosocial Behavior

Although the account so far has emphasized toddlers' internalization of standards and prohibitions, another critical aspect of morality that begins to emerge during this period is "prosocial behavior," defined as "acts that include provision of comfort or sympathy, helping, sharing, cooperation, rescue, protection and defense" (Zahn-Waxler & Smith, 1992, p. 229). Underlying these behaviors are prosocial thoughts and feelings, including, "empathy or emotional incorporation of the other's emotional experience . . . [as well as] moral reasoning and cognitive comprehension of the others' internal states and needs" (Zahn-Waxler & Smith, 1992, p. 229).

As toddlers develop the cognitive ability to comprehend others' perspectives, they also become capable of empathizing with the feelings of others. Many observational studies have demonstrated prosocial behavior in 2-year-olds (Zahn-Waxler & Smith, 1992). For example, a toddler in a child care setting sees another child fall off a slide and begin to cry, and goes over and pats or hugs her. This toddler empathizes with the other child's distress and, drawing on memories of being comforted himself, offers concern and comfort. Empathy is an essential element of later moral development. The toddler who responds to the distress or pain of another child is not acting in response to rules or prohibitions but rather to feelings of identification with the other child. The capacity to empathize with what it feels like to be hurt begins to play a role in the older toddler or preschooler's ability to inhibit aggression (Kagan, 1984). Through empathy and imaginative role taking an older toddler can sometimes control aggressive behavior, as if he is saying to himself, "I would not like to be hit or kicked, and so I will stop myself from kicking this kid."

Limits of Toddlers' Moral Development

The toddler period marks only the beginning of moral development. Consequently, the toddler's internalization of rules, self-control, and capacity for empathy are subject to frequent breakdown. It remains hard for a toddler to inhibit a strong wish or impulse (Kopp, 1982). Although internalization is proceeding, toddlers are not yet able to consistently comply with parents' expectations simply because it is the "right thing to do." Egocentrism and self-preoccupation impose limits on the toddlers' ability to empathize with another's point of view. In Kohlberg's (1984) formulation of moral development, the toddler's motivation for doing the right thing derives from wishes to gain approval and to avoid punishment, rather than from well-established internalized values or a sense of self as a good person.

For these reasons, contemporary books on parenting caution against having overexpectations about the toddler's moral abilities and self-control, suggesting that parents avoid control battles as well as coercion by structuring the child's choices and combining firm limits with diversions and alternatives. They suggest that parents be ready to move in and pick the child up when she does not respond to verbal limits (Comer & Poussaint, 1992; Brazelton, 1992).

The discussion thus far describes the first steps in the internalization of a positive morality. However, early socialization may also teach "immoral" values or create moral confusion. If parents fail to set limits on toddlers' aggression or rule breaking, give direct or implicit approval for impulsiveness, permit intense competition and aggression between siblings, model negative behavior, or present contradictions between their own behavior and moral injunctions, the toddler is likely to internalize those values and is unlikely to develop strong capacities for empathy and prosocial behavior. The development of self-control will also be attenuated (J. Dunn, 1987).

THE DEVELOPING SELF

The concepts "sense of self" and "development of the self" are abstractions. Whereas language or motor development can be tracked definitively, the evolution of the self is not so easily quantifiable. However, several milestones in the second half of the second year convince us that the toddler is developing a sense of self and beginning to differentiate that self from other selves. Between 18 and 24 months, toddlers begin to recognize themselves in a mirror. Prior to this, they may show interest in the reflected image but not be aware it is their own image (Lewis & Brooks-Gunn, 1979). *Self-recognition* is one of several indicators of the child's developing sense of self at this age. Another is *self-assertion*. Between 14 and 20 months, the toddler's behavior is increasingly directed by his own wishes and goals. He is clearly thinking more about what *he* wants to do, and somewhat less about coordinating his behavior with his parent's (Sander, 1975). The 2-year-old's awareness that other people have intentions, an awareness that probably arises out of experiences of conflict between his own intentions and his parents' wishes, contributes to the child's understanding that he has a self distinct from other selves. Awareness of self and awareness of other selves develop in tandem.

Mahler's Separation–Individuation Theory

Margaret Mahler studied the development of the sense of self in the context of the attachment relationship through longitudinal observations of infants and toddlers with their mothers. Mahler theorized that, up to about 16–18 months, the infant does not seem to have a full awareness that she and her mother are separate beings. Parental responsiveness has protected the child from having to rely on herself too much, and this has allowed her to experience herself as part of an adaptive unit, "my mother and me." Mahler argued that prior to 16–18 months the child's internal images or representations of the parents and the self are not yet separate and distinct (see Mahler et al., 1975). Stern (1983) and others have criticized this formulation, since there are many indicators that infants can distinguish themselves from parents during the first year. Nevertheless, Mahler's descriptions of the toddler's "separation–individuation" process during the second year provide understanding of how the sense of self develops.

Mahler and colleagues observed that, beginning at about 16–18 months, toddlers regularly became more anxious about their attachment with the mother. They were more easily distressed, more reactive to brief separations from the parent, more clingy and controlling, showed more negative affects such as depression or angry outbursts toward the mother. Mahler et al. (1975) explained these reactions as related to advances in the child's cognitive development that enable the toddler to understand reality ever more clearly. This includes being able to differentiate the intentions and feelings of others from one's own. Essentially, the toddler becomes aware that "My parent and I do not think the same thoughts, or always want the same things." When the toddler, intent on asserting his will or pursuing his own goals, runs into opposition from his parents, his awareness of psychological separation further intensifies. The toddler increasingly realizes that the parent has separate intentions and that he cannot control the parent.

Mahler theorized that this perturbed period, which she called the "rapprochement crisis," represented a struggle for the toddler over coming to terms with his actual and psychological autonomy from his mother. She argued that the feeling of being separate and individuated was exhilarating, because of the increase in autonomy and power, but also frightening because of separation anxiety. Eighteen-month-olds seem to alternate between acting powerful and invulnerable and feeling very vulnerable and unsure of themselves. Consequently, the rapprochement crisis is characterized by ambivalence, "By the rapidly alternating desire to push mother away and to cling to her" (Mahler et al., 1975, p. 95). Parents of toddlers observe rapprochement as conflicting behavior. The toddler at one moment refuses help with something she is not yet capable of doing, such as buckling a seat belt, insisting "Me do it!" But when they arrive a place the child has never been before, she refuses to walk on her own and whines, "Carry me." From the perspective of attachment theory, the toddler seems to be asking, "How can I be an autonomous individual and maintain the attachment?" These conflicting feelings are expressed behaviorally through shadowing the parent everywhere, ignoring the parent, darting away (often with the hope that the parent will chase), being demanding toward the parent, and becoming more vulnerable to frustration and temper tantrums. This is the period when parents exclaim, "I can't even go to the bathroom without him following me. If I lock the door, he sits against it and whines until I come out!" Yet at other times the toddler's loving feelings shine through without ambivalence and he is particularly responsive and interested in sharing feelings with his parents.

Steps in Mastering Separation Fears

What allows the young child to gradually master the frightening aspects of autonomy? First, when the parent remains a secure base, tolerates yet also sets limits on the toddler's demanding behavior, and welcomes his need for closeness, the child gradually understands that it is possible to be autonomous *and* connected. As in earlier periods of perturbation, the child is protected from negative psychological effects by the security and dyadic regulation of the attachment relationship (Sroufe, 1989). A second answer is found in the process of internalization. Mahler and others have pointed out that what allows the young child to tolerate the anxiety that comes with the awareness of being separate is the development of *object constancy*. This term refers to the internalization of a positive representation of the parent that is ultimately felt to be part of the self. The idea is that the child gradually takes into the self the caregiving and protective functions of the parents as well as aspects of the parents' ego functions, including the parents' defense mechanisms. Through this internalization the child gradually becomes able to use her own inner psychological resources to "take care of herself" and to become capable of regulating her anxiety without immediately needing to turn to the parent. This psychodynamic explanation has much in common with John Bowlby's (1973) description of working models of attachment.

Of course, if a parent responds negatively to the toddler's ambivalent behavior, there is risk that the "2's" really will be terrible. When parents react punitively or reject the toddler for being assertive, willful, and demanding, the toddler may feel disconnected and angry. Her separation anxiety may become more intense because of the parent's rejection. Consequently, her attempts to control the parent may also intensify, but with an angrier tone that in turn angers the parent. This spiral of negative interactions may lead to an attachment relationship characterized by mutual coercion and to the toddler's internalization of a negative self-representation.

Self-Awareness and Self-Consciousness

The shift to cognitive self-awareness around 18 months is paralleled by increasing awareness of the subjective states of others. As previously mentioned, an older toddler can empathize with another child's emotional distress, as well as feel guilt if he has hurt another child (Radke-Yarrow & Zahn-Waxler, 1984). In spite of evidence of these capacities for role taking and empathy, it should be emphasized that the toddler is egocentric and preoccupied with self. He thinks about himself more than about others and tends to assume his point of view is shared by others. Studies of the verbal discourse of 2-year-olds show that they refer to themselves not only much more often but in more complex and varied ways than they refer to others (Budwig & Wiley, 1995). The capacity to see the world from another's point of view does not emerge fully until school age.

Near age 2, the toddler is also developing self-consciousness, that is, becoming able to imagine how another person sees him. For example, a 2-year-old boy was brushing his teeth while looking in the mirror. He was enjoying watching himself doing what he had seen his parents do. His father was standing behind him, and several times he looked at his father. Each time when his father smiled and encouraged him, he looked very pleased and brushed more. It appeared that he was feeling, "I am doing what big people do, and my father sees that I'm doing it. He's proud of me, and that makes me feel proud of myself." It is out of such experiences of seeing oneself from another's point of view that the toddler begins to feel the human emotions associated with self-consciousness—pride in success, pleasure in receiving praise, but also embarrassment at failing and shame over being scolded. Self-consciousness allows the toddler to evaluate his performance through another's eyes. This opens the way to internalization of parental standards and expectations, which is the foundation of moral development. Gradually, older toddlers begin to show the capacity to monitor their own actions, which suggests that they are taking an outside perspective on themselves. For example, 2½-year-olds are self-aware enough to monitor their speech, as demonstrated when they spontaneously correct themselves after mispronouncing a word (Kagan, 1981).

The Intentional Self

The toddler's emerging sense of her self as an autonomous person is demonstrated by her urge to do things herself. She wants to feed herself, comb her own hair, and dress herself. The fact that she cannot do these things competently does not diminish her urge to assert control over her own activities and her own body. The toddler's behavior expresses the assertion "Do it myself!" even before she is able to say these words. By age 2, toddlers show considerable independence and persistence as they try to do things. They are more determined to do it their way and are not as easily deflected or distracted as they were at age 1. The toddler's insistence on doing things her way has been described as willfulness, oppositionalism, and a sign of "the terrible 2's." However, the toddler's having "a mind of her own" is a positive sign of cognitive development, indicating that she is now able to keep thinking about goals, persist at realizing them, and resist being distracted from them (Lyons-Ruth & Zeanah, 1993).

TODDLER PERSISTENCE: A BRIEF CASE EXAMPLE

An example of the toddler's persistence in pursuing her own goals appears in this vignette from a developmental testing. Tiffany was 2½-year-old referred for testing because child care providers worried about developmental delays, particularly in the area of language. The Stanford–Binet testing was conducted in the playroom at a child guidance clinic. Tiffany sat at the table and did the first three or four items of the testing with ease. It is possible to see on the videotape, however, that her eyes kept darting to the corner of the playroom where the toy stove and cooking utensils were. After the fourth test item, she got up and went to play at the stove. The tester, who was knowledgeable about toddlers, waited while she played for a minute, then coaxed her back to the table. Tiffany came back as he presented an item that tested memory. He showed her a toy kitty, which she briefly looked at with interest. Then she got up and went back to the stove. He coaxed her back again and put the kitty under one of three small boxes. Then he put a sheet of paper in front of the three boxes and started counting to 10. The idea is to see if the child can remember where the kitty is after 10 seconds. However, by the count of 2, Tiffany was back at the stove. Her mother commented wryly, "She likes those toys better than yours." The tester asked her to come back, and she did, but brought a plate, knife, and fork, and pretended to eat, seemingly ignoring the three boxes. The tester repeated the sequence while her mother sat beside her to keep her from leaving the table. Finally, almost as an afterthought, she correctly found the kitty under one of the boxes.

In watching this sequence, it is a matter of one's perspective in judging whether Tiffany is a willful and oppositional child or a child who has a clear idea of her own interests and goals—which happen not to coincide with the tester's objectives.

The Self at Age 3

By the end of the toddler period the child's sense of self as an individual seems clearly established. The older toddler uses the pronoun "I" regularly. He describes his own actions—"I eating now"—and gives herself credit when she succeeds—"I did it!" He is capable of describing internal psychological states: "I angry." She also uses the pronouns "you," "she," "he," and "we" appropriately, which indicates his ability to differentiate others from himself. She has learned her gender identity and can readily distinguish girls from boys (Thompson, 1975). Her experiences in the attachment relationship, assuming they have been consistent, have promoted a sense of internal continuity, the sense of being the same person over time. Alongside the working model of attachment, a working model of the self has developed. The content of the toddler's sense of self depends a great deal on the patterns of regulation of affect and behavior that have been internalized from the attachment relationship (Sroufe, 1989).

APPENDIX: SUMMARY OF TODDLER DEVELOPMENT, 1 TO 3 YEARS OF AGE

Information in parentheses shows when developmental features unfold and tasks become salient. Since there are individual differences in rate of development in children, I have indicated time ranges encompassing normal development. When a process is a salient part of development during the whole period, I have indicated this by including the whole period (1–3 years) in parentheses.

Overall Tasks

- Balancing attachment and exploration, with increasing movement toward autonomy and individuation
- Internalization of parental values and standards
- Developing the ability to symbolize, though mental representation, play and communication

Attachment

- Continuing transactional patterns of regulation of arousal and affect (1–3 years)
- Working models of attachment develop, allowing the toddler to develop some autonomous self-protective and self-soothing behaviors, especially between 24 and 36 months

- Use of transitional (comfort) objects for self-soothing and to cope with separation (16–36 months)
- Attachment relationship supports progressive development, including providing modeling for behavior, social referencing, helping the toddler understand the world, encouraging language and communication, support for autonomous behavior (1–3 years)

Social Development

- Toddlers' egocentric view of the world, combined with their need to feel autonomous and in control, limits their ability to share or acknowledge others' different intentions (16 months to 3 years)
- Beginning understanding of reciprocity develops through play with peers (2–3 years)
- Imitation of parental behavior implicitly incorporates a beginning understanding of social expectations (2–3 years)

Cognitive Development

- Intense interest in understanding and learning about the world (1–3 years)
- Development of conscious expectations, based on memory of prior experiences; awareness of violations of expectations (18 months to 3 years)
- Ability to observe and imitate others facilitates learning (1–3 years)
- Conscious goals and plans: toddlers can formulate plans, consciously remember them, and persist in trying to realize them (18 months +)

Language and Communication

- Language learning: after gradual growth in vocabulary from 12 to 18 months, there is a burst of language development; this burst is motivated by the toddler's growing wish to communicate her experience (1–3 years)
- Two- and three-word sentences are used (18–24 months)
- Rapid development of vocabulary, syntax, grammatical structures, as well as idiomatic usage and pronunciation patterns used by parents (2–3 years)
- Beginnings of mental representation using words, narrative, and verbally mediated thinking (18 months to 3 years)
- Use of language to understand and "construct" the world: asking questions, telling about experiences, talking to oneself, crib talk (2–3 years)
- Social uses of language develop: using language to share experiences, putting wishes into words, and a beginning ability to slow down impulses by verbalizing them (18 months to 3 years)
- Limitations in language ability are a common source of frustration (and angry behavior) over not being able to communicate (18 months to 3 years)

Symbolic Communication and Play

- Sensorimotor play: exploration of properties and functions of objects (1–2 years +)
- Pretend play: imitation of ordinary activities (pretending to eat) or caregiving behavior (1 year to 18 months +)
- Symbolic play: substituting one object for another, sequences of actions in pretend (16 months +)
- Play becomes used as the child's symbolic commentary on his experience, as well as a means to represent and emotionally discharge reactions to stressful situations (18 months to 3 years +)
- Play of toddlers often provides a more complex representation of experience than they are able to express in words (18 months to 3 years +)

Self-Regulation

- Beginnings of autonomous self-regulation emerge; however, toddlers' internal means of coping with stress are limited and consequently they continue to rely on dyadic strategies of coping, based on the attachment relationship (1–3 years)
- Toddlers are subject to many sources of uncertainty and anxiety, and have difficulty exerting autonomous control over impulses; impulse control slowly improves during the toddler period (1–3 years)
- Coping mechanisms of toddlers include the following: dyadic regulation through attachment relationships; self-stimulation as an outlet for tension; play as a vehicle for mastering stress; language as a means for communicating distress; imitating and internalizing parents' ways of regulating anxiety (1–3 years)

Moral Development

- Young toddlers' mobility and strong motivation to explore inevitably causes parents to limit their behavior, often to protect them from danger; the toddler begins to experience a discrepancy between his wishes and his parents' limits (1–2 years)
- Parents' direct approval and disapproval, especially when accompanied by strong affects, supports internalization of parents' rules; at this point, the toddler tries to control his behavior in order to gain the parents' approval and avoid punishment (1–3 years)
- Internalization of standards: toddlers notice deviations from expected norms and become concerned if their expectations are violated; they evaluate their own performance, feeling good if they have done well and bad if they have not; they have learned their parents' expectations for behavior—all these factors support the development of self-control (18 months to 3 years)

- Beginnings of prosocial behavior: beginning capacity for empathy may cause toddlers to comfort distressed peers and may help older toddlers inhibit aggressive impulses (18 months to 3 years)

Sense of Self

- Self-assertion: insistence on having things their own way and pursuing their own goals imply toddlers' increasing sense of self-importance (14–20 months)
- Self-recognition: midway through the second year, toddlers can recognize themselves in a mirror, confirming a new sense of consciousness of themselves (18 months to 2 years)
- Egocentrism dominates toddlers' view of self and others; they tend to emphasize their own needs and point of view over those of others (1–3 years)
- Separation–individuation: awareness of psychological differences and autonomy from parents; toddlers are more vulnerable to separation anxiety and more likely to activate attachment behavior during the most stressful period of separation–individuation, occurring at about 18–20 months (16 months to 3 years)
- Beginnings of an autonomous sense of self, symbolized by independent behavior and in language by the emerging use of the words "I," "me," "my," and "mine" (2–3 years)
- Gender identity: sense of self includes awareness of gender identity (2–3 years)

❖ CHAPTER 7 ❖

Practice with Toddlers

ASSESSMENT

As with infants, assessment of toddlers frequently combines observational with structured approaches. The toddler's capacity for symbolic expression through behavior, play, and—increasingly—words permits the clinician to observe how the toddler represents her experience. Observation of toddlers' representational play often becomes the vehicle for clarifying possible meanings of their behavioral symptoms. In the assessment of Jared (Chapter 6), for example, his repeated playing out of the incident when his father smashed the glass door demonstrated his ongoing fears and helped recast his "aggressive" behavior as symptomatic of anxiety about being attacked and hurt.

Developmental testing of toddlers may be more difficult than at other stages of development because toddlers frequently do not cooperate with an agenda that differs from their own. The toddler's desire to assert herself and to explore on her own terms sometimes conflicts with the demands of structured testing. These are not insurmountable obstacles, however. Clinicians who test toddlers usually become skilled at adapting the pace and order of test items to achieve a compromise with the toddler. They learn to engage parents to help the toddler stay on task. While testing is useful, especially when the presenting problems include possible developmental delays, observation and interaction with the toddler often provide the most telling information about psychological, interactional and developmental issues; see Table 7.1 (Meisels, 1996).

TABLE 7.1. Summary of Assessment Issues for Toddlers

- A balanced assessment aims to identify optimal levels of functioning and areas of strength and potential, as well as areas of deficit.

- Observation, rather than testing, is often the most useful approach to the assessment of many toddlers, including those with developmental delays. As with infants, observation of the toddler in multiple settings—home, child care center, and office—provides a full picture of the child's range of functioning.

- Emerging representational abilities in the toddler permit the clinician to learn directly how she has constructed and given meaning to experiences, particularly stressful or traumatic ones.

- Since the attachment relationship remains essential to the child's capacity for adaptive coping, toddlers should be observed with their primary caregivers. These observations should focus on the quality of attachment, the balance of exploratory and secure base behavior, and the caregivers' attitudes as to the toddler.

Assessing Secure Base Behavior

Although assessment must consider the full range of developmental tasks and accomplishments of toddlers, Lieberman and Pawl (1990, 1993) argue that secure base behavior and the balance of attachment and exploration are especially sensitive indicators of the toddler's functioning. Since these issues can only be assessed in the context of the toddler's primary relationships, *toddlers must be seen with their parents.* The function of attachment is to provide the child with a sense of protection and security. A lack of responsiveness or inappropriate responses by parents can interfere with the toddler's ability to internalize adaptive ways of managing fear and anxiety. When the toddler does not feel secure, because of a history of unreliable protection in the attachment and the resulting failure of internalization of self-protectiveness, "the child's ability to engage in a confident exploration of the environment is disrupted, and alterations in the balance between exploration and attachment behaviors (secure-base behavior) are observed" (Lieberman & Pawl, 1990, p. 379). Lieberman and Pawl identify three patterns of distortion of secure-base behavior: (1) counterphobic recklessness and accident proneness; (2) inhibition of exploration; and (3) precocious competence.

Counterphobic Recklessness and Accident Proneness

The attachment history of toddlers who put themselves in dangerous situations involves a failure of protection. Parents have exposed the child to danger or have discounted, minimized, or ignored the child's distress. Frequently, the attachment figure has been subjected to domestic abuse and has implicitly shown the child that she cannot protect herself. This leads the child to rely less on the attachment relationship for a sense of protection. When the infant becomes a toddler and the urge to explore becomes paramount, he seems to court danger, "as if trying to discover how much risk they have to endure before the mother intervenes" (Lieberman & Pawl, 1990, p. 382). These reckless toddlers have high levels of anxiety and reactivity to stress.

JARED: A BRIEF CASE EXAMPLE

Jared's presenting symptoms and the dynamics of his relationship with his mother illustrate the counterphobic, reckless style. He was referred after his family day care provider had expelled him from her program because of his wild, uncontrollable and aggressive behavior. He often hurt himself and would reverse his affect, laughing instead of crying or registering pain. He climbed high on the jungle gym and jumped off. He ran into the street during a field trip. His provider said, "I try to restrain him, but there is no way to discipline him unless you are right there to keep him quiet." Jared's experience throughout his first 18 months included frequent exposure to his father's violence toward his mother. His mother reinforced his reckless, aggressive behavior by failing to set limits on it, simultaneously conveying to him through her lack of firmness that she could not protect him or help him control his anxiety-based impulses.

Inhibition of Exploration

These children, in a manner surprising for toddlers, avoid exploring the environment and instead appear as passive, vigilant, or unemotional watchers. They cling to the parent and are very distressed by separation. Two types of distorted parenting were identified to explain the behavior of these inhibited toddlers: parents who "needed" their infants and discouraged or punished autonomous exploration, and parents who were unpredictable and abusive, which seemed to encourage their toddlers to withdraw and to be cautious about making a move.

Precocious Competence

The toddler reverses roles with her caregiver, as shown in vigilance of the parent's moods and caretaking of the parent (Lieberman & Pawl, 1990). The toddler gains a sense of security by staying close to and attending to the parent's needs, but at the cost of autonomous explora-tion. This pattern is associated with parents who are self-absorbed because of depression or other conflicts that make them emotionally unavailable. These toddlers perceive an emotional fragility in their parent that leads them to become precociously self-reliant because the parent cannot be depended upon. They direct their energies toward taking care of the parent and may become "compulsive caregivers" (Bowlby, 1980).

INTERVENTION

Intervention with toddlers involves an extension of the principles of infant–parent psychotherapy. Developmental attachment theory pro-vides a rationale for seeing the parents and child together, rather than either the toddler or parent alone. Even though the toddler is becom-ing an autonomous self, he still requires the support of the attachment relationship as it expands to include helping him understand the world. In joint therapy the therapist and parent observe the toddler's play and behavior in order to learn about the sources of his distress or difficulties in the child–parent relationship. An important contrast with infant work, however, is that toddlers, because of their more advanced development, become more active participants in the therapy (Bennett & Davies, 1981; Lieberman, 1992). The representational play of tod-dlers is usually clearer and less mediated by defensive processes than is the play of older children. The toddler's growing facility with lan-guage becomes available for therapeutic uses. Therapist and parents can name the toddler's feelings and describe stressful experiences in simple terms so that the toddler is helped to make sense of them. "Dia-logues" between the toddler's behavior and play and the parent's or therapist's words can become the vehicle for understanding and resolving the toddler's problems. For example, Jared specified the sources of his symptomatic behavior in play by repeatedly having the dinosaur break down a door and bite the baby inside. His mother real-ized that he was representing a frightening event that both of them had experienced. This allowed her to see beyond Jared's aggressive behavior to the fear and anxiety that were fueling it. The therapist and Jared's mother put the events and affects expressed in his play into words: "It was so scary when daddy broke the glass. The glass hit you. Mom's not going to let daddy do that again." The expression of empa-thy and clarification in words helped Jared represent his experience at a verbal level and provided him with reassurance that his mother was aware of his fears and intended to act protectively.

Lieberman (1992) points out, however, that it is important not to overestimate the toddler's ability to make use of verbal interventions and recommends that therapists find ways to talk about "big feelings in toddler-size words" (p. 570). The younger the toddler, the more strongly this caveat applies. It is frequently useful for the parent, with the therapist's coaching, to join in the toddler's play as a means of nonverbally dramatizing empathy and protective responses to the child's anxiety. For example, when Jared continued to raise questions and fears about his father's violence in play by having a father figure crash into the family in the middle of a meal, his mother picked up the mother figure and had her push the father figure out of the house, saying, "No, the mom's not going to let the daddy do that."

The toddler's advancing capacity for representing the self in the context of experience carries liabilities when the child encounters stressful or traumatic events. The toddler may construct images of stressful experiences that reflect misunderstandings, confusions of cause and effect, and egocentric perspectives. Jared, even though he had not seen his father for 6 months, implied an ongoing expectation of his father's violent return through his nightly checking to see if all the doors were locked. In the toddler, in contrast to the infant, anxiety can take the form of conscious mental imagery that influences the toddler's view of self and reality. The toddler remembers and thinks about difficult experiences, such as a long separation from a parent, and worries they will occur again. These ideas create anxiety and are often the basis for toddlers' symptomatic behavior.

The capacity for internal representation means that traumatic experiences may affect a toddler's working models, even when the parents are trying hard to provide a sense of security. The practice implication of this is that toddlers' misunderstandings and over-generalizations need to be addressed directly in treatment. Because the toddler forms her own impressions and thoughts, guidance-based intervention with the parent alone usually is not sufficient to mitigate the toddler's anxiety. Toddlers need an opportunity to represent their concerns and to have them responded to specifically, which means that in most cases the toddler will be included in sessions with the parent and that therapy will be structured to elicit the toddler's representations of her experience (Davies, 1991; Lieberman, 1992).

In the treatment of toddlers and parents, *a primary goal is to strengthen the adaptive features of the attachment* (Table 7.2). In some cases the focus will be on the parent's own negative or insecure attachment history as it contributes to his or her negative perceptions of the toddler. In less severe cases, the focus may be on the interaction between

TABLE 7.2. Toddler's Developmental Capacities That Can Be Utilized in Intervention

- Ability develops to represent and raise questions about experience through symbolic enactment and play (begins between 15 and 18 months).
- The toddler's strong motivation to know and understand experience makes him interested in pursuing salient issues in treatment.
- Receptive language ability permits the toddler to understand simple explanations of stressful experiences and reassurance (begins at 15–18 months).
- Receptive language ability also allows parents to prepare the child in advance for potentially stressful events, such as brief separations or doctor visits (begins at 15–18 months).
- Expressive language ability permits the toddler to articulate worries, questions, and concerns in simple ways (begins at 20–24 months, and increases rapidly with language development).

parental vulnerabilities and toddler's self-assertion. For example, some parents who have found pleasure in the child as an infant react negatively to the toddler's growing autonomy, experiencing the child's assertion as a struggle for control. Treatment concentrates on reframing the toddler's behavior as developmentally appropriate and exploring alternatives to the establishment of mutually coercive interaction patterns. In other cases, the work focuses on restoring function to a previously adaptive attachment that has been compromised by developmental changes, stress, or trauma.

ASSESSMENT OF TODDLER DEVELOPMENT: A CASE EXAMPLE

The evaluation presented here illustrates issues of toddler development when a child is not functioning at the expected developmental level. Marcel, age 2 years, 8 months, presented with intrinsic developmental difficulties. Marcel's difficulties in navigating the developmental tasks of the toddler were primarily caused by his deficits in language and affect regulation, though the parent–child transactions which had been shaped by his mother's responses to those deficits also played a role in Marcel's presentation.

In assessing children with atypical or delayed development, it is crucial to examine the child's optimal level of functioning and areas of developmental adequacy, as well as areas of delay (Greenspan &

Meisels, 1996). It is essential to identify areas where the child's functioning is age appropriate or has the potential to become age appropriate, because these areas of relative strength can become the basis of an
intervention plan to address the areas of delay. This case example
illustrates the uses of a careful developmental assessment. It also demonstrates how intertwined the toddler's developmental tasks are and
how difficulties in one area can interfere with the accomplishment of
tasks in another area. Marcel's development was very uneven, with
age-appropriate functioning in some domains and severely delayed
functioning in language and regulation of affect and behavior. These
delays led to severe symptoms that overshadowed Marcel's areas of
adequate functioning. Because of the severe language delays, it was
difficult to assess his overall cognitive abilities. Between the ages of 2
and 3 years, cognitive progress proceeds in tandem with advances in
verbal abilities. Marcel was moving ahead in the development of
awareness of self and other. He was not autistic. He wanted to communicate and was aware of the possibilities of communication. However, he was tremendously frustrated because he could not use words
to communicate, and thus experienced a great disparity between his
cognitive abilities and desire for interaction, on the one hand, and his
ability to communicate what he was thinking, on the other. Finally, the
case illustrates how consultation after evaluation became an important
intervention on behalf of a child. Following the assessment, I was able
to frame Marcel's difficulties and strengths in a way that helped a
school-based early intervention program plan services for him and his
mother.

Referral: A Toddler Out of Control

Marcel was the only child of his 24-year-old single mother. His father
rarely visited and was not involved in his life. Ms. Montgomery was
supported by AFDC (Aid to Families with Dependent Children) and
was not working outside the home. The family was African-American.
Marcel and his mother lived alone, but extended family members lived
in their neighborhood. A school early-intervention program referred
Marcel for evaluation at age 2 years, 8 months.

Presenting problems included severe language delays, short attention span, "hyperactive" behavior, and frequent severe tantrums. The
school district had attempted to evaluate him using standardized tests,
but he refused to cooperate with the examiners. His refusals were characterized as "lack of motivation." Estimates of his abilities were based
on observation and suggested delays in several areas. Language was
estimated at 15 months, a very significant delay since it represented

less than half his chronological age. A normal hearing test had previously ruled out hearing loss as a cause of his language delays. Cognitive abilities were estimated at 20 months, while self-help skills were at the 24-month level. His fine motor coordination was seen as significantly delayed, at about the 2-year level, while his gross motor abilities were judged age appropriate. His social abilities were seen as at the 10-month level. This extremely low estimate was based on his "antisocial" behavior, which the school program's report described in detail. Marcel ran around the classroom, threw toys, opened desk drawers and threw the contents about, pushed books and personal items off the teacher's desk, and tore pictures off the wall. When the teachers tried to restrain him, he hit and kicked them. He was, according to the report, "completely out of control." Apparently in desperation, a teacher put him on top of a tall file cabinet, which stopped his behavior briefly. The school intervention program referred him for a pediatric neurology examination in order to discover whether neurological dysfunction explained his extreme behavior and with the hope that medication could be prescribed.

The physical examination showed no clear signs of neurological dysfunction. The medical report contained imagery and tone similar to those in the school report. During the examination, Marcel ran against the door, hurtled around the room, fell on the floor, constantly screaming and crying. He refused to cooperate with the examination and was "completely impossible to control." The pediatric staff could not capture his attention, and the resident evaluator commented, "Not much interests him." Marcel did not comply with his mother's demands, but it was noted that she was very patient with and invested in him. The report ended with the awed and decidedly nonclinical impression that neither the resident evaluator nor his medical supervisor had "ever seen anything like Marcel." A psychiatric evaluation was recommended.

Impressions of Referral Reports

The reports of these previous evaluations made clear that Marcel showed difficulties in several areas of development. It appeared that he had few adaptive strategies for coping with stress. I wondered if he might be unusually sensitive to novel situations. My other impression was that the previous evaluators were perplexed and awed by his intense, disturbed behavior. Their descriptions conveyed that he was incomprehensible and very difficult to empathize with. Both reports described him as lacking in motivation. This is a very unusual comment about a toddler, since so much of a toddler's behavior reflects the strong motivation to master his environment. The school report referred to his "destructive and dangerous acting out behavior." Such language is commonly used to describe delinquent adolescents. It seemed extreme as a description of a 2½-year-old. Because Marcel was African-American, I was concerned about this characterization, since it might later contribute to stigmatization based on racist stereotypes of African-American males.

The image of Marcel that emerged was a child who was incomprehensible, out of control, and dangerous. A child like Marcel understandably evokes in adults strong reactions that cause them to want to restrain and control him. The parent of a young child with serious behavioral problems often feels helpless and alarmed by the intensity of the child's behavior. However, a focus on the surface of behavior may prevent parents and others from understanding its potential meanings and may lead to controlling and punitive responses. But efforts at restraint, which ignore the sources of the child's distress, often elicit an escalation of the behavior. Marcel's behavior was so extreme that even seasoned evaluators were emphasizing the need to control him, rather than formulating an understanding of his behavior.

Since Marcel seemed incomprehensible and possibly unreachable, the school had not been able to develop an intervention plan. Their request to our program was for intervention recommendations and medication. In my experience it is unusual for a request for medication to figure so prominently in a referral of a child so young. When such a request comes in, it is usually because the child's behavior is not only extreme but also unexplained. When extreme behavior in a toddler does not yield to a biological, developmental, or psychosocial explanation, parents and professionals, in desperation, may hope that a medication can be prescribed that will at least moderate his behavior.

Assessment Plan

I decided to spend my limited evaluation time observing Marcel in free play and interaction with his mother. This approach was consistent with current thinking on the developmental assessment of young children: "The cornerstone of assessment should be the observation of the child in interaction with trusted caregivers and the appreciation of the child's core functional capacities" (Greenspan & Meisels, 1996, pp. 25–26). The interview was videotaped so that I could carefully review Marcel's developmental abilities later.

Marcel's "deficits" had already been described in the two previous evaluations that attempted to impose structure on his behavior. These attempts at formal evaluation had not succeeded and had yielded only estimates of his developmental levels. There are a number of limitations in the use of structured testing for toddlers, not least of which is the toddler's frequent refusal to cooperate. Furthermore, formal tests, which have been standardized on samples of normal children, may not "bring out the unique abilities and potential of children with atypical or challenging developmental patterns" (Greenspan & Meisels, 1996, pp. 24–25). Since most test instruments designed to assess development after age 2 rely heavily on *verbal* directions and therefore on the child's ability to understand language, Marcel's language delays put him at a great disadvantage. I speculated that language-based tests—even assuming that Marcel would cooperate with them—would reveal his already-known language deficits but perhaps obscure his capacities in other domains. I wanted to see what he was like in a more relaxed situation, without the pressure of formal testing. I wanted to see if his behavior told a story that made sense and to learn if he demonstrated areas of strength upon which an intervention plan could be built.

Parent–Toddler Interview and Observation

For the first 20 minutes of the 90-minute interview, Marcel did not fit the image of the previous evaluations. While I spoke to his mother and the school social worker who had driven them to my office, Marcel played with toys on the floor. He sustained his play and only approached his mother a few times to show her a toy. His preference for exploratory play was typical for a toddler. I did not observe any evidence of distress or attachment-seeking behavior. He seemed to regard his mother as a secure base and to feel comfortable exploring a new environment in her presence. However, other observations immediately raised questions of developmental delays.

- Marcel played exclusively at the sensorimotor level, looking at the toys, seeing what noises he could make with them. He moved from toy to toy in a restless way. I did not see any clear examples of symbolic play or imitation of adult behavior that would be typical for an older toddler.
- He said nothing. Toddlers often accompany their play with noises or verbal commentary, but Marcel was strikingly silent for nearly 20 minutes.
- He did not show evidence of understanding what we were saying. An older toddler with normal language development often responds to adult conversation about himself, especially when a parent expresses anxiety, concern, or negative feelings about him. His play may become more agitated, or he may become distressed and approach

his parent. When Ms. Montgomery gave a concerned description of his frequent extreme tantrums, Marcel continued to play by himself. I suspected that his lack of reactiveness meant that he could not understand his mother's words.

• During his solitary play, his affect was serious and subdued. Playing did not evoke a range of affects. His affect did not change when he was spoken to. He seemed alone and out of contact with us.

History Taking

While I observed Marcel, I asked Ms. Montgomery about his development. I learned that pregnancy and delivery were normal, and, except for colic during the early months, she did not recall any problems during the first year. Motor milestones were on target. She said that her sister had thought that Marcel was not a very responsive infant. However, she had not been concerned during the first year because she usually knew what Marcel wanted and he seemed to enjoy being held and cuddled. There were a few words at age 1. During the second year, the capacity for imitation was present, but language and symbolic play did not develop. By 18 months, Ms. Montgomery had become concerned about Marcel's lack of social responsiveness and his lack of language. He was increasingly oppositional and began to have tantrums that she could not help modulate. Ms. Montgomery seemed highly invested in Marcel but perplexed and dismayed by his behavior.

Family history was positive for speech delays and severe stuttering by Ms. Montgomery during early childhood. Her younger brother was diagnosed with hyperactivity and learning disability in middle childhood. Ms. Montgomery was poor but received emotional support from her mother and sister who lived nearby. However, she said that recently her mother had been pressuring her to spank Marcel when he had a tantrum. She said she was reluctant to do so because "I know there's something more wrong than just being contrary." Marcel's mother was a gentle woman who was trying very hard to understand him. She was a good informant about his development, which suggested she had come to know him well by being engaged with him over time. As she reported the developmental history, there were no holes in the information, as occurs when a parent has been neglectful, depressed, or abusing drugs or alcohol. Her descriptions of his development also seemed consistent with Marcel's current presentation, which suggested that her perceptions of him had been free of distortion. Her account was factual and free of attributions that connoted negative working models or unrealistic expectations of him.

Risk factors, including poverty and single parenthood, were present, but Ms. Montgomery had apparently been able to mediate the impact of these stressors up to this point. There was no evidence of risk factors such as parental psychopathology or substance abuse, which are particularly damaging to early development. Nor were there clear signs of physical or sexual abuse. These findings pointed away from a primarily psychosocial explanation for Marcel's difficulties and in the direction of intrinsic developmental problems.

Observation of Normal Behavior: Social Referencing

I noticed that as Mrs. Montgomery began to feel increasingly comfortable with me during the first 10 minutes of the interview, Marcel's use of the play space changed. At the beginning of the interview, he played near his mother, a few feet from her chair. Gradually he moved away from her, while staying on her side of the room and at a distance from me. When his mother began to relate to me in a more warm and relaxed manner, Marcel moved to the center of the room and a few minutes later picked up a Fisher–Price house and put it on the table between us. He was relaxed and curious as I showed him how the house opened up and pointed to the small figures and furniture inside. Marcel's willingness to move closer to me as his mother became comfortable with me was another encouraging sign of a "normal" behavior, a clear demonstration of social referencing. Toddlers assess the safety of a new situation or person by paying attention to their parent's affective cues. If the parent expresses coolness or wariness, the toddler tends to avoid closeness or contact with the stranger. If the parent's affect is warm and relaxed, the toddler gets the message that the stranger is a safe person (Feiring, Lewis, & Starr, 1984). Social referencing has been studied in young toddlers who still understand very little language. The toddler's acceptance of the stranger depends not on language but on the affective tone the parent conveys to the new person (Emde, 1989; Hornik & Gunnar, 1988). Marcel used his mother's responses to guide his own behavior, suggesting he saw her as a reliable beacon and secure base. Since such trust of the parent is based on a positive attachment, this was an encouraging observation.

A Critical Incident

As Marcel played with the house, he suddenly became upset. He screamed and banged his fist against the house. His mother thought he'd had trouble fitting a car into the garage and pointed to the garage opening, saying, "That car goes right there." Marcel looked at the house and screeched again. He tried to push the house off the table, then began to jump up and down. He jumped so hard he fell down. He began to cry loudly. He slammed the car against the house. Then he approached his mother crying very loudly and signaling gesturally that he wanted to be picked up. She picked him up, and for a few seconds he seemed to feel comforted. Then he arched away from his mother, crying harder and kicking. Ms. Montgomery held him for several seconds, trying to restrain him from bucking, then became frustrated and put him down. He lay on the floor, crying and kicking at the legs of her chair. She became angry and told him to stop it. He stopped kicking and began moving around the room in a "hyperactive" way, still crying. While this tantrum was going on, his mother confirmed that they occurred often, and she frequently did not know what caused these catastrophic reactions.

Marcel's tantrum was stunning in its intensity and duration. At first he had tried to use his attachment relationship to modulate his apparent frustration with the house. When that failed he was unable to regulate his own affects and became disorganized, collapsing into helpless, rageful jumping and screaming. He had almost no capacity to control the escalation of a negative feeling once it had started. His mother looked perplexed by his intense behavior and also demoralized because she did not know how to help him modulate it. I could identify with her sense of helplessness and with the reactions of professionals who had previously evaluated him. This was the behavior that had been seen as "completely out of control," dangerous, and inexplicable.

However, I had paid careful attention to the sequence of Marcel's behavior and formed a hypothesis about the causes of his extended tantrum. My position differed from that of an evaluator who assesses a child by trying to get him to do a structured task. I was free of the pressure—and frustration—an evaluator can feel when a child refuses to perform. It looked like Marcel's tantrum had been precipitated by his inability to do something with the garage door of the house. I wanted to assess whether he could regulate affect and behavior if he was helped to refocus on the point where things began to go wrong. I encouraged him to come back to the house, pointed to the garage, and said, "Let's figure this out. Did something go wrong with the house?" In response, he banged the truck against the house and tried to push it into the garage. His angry response seemed a way of saying, "Yes!" Already this was encouraging because his anger focused on a problem, instead of being expressed in diffuse and aggressive discharge. When I helped him put the truck in the garage, Marcel's affect changed dramatically. He calmed down and became interested in play again. For a minute we played together at the sensorimotor level, moving the truck in and out of the garage. When he started another tantrum because he could not get the garage door closed, I helped him by showing him the small handle and he quickly calmed again. Marcel could remain calm and focused if I physically demonstrated solutions to what had frustrated him and put into words what was happening. After the frustration was mastered, he was able to follow my suggestions about where to put people and furniture in the house. He also imitated me when I showed him how to ring the doorbell. As Marcel continued to play with the house he said, "Dee, dee, dee" in an excited and pleased tone, and then said two words, "uh car, uh truck." Afterward, Marcel played independently with the house and other toys for about 15 minutes without the need for outside support.

Making Sense of Marcel

A different view of Marcel emerged from this interaction. His behavior was no longer incomprehensible. When I responded to him in terms of the actual source of his frustration (the truck that wouldn't fit, the garage door he couldn't close), and helped him master a previously difficult task, his affect modulated and his behavior became much more organized. I immediately pointed out to his mother that his extreme behavior was a response to frustration with the house and that she had been correct in seeing that. His response to my help with the garage door made clear that he was not an "unreachable" child. On the contrary, he was very responsive to my support and suggestions. This suggested he could be open to instruction based on a reciprocal relationship. When I framed his tantrum as caused by a frustration with the house, he responded positively. This response suggested that it would be fruitful to think of his problems as based on a primary deficit in communication that had secondary effects on his relationships and his ability to regulate affects.

Formulation

The observation of Marcel's behavior told a story that permitted a formulation of his problems that encompassed his intrinsic developmental problems and the transactional difficulties they created. Marcel was hyperreactive and easily distressed. He was motivated to communicate his distress. His approaches to his mother indicated that he saw her as a resource for dyadic regulation of affect. But his deficits in communication made this nearly impossible. His mother, who was strongly invested in him, frequently could not understand him. This made Marcel feel out of touch with her, which had a disorganizing effect on him and led to or at least intensified his tantrums. Unlike an autistic child, Marcel was clearly motivated to communicate and be understood by others, but he was unable to convey his internal states in understandable ways. He had so few words that he could not use language to help his mother and others understand his needs.

Interactive coping depends on the ability of the toddler to signal and engage a caregiver, who can then take steps to help the child cope with a stressor (Williamson, 1996). Marcel and his mother had not been able to evolve the more complex communication system one expects to see between toddlers and parents. As a result, their ability to use their attachment to help Marcel deal with distress was seriously compromised. The lack of dyadic regulation strategies led to many interchanges that were frustrating on both sides. For his mother and other adults, it was distressing to try to understand and fail; for Marcel, it was affectively disorganizing to try to communicate and fail. By the time of the evaluation at age 2 years, 8 months, this communication failure had a long history, resulting in negative expectations for both Marcel and Ms. Montgomery, not only about their ability to communicate but increasingly about the viability of their relationship.

The interactional sequence following Marcel's difficulty with the house was not only frustrating for Marcel and his mother but led to an escalation of mismatched responses and ultimately to demoralization in Ms. Montgomery and what appeared to be a profound sense of abandonment in Marcel. When Marcel first became distressed he demonstrated secure-base behavior by turning to his mother for help. This was an appropriate use of their attachment relationship and was typical for a toddler who becomes anxious or encounters difficulty during exploratory play. However, Marcel was unable to communicate the particular meaning of his distress, which might be stated as "I can't get this truck in the garage, and I'm feeling angry and helpless. I need help both with the truck and to get control of my feelings." Lacking the linguistic means to convey this, he simply approached his mother for comforting. His mother then *thought* he wanted to be cuddled and picked him up. Marcel immediately became angry, feeling his mother had failed to understand him. His mother also began to feel helpless and responded by trying to control the symptomatic behavior by restraining him. Then she gave up and pushed him away. In this disturbed interaction, the desire of both to communicate was thwarted by Marcel's diffuse signals and by his mother's inability to decipher what they meant. The interaction became aversive for both, and the original tension, instead of being resolved, increased and was transformed into an interactional tension. In this type of interaction, there is no closure, and Marcel had to fall back on his own capacity for regulation of affect, which, when he was under stress, was limited to diffuse or aggressive motoric activity that others tended to view as "out of control" and incomprehensible.

Assessing Areas of Developmental Adequacy or Potential

My observations confirmed the developmental deficits or delays found in the previous evaluations. Marcel showed serious delays in receptive and expressive language, which were likely related to deficits in auditory processing. He was hyperreactive to external stressors and internal frustration. His capacity for self-regulation even under mild stress was poor. Because of his difficulty in communicating in ways his mother could understand, dyadic regulation of affect was also compromised. However, assessment must also define areas of developmental strength or potential. Identifying areas of normal development not only provides the parent with a sense of hope about her child but also helps the practitioner frame a treatment plan that uses the child's areas of strength to approach the areas of deficit.

A crucial aspect of my assessment of Marcel was seeing that he was capable of joint attention. In fact he was highly motivated to share my focus on the house. He could not express this interest in words, but he demonstrated it by looking where I looked and imitating my behavior. Joint attentional behavior has been identified as an important condition for language learning (D. A. Baldwin, 1995). Typically, when parents look at an object or an event with a child, they talk about what they are seeing, implicitly teaching the child the names of objects and actions, and gradually helping the child think about what she is seeing in words. This process had probably been derailed for Ms. Montgomery and Marcel because his language deficits prevented him from taking up the child's role in the process, which is to imitate the parent's utterances. Ms. Montgomery acknowledged that her behavior had been shaped by Marcel's lack of response. She had decided that he was "not ready to talk yet, or maybe he didn't like talking," and had talked to him less and less. I had engaged him as one might engage a very young toddler. Instead of relying primarily on words, I pointed out parts of the house and physically demonstrated how to do things that had previously frustrated him. I accompanied my actions with words but did not expect Marcel to grasp what I said. It was helpful to think of him as being like a toddler early in the second year, who is beginning to learn language but who needs concrete demonstrations as a bridge to language learning.

The assessment of Marcel's motivation was another crucial issue.

It was very important to notice that, although he constantly struggled with feelings of failure and incompetence, he was still trying hard to communicate and master his environment. Marcel was not an unmotivated or apathetic child; rather, he appeared to have strong wishes to express himself and be understood. From this perspective it was possible to think about the intensity of his tantrums as a measure of his frustration about not being able to communicate. Further, seeing Marcel as motivated to make sense of the world and to communicate his feelings and ideas made him seem much more like a normal toddler, rather than a child whose behavior was beyond comprehension. Marcel certainly was not "normal" because of his severely delayed language development and auditory processing skills, yet his motivations were typical for a toddler. The observational assessment of Marcel illuminated several areas of developmental adequacy or potential. These included the following:

- Strong motivation to communicate and master his environment.
- Positive (though not always functional) attachment with his mother.
- Interest in exploratory behavior.
- Capacity for autonomous affect regulation when not under stress.
- Capacity to use interactive coping to deal with distress.
- Capacity for joint attention.

These observations confirmed that Marcel's overall developmental maturation had been proceeding, even though one area, language and symbolic communication, was seriously impaired. Brazelton (1990) notes that "the force of the central nervous system as it develops is relentless" (p. 1664). Even in an infant or young child with deficits, the maturational thrust "tries to force around that defect, to push beyond what's holding the infant back" (Brazelton, 1990, pp. 1664–1655). Marcel's strong desire to communicate, marked by the intensity of his anger, frustration, and behavioral disorganization, could be seen as the force of development as it tried to overcome a defect. Brazelton (1990) also notes: "This is a critical force for recovery from a defect in an impaired infant, if it can be harnessed properly" (p. 1665).

An Intervention Plan Based on Developmental Understanding

This observational assessment, combined with the findings of the previous evaluations, suggested an approach to intervention that addressed Marcel's deficits by making use of his existing developmental strengths and potentials, as well as the strengths in the parent–toddler relationship. To be effective, the intervention would need to address transactional issues between Marcel and his mother as well as Marcel's language and communication deficits. The following recommendations were offered to the early intervention program:

Toddler–Parent Developmental Guidance with a Specialist Trained in Infant Mental Health

This part of the intervention would attempt to build upon Ms. Montgomery's investment in Marcel and the adaptive aspects of their attachment relationship. Goals would include the following: helping Ms. Montgomery learn to observe and understand Marcel's behavior as reflecting attempts to communicate; helping her develop more empathic communication with him as she came to understand him better; and helping the two of them move toward an increasingly shared affective experience and "vocabulary" of gestures and words. The communication difficulties between Marcel and his mother had caused a relative failure in the functioning of the secure base. Marcel wanted to use his mother as a secure base when distressed, but since he could not communicate the content of his distress, he experienced his mother's caregiving as frequently off the mark and unreliable. The essential aim of the parent–child work would be to help Ms. Montgomery read Marcel's behavior accurately so that she would respond to him more contingently. If Marcel could feel that his mother understood him more often, his ability to use her as a secure base would be strengthened.

Speech Therapy in the Context of an Intensive Early Intervention Program

Because of Marcel's severe language deficits and possible deficits in auditory processing, he needed speech therapy carried out at a basic language-learning level. I suggested in my report that "those who work with him will need to start where he is developmentally, responding to him much as one would to a young toddler. This will involve putting everything he does into words, providing a kind of running commentary, and being ready to provide concrete, hands-on help if he becomes frustrated." I also suggested that if his progress in spoken language was slow, it would be useful to teach him some basic hand signing in order to give him some means of communication. This would lay the groundwork for verbal communication as his language skills developed.

Continuing Periodic Assessment

I suggested that I evaluate Marcel periodically to assess the effects of interventions and to provide consultation to the practitioners working with him and his mother. I hoped that periodic assessments—approximately every 6 months—would help Mrs. Montgomery see Marcel's progress. During the first 3 years of life, development is rapid and responses to intervention are often more obvious than at later stages of development. Periodic assessments can provide a sense of progress and hope to the parent, since the evaluator can often point out real signs of developmental advances (Parker & Zuckerman, 1990).

No Medication

The request for medication to control Marcel's extreme behavior had figured prominently in the referral. This was a delicate issue, since the referring professionals hoped that medication would be recommended. My report carefully detailed the dynamics of Marcel's extreme behavior. My intent was to provide a framework for understanding his tantrums and aggressive behavior in terms of developmental delays and interactional problems. I hoped that if Marcel's behavior could be seen as making sense and if the parent–toddler and speech therapy interventions began to show results, there would be less pressure to medicate him. In my report I indicated that I had consulted with our psychiatric staff and noted that we were unwilling to recommend medication for a child as young as Marcel unless other types of intervention were unsuccessful.

Follow-Up

Marcel entered a preprimary early-intervention program. He established a good relationship with his primary teacher and made steady progress in language development, with slower improvement in reactivity and affect regulation. His mother had attended school with him frequently and was borrowing some of the teacher's approaches to playing with him and setting limits. At the time of the follow-up assessment, 6 months after the first, Marcel's play was more organized and accompanied by more verbalization. He did not have any tantrums during the session. Mrs. Montgomery played with him in a more sustained way, yet she said that she still often felt at a loss to understand his behavior. Significantly, the infant mental health referral had only just been made and Mrs. Montgomery had not yet begun to receive the same level of intervention and support that Marcel was receiving at school.

❖

OBSERVATION EXERCISES

1. Spend 1 hour observing toddlers and parents in a public place. A park or playground would be best, though a shopping mall or fast food restaurant would also be interesting sites for observation. Observe for the following:

   a. *Secure base, attachment, and exploration.* If the toddler is in a place where she can play freely, note the balance she establishes between exploration and attachment. Do you see the toddler "checking in" with the parent, either visually or verbally, while she plays? How far does she move away from the parent? What does the parent do to stay in touch with the exploring toddler? What is the toddler's activity level? What evidence do you see that supports the idea that toddlers are intensely interested in learning about their immediate world?

   b. *Autonomy.* What examples do you see where the toddler takes the initiative or insists on doing things his own way? How do toddler and parent react when the toddler's assertion of will runs contrary to the parents wishes or intentions? How do the parent and toddler negotiate conflicts over safety?

2. Spend 30–60 minutes observing in a toddler room in a child care center or preschool.

   a. What individual differences among children do you notice in the areas of motor skills and language ability?

   b. What kinds of play do you observe? Note examples of sensorimotor, imitative, symbolic, and interactive play.

   c. Observe for the "Mine" phenomenon, looking for instances of possessiveness or conflicts over toys. How do toddlers respond to such conflicts? How do caregivers respond when a conflict occurs?

   d. Do you see instances of empathy and prosocial behavior?

   e. Do you see instances of the presence or absence of self-control? What forms does self-control take? What appears to precipitate breakdown in the control of impulses?

INTERVIEW EXERCISE

Spend 30–60 minutes interviewing the parent(s) of an older toddler (between 2 and 3 years of age). Ask the parents to reflect on the differences between their child as an infant and toddler.

1. In general, how is she different at age 2, compared with age 6–9 months?
2. How has your relationship with her changed during the past 1–1½ years?

3. What do you recall about her during the 3–4 months immediately after she learned to walk?
4. How has her ability to communicate changed? How has her new ability to understand and use words changed your relationship?
5. Do you find it easier or harder (or perhaps some of each) to parent a toddler, compared to an infant?

❖ CHAPTER 8 ❖

Preschool Development

The preschool period, encompassing ages 3–6, is a great transition in development. The child evolves from an egocentric toddler with limited capacity for understanding the self and the world into a child of the middle years, who has much in common with adults, in that she can think logically, maintain self-control, and empathize with others. Cognitively, the preschool child moves gradually from magical thinking to thinking that is more logical, shows understanding of cause and effect, and distinguishes between fantasy and reality. A major effect of these cognitive changes is that by age 6 the child's view of self begins to be more realistic. So there is a corresponding movement from an egocentric, self-centered view of the world to a decentered, more objective view that understands that many events happen without reference to the self.

The preschool child's relationships change as he becomes more autonomous. Relationships with peers become very interesting to the preschooler and have implications for development. In interactions and play with age mates the preschooler gains skill in empathy, perspective taking, negotiation, and cooperation, and begins to experience the pleasures of friendship. Through these interactions, the child begins to measure himself against others, introducing for the first time social comparison as a component of the sense of self.

The capacity for self-regulation and impulse control improves a great deal between 3 and 6, as the child learns interpersonal coping skills and internalizes cognitive controls and unconscious defenses. She still depends on her attachment relationships, but she slowly learns to manage anxiety by using internal resources and by gaining support from others, based on generalizing her working models of attachment. In moral development there is a movement from reliance

227

on outside approval or disapproval to a more internalized sense of values. The child gradually develops a superego or conscience, which imposes internal standards for judging her behavior, creates possibilities for deriving self-esteem based on self-approval, and helps consolidate the child's internalization of the values, expectations, and rules of her family and culture.

The preschool child lives to play. This is the age of individual fantasy play and dramatic play with peers. As with the older toddler, play continues to serve the functions of skill development, exploration of reality, and mastery of anxiety. But imaginative play takes center stage in development, becoming an essential vehicle for constructing and understanding the world, as well as facilitating cognitive and socioemotional growth (Piaget, 1962). The central role of play in preschool development will be emphasized and illustrated in this chapter, as well as following Chapter 9, which presents a detailed account of play therapy with a preschool child.

PHYSICAL DEVELOPMENT

The preschooler grows steadily but at a slower rate than the infant and toddler rates. A comparison of 2- and 5-year-olds shows that the 5-year-old is not just taller but more slender and has proportionately longer legs than the toddler. Physical skills continue to develop steadily. Preschoolers can coordinate the movements of their muscles in gross motor activities like climbing, skipping, hopping, and running. They can throw or kick a ball and ride a tricycle. Because they are stronger and more coordinated, preschoolers thrive on physical activity. In the fine motor area, they become more and more adept at guiding their hands with their eyes. Improving eye–hand coordination enables them to cut with scissors, draw shapes such as a circle and a square, and by age 4 draw human figures that are recognizable. A 2½-year-old may draw a series of straight or circular lines and label them a person, but without the child's description one would not see a person in the drawing. A 4-year-old, by contrast, draws a person as two crossed lines with a circle on top—body, arms, head. She may also add details—fingers, eyes, mouth, hair. A 5-year-old can draw human figure that have more realistic proportions. (See Figures 8.1, 8.2, and 8.3.) Between 4 and 5, fine motor coordination improves enough for the child to be able to handle the fine points of dressing—zippers, buttons, and Velcro straps. Shoelace tying is harder and is usually not mastered until age 6 or 7. Overall, preschoolers take pleasure in the use of their bodies, which work much better than when they were toddlers.

FIGURES 8.1, 8.2, and 8.3. The progression of children's drawing abilities. Figure 8.1 (top left). Age 2 years, 11 months: "Me, my eyeballs, and my body." Figure 8.2 (bottom left). Age 4: "Me." Figure 8.3. (Bottom right). Age 5: "Me when I grow up."

ATTACHMENT

The preschooler continues to depend on the attachment relationship for feelings of security. The preschool child who has a history of secure attachment may show attachment behavior much like a 2-year-old's if she is feeling particularly distressed or anxious, very fatigued, ill or in pain. He may run to the parent and cling to her, crying and demanding the parent's attention. More often, however, securely attached preschoolers manage their attachment needs differently from infants and toddlers (Schneider-Rosen, 1990). Because a preschooler can verbalize his wishes, he is increasingly able to negotiate attachment issues with a parent. Bowlby (1969) pointed out that the preschool child's cognitive and verbal skills allow him to enter into a "partnership" with the parent around the goal of maintaining attachment. A familiar example of the child's negotiating ability happens at bedtime. The 4-year-old may say to his father, "I don't want you to go yet. Just read me one more story." His father may respond, "OK, I'll stay a couple more minutes, but then it's time to sleep." Increasing linguistic sophistication allows preschoolers to communicate their needs much more specifically than the toddler can. A child who has been upset by a separation can say, "Mommy, I wanted you and you weren't there!" Being able to communicate directly in words, with the assurance that the parent will understand those words, allows the child to feel more secure and in control (Crittenden, 1992b).

At the same time, improved memory, sense of time, and understanding of daily routines allows the child to use the parent's explanations to promote feelings of security. The 4-year-old can take in and remember a parent's words: "I'm going to be gone all day. You'll have lunch, take your nap, get up and have a snack, play with your friends, and *then* I'll come and pick you up." Cognitively, the 4-year-old is capable of using events in the routine of the child care center as markers in the progress of the day that tell her when to expect her parent to return. She may still miss her parent, but she now has a cognitive means of coping with a separation that the 2-year-old does not yet have. Although the child does not have a choice about the parent's leaving, she now has the ability to gain mastery over separation anxiety by thinking about the parent's absence, by understanding it as part of a plan. Further, the preschooler can draw on internal resources, which include her internal working models of attachment, without needing the actual help of the parent. Instead of needing the physical presence of the parent, she may represent and dramatize attachment seeking through doll play or family play with peers. Working models of secure attachment also give the child confidence in seeking support from other adults and peers.

Studies of Attachment History and Preschool Development

The quality of attachment during the first 3 years has important implications for preschoolers' development. Several longitudinal studies have assessed the effects of secure and insecure attachment patterns on later development. These studies have found consistency in attachment classification from infancy to age 6. Types of attachment at 12 and 18 months tend to persist through the preschool years, suggesting that parental caregiving styles, working models, and transactional patterns tend to be continuous, and also that internalized working models of attachment and self are being generalized by the child (Main & Cassidy, 1988). A consistent finding across studies is that secure attach-

TABLE 8.1. Research on Relationships between Attachment Patterns in Infancy and Functioning of Preschoolers

Preschool children with histories of secure attachment

Affect: emotional openness, more positive affect, full range of affects, good memories of attachment experiences, at age 6 (Main, Kaplan, & Cassidy, 1985; Main & Cassidy, 1988); capacity for modulation of affects and "situationally appropriate" expression of affects (Easterbrooks & Goldberg, 1990).

Self-regulation: ability to cope with anxiety adaptively, either by drawing of internal coping resources or by turning to an adult for help. This capacity for self-regulation, in turn, enables preschoolers to sustain exploration, play, and learning (Maslin-Cole & Spieker, 1990).

Generalization of attachment: readily turn to adult caregivers for support when parents are not available (Sroufe, 1983).

Peer relationships: show more positive affect in peer play and more engagement with peers; show positive expectations of interactions, have more friends, and become more popular with peers (Sroufe, 1989).

Sense of self: confident in solving problems, self-directed, appropriately independent and resourceful; adequate to high self-esteem (Sroufe, 1989).

Preschool children with histories of insecure attachment

Affect: defensive restrictions on affect and on memories of attachment experiences (Main, Kaplan, & Cassidy, 1985)

Self-regulation: difficulties in affect and behavior regulation, including over- or undercontrol of impulses, lower frustration tolerance, higher levels of anxiety, more negative affect (Easterbrooks & Goldberg, 1990)

Generalization of attachment: negative attention seeking, provocative or oppositional behavior toward adults, less comfort seeking from adults, precocious self-reliance, social withdrawal, tendencies to anxiously monitor caregivers' availability at the expense of developing relationships with peers; negative behavior tends to elicit controlling behavior by teachers, which often feels punitive to the child (Sroufe, 1983; J. E. Bates & Bayles, 1988; Cassidy, 1986)

Peer relationships: aggression and negative behavior toward peers; emotional distance, especially in preschoolers with avoidant attachment; exploitative and coercive peer interactions, often with an avoidantly attached child dominating an ambivalently attached child (La Freniere & Sroufe, 1985; Troy & Sroufe, 1987)

Sense of self: view of the self as incompetent, based on a history of feeling unable to elicit caretaking from parents; view of the self as not valuable or lovable, which contributes to depression as well as to angry, mistrustful, and oppositional behavior toward caregivers; negative behavior results in rejection by peers, further damaging self-esteem (Greenberg & Speltz, 1988; Sroufe, 1983) ment in infancy and toddlerhood predicts adaptive functioning during the preschool years whereas insecure attachment predicts some difficulties in functioning. A summary of these studies is presented in Table 8.1.

SOCIAL DEVELOPMENT

The preschool years are a bridge between the egocentric toddler and the more socially adept and aware child of the middle years. Preschoolers are learning how to be social, how to take others' perspectives into account. The tasks of social development for the preschooler include learning social skills, prosocial behavior and values, learning how to play with peers and how to establish friendships.

Preschoolers encounter many situations requiring social competence. New circumstances and developmental change contribute to the need to develop social abilities. Preschoolers are more likely than infants and toddlers to be cared for in large groups. At the same time, the preschool child's growing orientation toward peer relationships and cooperative play with peers motivates him to learn to get along with other children. A 3- to 4-year-old enters a new day care setting and has to find a way to break into an established peer group; or he wants to play with the blocks another child is already using.

Across the preschool years children advance in their strategies for reaching goals in social situations. Young preschoolers may try to get what they want in ways similar to those toddlers employ. A 3-year-old wants the toy another child is playing with and looks for an opportunity to simply take it. By age 4½, such physical means are increasingly supplanted by verbal strategies. She may say, "I want to play with that," or, in a more sophisticated approach, "Let's both play with the dishes, OK? I'll make spaghetti." New developments in communication skills and social understanding allow for this change in strategy. The child can express herself more easily now, and she is more able to take another's perspective, which means that she is aware that the other child would resent having the dishes taken away from her.

Prosocial Behavior

Although toddlers act in prosocial ways occasionally, they are most often concerned about their own self-interest and needs. Preschoolers show increases in prosocial actions between 3 and 6. Children learn values about prosocial behavior—sharing, comforting, helping, controlling aggression—through the ways they have been responded to by parents and others. Parents who model prosocial behavior through their caregiving and provide warmth, nurturance, and clear limits encourage incorporation of prosocial values as part of the child's over-all identification with parents (Clary & Miller, 1986). In addition, new cognitive skills such as role taking (the ability to see things from another's perspective), exposure to rules and expectations in the family and preschool settings, and exposure to peer group situations that require cooperation all influence the development of prosocial behavior.

Peer Relationships

During the preschool years, the child's relationships begin to focus more on peers, although parents remain the central people in the preschooler's life. This shift in orientation can be observed in preschools. A toddler who is dropped off at child care tends to look for a teacher as a substitute attachment figure. A 4-year-old, even though she may have warm relationships with her teachers, looks for her friends. She may see two other children she regularly plays with and ask, "What are you playing?"—or she may propose her own scenario. A 4- or 5-year-old identifies with her peers, intuitively seeing them as the people most like herself. Therefore, she comes to school oriented to telling them what is emotionally important to her—"Look at my new shoes," or, for a child who was scared and excited by fire engine sirens on her street the night before, "Let's say there was a big fire and we're firemen." She has come to expect responses from her peers, to be noticed, accepted, and praised by them.

The increasing valuation placed on the opinions of peers supports the preschooler's cognitive shift toward a more objective and complex view of the world. Egocentrism decreases as cognitive development proceeds. The 5- or 6-year-old is less egocentric because he is more able to take another's perspective. He sees that his point of view is not the only possible one and that the ideas of others must be taken into account. However, the decline of egocentrism is not simply a result of cognitive maturation, but rather is influenced transactionally by the child's experiences with peers (Piaget, 1951). The relative equality of power among peers, as compared with the child's relationships with adults, requires the child to take other children's wishes and ideas into account. As peer relationships become more important, beginning at about age 3, the child is increasingly motivated to have enjoyable interactions with peers and to be accepted by them. This motivation fuels the development of skills in perspective taking, negotiation, sharing, and cooperating (Piaget, 1951).

Many studies find links between the quality of early relationships with parents and the quality of preschoolers' peer relationships. If a child has had secure and satisfying relationships with parents during the first 3 years, he is likely to be oriented toward peers, to expect that contacts with others will be pleasurable. Toddlers who have experienced a secure base in the attachment relationship explore the environment more confidently, and this includes making contact with other children (Hartup, 1992). Preschoolers with histories of secure attachment have more advanced social abilities, in part because their working models contain positive expectations about relationships and in part because they have developed social skills through interactions with parents (Sroufe & Fleeson, 1986).

By contrast, insecure working models lead to assumptions that make it more difficult for the preschool child to enter the world of peers and to learn social skills in the context of peer interactions. Preschoolers with working models that assume a lack of responsiveness from others may not reach out socially because they are unsure of the response. Those with working models organized around assumptions of interpersonal anger and coercion may seek out or create conflictual situations that confirm their working models. These children may want to interact with peers; however, their efforts to control interactions combine with their impulsiveness and aggression to alienate other children (Rubin, Coplan, Fox, & Calkins, 1995). They may also misinterpret others' intentions, seeing aggression when none is intended, as a projection of their own aggressive feelings. Impulsive, aggressive behavior in the preschool is one of the most common reasons that preschool children are referred for evaluation. Both withdrawn and aggressive children have difficulty gaining skills though peer interactions during the preschool years. Children who shrink back from contact miss out on "the positive outcomes associated with exploration and peer play," whereas those who fight with and coerce their peers are rejected and miss out on "the benefits of cooperative peer play, peer negotiation and competition" (Rubin & Rose-Krasnor, 1992, p. 304).

In peer interactions, the preschool child learns a great deal about social behavior, building on what she has learned in her family: "Turn taking, sharing, control of aggression, empathy, helping, sex role learning, role taking, strategies of conflict resolution and moral reasoning all develop within the peer group as well as the family and appear to be central to the ability to establish friendships and maintain relationships with others" (Campbell, 1990, p. 142).

It should be emphasized, however, that these skills are in the process of developing during the preschool years. Observations of preschool children playing together document frequent conflicts, dis-agreements, aggressive actions, falling-outs, and disruptions of cooperative play (Shantz, 1987). Triangular dynamics emerge as children vie for each other's attention. Children's feelings are hurt because they are excluded or rebuffed. Egocentrism and possessiveness are common, as children try to force their fantasies on others or refuse to share toys. When conflict erupts, children may become physically aggressive or verbally rejecting (e.g., "You're not my friend!" or "I'm not inviting you to my birthday!"). Because of preschooler's wishes to be accepted and valued by peers, however, such conflicts become a laboratory for learning how to resolve conflicts (Shantz, 1987).

The inherent pleasure of fantasy play provides an additional motive for resolving conflict—if the conflict is overcome, play continues (Pellegrini & Jones, 1993). In one of many lovely examples in *Bad Guys Don't Have Birthdays: Fantasy Play at Four*, Vivian Gussen Paley (1988), a preschool and kindergarten teacher in Chicago, describes a conflict between three boys in a passionate disagreement about whether the play will be about Batman or He-Man. Two of the boys have ganged up on the other and are belittling his ideas. The interactional dynamic is complex because, in addition to the attempt to exclude one boy, there is a rivalry for the attention of Mollie, with each side appealing to her to join its fantasy:

CHRISTOPHER: What are you talkin' about? Mollie's never going to play with you. She's *my* friend.

BARNEY: Are you playing with him or us?

FREDERICK: Say us, say us.

In response, "Mollie purses her lips primly. 'I'm still friends with the whole of everyone. Nighttime, nighttime, everyone goes to bed. The rainbow is outside the window.'" (Paley, 1986, pp. 17–18). Mollie defuses the conflict by accepting all of them and then adeptly shifting the fantasy to include her favorite character, Rainbow Brite. The three boys, evidently relieved to be out of conflict and back in play, join her idea by agreeing to go to bed. Then they begin discussing the need for guards during the night and play resumes. Children like Mollie, who have a positive attitude and skills negotiating conflict, are usually popular among their peers, which in turn supports the development of their social competence (Campbell, 1990).

While preschool children popular with peers are friendly and socially competent, "aggressive and disruptive behavior enhance[s] the likelihood of social rejection, especially among boys" (Hartup, 1992,

p. 264). Preschoolers who are negative and aggressive toward others are often avoided and excluded by their peers, fueling a cycle of anger and further rejection. Without prompt and consistent intervention, the aggressive preschooler is likely to remain aggressive because, from his point of view, aggression works. Threats and physical aggression often cause other children to give up the toy he wants, so his behavior is reinforced (Rubin, Bream, & Rose-Krasnor, 1991). Longitudinal studies of peer relationships confirm that the quality of relationships developed during the preschool years persists into middle childhood (Dodge, 1983). The child who enters middle childhood with poor peer skills faces a big disadvantage, because then peer relationships become even more important as a source of personal competence and self-esteem.

Friendships

Although toddlers show preference for some peers over others, pre-school children begin to develop real friendships. Between 4 and 5, children begin to label other children as their friends and in group settings prefer to play with them (Hartup, 1992). For a young preschooler, a friend is someone she likes to play with. Older preschool children often pair up with a close friend in relationships that show other characteristics of friendship, including concern for the other child's feelings, wishes for approval, and displays of affection. These friendships are beginning forays into having a "best friend," which becomes so common during middle childhood. Hartup (1992) notes that because friends spend more time playing together, they have more conflicts, frequently over whose fantasy agenda will control the direction of play. Friends, as opposed to nonfriends, will work on solving these conflicts not just to keep the play going but because of mutual investment in the friendship (Hartup, 1992). Because friends have come to know each other's interests and preferences, they are more adept at keeping play going because they know what to do to reduce conflict.

At the same time, preschoolers with quiet, withdrawn temperaments or histories of insecure attachment may already be showing difficulty in establishing friendships. For example, a fearful or withdrawn child may shrink back from social play and become an outsider in the group. This reinforces his withdrawal and prevents him from learning the pleasures of friendship. Resiliency research has identified having friends as a protective factor and not having friends as a risk factor (Parker & Asher, 1987). Hartup (1996) summarizes these findings: "Children who have friends are more socially competent and less troubled than children who do not; they are more sociable, cooperative, altruistic, self-competent and less lonely" (p. 4). Children without friends have much higher rates of referral to mental health clinics (Rutter & Garmezy, 1983). The ability to make and keep friends depends on having good social skills; in turn, friendships support social development because they give children chances to learn how to interact, negotiate, and solve conflicts in order to keep the friend (Hartup, 1996). Having friends helps children cope with developmental transitions and other stressful situations. For example, children who enter kindergarten with friends or who make friends early in the year and maintain them show better attitudes toward school and better academic performance than those children who have difficulty making friends (Ladd, 1990).

Play and Social Development

The parallel play of toddlers persists into the early preschool years but is gradually replaced by more cooperative play. Two 3-year-olds riding tricycles side by side on the playground enjoy doing the same thing in parallel, but they do not say much to each other or give evidence of sharing a fantasy. By age 4 these children riding tricycles together may be engaged in a more complex and interactive form of play based on a shared idea. For example, they might be playing out a superhero fantasy; rather than simply riding together they are chasing bad guys, and their words and actions create a joint story:

CHILD 1: Batman, they went out by the swings. Let's get 'em.

CHILD 2: No, Robin, they've got laser guns. Let's go back to the Batcave and get our bazookas!

CHILD 1: OK! (*They turn and ride off in another direction.*)

Similarly, the "conversations" of 3-year-olds often sound like joint monologues, but they evolve into dialogues as the children move closer to 4.

Three-year-olds make the transition to cooperative play by watching the play of other children, gradually learning its forms, rituals, and "rules," and then beginning to take roles in it (Paley, 1986). By ages 4 and 5, a great deal of a child's play involves other children as they take roles in a shared scenario. Their conversations often sound like real dialogue, in which the perspective of the other is increasingly taken into account, as they plan and negotiate roles in fantasy play. Here is an example of three 4-year-olds getting started in fantasy play (Paley, 1986, p. 141):

CHRISTOPHER: Come on, Rainbow Brite, I hear a sound in the doll corner. I think it's the good witch.

MOLLIE: OK, Starlite. Margaret, you can be Rainbow's kitty . . . Starlite horsey, come get your food now. Once more now. Time for bed now, horsey. Go to sleep.

CHRISTOPHER: I tricked you Rainbow Brite . . . Lurky is coming! He's coming in the back of us. He might be scaring us!

MOLLIE: Don't worry, Starlite. I put the magic trap under the door. Then we'll give him the poison drink. Don't touch this. It's the poison drink.

CHRISTOPHER: It's poison mud.

MARGARET: Meow, I'm afraid of Lurky.

MOLLIE: I'll keep you safe, little kitty, because Rainbow Brite has powers.

CHRISTOPHER: Yeah, but I got superpower . . . I'm super Starlite! Super Starlite! I never go to sleep to watch for bad guys. I kick at them with my hind legs!

In this brief interchange a number of things occur. One child announces a theme for the play based on characters and scenarios the other two children are familiar with. They quickly assign or take roles and the play begins, with turns in the plot being negotiated on the fly as the drama unfolds. The two principal actors, Mollie and Christopher, have different, gender-influenced ideas about what the story should be about (caretaking vs. danger), but they accept each other's fantasy and Mollie, in particular, finds ways to accommodate Christopher's wishes in order to keep the story going. Implicitly these 4-year-olds are learning and practicing skills in perspective taking, negotiation of differences, problem solving, and cooperation.

LANGUAGE DEVELOPMENT

At the beginning of the preschool period at age 3, the rapid acquisition of words between 2 and 3 has resulted in a vocabulary of 1,000 words. Vocabulary continues to increase by about 50 words each month. By age 3, the child has learned the question form. His ability to ask "why" and "what" gives him power over his own learning. The responses of parents and caregivers to his frequent questions increase his vocabulary. The normal 3-year-old's speech is clear and easy to understand.

By age 4, he is speaking in long sentences (8–10 words) that are gram-matically complex and include relative and dependent clauses. By age 7, it is estimated that the child understands about 14,000 words (Rice, 1989).

By age 4, children have mastered language sufficiently to tell a story using words alone. By contrast, toddlers, because they know fewer words and have not mastered grammar, tend to combine words with actions in order to communicate. Increasingly, during the pre-school years, children rely on language over action to express them-selves. Older preschoolers have learned that words are useful and powerful. Their ability to use language has become creative and flexi-ble. Imaginative play also relies more on language.

One of the most salient tasks of the preschooler is to learn to dis-tinguish between fantasy and reality. The development of language supports the development of reality testing. However, between 3 and 4 years of age, the struggle is compounded by the fact that the child is still trying to define and remember the meaning of words. Although the development of language lays the groundwork for an increasingly clear and consensual understanding of reality, at age 3 a child is both wondering if monsters exist and what the word "monster" actually means. It is easy to get confused. Words still have an abstract quality, on the one hand, and they do not mean the same thing to each child, on the other. It is often difficult for young preschoolers to see words as representing a consensual reality; rather, their meanings are more linked to the idiosyncratic reality of each child's experience. This is another reason why play is so important to young preschoolers. By acting out their ideas in play, they can show others what they mean. Action for a 3-year-old is a much more real and reliable mode of self-expression than mere words. However, by 4 and 5 years of age the child's ability to express meaning through language has improved a great deal, and play interactions increasingly rely on words to set the scene and maintain the themes of the play scenario. For example, one 4-year-old boy says to another, "Let's say I'm Jim and you're Long John Silver, and we're going to get to the island, but there are croco-diles in the ocean." They kill the crocodiles and reach the island, but one child continues to shoot his gun at the crocodiles. The other child redirects the play, in accordance with his fantasy, by saying, "No, we killed the crocodiles and now we're gonna' look for the treasure!" If his playmate now agrees, as he presumably does, language has served to organize and perpetuate the play.

Preschoolers talk to themselves a great deal, saying out loud what older children and adults say to themselves in silent thought. "Private speech" accompanies preschoolers' activities and seems to function as self-direction (Berk, 1992). The 4-year-old girl playing by herself with a dollhouse carries out a running commentary that describes what is happening and plans what will happen next: "Now the mommy is going to change the baby's diaper. The baby says, 'Ma-ma, I want my dinner now.' So the mommy goes to the store to get food." Or a 4-year-old boy building with blocks says to himself, "I gotta put the triangle one up here—carefully, so it doesn't fall." Private speech also helps the child exert self-control, as when a child repeats parents' limit-setting words to himself: "Don't run in the house, Amani."

SYMBOLIC COMMUNICATION AND PLAY

Preschool children love to play. Their play is more complex and imaginative than a toddler's, but it is less constrained by rules and adherence to reality than is the play of a school-age child. Play takes on a number of functions that support progressive development. During the preschool period, play takes two primary directions, which in practice are often combined. The first involves exploration of reality and especially social roles. By dressing up as adults or even as Teenage Mutant Ninja Turtles, the preschooler is exploring in fantasy what he may become. The second direction of preschool play involves using play for the mastery of stress and anxiety, as well as for the expression of wishes and fears. The 4-year-old boy's superhero play represents an attempt to master anxiety connected with the young child's growing perception that he's a small person in a big world who is incompetent compared to adults. The process of imagining and carrying out play scenarios supports the development of cognitive skills, such as planning and problem solving, as well as providing the child with opportunities to exercise autonomy and initiative (Piaget, 1962). Play facilitates understanding of emotions and perspective taking: children in dramatic play express strong emotions and must empathize to some degree with each others' ideas and feelings. The negotiation and cooperative planning that occur spontaneously in dramatic play strengthens the child's capacity for self-control. In order to stay within the play scenario, preschoolers will control impulses to act in ways that do not fit the drama they are acting in.

Play Reflects Reality But Is Outside Reality

Winnicott (1971) described play as transitional activity that takes place in a zone between the individual's subjective reality and external reality. The preschool child's play expresses her private fantasies in the public forum of the group of players, yet the play they create is not bound by the rules of reality. In dramatic play, the imaginable is possible. Bad guys can be killed by laser swords, then rise from the dead to fight again. Princesses are transformed into mothers and then into superheroines. Anger, rudeness, competitive feelings, disappointment, affection, and grandiosity can be expressed in the pretend scenario without eliciting the same responses they might if expressed in reality. Play allows the child to comment on and try to understand reality through a make-believe medium that is under the child's control and therefore more easily manipulated than the actual world (J. L. Singer, 1993).

Increasingly, the players acknowledge that they are pretending. While preschoolers sometimes have difficulty distinguishing between fantasy and reality, when they are playing they have no trouble with this distinction. Children know very well when they are intentionally operating within the play frame and when they are not (Bretherton, 1986). The imaginative social play of 4- and 5-year-olds almost always begins with the establishment of roles: "I'll be Robin and you be Batgirl, OK?" Preschoolers signal the beginning of play in many ways—by saying "We're playing now" or "Let's say we're on the ice planet" or by a dramatic look or gesture. In the pretend scenario, the child sets his personal identity aside and becomes a character sometimes inspired by adult models, sometimes by figures from the media.

Even though the preschooler changes his identity in play, the play almost always reflects psychological themes and issues that are salient for the preschool child: the imitation of adult behavior; caretaking; practicing of parental, gender, and occupational roles; concerns about body damage and physical vulnerability; and mastery of danger. At times, however, both in peer play and play therapy, the play frame is not strong enough to contain frightening affects and a child breaks off the play. If one child begins to inject too much aggression into play or becomes a particularly frightening character, another child may step out of the play frame and say, "No, I don't want to play that. It's too scary" (Bretherton, 1986). Play therapists are also familiar with play disruption when the content of the play produces so much anxiety for the child that he must stop it. This frequently occurs when a child unconsciously realizes that he is "going too far." For example, Gregory, a 4-year-old boy I was seeing in therapy, was having two puppets fight: one was a shark, and the other a girl. The shark took the girl's head in its mouth, and Gregory shouted, "He bit her head off!" Then he abruptly put the puppets down and said, "I want to play with the house now." It was unclear to me whether this play disruption was caused by aggressive feelings (toward his younger sister) that felt too strong or by anxiety about body damage. Probably both factors were involved.

Play and Cognitive Development

Play and fantasy create opportunities for the development of cognitive skills during the preschool years. The preschool child uses play to "think" about her experience, considering alternative ways of viewing it, and exploring new ways of acting (J. L. Singer, 1993). In symbolic play, the preschooler practices and increases her understanding of cause-and-effect thinking, construction of narrative, and perspective taking (Connolly & Doyle, 1984). By 5 and 6 years of age, children can increasingly describe their experiences in words. This development is not related simply to the accumulation of vocabulary. Rather, it is a result of cognitive abilities supported by and in part developed through playing. Play increases the child's capacity for mental representation by dramatizing in action the child's thoughts and feelings, putting what starts out as an imagined idea into a tangible scenario the child can see in front of her. After a few years of such practice it becomes easier to organize one's thoughts in more purely mental ways, using words rather than action. The ability to mentally organize experience in narrative form promotes clarity of understanding, which in turn has been identified as a protective factor for school-age children who are exposed to stress. Such "representational competence" mitigates the impact of stress and may prevent traumatization, because the child is able to take a more objective and comprehensive view of what has happened (Anthony & Cohler, 1987; Beardslee, 1989). Such findings about the transactional relationship between play and cognitive development suggest that imaginative play and fantasy, rather than simply being regarded as entertainment for the child, should be strongly supported by parents and caregivers during the preschool years (D. G. Singer & J. L. Singer, 1990).

COGNITIVE DEVELOPMENT

Between 3 and 6 years of age, the preschooler's thought gradually matures to allow for clearer perception of reality. Memory improves because the child has a bigger knowledge base that provides associations and categories for new information. Unlike the toddler, for whom new experiences often seem individual and different from one another, the preschool child generalizes similar experiences. Increasingly, he thinks categorically, using mental representations of previous similar experiences to understand new ones. If a child can link a new experience or piece of information to an existing mental category, he is more likely to remember it.

In turn, having a larger fund of knowledge allows the preschooler to be a more flexible thinker than the toddler. As a result, preschool children are more adept at assimilating new experiences and unexpected events into their play and thought. For example, a 3½-year-old girl is loading a doll family into a toy plastic van to go on a shopping trip. As she is tipping the top section of the van open so that the doll family will go in more easily, the top unexpectedly comes off, leaving just the floor and seats attached to the wheels. A glimmer of surprise crosses her face; then she says, "They wanted the top off so the sun can shine in. They're going to the beach."

The motivation to assimilate new information is based in turn on the child's increasing perception of the complexities of the world. It is useful to think of a 4- to 5-year-old as a person who is realizing that reality is more complicated than he thought, that causality is mysterious, that there are surprising connections between things, and that there is a great deal he does not know. In response to this awareness, he asks many questions and tries out different versions of reality as he plays. The 4- or 5-year-old's questions about "the big questions" imply surprise, curiosity, and anxiety. He wants to know how God makes rain fall from the sky and what kind of germs make people die. How does a small seed buried in the ground become a bush with tomatoes covering it? A 5-year-old asked his parents, "*How* do you love each other?" Paley (1988) points out that "a relentless connection-making" (p. 12) goes on in the play and dialogue of preschoolers as they attempt to understand reality.

Egocentric Thinking: The Preschooler's Perspective

Jean Piaget (1962) described toddlers and preschoolers (his *preoperational period* encompassing the ages of 2–7) as characterized by egocentric thinking. Egocentrism means that the child sees the world from her own perspective and has difficulty seeing another person's point of view. An aspect of egocentrism is an assumption that everyone thinks and feels the same way as she does. Piaget argued that children during this stage are not able to take another person's perspective. More recent experimental research suggests that the capacity to see things from another person's point of view is gradually developing during the preschool period. At 4½ and 5, children can frequently acknowledge another's ideas, particularly in the context of cooperative play (Mossler, Marvin, & Greenberg, 1976). Researchers on prosocial behavior have demonstrated that, as early as age 2, children can sometimes empathize with the feelings of others.

A well-known recent Piaget-like experiment documents that age 4 may be an important dividing line for perspective taking. In this experiment an adult and a child watch an experimenter put a toy under a box. After the adult leaves the room, the experimenter removes the toy, puts it under a second box, and asks the child, "Where will she look for the toy when she comes back?" Children under 4 point to the second box, where the toy is currently. They focus on the toy's present location and are unable to imagine that the person who does not know the toy as been moved would still think it was under the first box. Increasing numbers of 4- and 5-year-olds understand that the adult will look where the toy was when she left the room, and 6-year-olds universally realize this. This experiment suggests that between 4 and 6 years of age, children are increasingly capable of imagining another's perspective even though it differs from their own (Wellman, 1990).

In spite of these refinements of Piaget's theory, the consistent capacity for nonegocentric thinking does not seem to be fully available to the child until near the end of the preschool period. We often see in clinical cases that the capacity to think in nonegocentric ways is influenced by emotionality, arousal, and stress. A 5-year-old who can show perspective-taking skills in an experimental situation may think egocentrically in a stressful real situation that causes arousal and fear. For example, 5-year-old who is put in time-out because he has hit another child is likely to feel unfairly treated. Although he may have some notion that he is being punished for aggressive behavior, his primary response will be egocentric—at an emotional level in the immediate moment he will feel mistreated. Preschool children also have difficulty sorting out the intentions of others (Shantz, 1987). For example, if another child bumps into a preschooler accidentally, the latter may assume that the act was done on purpose because he was hurt. The ability for perspective taking is present but fragile during the preschool years. In social work practice, it is important to watch for evidence of distortions and misunderstandings based on egocentric thinking, especially for children who have been exposed to stressful or traumatic events and relationships.

Characteristics of Egocentric Thinking

The following features of egocentric thinking decrease as the child gets older, but they are also subject to the impact of stress:

Understanding of Cause and Effect

The preschooler tends to see a cause-and-effect relationship between things that happen at about the same time. He cannot understand that there can be remote or unseen causes. When combined with an egocentric viewpoint, this can lead to serious misunderstandings of reality. For example, a 3-year-old girl whose parents had recently separated said, "Daddy left because we were jumping on the bed that night." In situations of high arousal or strong affect, preschoolers may reverse cause and effect, seeing themselves egocentrically as causative agents. For example, another 4-year-old boy whose parents had divorced explained, "My mommy and daddy got a divorce because they both wanted me to live at their house." It is a short step from thoughts like this to feeling responsible for the parents' separation.

Transductive Reasoning

This is a form of associational thinking in which the child over-generalizes the results of past experiences. Elkind and Weiner (1978) describe this associational logic as follows:

> A and B occur together
> A is present
> [Therefore] B must be present. (p. 243)

For example, a preschooler was scared by a loud thunderclap and tornado-warning sirens just as she was entering her child care center. The next day she fearfully refused to get out of the car when they arrived at the center. Her father was perceptive in connecting her present anxiety with what happened the previous day and reassured her that there would not be a storm. He pointed out that the sky was clear. It is not always so easy to understand when a child is using transductive reasoning, yet preschoolers' stubborn or seemingly irrational behavior is frequently caused by this type of thinking (Elkind & Weiner, 1978).

Personalism

Evident in the previous examples is the preschooler's tendency to personalize events. Rather than being able to think in generalizing or universalizing terms, the preschooler thinks in terms of himself. Paley (1988) writes about a 4-year-old, "Frederick responds to questions about boys and their grandfathers as if they are about himself and *his* grandfather" (p. 12). This characteristic has implications for storytell-ing in therapy. It is often useful for the therapist to tell a story about "another kid I knew" that presents the issues a child is struggling with. The story can present an adaptive solution or more accurate explanation for the child's problem. Preschoolers, as well as somewhat older children, will feel less anxious if the story is about someone else, yet will personalize the story and apply it to themselves.

Animism

The younger preschooler projects her own feelings and characteristics onto inanimate objects, believing that a wave that splashed in her face did it on purpose or that a scratch on the face of a plastic doll must hurt.

Judging Reality by Surface Appearances Rather Than Using Reasoning

Some of Piaget's best-known experiments involved conservation of number and quantity. In one test preschool children were shown 10 vases, each with a single flower in it. The flowers were removed and bunched together. When the flowers are closer together, the preschool child will say there are fewer flowers, whereas a 7-year-old will say that the number of flowers remains the same. For the preschooler appearance alters perception, whereas the 7-year-old uses logic to understand that if none of the flowers have been taken away, the same number remains no matter how they are arranged. In another test, Piaget showed children two identical short, wide glasses filled with equal amounts of water. When he poured the contents of one into a taller, slender glass and asked if one of the glasses had more water in it, preschool children said that there was more in the taller glass. Older children, by contrast, said the amount in each glass was the same because they knew that the actual amount of water had not changed (Piaget & Inhelder, 1969). More recent researchers have documented earlier conservation abilities and have argued that "given the appro-priate wording and context, the child seems capable of demonstrating at least some of the abilities which, in Piaget's view, would not appear until later" (Smith & Cowie, 1991, p. 334). Nevertheless, it is useful to keep in mind the broader implications of Piaget's research: preschool children tend to interpret reality by observing surface qualities, and their capacity for reasoning about changes in reality has not yet devel-oped.

Magical Thinking and the Fusion of Fantasy and Reality

The characteristics of preschool thinking described above cause preschoolers to think in magical terms that compromise accurate perceptions of reality. Although they are working to understand reality, their capacity for reality testing is not well established. They have difficulty distinguishing between wishes and what really happens; they tend to impose wishes onto reality, often because they want to feel powerful and in control; and they still believe that thoughts and strong feelings can cause things to happen. They tend to believe that dreams can come true. When they have a frightening dream, they often believe it really happened. Since dreams are not under the child's conscious control, he cannot easily see them as imaginary. Rather, they have the power of reality because they seem to the young child to come from outside himself (Estes, Wellman, & Wooley, 1989).

MAGICAL THINKING IN A 4-YEAR-OLD:
A BRIEF CASE EXAMPLE

To demonstrate the qualities of magical thinking, here is an example from a treatment session with a 4-year-old boy. Brandon had a close relationship with his mother, which was changed by the mother's remarriage. His new stepfather was somewhat distant from him. He felt left out because of his mother's new relationship, and he wanted to regain a more exclusive relationship with his mother by getting rid of his stepfather. He had confided to his mother that he wished his stepfather would go away. But his fantasies of getting rid of his step-father would provoke counterfantasies involving Brandon's being retaliated against by powerful monsters or robbers. As E. H. Erikson (1963) notes, the preschooler's wish to be powerful competes with feelings of vulnerability based on guilt over aggressive thoughts: "The child indulges in fantasies of being a giant and a tiger, but in his dreams he runs in terror for dear life" (p. 256). Brandon was having scary dreams, which caused him to feel very anxious, because he still believed that dreams might come true. I had told him that I often learned about kids' feelings by hearing about their dreams, and Brandon sometimes described his dreams. In this session, Brandon said, "Lets talk about dreams some more. I have a burning sword that can chop people's necks." I said, "I don't think you've really got a burning sword, but was that in a dream?" "Yeah, I took my sword and chopped everybody on the neck, every robber. But a skeleton knocked the sword out my hand. Then he chased me." I said, "Sometimes when boys have chopping feelings, they get worried that something bad could happen to them because they have those feelings. In your dream, you chopped the robber's neck and then got worried, and the skeleton shows your worry."

Brandon said, "I had another dream. A king cobra with a hood came up from a hole at the end of my bed and bit my feet." I said, "That sounds like a scary dream." He said, "In fact there really was a king cobra in my bed because I saw it and I could feel it biting my feet." He pointed to his heels. "Right now I can feel those bites, they're still hurting." I said, "I'm sure there wasn't a king cobra in your bed and you weren't really bitten, but your dream must have seemed very real." He said, "No, there's a hole in my bed where the snake came out!" I said, "I don't think that's true." He said, "That's right, really I peed my bed and my pee spot looked like a hole." I said, "Yes, the hole was really your pee spot, but the dream seemed so real that you started to get mixed up and think that the dream really happened."

For Brandon, a real event—waking up to find he'd wet the bed— became the inspiration for a fantasy. This particular fantasy—being bitten by a cobra that crawled up through the "pee spot" hole—may be influenced by guilty feelings about having wet the bed. The technique I have illustrated focuses on empathizing with the child's fears but clarifying what is real and what is not. Some therapists emphasize the control of fears through symbolic means, for example, by asking a child to draw a picture of a bad dream and then destroy it (Webb, 1996), or putting a picture of nighttime fears into a locked box (White & Epston, 1990).

The Influence of Affective Arousal on Preschoolers' Reality Testing

Academic studies show that by age 4 children know the distinction between an imaginary object and a real, physical object. For example, 4-year-olds know they can change a pretend scenario by imagining it differently. They realize that "mental images can be manipulated by mental effort" (Wooley, 1995, p. 185). A 4-year-old can imagine herself lifting a heavy boulder—she makes it light with her imagination. This same child knows that she could not lift a real boulder. When asked why she could lift the pretend rock but not a real one, a 4-year-old will readily answer, "because it's make-believe." However, this apparently firm distinction between fantasy and reality can become tenuous when a preschooler is under stress or influenced by fearful affects. Even in academic experimental studies, if frightening images such as monsters or other images with strong emotional content are introduced, preschoolers' ability to differentiate between fantasy and reality becomes compromised (Samuels & Taylor, 1994).

Context influences preschoolers' reality testing more than older children's. For example, preschoolers are more likely to believe in monsters or witches at bedtime, when it is dark and they are in the position of having to give themselves up to sleep. Every night a 4-year-old girl would leap onto her bed from a distance of a few feet. She explained that if she jumped the witch under the bed would not be able to grab her feet. During the day if she was asked if the witch was real, she would say, "Well, not really." A 6-year-old boy told me his nightmares were caused by a blank space on his wall next to his bed. He said, "Everywhere else in my room there are toys, and if I look at them I get happy dreams, but if I look at the blank space, I'll have bad dreams." He said maybe the person who built the apartment had put bad stuff in the wall that makes him have the bad dreams. When I asked what he thought was in the wall, he said, "I really don't think there's something in there really. It's my imagination." However, this child's capacity to distinguish fantasy from reality was only of limited use to him, because he was still having bad dreams. Since he had attributed them to the blank space, he was no less afraid to look at it before he fell asleep.

Experimental studies have shown that preschoolers have more difficulty than school-age children in differentiating between memories of actual events and imaginary events or dreams. A 4-year-old is much more likely than an 8-year-old to say that an imagined event really happened (Foley, Harris, & Hermann, 1994). The relationship between fantasy and reality for a preschooler is fluid, and in memory images of what really happened and what the child imagines tend to merge with one another. This has important implications for the treatment of preschoolers who have experienced disturbing or traumatic events. Traumatized individuals benefit from help in creating a trauma story—an account of what happened—and from the systematic correction of distortions of thinking and perception based on posttraumatic internal imagery and environmental reminders. For young children, a focus on distortions and misunderstandings is particularly important because of their developmentally based tendency to fuse fantasy and reality (Terr, 1991).

Preschoolers' behavioral symptoms are sometimes based on such distortions. For example, teachers at 3½-year-old Tisha's child care center asked me to interview her because she had suddenly become aggressive toward other children and had been trying to paint the mouths of other children with red paint. When I asked if she had any worried or scary feelings, she told me about a physical fight between her estranged parents: "My daddy came over. He fought my mama. My mama fell down, and her mouth got bloody. My daddy fell down. His mouth got bloody. I fell down, and my mouth got bloody. I fell out of the car on my mouth. It got all bloody." Tisha's mental representation of this frightening scene turned out to contain cognitive distortions. Her mother confirmed that Tisha's father had in fact hit her (the mother) and bloodied her mouth, and that she had fallen down. That much was an accurate description of what happened, but the rest of Tisha's account was not. Her father had not fallen down, nor had she, nor had she fallen out of a car. The only person bleeding had been her mother. Fear and confusion about what happened became generalized for Tisha, in the form of distorted memories, fears about future vulnerability at school or in the car, anxiety-based aggression at school, and "action memories" of putting red paint on other kids' mouths.

Tension between Fantasy and Reality

The preschooler lives with a tension between different ways of thinking about the world. The first way is the egocentric and magical thought of the toddler. In this mode, the child's wishes, fantasies, and dreams influence and sometimes dominate perception. The second way resembles the more mature thought of the school-age child. It is more objective and logical, and reflects the child's strong motivation to understand reality. During the preschool years these modes of thinking coexist and alternate. The direction is toward logical thinking, but during this transitional period, when magical thinking remains prominent, the young child's capacity to think logically is frequently compromised by stress, emotionality, disappointments, and compensatory wishes.

Preschoolers demonstrate their wish to hold on to a magical view of the world through their fascination with events that occur miraculously and beings that cannot be seen. Preschool children believe in things they cannot see, like the tooth fairy, and they love to create fantasies about unseen things. These fantasies often reflect their wishes. Paley, in her book *Wally's Stories* (1981), quotes extensively from conversations between five 5-year-olds. For example, she asked children how they knew the tooth fairy was real, and the following discussion ensued (pp. 41–42):

WALLY: The tooth fairy came into my room and woke me up.

TEACHER: What did she look like?

WALLY: She was pretty and had long hair.

TEACHER: Was she old?

WALLY: Not as old as a grand person. As old as you. She put an envelope with money under my pillow.

TEACHER: Tanya says the tooth fairy can't get into her house. Her daddy locks all the doors and windows.

WARREN: She flies through the glass.

WALLY: No, she comes in through the roof.

TEACHER: Where does she get all the money?

WALLY: From the bank.

DEANA: He's right. I *saw* her at the bank. She had purple shoes and red hair.

ANDY: Did she talk to you?

DEANA: She doesn't speak English. I think she talks in Chinese.

EDDIE: Does she, Warren? [Warren is Chinese-American.]

WARREN: Probably she does.

This conversation reveals the preschool child's tendency to interweave fantasy and reality, and presents the tension between the two modes of thinking. The tooth fairy can fly through closed windows, yet she gets her money from the bank. Perhaps Deana did see a woman with red hair and purple shoes who looked exotic enough to be the tooth fairy, and so Deana (at least for the purpose of this discussion) assumed that she was. These children simultaneously show their belief in magic and their attempt to assimilate magic with the concrete reality of everyday experience.

REGULATION OF AFFECT AND BEHAVIOR

Increased Self-Control and Inhibition of Impulses

During the preschool years, the child continues to rely on attachment behavior when under stress, but she also makes considerable gains in regulating feelings and impulses on her own. The preschool child increasingly makes use of interpersonal coping skills, internalized defense mechanisms, and even cognitive strategies for dealing with anxiety and distress. Cognitive development makes contributions to the preschool child's ability to exert self-control and inhibit impulses. In part these new cognitive abilities promote feelings of control because they allow the child to understand reality better, so that she is less frequently reactive in the face of experiences that are new or surprising. Factors contributing to increasing capacity to delay or inhibit impulses include the following:

Ability to Imagine and Anticipate Consequences of Behavior

Improving memory and previous social learning allow the child to remember previous consequences and to make choices about future actions on the basis of those memories. A child rejected by peers for destroying their fort by pulling a blanket off the chairs it was draped over sometimes is able to inhibit his impulse the next time because he does not want to be rejected again. It is important to note, however, that having an ability does not mean the preschooler always uses it. The intensity of the preschooler's wishes often causes impulsive actions.

Increasing Categorization of Experience

Increasing categorization of experience permits generalization across similar experiences. For example, a child who has had several baby-sitters is able to control her apprehension about what the new babysitter will be like.

Inner Speech and Private Speech

The preschool child can talk to herself in order to sort out what is happening and what she plans to do. This gives her a sense of control. She can also remind herself about rules, prohibitions, and expectations, either silently or out loud, in order to guide her behavior.

Increasing Awareness of Social Expectations

The child has internalized ideas about acceptable behavior and is beginning to recognize when he has the impulse to break the rules.

Ability to Displace Real World Concerns and Anxiety into Fantasy Play

Children use play to compensate for feelings of inadequacy and fears. The 4-year-old, for example, may be anxious about the fact that she is smaller and less competent than adults but compensates by playing adult roles or becoming idealized characters who represent power in her dramatic play. By becoming the powerful queen or heroine, she temporarily diminishes and masters feelings of inadequacy.

Sources of Anxiety for Preschoolers

Some of the sources of anxiety for toddlers—separation fears, problems with self-expression, fear of losing control—cause less pronounced anxiety in preschoolers. Developmental advances have rendered these concerns less stressful. But the preschooler experiences other typical sources of distress and anxiety:

Reactions to Aggressive Feelings

Preschool children are working hard to develop self-control, particularly over aggression, but also over wishes to be dependent. When they are unsuccessful at controlling aggression, they may become anxious about the results of their aggressive behavior and about the internal experience of being overwhelmed by anger. The child who is aggressive may already be a fearful child, particularly if he has been treated harshly or exposed to violence; however, the child's egocentric view of his aggressive thoughts and behavior may intensify his anxiety because he assumes that others have similar impulses.

Fear of Being Displaced in the Parents' Affections

Given that many families space their children at 2- to 3-year intervals, the birth of a sibling is a normative event—and a normative source of anxiety—for many preschoolers. During the mother's pregnancy the young child thinks about the baby and worries about being displaced. Volterra (1984) documents the thoughts and behavior of a 2½-year-old boy. After this child learned about the coming baby, he became aggressive toward his dolls and younger children. He developed a play scenario in which he, as a policeman, kicked a "bad boy" out of the house (Volterra, 1984). The timing of the baby may temporarily interfere with the preschooler's movement toward autonomy. In response to anxiety about being less loved, he may show regressive behavior that aims to get his mother to take care of him, as proof that she loves him. When he is at child care or nursery school, he may imagine that his mother and his younger sibling are at home having a wonderful time together. As his sibling gets older he may feel threatened by her developing motor skills and his parents' admiration of them. Finally, he must cope with unacceptable anger toward his mother and the baby, which increases his anxiety. Of course, parents find many ways to help the older child cope, by continuing to support his autonomous functioning, tolerating his temporary regressions, and encouraging his relationship with the baby.

Failures in the Control of Bodily Functions

A preschooler who has mastered urinary and bowel control is upset by lapses in toilet training. The child who wets himself during the day or wets the bed after a period of dryness is distressed by such lapses. Often failures in control indicate reactions to other types of stress—a separation from a parent, the birth of a sibling, or intense arguments between parents. However, parents may increase the child's anxiety by putting pressure on him to stay dry. Brazelton (1992) recommends addressing the primary sources of the child's anxiety, rather than focusing on the lapse in toilet training.

Fear and Distress about Being Rejected by Peers

The increasing social orientation of the preschool child means that she is sensitive to how peers perceive her, and by age 5 she may be aware of her reputation and standing in the peer group. To be rejected, teased, or excluded can cause great pain and anger. Because a preschool child thinks egocentrically and still lacks the ability to evaluate the intentions of others, she may hear another child's insult—"You're a stupid poopy-diaper baby"—as if it were true, and react with humiliation and rage. They experience such insults as attacks on their whole person.

Fears Caused by Inadequate Reality Testing and Magical Thinking

The preschooler's ability to distinguish fantasy and reality, especially under conditions of stress, is not reliable. Consequently, young children may become anxious in response to bad dreams, or films or TV programs that show graphic violence or scenes of horror, because they experience the content as if it were reality. Increasing knowledge of the frightening aspects of life can also become a source of anxiety. Learning about death, kidnapping, burglars, or plane crashes can create anxiety because the child personalizes these catastrophes imagining them as happening to himself or his parents. For example, a 4-year-old whose babysitter told him that he could not stay in the car alone at a shopping center because children were sometimes kidnapped out of cars began to shadow his mother everywhere at home because he was afraid of being kidnapped. The preschooler's dilemma is that his cognitive development is advanced enough to allow him to create images of unseen danger, yet not advanced enough to appraise how realistic his fear is.

Attachment History and Self-Regulation

L. A. Sroufe's longitudinal study of attachment has demonstrated that preschoolers with secure attachment histories continue to turn to adults, such as child care providers and teachers, for support when they are distressed. Their working models lead them to anticipate that they will receive help when they need it. Consequently they seek attention in positive rather than negative ways. Preschoolers with secure attachment histories also show good ability to manage impulses. They are assertive but not aggressive.

By contrast, preschoolers with avoidant attachment histories tend not to turn to adults for help in regulating distress. The working models of attachment and self that develop out of the avoidant pattern suggest that others cannot be relied upon for support and that the self is not worthy of being helped. Preschool children with avoidant attachments may turn away from caregivers if they fall and hurt themselves, or huddle in a corner if they are feeling ill. These children also have much higher rates of aggression than children with secure attachments, suggesting both that they feel more hostility and have less ability to regulate aggressive impulses (Sroufe, 1983, 1989).

Preschoolers with such difficulties can be helped to move toward more adaptive social relationships if a preschool teacher makes extraordinary efforts to establish an an attachment with the child. When a therapist is working with a preschooler with behavioral problems secondary to attachment difficulties, intervention must include not only work with parents but also consultation with the child's day care providers.

Strategies for Self-Regulation and Coping

New self-regulatory capacities emerge during the preschool years that make autonomous self-regulation more and more possible. Nevertheless, we should think of the preschooler as on the way to self-regulation, rather than having achieved it. Compared with school-age children, preschoolers are more volatile and less able to maintain consistent self-control. The preschooler increasingly relies on the following self-regulatory strategies:

Play and Fantasy as Displacement of Negative Affects and Impulses

Play increasingly has the function of containing anxiety through displacement. Rather than risk the anxiety that accompanies the direct expression of forbidden aggression, the child displaces aggressive and other negative impulses into play. Paley (1988) catches this idea as she describes the dramatic play of 4-year-olds: "How easy, in play, to disguise the feelings represented by the actions. The more I listen, the more the play seems motivated by that which *cannot* be discussed" (p. 45; emphasis in original).

> In a play therapy example, 5-year-old Andrew had become very rivalrous toward his 2½-year-old brother. His brother had recently been praised by their parents for his successful toilet training. Andrew's play became a vehicle for representing his angry perception that his parents appreciated his brother more than himself. Andrew brought a dinosaur he called Chompers to the session. Chompers attacked family dolls, especially a little brother doll, who was punished for unnamed reasons by being thrown across the room and given a potion that would keep him at the age of 1 forever. Chompers's aggression toward the dolls gave Andrew a vicarious outlet for angry feelings toward his parents and his younger brother. His anger was expressed through the play, rather than directly and consciously. I commented on his play as representing the difficult feelings children have when they feel their parents favor a sibling. Like Andrew, I used displacement, couching my statements in universalizing terms about the feelings of children in general rather than Andrew in particular.

Internalization of Dyadic Regulatory Strategies

During the first 3 years of life, the child, and parents have established transactional strategies for regulating affect. These strategies, which originated in the attachment relationship, may generalize into behavioral styles of managing anxiety. The preschooler begins to use the social abilities and prosocial attitudes learned in the attachment relationship in peer relations. Children who use these skills to mediate conflicts and disputes with peers feel successful and more in control. They are also popular with other children (La Freniere & Sroufe, 1985).

Conscious Inhibition of Emotional Expression and Arousal

Preschool children have a beginning ability to consciously control their emotional responses. One can see 4- to 5-year-olds, especially boys who are socialized not to cry, working to suppress the urge to cry after being hurt. Older preschoolers develop the ability to express "appropriate" feelings and hold "inappropriate" feelings in check (Izard & Malatesta, 1987). However, conscious self-regulation is a difficult task for preschoolers. Reliable control over affects does not develop until midway through school age. Preschoolers swing back and forth between self-control and strong expression. In fact, the degree of strain they feel is suggested by how excited they become in situations where a full range of emotions can be revealed. This is one reason that pre-school children love dramatic play. Play is an arena outside the demands of reality where all sorts of intense feelings—exuberance, silliness, aggression, disappointment—can be expressed in pretend scenarios that feel affectively real. Child therapists also observe the preschooler's excitement when she realizes that play therapy permits a wide range of emotional expression.

Establishment of Psychological Defense Mechanisms

Defenses, as defined by psychoanalytic theory, are unconscious mental operations that serve to protect the child from experiencing anxiety or psychic pain (A. Freud, 1966). When mobilized in response to internal or external cues of anxiety or danger, defenses help the individual regulate affects and maintain a sense of psychic organization. The motivation for the establishment of defenses in the toddler period comes from awareness of conflicts between the toddler's wishes and his parents'. In order to avoid the anxiety associated with being angry at his parent, the toddler uses the defense of projection, which involves attributing one's negative feelings and impulse to someone else. So the toddler who is angry at her father says, "You're angry at me!" As development proceeds, more sophisticated and adaptive defenses gradually supplant the "primitive" defenses of early childhood. Defenses are one of the normal means of regulating affect and impulse. They only become problematic when they become overgeneralized to situations where they are not appropriate or when they supplant other coping mechanisms such as cognitive and interpersonal skills. Defenses prominently used by pre-school children include the following:

Projection. The child attributes his own feelings—especially hostile or aggressive ones—to someone else. A 3- or 4-year-old may accuse a peer he has just pushed as having intended to hurt him.

Displacement. A child who becomes anxious about negative feelings toward a person he cares about directs these feelings toward someone else. Angie, 3½-year-old whose mother was pregnant became rude and defiant toward one of her child care providers, who was also pregnant. In her own family she was seemingly happy and showed interest in the coming baby. During a brief evaluation this little girl repeatedly played out a scenario in which a baby figure was burned up and then a mother and girl figure held each other close. This child had displaced hostile and ambivalent feelings toward the baby (and her mother) onto another pregnant woman.

Denial. Denial involves saying, believing, or acting as if some painful or anxiety-generating event did not happen. A child may deny to himself that he has violated a parent's rule. Or he may overtly state to another person that he did not violate the rule. This defense, though clearly unrealistic when used just after a teacher or parent has seen him do something wrong, demonstrates the young child's strong need to avoid disapproval. In the therapeutic situation, denial is common if the therapist asks directly about a child's negative behavior. For example, I said to a 5-year-old boy, "Your mom told me you got in a fight with another boy at the park." He replied, "No, I didn't." Another child expressed denial in response to a similar question by completely ignoring it and talking about something else. Denial is a common defense for older children as well, but it is particularly utilized by pre-school children. For this reason, it is best to approach anxiety-laden material indirectly, though displacement in fantasy or play.

Regression. This defense involves "turning back to acts, thoughts or feelings which belonged to an earlier stage of development" (Berman, 1979, p. 10). The stereotypical example of regression is when a child whose mother has just had a baby becomes less autonomous, demanding that her mother pick her up, dress her, or feed her. Regression in this example represents anxiety about attachment. The child seeks reassurance that the parent still cares about her, and she communicates this by reverting to attachment-seeking behaviors that had been set aside. Regression can also be used to deny aggressive behavior. For example, a 4-year-old boy who had just wildly thrown dolls and furniture out of the dollhouse in my office began talking "baby talk," apparently in order to suppress the anxiety aroused by his aggressive behavior. Regression is also common at times of developmental transitions. Many children temporarily cope with the stress of beginning kindergarten by becoming more demanding and dependent at home.

MORAL DEVELOPMENT

During the preschool period, the child moves from a moral sense that is based on outside approval to a more internalized sense of right and wrong. At 2 and 3 years of age, children's sense of morality is determined by their wishes for love and approval and their avoidance of disapproval, so they try to avoid behavior that will bring disapproval. Kohlberg (1984) calls this a "punishment and obedience orientation." Although toddlers are aware of parental standards, their internal controls are not well developed and they rely on parents to function as auxiliary consciences (Emde, Johnson, & Easterbrooks, 1987; Emde & Buchsbaum, 1990). This is quite different from having an internalized sense of values or conscience. During the preschool years, progression in cognitive and social development makes possible an internalization of morality. The following discussion presents some characteristics and trends of moral development in children between 3 and 6 years of age.

Distinctions between Intention and Result

Early preschoolers are unable to distinguish between intention and result. (According to our system of law, a crime is worse if someone intended to do it than if it was done accidentally or through negligence, e.g., the distinction between murder and manslaughter.) The young preschool child only looks at the surface of behavior and can't understand motives. Piaget (1948) gave 3-year-olds the following problem: One boy was told by his mother not to touch a nice cup. But he was mad at his mother, so he threw it down and broke it on purpose. Another boy was carrying 12 cups on a tray to help his mother get ready for a party. He tripped and all the cups got broken. Piaget asked the children, "Is one of the boys more naughty than the other?" Preschool children regularly answered that the boy who broke 12 cups is naughtier because he broke *more* cups. By contrast, school-age children, who understand the distinction between intention and result, regularly said that the first boy was naughtier because he did it *on purpose.*

Increased Self-Monitoring

The toddler has become aware of parental standards and expectations. During the preschool years, this awareness is increasingly acute. Preschool children usually know when they have violated a rule or acted aggressively. As they internalize standards, they begin to monitor their own behavior.

The Development of Guilt as a Distinct Emotion

The capacity to feel bad "on the inside" develops during the preschool years. Unlike the toddler, who may feel anxious if he violates a parental rule because he is afraid of punishment, the preschool child begins to understand that he is wrong whether the parent knows or not. This internal awareness of wrong and the painful feeling that accompanies it is the feeling of guilt. Kagan (1984) argues that the emergence of guilt is related to cognitive maturation, specifically to the preschooler's awareness that he can choose among alternative actions: "A two-year-old is not capable of recognizing that he could have behaved in a way different from the one he has chosen. But the four-year-old has this ability and so experiences the emotion we call *guilt*" (p. 175). Preschoolers understand that they have choices about how to behave, as well as having a beginning awareness that they are responsible for their actions. Consequently, they can blame themselves when they do not choose to do the "right" thing.

Play as Practice for Morality

As preschoolers begin to think about "good" and "bad" their interactions and fantasy play begin to address explicit questions of what is good behavior and what is not. Because they are trying to figure out these questions on a conscious level, they can easily have their feelings hurt if they think another child is accusing them of being bad. Fantasy play becomes an important vehicle for exploring these questions. In play, one can pretend to be a bad guy without being bad in reality, or one can be Wonderwoman or Batman, whose job is to stop the bad guy.

Play also allows children to discharge aggressive impulses in safe ways. For example, two boys have been fighting over a toy and have pushed each other. One threatens to throw the other into the river. The other says, "Like a troll?" and this shifts the focus into play based on the story "Three Billy Goats Gruff." What began as real aggression is displaced into fantasy aggression in which both boys are "safe" and neither has to experience himself as actually bad (Paley, 1986). Through play "antisocial" behavior is transformed into a shared social experience.

Understanding and Following of Rules

Through frequent reminders and limit setting, preschoolers learn the rules of behavior established by parents and caregivers. However, they have trouble understanding the rules of a game. Even when a preschooler understands the rules cognitively, he tends to see games as vehicles for fantasy. Adults who play simple board games with preschool children find that they often change rules or make them up as they go along. They have almost no sense yet of the importance of following the rules for the sake of making the game fair. For example, a 5-year-old boy I saw in therapy had learned the rules of checkers and often asked me to play. The game would always begin politely, with several moves that followed the rules. But then he would pick up a checker, raise it high above the board, and shout, "Superchecker!" Then Superchecker would fly down and knock all my checkers off the board. Another issue implied in this story is that preschoolers know that adults are bigger and more competent than themselves. Their frequent tendency to "cheat" and their insistence on winning reflects their attempt to level the playing field by giving themselves advantages over a clearly superior competitor. Young children who become angry at a parent who wins a game sometimes complain bitterly, "It's not fair!" From their perspective as a small person competing against a bigger, more accomplished person, they are right, even when the adult is playing by the "rules." This has implications for parent guidance. If a parent is expecting a 4- to 6-year-old to play by the rules, it might be pointed out that that is expecting too much of a preschool child and might be suggested that the child's interest in playing fairly will develop over the next few years.

Social Relationships

The growing importance of social relationships gradually contributes to the development of the superego. In the early part of the preschool period, the child's egocentrism leads to attempts to get other kids to fit themselves into the particular fantasy she is having. There is often conflict about whose fantasy should dominate; because of this the collaborative play of preschoolers is unstable. Gradually, however, children come to value relationships over egocentrism. They become more able to negotiate because they can increasingly take the other child's role and empathize with her point of view.

Transformations in Children's Ability to Accept Responsibility for Their Actions

Young preschoolers have trouble tolerating feeling they have been bad; consequently, they rely a lot on defenses of projection and denial. They are very likely, for example, to deny that they have hurt another kid, and in fact are likely to blame the victim, saying, "He hit me first," or "He was going to hit me." Between 5 and 6 years of age they gradually take more responsibility for their actions. In work with parents, it is often useful to point out that the "lies" preschoolers tell often represent wishes or attempts at self-protection. We can suggest that parents contradict the "lie" without punishing the child for lying.

How Do Moral Controls, Rules, and Values Become Internalized?

A number of processes, both in the environment and within the child, support moral development. These include the following:

Parental Consistency

Parents and others repeatedly define expectations and rules for the child. Preschoolers regularly test boundaries, and adults repeatedly clarify what the boundaries are. Although psychoanalytic theory has characterized discipline as a process of taming the "instincts" of the child, this tells only part of the story. The child's internal awareness of standards, need for parents' love and approval, and need for regularity and help with self-regulation makes her receptive to parents' limit setting. If discipline is neither harsh nor absent, the preschool child shows a readiness to take in the parents' rules. Baumrind (1993) notes: "When parents consistently arouse sufficient empathy and guilt in disciplinary encounters to capture the child's attentions, but not sufficient to be disruptively arousing, the child is likely to successively assimilate the parents' moral norms" (p. 1307).

Identification

The child who loves and admires his parents comes to identify with them and takes their values into the self. Particularly through identification the child learns "acceptable" ways of expressing autonomy and initiative, as well as ways of controlling negative impulses (Kagan, 1984). Toddlers with histories of secure attachments and reciprocal positive feelings are more receptive to the limits their parents set. As preschoolers, they show more evidence of having internalized their parents' expectations and rules, based on positive identifications (Kochanska, Aksan, & Koenig, 1995). On the other hand, the power of identification is so strong that if a parent models dishonest or antisocial behavior, the child will come to feel that he cannot avoid being like his parent even though he may be aware of the parent's violation of social norms. Such a child may experience confusion and shame over differences between parental and social norms, especially when he enters school.

Increasing Parental Expectations

Parents intuitively recognize the older preschooler's growing capacity to distinguish between intention and result and to empathize with others. In response they increase their attempts to help the child realize the importance of taking the needs and feelings of others into account. In this way, emerging moral abilities based on cognitive development are reinforced by socialization (Grusec & Lytton, 1988).

Increasing Empathy

The capacity to empathize continues to develop. The child becomes more able to put herself in another's place and to imagine how it feels to be hurt or teased. Through empathy, the child can understand why she should limit her aggressive impulses toward others.

Increasing Peer Orientation

As peers become more important, it becomes necessary to recognize that others have needs too. Older preschoolers find it quite disturbing if another kid tells them, "I won't be your friend," because friends are becoming so important to them. So they gradually internalize values about treating others fairly.

Internalization of the Superego

The progress of moral development during the preschool years involves a shift from external to internal control. Through the influences and developmental processes described above, the child's control of self moves from outside dependence on parents and other authorities to the inside—to an internal locus of control called the conscience or superego. The implications of superego development will be described more fully in Chapter 10 on middle childhood.

THE DEVELOPING SELF

The tension between fantasy and reality in the preschooler's thinking is also reflected in his views of self. The preschool child seems to alternate between grandiose and realistic views of the self. The more grandiose perspective, which is often expressed in fantasy play, serves to temper the child's realistic awareness of how much smaller and less capable he is compared with older children and adults. The compensatory nature of the child's fantasy can be heard in statements of a 5-year-old boy who was anxious about entering kindergarten: "I'm the best basketball player. I already know how to read, even hard books like *Goosebumps.*" These inaccurate statements reflected his worry that he would not be able to meet the demands of the "big school."

In spite of normal doubts about the self based on realistic perceptions of inadequacy compared to adults, the preschool child draws on several resources that support the development of feelings of competence and self-esteem. Self-esteem is supported by the child's growing sense of autonomy and coping ability. Preschool children often insist on doing things themselves. They frequently challenge themselves physically. Growing self-awareness allows children to evaluate and value themselves. If they succeed often enough in meeting their goals, they begin to develop an internal locus of control, seeing themselves as competent to make things happen. The sense of competence and self-esteem are also supported by the child's historical and continuing relationship with her parents. Psychoanalytic theory points out that the child's self-love is based on a history of secure attachment, parental availability, and emotional support, as well as the child's internalization of her parents' basically positive view of her (Gemelli, 1996).

The preschooler's ability to maintain a positive view of self can be compromised by a number of maladaptive parenting behaviors, including insecure attachment, parental overexpectations that the child repeatedly fails to measure up to, parents' harsh punishment or expression of negative views of the child, and frequent rejection of the child. Such parenting behavior is often the result of intergenerational transmission of insecure and negative attachment patterns, mediated particularly by projective identification, in which the parent projects negative views of the self onto the child (Lieberman & Pawl, 1990). Such projections can be understood as the expression of the parents' working models of attachment. They encourage negative or anxious self-representations in the child that interfere with the development of self-love. The child's resulting difficulties with self-esteem confirm Bowlby's (1973) point that the working model of attachment creates the working model of the self as the parent's view of the child becomes internalized. The toddler who has received the parents' support and love, as well as limits, emerges as a preschooler with self-esteem and confidence in his autonomous abilities. The toddler who has been shamed, criticized, negatively characterized, harshly punished, or abused, enters the preschool period with a sense of inadequacy, poor self-esteem, and self-doubt.

Identification

During the preschool years, identification with parents becomes a primary means of defining the self. Toddlers imitate their parents' behavior, but identification reflects a more global idea: I am like my parent. Between 3 and 4 years of age, the child begins to be aware, both consciously and unconsciously, of similarities between herself and her parents, as well as other important persons in her life. She not only imitates her mother's behavior but now sees herself as having psychological qualities like her mother's. Through identification, the preschooler takes on some of the characteristics of the parent. Although the child's primary identification may be based on the most obvious similarities, such as gender and physical attributes, identifications occur in many more subtle ways as well and a child in a two-parent family will identify with aspects of both parents. Whether a child develops these more flexible identifications depends on how sex-stereotyped behavior is reinforced within the family. In families adhering to rigid gender roles, children are likely to be reinforced for identifying with the same-sex parent and discouraged from being like the opposite-sex parent (Elkind & Weiner, 1978). Although children consciously strive to be like their parents, they also unconsciously assimilate parental characteristics. For example, the son of a thoughtful and rather taciturn father spoke in thoughtful, reasoned tones, constraining his affects, in an eerily perfect imitation of his father. A candid photo of them together showed the father with a quizzical facial expression and the 5-year-old son looking up at his dad with the same look on his face.

An important impetus for identification is the preschooler's growing awareness of the adult's power and competence: "One reason that children want to move toward maturity is that the adult role is attractive to them" (Kagan, 1984, p. 142). Although the child is aware that she cannot do the things her father can do, identifying with him allows her to share vicariously in his power and accomplishments. A strong identification helps allay the anxiety young children feel as they become aware of their relative inadequacies compared to older children and adults. The child with a positive identification with one or both parents and a history of secure attachment tends to have confidence that she will eventually be able to do things as well as her parent can. Further, strong, positive identifications support moral development, since the child who feels a strong identification with a parent is more likely to assimilate the parent's values and morality. However, if a parent behaves in antisocial, aggressive ways, the preschooler is at risk for incorporating those characteristics as part of her identification

Gender Identity

During the preschool years, gender identity and sex-role learning become important to the child's definition of self. There are many studies of parental behavior that suggest that sex typing begins at birth. Parents tend to project gender stereotypes onto very young infants, seeing boys as more active and stronger and girls as more fragile and sensitive. Parents respond to girls and boys differently, talking and cuddling more with girls and playing more actively with boys (O'Brien, 1992). By the age of 2, toddlers have learned their gender and, through socialization, are beginning to be aware of the characteristics associated with each gender. Once toddlers are aware of their gender, they tend to identify with and imitate the behavior of the same-sex parent. They begin to attend to and assimilate gender-based attributes as defined by their culture (Martin & Halverson, 1981).

This understanding of gender characteristics specific to the child's culture continues to grow during the preschool years. The dramatic play of 4- and 5-year-olds at times seems to take on exaggerated gender-stereotyped behavior, with girls emphasizing nurturant roles and boys aggressively confronting the dangers of the world. Further, preschool children begin to show a strong preference for play with same-sex peers. In nursery schools and child care centers, 4- and 5-year-old girls enjoy playing together in the doll corner, emphasizing themes of nurturance and caretaking, and becoming brides, whereas boys may act out superhero play involving aggression, magical powers, and overcoming danger. Although boys may join in girls' family play and girls may take roles in boys' superhero play at times, there is a strong tendency during the preschool years for play to be sex stereotyped (O'Brien, 1992). Preschoolers tend to support and admire peers who maintain sex-stereotyped behavior and to criticize or reject those who do not (Lamb & Roopnarine, 1979).

In spite of this general trend, observations in preschools suggest that girls and boys do play together and that the roles they take sometimes blend stereotyped masculine and feminine characteristics, with girls combining magical superpowers with caretaking and boys, who usually focus on fighting bad guys, occasionally showing concern about babies. Observational studies in group settings have found that about two-thirds of preschoolers' play is same-sex and about one-third involves both sexes. The amount of cross-sex play is influenced by the values of teachers. If teachers encourage it, there is more cross-sex play (Smith & Cowie, 1991). Overall, in the preschool years, there are strong tendencies toward same-sex play, but there is more fluidity in the amount of cross-sex play and sex-role behavior than in middle childhood, when sex segregation is much more rigidly adhered to.

Studies of gender identity suggest that *gender constancy*, the awareness that one's gender cannot change, does not develop until about age 6 (Marcus & Overton, 1978). Younger preschoolers may believe that girls may turn into boys, boys into girls. This is consistent with the preschooler's emphasis on imaginative thinking, as well as the awareness that many things about the self do change, including height, weight, strength, and coordination abilities. Harter (1983b) points out that "most of the physical characteristics that define the young child's bodily self actually do change. . . . With this tremendous emphasis on change, it isn't surprising that the young child may assume that gender may also undergo transformation" (p. 296).

Sexual Interests and Gender

Preschoolers show increasing interest in their genitals, realizing through experimentation that the genitals are a source of pleasure. In general, they are interested in the ways their bodies work, but the genitals hold particular interest. Masturbation becomes more frequent not just as a means of self-soothing but as a way of getting sexual pleasure. During this period, children play "doctor" and want to see and touch their parents' bodies. It is not unusual to hear from the mother of a preschool boy, "He said he wanted me to take off my shirt so he could touch my breasts," or to hear from a father that his daughter's (or son's) sexual excitement at bath time has led to a request that the father take off his clothes and get in the tub.

As children imagine themselves growing into adult roles, they think first of their parents—usually the opposite-sex parent—as love partners. For the preschool child the fantasy of the Oedipus complex makes sense: who could be a better partner than the person who has loved and cared for you and whom you feel close to and admire? Who better to feel sexual toward than a person who has held you, caressed you, allowed you to snuggle against his or her body? The notion that the Oedipus complex consists of the child's falling in love with the opposite-sex parent and wanting to get rid of the same-sex parent is an important but only partial description of the wishes of preschoolers. The girl who imagines marrying her father also wants to be just like her mother. Since the preschool child cannot maintain these competing fantasies simultaneously, she may alternate between which parent she demands an exclusive relationship with and which she treats as a rival. Positive identification tempers and alternates with rivalry. Nevertheless many parents observe that between 4 and 5, children go through a period of possessiveness toward the opposite-sex parent and competition with the same-sex parent. Children in families where fathers are absent play out these dynamics with other males in the extended family. In the dramatic play of preschoolers, one can observe triangular, exclusionary themes as children, trying to compensate for their actual status in the family, compete for the more grown-up role. So one boy says to another, "*I'm* the daddy—you have to be the little boy."

There is a curious dichotomy between classic psychoanalytic thinking, which characterizes the preschool period as the Oedipal phase or "infantile genital phase" (Tyson & Tyson, 1991), and academic developmental psychology, which virtually ignores the preschooler's body and sexual interests in favor of studying cognitive and social development. Although we see behaviors that seem to fit classical Oedipal theory—preference for the opposite-sex parent, jealousy toward the same-sex parent, "triangular" play among preschoolers—for most children the Oedipal drama does not cause irresolvable conflict. A more balanced approach would acknowledge that preschoolers are very interested in their genitals and sexuality, but would not argue that the Oedipus complex is the central developmental process of the preschool years. Practitioners familiar with attachment theory tend to see "Oedipal conflicts" as the outcomes of problems of attachment. Children whose play and "transferences" are cast in Oedipal imagery are most often those who have developed an insecure–resistant/ambivalent attachment or who have experienced disruptions of attachment that have put the security of their attachments into doubt (M. T. Erickson, 1993).

Psychoanalytic theory has also emphasized the developmental significance of young children's reactions to anatomic sex differences. Between 2 and 3 years of age, children know that they are girls or boys and that the other sex is somehow different from them. Between 3 and 5, children become aware of the physical differences between the sexes. Preschool children commonly have some worries and questions about sex differences. The awareness of sex differences is a strong challenge to the child's egocentric view that "everyone is like me." Because of the limits of their cognitive abilities, preschoolers may develop wrong and worrisome theories about the reasons for sex differences. Girls, upon seeing boys, wonder if they once had a penis and imagine it was stolen, cut off, or maybe went inside. A 4-year-old girl told me as we discussed sex differences, "I used to have one when I was 1, but somebody took it from me when I was asleep." Boys, seeing girls, imagine they could lose their penis. Psychoanalytic theory presented this issue as a central issue in preschool development. However, I think it makes more sense to see children's theories and concerns about sex differences as a specific example of how preschoolers think, in this case about an issue that is interesting and exciting. Preschoolers work very hard to come up with explanations for what they observe. In part their thinking is a generalization on the accurate view that many things about the body do change. However, their attempt to understand sex differences is also based on a mistaken premise of egocentrism: that all people are the same. Within this premise the theories they develop about sex differences are not so strange.

Racial Identity and the Self

During the preschool years children's cognitive skills in generalization and categorization develop. Children differentiate between girls and boys, younger and older children, and other obvious physical differences between people. By about age 4, children remark on differences based on skin color and begin to identify themselves as members of a particular ethnic group. Racial/ethnic identity becomes an element in the child's emerging sense of self. Early studies of race awareness among American preschoolers showed that African-American children were aware of racial differences at younger ages than white children (K. Clark, 1955).

Experimental studies asking white and African-American preschoolers to indicate a preference between white and black dolls have consistently shown that both groups of children preferred the white dolls (Spencer & Horowitz, 1973). These findings have been interpreted as responses to exposure to racism (I. Katz, 1996). However, the preference for white dolls should not be equated with negative self-images in individual African-American children, since studies of young African-American children have found that their level of self-esteem does not differ from that of white children (Powell, 1985; Spencer, 1985). Instead the preference for white imagery "may reflect young children's identification (of the self) with the (perceived) more valued stimuli" (Spencer & Markstrom-Adams, 1990). Spencer (1985) found that although African-American preschoolers were aware of negative racial stereotypes and may have been directly subjected to racial prejudice, they did not tend to apply these negative views to themselves. Unlike earlier researchers, who assumed that awareness of negative stereotypes must contribute to a negative view of the self, Spencer concluded, "Racial stereotyping in black children should be viewed as objectively held information about the environment and not as a manifestation of personal identity" (1985, p. 220).

APPENDIX: SUMMARY OF PRESCHOOL DEVELOPMENT, 3 TO 6 YEARS OF AGE

Overall Tasks

- Development of play as a vehicle for exploring reality
- Make transition from view of world based on egocentric and magical thinking to a more logical and reality-based view

Attachment

- Attachment continues to provide security when child is under stress (3–6 years)
- Attachment needs are frequently verbalized, rather than simply being expressed in action (4–6 years)
- Improving memory and sense of time allow child to cope with separations— the child can understand better when a parent will return (4–6 years)
- Working models of attachment are firmly established and can be generalized to relationships with nonparental caregivers and peers (3–6 years)

Social Development

- Development of social skill through interaction and play with peers; social competence gradually develops through peer interactions involving negotiation about play scenarios, conflicts based on egocentrism and possessiveness, and triangular dynamics involving competition and exclusion (3–6 years)
- Development of verbal approaches to social interaction and conflict resolution (4–6 years)

- Prosocial interaction is elaborated and more frequent, based on increasing identification with adult models and growing skills in empathy and perspective taking (3–6 years)
- Exposure to peer group and prosocial values in preschool settings encourages cooperation, sharing and problem-solving skills (3–6 years)
- Peers become more important; sustained exposure to peers leads to decreases in egocentrism; the preschooler identifies with peers and is motivated to make interactions with them pleasurable (4–6 years)
- Friendships based on common play interests develop (4–6 years)

Language and Communication

- Vocabulary at age 3 equals about 1,000 words and continues to increase at a rate of about 50 words each month (3–6 years)
- Speech becomes clear and easy to understand in most preschoolers (3–4 years)
- Long, grammatically complex sentences involving 8–10 words and dependent clauses is typical of the speech of preschoolers (4–5 years)
- Out loud self-talk, or private speech, accompanies behavior and play; the child describes and directs his behavior in this way (3–5 years)
- Interactive play increasingly depends on language (4–6 years)
- Language gradually supplants action as the child's primary means of communication (4–6 years)

Symbolic Communication and Play

- Preschooler's play tends to be imaginative, dramatic, and interactive (3–6 years)
- Functions of preschool play: exploration of reality and social roles; mastery of stress; expression of fantasies, wishes, and negative, forbidden or "impossible" impulses (3–6 years)
- Distinction between real and pretend: this distinction becomes increasingly clear as the preschool period proceeds; play, which children understand is pretend, helps them begin to distinguish between fantasy and reality (4–6 years)
- Play provides opportunities for practicing emerging cognitive skills, including cause and effect thinking, construction of narrative, perspective taking, problem solving, and exploring alternative interpretations of reality (4–6 years)

Cognitive Development

- Generalization and thinking in categories increases (3–6 years)
- Improving memory provides a greater knowledge base for categorizing new

information; at the same time, a wider range of categories for information storage increases the chance the child will remember new information (3–6 years)
- Cause-and-effect thinking: increasing awareness of causality leads the preschooler to look for causal connections between events; however, limitations
in the ability to think logically or emotional arousal may lead the preschooler
to mix up cause and effect (4–6 years)
- Egocentric thinking persists, causing limitations in accurate understanding of
reality; types of egocentric perceptions include the following: inability to take
another's perspective; reversal of cause and effect; attributing the causes of
events to the self; transductive reasoning; personalism; animism (3–6 years)
- Magical thinking and the fusion of fantasy and reality are common, especially
when affective arousal, as in trauma, influences thinking. In situations where
there is need for "hidden" information, such as figuring out how a seed
becomes a plant, the preschool child is likely to utilize fantasy as a way of trying to explain reality (3–6 years)

Self-Regulation

- Increasing ability to categorize experience reduces sense of novelty in new situations, resulting in feelings of control and less vulnerability to anxiety (4–6
years)
- Cognitive ability to imagine and anticipate the consequences of behavior contributes to improving impulse control; this ability is increasingly supported by
the child's internalization of social expectations (4–6 years)
- Inner speech and private speech are used to sort out experience and provide
reminders of rules, prohibitions, and expectations (3–6 years)
- Ability to displace real-world concerns and anxiety into fantasy play and other
forms of symbolic expression (3–6 years)
- Internalization of dyadic strategies of regulation: working models of dyadic
regulation are generalized to self-regulation (3–6 years)
- Beginnings of conscious inhibition of emotional expression and arousal (4–6
years)
- Psychological defense mechanisms: projection, denial, regression

Moral Development

- Gradual internalization of moral values, resulting in the establishment of a
conscience or superego by about age 6 (3–6 years)
- Increased self-monitoring: older preschoolers monitor their behavior, applying
standards of morality to themselves; however, this is not done consistently (5–
6 years)
- Guilt develops as a distinct emotion (4–6 years)
- Rule-governed behavior: with reminders and reinforcement, preschoolers can

follow the rules at school or home; however, they have difficulty abiding by the rules of a game, in part because they cannot emotionally tolerate losing, and in part because the fantasies games evoke seem more important to them than the rules (4–6 years)

- Increasing importance of peer relationships helps children control negative or impulsive behavior because they want to maintain the friendship and approval of peers (4–6 years)
- Moral controls are gradually internalized by age 6 through the following influences: consistent parental monitoring, limit setting, and praising of good behavior; increasing parental expectations as the child's capacity for self-control matures; identification with parental values; increasing capacity for empathy; increasing peer orientation (3–6 years)

Sense of Self

- Self-esteem is supported by child's growing sense of competence, autonomy, and coping abilities (5–6 years)
- Preschool children who have received parental love and support over time tend to have a positive view of self (5–6 years)
- Identification becomes a basis for defining the self; children consciously strive to be like their parents and also unconsciously assimilate parental characteristics (3–6 years)
- Positive identification helps allay the child's anxiety about being small and incompetent relative to adults (4–6 years)
- Sexual sense of self: during the preschool years sexual interests develop, as manifested in preoccupations with the body, increased masturbation, Oedipal interests, and curiosity and anxiety about sex differences (4–6 years)
- Racial identity: minority children are aware of prejudicial racial stereotypes; the impact of this awareness for self-esteem, however, depends on whether minority children have experienced the positive processes contributing to self-esteem described above (5–6 years)

CHAPTER 9

Practice with Preschoolers

ASSESSMENT

Preschool children are more autonomous than toddlers. They can express themselves in play, art activities, and words. Consequently, assessment approaches that combine parent–child sessions and individual sessions with the child are both possible and useful. In individual sessions a preschool child may be able to represent her concerns in play more freely than with her parent present.

As always, assessment must consider all of the developmental domains. Areas particularly useful to observe in the assessment of preschoolers are cognitive processes, play ability, and self-regulation, particularly in terms of impulse control and anxiety management. Children who have difficulties controlling impulses during the preschool years are at risk for problems in social development. Cognitive processes should be observed with an eye to possible distortions of experience based on egocentric thinking. Since play supports so many aspects of preschool development, it is important to investigate the child's capacity to use play to create stories, represent ideas about cause and effect, and organize her view of reality. Children who are inhibited in their play may need help to express themselves more freely. Children who are impulsive or have attentional difficulties may benefit from interventions that help them organize their play. Studies of the play of preschoolers diagnosed with attention-deficit/hyperactivity disorder (ADHD) suggest that their problems with inattention and impulsivity cause them difficulty in organizing and sustaining play. They tend to discard toys as soon as the novelty wears off, and they move quickly from one play theme to the next, without creating themes or narratives. The child whose problems with attention, concentration, and impulsivity interfere with play development does not get the practice with organizing the world and thus may be less prepared for more advanced forms of thinking that build on play thinking (Mayes, 1991).

INTERVENTION GOALS WITH PRESCHOOLERS

From a developmental perspective, the aims of therapy with preschoolers often include addressing troubling ideas and feelings based on the child's cognitive limitations and encouraging the child to move toward verbally mediated understanding of his experience. Here are some characteristic objectives in the treatment of preschoolers:

Help the Child Clear Up Misunderstandings

The preschooler's tendency to try to understand reality through fantasy can generate anxiety which leads to symptomatic behavior. For example, Angie, the child described in Chapter 8 who displaced her anger about her mother's pregnancy into defiant behavior toward her pregnant child care provider, had evidently come to the idea that the new baby would take her mother away from her. This fear was expressed clearly in her play involving the girl who went everywhere side by side with her mother while the baby was left behind in the stove to burn up. I asked Angie if she would show her mother the story she had made up with the small people. Angie was pleased. With her mother watching, once again the baby was put into the stove and the girl and mother flew together. I said to Mrs. Browne, "I think Angie's play shows she has some worries and a question: when the baby is born, will you still hold Angie close and play with her?" Mrs. Browne reassured Angie and they played together. Angie seemed very happy that her mother now knew that she was worried that she would lose their closeness when the baby was born.

Clarify Overgeneralizations

Preschoolers tend to overgeneralize on the basis of their stressful experiences. While generalization and categorization are normal aspects of cognitive development, generalization of stressful events can disturb the child's ability to assess reality accurately (Crittenden, 1992c). As a result children may become anxious in situations that have associational reminders of the stressful or traumatic situation, or even come to associate any anxiety-provoking situation with the traumatic situation.

For example, it is common for young children who have witnessed violence to become hypervigilant and expect that violence can occur at any time, even in situations far removed from the original situation. Tisha, the child described in Chapter 8 who was very aggressive with other children at her child care center after witnessing domestic violence, needed explanations from her mother and teachers to understand that she was safe at the child care center and that her teachers would not allow the type of violence she had witnessed to occur there. Her mother, in a joint parent–child session, explained to Tisha what had happened: "Daddy hit me, and my mouth was bleeding." I pointed out to Tisha that she had been very scared and had worried about everybody getting hurt, but that she didn't fall down and that her mouth did not bleed. Her teachers later told her that they knew what she had witnessed and that they would not allow grown-ups to hurt anyone at the center. These interventions validated Tisha's perceptions and feelings, but identified her overgeneralization as invalid.

Help the Child Move to Verbally Mediated Understanding of Experience

Talking with a child about her experience by organizing it into verbal narratives that specify cause-and-effect relationships and distinguish between past and present allows her to gain a sense of control and cognitive competence. Verbalizing feelings allows the child to get some distance from strong impulses and affects, so that she does not have to act on them immediately. Being able to substitute thinking for acting promotes a sense of mastery and self-control. As the child gains some verbally mediated mastery over anxiety-producing internal feelings and impulses or stressful past situations, she is likely to become less symptomatic. This objective is particularly important in therapy of children who have difficulty controlling impulses. Since preschoolers are not able to represent all their feelings verbally, the therapist needs to encourage the process of verbalization and verbally mediated thinking by putting into words what the child symbolizes in play. This accomplishes several things:

- The child feels she is not alone with her problems; as the therapist puts thoughts and feelings into words, she feels that someone else understands.
- Her experience is given shape and meaning, giving her a clearer sense of reality and of the distinctions between past and present.
- She gains a means of thinking about her experience and gradu-

ally can begin to talk about it herself; she is developing representational competence.

- Her experiences and affects are linked together in a way that makes sense.

USING PLAY IN THE TREATMENT OF PRESCHOOLERS

Since preschoolers readily utilize pretend play to represent experience, play can be the social worker's entry point for a dialogue—involving both action and words—about the child's difficulties. This displacement of real experiences into play creates a safe vehicle for mastering stress or confusion. In part, play provides a means of dramatizing one's concerns beyond mere words; in another way, play provides protection: play is about fantasy characters, not about the self. Practitioners should pay attention to the story and themes represented in preschoolers' play. It is useful to assume that the child's play is telling a story that reflects his concerns.

Preschool children understand the distinction between real and pretend. They are also able to step out of play temporarily, much like the movie director who yells "Cut!" and tells the actors what she wants them to do, and then shouts "Action!" to resume the drama. Therapists can make use of the preschooler's ability to distinguish between the play frame and the reality frame. The therapist can at times stop the play briefly and comment on its content and then resume play. Even though a child may not welcome such breaks in the play, they feel normal to her.

Most preschool children, once they have begun to feel some trust in a therapist, prefer that the therapist play with them, as opposed to passively observing their play. A smaller number of children prefer that the therapist stay outside the play, and this must be respected. During the preschool period, players take roles and act them out, which means a preschool child will expect the therapist to become an actor in his play scenario. The therapist must be willing to become a player. As a participant-observer in the play, the therapist can learn how the child constructs his experience and is in a unique position to make interventions, both within the flow of play and by stepping out of the play to comment on it (Chethik, 1989).

In the case that follows, we examine the use of play therapy with a 4½-year-old girl whose development was interfered with by medical treatment for a cancerous brain tumor. We look at the preschooler's ability to use play to communicate concerns she is not yet able to express in words, as well as the therapeutic potential of play interpretation. Before presenting the case, I will discuss the problem of developmental interference, with particular reference to the interaction between extended medical treatment and the preschooler's developmental tasks.

MEDICAL TREATMENT AS A
DEVELOPMENTAL INTERFERENCE

As medical treatment for childhood cancer has improved, larger numbers of children are surviving malignancies that previously were almost always fatal. Paradoxically, successful medical treatment may produce negative developmental side effects. The prolonged and invasive treatment common to cancer therapy protocols may constitute an interference to subsequent development in young cancer survivors (Rowland, 1989; Van Dongen-Melman & Sanders-Woudstra, 1986). Children treated during the toddler and preschool years are particularly vulnerable to developmental interference (Mulhern, Wasserman, Friedman, & Fairclough, 1989). This is consistent with the general findings of developmental research suggesting that the younger the child, the fewer internal resources he has for coping with stress (Maccoby, 1983; Kagan, 1983).

Cancer treatment typically involves the onslaught of a number of stressors, including hospitalization, anxiety about dying, pain from spinal taps, bone marrow aspirations and other procedures, nausea and weakness as side effects of chemotherapy, bodily changes such as hair loss, loss of familiar routines, disruption of friendships, and in some cases separation from parents (Van Dongen-Melman & Sanders-Woudstra, 1986; Goodman, 1991). Rutter (1981) noted that the capacity of preschool children to cope with future stresses was altered by the stress of multiple hospitalizations. Coping styles developed in response to the stress experienced during hospitalizations tended to persist even if they were not adaptive from the perspective of the tasks of future development (Rutter, 1981; Trad & Greenblatt, 1990). Many preschoolers develop a precocious maturity, becoming unexpectedly compliant with treatment; however, this precocity may become generalized and show up later as inhibitions and behavioral rigidities that interfere with development (E. R. Katz, 1980; Rowland, 1989).

Compared to the school-age child, the preschooler's internal mechanisms for coping with stress are not yet well developed. The more sophisticated defenses characteristic of the school-age child—repression, rationalization, denial in fantasy—are not yet in place. Lacking adequate coping strategies, the preschooler is more likely to become overwhelmed during stressful procedures and may either shut down emotionally or lose control and dissolve into tantrums (Jay, 1988; Gauvain-Piquard, Rodary, Rezvani, & Lemerle, 1987).

Prolonged invasive medical treatment is likely to interfere with a number of developmental tasks of the preschool child, including the development of an autonomous self, beginning peer relationships, elaboration of play and fantasy, and control of one's body in terms of regulation of body functions, physical activity, and mobility (Rowland, 1989; Brunnquell & Hall, 1982). At a time when these developmental issues are in ascendancy and therefore subject to disturbance, cancer treatment and hospitalization cause the preschooler to experience a loss of autonomy and self-control, increased dependency, isolation from peers, restrictions on freedom to play, restrictions on physical activity and mobility, and physical vulnerability because of invasive procedures and the side effects of chemotherapy (Van Dongen-Melman & Sanders-Woudstra, 1986; Chang, 1990).

During the preschool period the ability to play imaginatively is a major adaptive mechanism for the mastery of stress, as well as the primary pathway for exploration that facilitates learning and socio-emotional development. Play supports the development of autonomy and initiative (Piaget, 1962). Cancer treatment disrupts the child's ability to play actively and strenuously, and has inhibiting effects on her ability to fantasize (Lansky, List, Lansky, Cohen, & Sinks, 1985; Zeltzer & LeBaron, 1986). When young cancer survivors return to school they may be inhibited in expressing feelings and take passive roles in peer interactions (Deasy-Spinetta, 1981).

Such inhibited behavior can be understood from the perspective of attachment. Although still reliant on the attachment relationship when under stress, the preschool child is moving toward a sense of the self as autonomous, self-reliant, and purposeful. This movement is supported by an internalized secure base of positive working models of attachment (Main et al., 1985). The child who has internalized a secure attachment relationship is able to explore reality with more confidence and interact with the world in ways that further the development of autonomy and individuation (Matas et al., 1978; M. F. Erickson et al., 1985). But when a preschool child experiences prolonged stress due to illness and medical treatment and must revert to dependency on parents and other caregivers, his developmental progression toward autonomy may be compromised. Behavioral and affective inhibition can be based on other factors, including temperament and a history of insecure attachment; however, even a preschooler with a history of secure attachment and adequate development can be thrown off track by exposure to severe stressors and may adopt an inhibited style that emphasizes security at the expense of exploration and autonomy (Lieberman & Pawl, 1990. There is a considerable intervention literature dealing with behavior problems of preschoolers (e.g., see Speltz, 1990; Cambell, 1990); much less has been written about problems of inhibition. An inhibited child does not compel attention as dramatically as a child whose behavior is impulsive or out of control. However, serious inhibitions during the preschool years may have a negative impact on the child's ability to interact with the world and thus foreclose many normal developmental opportunities.

The likelihood of developmental interference is increased by the preschooler's cognitive characteristics, including egocentrism and prelogical, magical thinking, which does not distinguish clearly between intention and result or between cause and effect, especially when stressors are operating. Consequently, a preschooler may develop distorted notions about the causes of her illness, including mistaken associations between the onset of the illness and coincidental external events, and is likely to regard invasive and painful medical procedures either as sadistic abuse or as punishment for misdeeds (Bibace & Walsh, 1980; Jay, 1988). Further, the preschooler has limited ability to understand abstract explanations of medical issues that she may overhear in the hospital and is prone to impose idiosyncratic constructions on them (Bergmann & Freud, 1965).

PLAY THERAPY WITH A PRESCHOOL CHILD: A CASE EXAMPLE

The case of Katy is an interesting example of a developmental arrest caused by a preschooler's reactions to a serious illness following an early history of excellent development in the context of a stable and loving family. Although the cancer treatment was sometimes traumatic and at other times quite stressful for this 3- to 4-year-old girl, her previous excellent developmental progress and remarkably supportive parents combined to protect her from more severe effects of the treatment. Katy was buffered by other protective factors, including middle-class status, her parents' high levels of education, and family and friends who supported the family in many ways, including providing care for her younger brother. Nevertheless, she did show evidence, at age 4½, of developmental arrest in the social and affective areas.

Medical History

Up to the onset of her medical symptoms at age 3, Katy was a vivacious, outgoing child, who played vigorously and had a good sense of humor. Near her third birthday, her parents noticed that Katy seemed to become moody and that she "stopped playing." Over the next 3 months she became more and more somber and less and less active. She complained of feeling weak and began to have headaches. However, her pediatrician could not find any evidence of illness. When she refused to get out of bed because her head hurt, her parents took her to the emergency room, where she was diagnosed with a malignant brain tumor.

The tumor was removed in an 8-hour surgery. Katy was in considerable pain for 10 days following surgery. Over the next 7 weeks of hospitalization she had several minor surgeries, including the placement of a shunt to drain fluid from the surgical site, two repairs of the incision, and the placement of a Broviac catheter in her chest wall. (A Broviac is a catheter tube that is inserted into the vena cava, the large vein near the heart. It is used for the administration of chemotherapy. The toxic cancer medications would have severely damaged Katy's veins if dripped into her arms; by using the vena cava, where the volume of blood is much higher than in the arm veins, the medications were diluted more quickly and did not cause vascular damage.) Altogether she underwent general anesthesia six times. One repair of the incision was done without anesthesia and seems to have been traumatic: Katy became hysterical and had to be held down, and the doctor yelled at her to stop crying as she restitched the wound. She also received cranial radiation, which caused her to lose her hair.

Over the next 15 months, Katy was hospitalized 10 times for 2-day periods for chemotherapy. As she realized that the chemotherapy made her feel terribly ill, she began to resist it and had to be coaxed by her parents. She told her parents that she thought the chemotherapy might make her die. Most of the time, however, she seemed to submit passively. There were also many other invasive procedures, ranging from extremely uncomfortable and at times painful spinal taps to needle pokes for i.v. (intravenous) intubation and blood draws. Her parents reported that Katy was forced in the hospital to do things she didn't want to do—to have i.v. needles changed, to be awakened at night to go to the bathroom, and in general to adapt to the hospital routines. Another consequence of her illness was that she had to be kept away from other children when she was out of the hospital. The chemotherapy seriously compromised her immune system, so that an ordinarily mild illness like measles would be life threatening to Katy.

Her parents and the medical staff, however, had explained what was happening to her, and her parents had been remarkably supportive and consistent with her in spite of the tremendous stress her illness imposed on them. One of her parents had been with her at all times when she was hospitalized. Katy, for her part, had been cooperative or stoic in response to all but the most surprising or painful procedures. By the standard of overt distress, which is commonly seen in the literature as a measure of coping (Blount, Davis, Powers, & Roberts, 1991), Katy seemed to have tolerated her medical experiences well. She had used an array of coping mechanisms, including using the support of her parents and the medical staff, complying with medical procedures, and defense strategies such as denial and blocking of affects.

Assessment Impressions

I began seeing Katy when she was 4 years, 8 months. At that point her cancer treatment was completed and medically she was doing well. Her parents were aware that her cancer could recur and also that she would be at risk for developing leukemia later on. They referred her because she had become such a serious, quiet, inhibited child, quite different from the vivacious 2-year-old they remembered. They were concerned that she had reactions to her hospitalizations and fears of death that she could not talk about. She was extremely cautious physically and no longer threw herself into play. She refused to do "risky" play like swinging, jumping, or climbing. Katy told me she thought she'd gotten cancer because she fell off the jungle gym when she was 3. She was enrolled in part-time day care but was standoffish with other children and played mostly by herself, probably because she had missed out on learning to play with other children over the previous year and a half, and also because she was still afraid of catching a disease from another child. She also seemed arrested in her ability to play. At home, at day care, and in the early treatment sessions, her play had a constrained, tentative and obsessional quality and lacked the rich fantasy themes typical of a 4-year-old. These were indicators that her experience with cancer treatment was interfering with her development. My impression on meeting Katy, however, was that she had a full range of affect and fantasy available to herself but that she kept them under wraps. She was nearly silent in sessions. Nevertheless, I felt engaged with her and believed that underneath her inhibitions and affective constriction she might be imaginative and articulate.

A Developmental Treatment Approach

The treatment goals were as follows:

- To help her recover the ability to play. This would open up for her an age-appropriate pathway for developmental progress and the mastery of stress.

- To help her gain some mastery over the traumatic aspects of cancer treatment by playing out in an active way those experiences she had previously had to submit to passively. An essential part of this goal would be to give Katy a chance to present a range of affects—especially anger and negativism—which she had suppressed during her medical treatment.
- To help her differentiate her experience with cancer from her present experience. This would involve helping her see cancer treatment as a past experience, not a lens for viewing the present.

I did not assume that Katy had a psychiatric disturbance, although her parents' description of her as quieter, more inhibited and self-contained, less active physically, and less social raised the possibility that her reactions to cancer treatment had interfered significantly with the precancer trajectory of her development and might lead to more serious difficulties when she entered middle childhood (Susman, Hollenbeck, Nannis, & Strope, 1980).

The therapeutic approach in this case was a focal psychotherapy to help a child master a potential developmental interference (Chethik, 1989). The treatment modality was individual play therapy and parent guidance. (The parent work will not be described because it was minimal. The case is atypical in this respect. Ordinarily, parents also need a chance to work through the traumatic impact of their child's life-threatening illness. Katy's parents had done a remarkable job in helping Katy cope with her illness and in coping with it themselves. They had already made extensive use of outside supports, including a family intervention during Katy's illness.)

The play of preschoolers in the therapeutic situation is best seen as the child's representation of significant aspects of her experience and as a commentary on what her experience has meant to her. Starting from this assumption, the practitioner attempts to understand the meaning of the play and then to provide interpretive commentary that helps the child take a new perspective on her experience, with the aim of reducing developmental interferences. At the outset, the therapist makes statements about the problem for which the child has been referred. I told Katy, "Your mom and dad wanted you to see me because they think you might have some worries and scary feelings about cancer and the hospital. My job is to help girls with their worries, and your mom and dad thought I might be able to help you." If this problem statement is salient for the child, play representing the child's experience of the problem begins to emerge, often in the first session. For Katy, this took the form of her laying out 20 or so rectangular blocks and then placing small dolls lying down on each of them.

I watched her and said, "This is too big to be a family; there are so many beds, I wonder if it's a hospital." Katy looked me in the eye and said, "Yes." Through this process the play becomes focused, organized, and meaningful. The child preconsciously understands that the therapist sees play as a representation of experience and begins to use it to express what has been difficult for her. In order to help focus the treatment I had a toy doctor's kit and some medical paraphernalia—surgeon's mask and cap, i.v. tubing, tape, etc.—available for Katy's use. I never directed her to play with these materials but pointed out that she could use them to show me her worries, just as she could use the more standard child therapy toys.

Course of Treatment

Katy's early play was inhibited and constrained. She chose to draw and play board games, speaking little, and avoided developing any fantasies in her play. I was content to give Katy some time to acclimate to the therapeutic situation. Feeling forced and controlled had been inevitable features of her medical treatment. I felt that it was particularly important that Katy not feel forced in this relationship. I saw the early sessions as an opportunity to establish a friendly and supportive relationship with Katy. Her drawings were mostly of rainbows and hearts. As she drew we spoke about the bright colors she liked to use and I commented that she seemed interested in practicing getting her rainbows just right. We also played Candyland, a simple board game appropriate for preschoolers, since it is based on chance and does not require the use of strategy, which is generally beyond the cognitive level of preschoolers (Schaefer & Reid, 1986). Katy took pleasure in winning the game, though she seemed to be working to keep her affects in check. This was consistent with the affective restraint that had been an adaptive coping device when she was in the hospital. My main intervention during these early sessions was to mirror her excitement and pleasure in a slightly exaggerated manner in order to model the possibility of a wider range of affect.

After Katy became more comfortable showing pleasurable feelings, I began to model negatively toned feelings. For example, in the third session, I offered her Play-Doh. Play-Doh is a good material for eliciting affects of anger and frustration. Children like to pound on it and work it vigorously. As Katy worked with Play-Doh, small breakthroughs of affect began to occur. For example, she began to pound on it with her fist. When a piece dropped on the floor and Katy looked displeased, I amplified her facial affect by saying, "That stupid Play-Doh! It fell on the floor!" Katy was pleased and repeatedly dropped the Play-Doh, while I continued to express irritation. My aim was to demonstrate to Katy that negative affects could also be safely expressed within the therapeutic situation.

The first significant play commentary Katy made on her hospital experience appeared in the third session, after we had played with the Play-Doh. In the course of playing catch, Katy began hitting me on the head repeatedly with a foam ball. Given that Katy had had many hurtful things done to her head, I did not think this was random or merely diffusely aggressive behavior. I told her that of course it didn't hurt to be hit with the soft foam ball but that I would pretend to be hurt. I complained a lot about being hurt, and she continued to hit me with the ball with a grim expression on her face. I also pretended to be mad, which she thought very funny. When she took up this play in the next session, I focused it around her medical treatment. I told her I would pretend to be a kid at the doctor's office who was getting hurt by what the doctor was doing. As she hit me with the ball, I said, "Doctor, that hurts. I don't like you to hurt me. I'm getting mad at you for hurting me." After a bit I stepped out of the play and said, "I'm showing how kids get very angry when the doctor hurts them." At this point, Katy got a girl doll, took off its clothes, and began taping an i.v. tube to its chest. I spoke for the doll and asked if what the doctor was doing would hurt. Katy, as the doctor, gave a small, enigmatic smile and mumbled incomprehensibly. (This, it appeared, was her representation of the doctor—someone who did hurtful things, all the while smiling and mumbling, but not being responsive to her feelings or questions.)

Following this direct representation of medical procedures, Katy's play became more symbolic but still affectively salient. She developed a game of throwing markers on the floor and telling me, "Pick 'em up!" This was repeated many times. I asked her how I was supposed to feel about having to pick the markers up all the time, and she said, "You don't like it." I echoed this feeling each time she threw them on the floor. I commented that she was helping me understand how it felt to be forced to do something you don't want to do. I said her mom had told me she'd been forced to do a lot of things when she was in the hospital. Over the next few sessions, she elaborated the game. We would both pretend to go to sleep in my chairs. While I remained asleep, she would get up and throw markers and crayons all over the floor. Then she would turn over the play chairs with a big thump, which would be my signal to wake up and pick everything up. Within the play, I said, "I hate to be woken up. I don't like to be forced to pick all this stuff up." Katy said, "You have to." I commented that a kid in the hospital wouldn't like it when the nurse woke her up and forced her to have a shot or made her get up and go to the bathroom.

This hospital play scenario was fully elaborated in a session 2 months into the treatment. As usual, Katy threw markers on the floor and turned the chairs over. While I was sleepily picking things up, I complained that I hated being awakened in the middle of the night and that I wanted to be home in my own bed. I didn't want to be in this stupid hospital. She said, "Now you have to get up and pee." I said, "I'm not going to, and I'm not going to take my medicine either!" Katy looked very grim and said, "You can't say that." I said, "I don't care! I hate this hospital!" She hit me on the shoulder, looking very stern. I said, "Why am I in this hospital?" She said, "You have cancer." I said, "I hate cancer and I hate chemotherapy, because it makes me feel so awful. I'm not having any more chemotherapy or radiation!" She said, "You have to have surgery." I said, "No!" She hit me again and said, "You already had your surgery." I said, "Yes, and it hurt so much after I woke up." She said, "Now you're going to get a Broviac." I said, "What's a Broviac?" She said, "It's just a little tube that goes into your chest." I said, "I'm not getting any Broviac!" She hit me again and said, "Yes you are, and you're going to get an i.v. and a shot too." I made several comments at the end of this hour—that she had helped me know how it felt to be in the hospital and shown me many of the things that she hadn't liked, that she had helped me feel how scary it could be for a kid, how mad a kid could get about having all kinds of hurting and scary things done to her, how a kid hated to be forced, and how confusing it felt when doctors, who were supposed to be helping, sometimes did things that hurt a kid.

In the sessions immediately following, Katy began to take the role of the patient. For example, she took the cushions off my office chairs and lay down on them. She instructed me to get some puppets who should wake her up. The puppets told her it was time to wake up, and she woke up with a vengeful look and began pummeling the puppets until they were knocked off my hands and flung across the room. When I had the puppets say, "Wake up. It's time to take your temperature and go to the bathroom," Katy bit the puppets and threw them against the wall. She represented the pain she experienced in the hospital using the doll figures and blocks. She made a bed out of blocks and put a girl figure on the bed. Then she built up the sides of the bed and placed other figures there, standing over the girl. I commented that the girl looked as though she was in the hospital, and Katy confirmed this. Then the figures standing over the girl pushed blocks on top of her. I said, "I think you're remembering about doctors and nurses looking down at you. What happened to the girl showed me how confusing it could be to have doctors hurt you when they were supposed to be taking care of you."

Over the next several sessions, Katy's play shifted from hospital themes to themes of protection and safety. She crawled under a chair and refused to talk to me. She brought her hand out from under the chair and motioned that I was to chase it with my hand. My hand chased hers but was never able to catch it. Then she began grabbing my intruding hand and throwing it out from under the chair, and looked very pleased with her ability to repulse me. I commented that it looked like she was in a very safe spot under the chair and that it must feel good to be in a safe spot. She probably felt in the hospital that there weren't any safe spots. She couldn't get away from having people do things that scared her and hurt her, and she must have wished then for a safe spot. I said, "In our game, you're the one in control. When my hand comes in, yours is too fast and always gets away. Or else your hand is too strong and throws mine out. I bet you wished that you could have thrown those doctors and nurses away from your bed in the hospital."

By now the therapy was in its third month and Katy's parents were reporting that she was much more social at school, that she was less inhibited, and that she was expressing negative or angry feelings much more openly. She was becoming very bossy to her brother and had some angry outbursts toward her mother. Her mother had been taken aback, because this was so unlike Katy. Her parents were pleased, however, because Katy was expressing a wider range of feelings.

The last month and a half of treatment focused on themes of mastery and putting her illness in perspective. I have selected 3 hours during this final phase that seem not only to summarize these issues but also to underscore the strong progressive developmental forces in Katy, which were becoming more available to her.

In the first of these hours, Katy pushed a chair over to the window, got up on it, and looked out at a nearby park. She pointed out a playground. Then she began jumping off the chair. At first she held my hand each time, then began jumping off on her own. I said, "This reminds me of how you used to be afraid of jumping or falling, because you had the mix-up that falling off the jungle gym made you get cancer. Now I, see that you can jump without being too scared." Katy did not respond verbally but went into the closet and pulled the door shut. She pretended to be a kitten locked in the closet, and it was my job to let her out. Several times when I opened the door, she had a very somber expression and I commented that the kitty was looking sad. About the fifth time I opened the door, she had a very happy expression and pranced around the room, flapping her arms, pretending to fly. This scenario was repeated about four times. Then, when I opened the door, her expression was threatening and she poked at me with a coat hanger. Next she huddled up in the corner, hiding her head. Finally, the flying girl came out again. I commented that her happy play reminded me about how she felt before she got cancer. But then she got sick and felt awful and scared and sad and just wanted to huddle up and hide from people who might hurt her. Sometimes she was also very angry but was afraid to let people know she was mad. I said, "Now that you're feeling much better, it seems like you can be a happy, flying girl again, who can do lots of things. Maybe you're not so worried now about getting sick again."

A few days before the second significant hour in the final phase Katy had had her 6-month CAT scan and it had been normal. Katy spent much of the hour showing me tricks she could do. She jumped off the chair in a number of different ways: first off the seat, then higher from the arm, then backward off the seat. She did somersaults and pretended to be a ballet dancer. I admired all the things she could do and complimented her abilities and her initiative. She also spent a good deal of time carefully building a house out of Lincoln Logs. I was pleased to see this kind of play because it is a normal type of skill-building play for a 5-year-old. A shift from play referring to trauma to such developmentally appropriate and conflict-free play is one of the signs that a child is becoming free from the preoccupation with trauma-based anxiety.

At the beginning of the third significant hour, which occurred a few sessions before treatment was concluded, I began by saying, "Your mom told me that your CAT scan showed you don't have any more cancer." Katy said, "Yes," and immediately became the kitty. She had me pull the two office chairs together to make a bed. The kitty climbed on to the bed, yawned, stretched luxuriously, and went to sleep. She smiled in her sleep, and I commented that the kitty looked like she was having nice dreams. Then the kitty climbed down and frolicked around on the floor. I said, "The kitty looks like she's feeling very good. I bet she's happy now because she doesn't have to go to the vet all the time or stay in the kitty hospital." The kitty answered by rolling around on the floor, stretching, and going to sleep. Then kitty woke up, looked very alert, and began bringing me things in her teeth: a plastic dinosaur, a little plastic table, a piece of string. I said, "The kitty's very good at picking things up with her teeth." Then I decided to reintroduce the medical theme into the play, saying, "I don't know if you can carry that big doctor's kit in your teeth—it might be too heavy." Katy grinned at this challenge and picked it up in her teeth and carried it over to me. Then she opened the kit and immediately took on an angry expression. She dumped everything out and scattered it across the floor. I said, "The kitty doesn't like all that doctor's stuff. Maybe it reminds her of the vets and the kitty hospital." She took a surgeon's cap and mask and stuffed them in a drawer and slammed it shut. I said, "The kitty hates all that doctor's stuff. She doesn't even want to see it." Then she initiated a game of chasing a ball and bringing it back to me. Once, while chasing the ball, she came across the doctor's kit and flung it across the room. I said, "The kitty doesn't like that doctor stuff because it reminds her of when she was in the hospital and people did things that hurt her. But it's very good that the kitty is healthy now because it means she won't have to stay in the hospital. She'll still have to go to the doctor for checkups and tests, but that won't be like staying in the hospital." Katy handed me a toy syringe and motioned for me to give her a shot. I did and said, "That shot was to keep you from getting sick. It didn't seem to hurt too much." She handed me the stethoscope, and I listened to her heart and said, "It sounds very good." The kitty yawned and stretched contentedly. I summarized this play by saying, "I know that you're just like the kitty—you're very happy to be feeling good again."

During the remaining few hours before termination, the medical themes were absent from Katy's play. However, more generalized issues of anxiety about being hurt and feeling safe were brought up, particularly in response to the pressure of termination. For example, Katy spent a lot of time standing on the arm of the chair looking out the window and she wanted me to be close to her. She repeatedly pretended to lose her balance and had to grab onto me to keep from falling. I said, "This reminds me how you used to be afraid of falling because you thought that had caused your cancer. But that's not true. Falling down didn't cause it." I also said, "Since you've been seeing me, you've been feeling lots better, lots happier, and you can do more fun things, like play games with other kids and even climb to the top of the jungle gym. Maybe you're worried that when you stop seeing me, you'll start falling again. But that's not going to happen because you've been practicing and you've gotten very good at climbing and jumping and at keeping yourself safe. And now you don't need to get extra worried about falls and bumps because you know that even though they might hurt they're not going to make you sick."

Discussion

At the end of this 5-month-long therapy Katy was far more expressive, showed a fuller range of affects, was much less anxious about her physical safety, was more active physically, and was more social. The intervention helped her give up her internal preoccupation with and anxiety about her medical experiences. There are other factors besides therapy that contributed to her resumption of an apparently normal developmental trajectory. These included her relief that she was feeling better physically, her opportunity in the day care center to become a "regular kid" interacting with other kids, and her parents' ability to support her assertiveness and expressiveness.

Play therapy enabled Katy to represent in play her subjective account of cancer treatment. Her play presented a story of a young child who felt frightened, helpless, and rageful, was confused by the pain of treatment that was supposed to help, and viewed herself as a victim of sadism and perhaps as deserving punishment for being bad. This affectively rich play representation was very different from her self-presentation while hospitalized, when for the most part she was subdued, compliant, and cooperative. Out of necessity, Katy had developed the ability to modulate and contain anxious reactions to all but the most painful or frightening procedures. Her precocious defenses and her ability to accept the support of her empathic and competent parents made it appear that she was coping well with her difficult medical treatment. However, as the story of her play suggests, it is important to distinguish between immediate coping and actual mastery.

Katy's play in therapy suggested that her coping capacity represented a self-protective process developed in a series of psychic emergencies, not psychological mastery of the experiences. After her medical treatment ended, the need to understand, master and integrate her experience with cancer still remained. Paradoxically, her defenses had become organized around the need to suppress activity and affect; consequently, the normal means a preschooler uses to master and understand experience—play and fantasy—had become inhibited and were less available to Katy as vehicles for mastery. For this reason, *restoring the ability to play became an essential goal of the early stage of therapy.*

Katy's continuing reliance on the emergency-based defenses was having more pervasive effects on her development because she tended to overgeneralize them to nonemergency situations. The inhibitive strategies she developed during hospitalizations—compliance, overcontrol of affects, emotional withdrawal—became maladaptive when applied to normal tasks of preschool development such as entering into peer relations and developing the capacity for initiative through imagination and physical activity.

By abstracting the main trends of the therapy, we can see how Katy gradually mastered these developmental interferences. At first Katy was inhibited in affect, fantasy, and activity level. After I indicated interest in her hospital experiences and encouraged the expression of affect, Katy progressively found ways to represent the negative feelings associated with cancer treatment. In the hospital play, Katy first attempted mastery through role reversal, putting me in the position of the hurt, frightened, angry child. Such role reversal was typical of preschoolers' tendency to represent anxious or traumatic experiences in compensatory ways. They try to deny and master real-life experiences of anxiety and helplessness by taking the roles of powerful, magical figures. By taking the role of the sick child I had the opportunity to put Katy's unspoken story into words and to empathize with her experience. Essentially, Katy "taught" me how it felt to be helpless, scared, and impotently angry, and I responded by acting out and articulating those feelings in order to convey understanding of what she had been through. Once a play dialogue had been built up, with Katy in the powerful role and myself taking the weak role, I began to conceptualize her experience of medical treatment, define its limits, and differentiate it from present reality.

An important shift occurred when Katy gave up the medical play and established her "safe spot" under the chair. By controlling and repelling my play intrusions into her safe spot, Katy was mastering the repeated intrusions during her hospitalizations. I emphasized her ability to gain control. During the last phase of treatment two themes coexisted. One was oriented to the present and involved testing her physical abilities by jumping off the chair and doing somersaults. I acknowledged Katy's physical competence and used her physical activity as an opportunity to contradict her earlier belief that physical daring had been the cause of her cancer. Occurring in the context of therapy, Katy's physical activity represented her struggle to master fears of body damage. (During this period, her parents reported that she had resumed climbing on the jungle gym and was swinging again.) The second theme was play that "summarized" her experience with cancer and placed it in the context of her life. This was expressed through the kitty character who seemed to go through cycles of intense anxiety and anger followed by relief and contentment. I interpreted this play to help her construct a view of her illness as a painful and frightening past experience that she would remember but was separate from her current life.

As she was able to represent the story of her cancer treatment and have it confirmed and then interpretively differentiated from her current experience by a therapist to whom she had become attached, Katy was gradually able to gain a significant degree of mastery over a series of extremely stressful experiences and to resume an adaptive developmental trajectory. The preschool child—because of her egocentric perspective, limited internalized coping mechanisms, and limited abilities in understanding and communicating verbally—may especially benefit from *play* interventions that help promote mastery of developmental interferences.

OBSERVATION EXERCISE

Spend 1 hour or more observing in a preschool or child care center. Focus on the following:

1. *Dramatic play.* Choose a group of children who are playing together. What are the themes and plots of the play? What roles do children choose or assign each other? Is the play gender segregated or not? How do the children deal with disruptions of the play scenario caused by conflicts over whose fantasy will prevail? What reflections of the mass media do you see in the play?

2. *Peer relationships.* Choose two or three children who are playing together, either in dramatic play, building play, or other activities. Can you discern elements of friendship in the way they relate to one another? How do they resolve conflicts that arise? To what extent are other children allowed to enter or excluded from the play activity?

3. *Relationships with adults.* How much do children interact with their teachers versus other children? Do you see attachment-seeking behavior? How do children cope with separation when their parents drop them off at the center? Do you see different styles of relating to teachers—friendly interaction, clinging, withdrawal, etc.

4. *Self-control.* Observe for potentially stressful situations—separation from parents, conflict with another child, having to wait to get the teacher's attention, etc. What strategies for self-regulation do you observe? Do you see instances of aggression? What seems to have precipitated aggressive behavior? Do you see instances of prosocial behavior?

CHAPTER 10

Middle Childhood Development

The school-age child seems calmer, somewhat more serious, and less spontaneous than the preschooler. The preschooler handles the need to learn about the "real world" by assimilating reality into fantasies driven by her wishes and needs. In middle childhood, extending from age 6 to the onset of puberty between 10 and 12, the child gradually comes to see the world as a place with its own laws and customs, which she must learn about and assimilate herself into. The child shifts from seeing herself as at the center of the world to realizing that the world is complex and that she must find her place in it.

The preschooler creates himself through his imagination; while imagination and play remain important to the school-age child, he increasingly establishes his sense of self through a long apprenticeship of gaining skills. This theme is most clearly symbolized by the progressively more complex skills learned in school, but the themes of "learning how to" and "getting good at" increasingly inform the child's efforts in other activities, such as sports and hobbies. School-age children learn that success is based on practice, which helps explain their intensity and persistence as they work on building skills. For example, a 10-year-old neighbor boy was shooting baskets in my driveway, over and over, when it began to rain. During a 10-minute period, it rained harder and harder, but he still kept shooting. My wife came home and said, "Hey, Liam, don't you know it's raining?" He said, "I've been through this before. All I have to do is keep focused." This boy's behavior, although funny because he was standing out in the rain, illustrates many of the capacities of school-age children: sustained concentration, belief in practice, and keeping a purpose in mind in spite of distractions.

Middle childhood, also referred to as the "latency" period in psychoanalytic theory, is defined by the child's capacity to maintain states of self-control, calm, pliability, and educability (Sarnoff, 1976). The ability to maintain such states is essential to the developmental tasks of school age, which involve the child's developing a sense of her capacity to work, to learn skills through practice, and to develop feelings of competence and self-esteem based on how she compares with peers. "Latency," a term first used by Sigmund Freud (1926/1959), refers to the decreasing intensity of emotions and impulses the elementary school years; within his theory of sexuality, Freud argued that the child's sexual impulses become quiescent, remaining "latent" until puberty. More recent developmental research, including some by psychoanalytic writers, makes clear that a broad range of developmental changes, not simply a diminishing of sexual impulses, contribute to the changes children undergo between 6 and 10 (T. Shapiro & Perry, 1976; Sameroff & Haith, 1996). Although the term latency is familiar to many in mental health disciplines, I will use "middle childhood" and "school age" in this chapter, since these terms are used in the broader developmental literature and are not tied to a particular theory of development.

What is happening within the school-age child that supports the development of calm, educability, and self-control? The following overlapping advances in development occur during the middle years:

• *Improved self-regulation.* The child can use many cognitive strategies to assert conscious control over impulses. Unconscious defense mechanisms are regularly utilized to control impulses and fears.

• *Internalization of the superego and related advances in moral development.* The child now has an inner sense of right and wrong, so that she approves of herself when she does something right or resists a bad impulse and feels guilty when she does something wrong. This internalized conscience helps the child control negative or antisocial impulses. The child gradually accepts personal responsibility for her behavior, with correspondingly less reliance on projection and displacement of blame (Zahn-Waxler & Kochanska, 1990). Moral controls are also supported by identification with parents' and peer group's values, by a growing sense of fairness and awareness of the social value adhering to rules, and by a growing capacity to see things from another's point of view.

• *Advances in reality testing and cognitive development.* Egocentrism diminishes, with the child increasingly able to take the "decentered" view of the observer, seeing events more objectively and in context, with less reference to the self. Basic reality testing capacity is now established: the child makes increasingly clear distinctions between fantasy and reality, thought and action, his thoughts and feelings and those of others. Attention span, concentration, and the ability to focus on a task all improve. Learning can now be based on observational ability, logic, and cause-and-effect reasoning.

• *Increased ability to substitute thinking, words, and fantasy for impulsive action.* Increasingly during middle childhood the child becomes capable of substituting thinking for doing, and of using reflection and fantasy as a means of rehearsing actions.

• *Increasing peer orientation.* The child moves into the social world of peers. The child's self-esteem and view of self are increasingly based on recognition and acceptance by the peer group and by the child's inner assessment of how she is doing compared to peers. Desire to fit into the peer group becomes a powerful motive for following rules and maintaining self-control.

PHYSICAL DEVELOPMENT

The child's rate of growth during middle childhood is steady and occurs at a slower rate than during early childhood. At age 6 children weigh an average of 48–49 pounds and are an average of 42 inches tall. By age 11, they have reached about 58 inches in height and weigh about 80 pounds. These figures are based on the 50th percentile for height and weight, and there are considerable variations around this mean. Boys are on average slightly larger than girls until about age 11, when the girl's earlier growth spurt begins. Since this growth spurt is linked to puberty, which occurs approximately a year earlier for girls, girls begin to develop secondary sex characteristics during the last part of middle childhood, whereas boys retain the prepubescent body shape until about age 12 or 13 (Elkind, 1994).

Gross motor skills—running, climbing, kicking, throwing—are well developed at the beginning of middle childhood and continue to improve throughout the period. Individual differences in gross motor coordination become important because in middle childhood athletic ability becomes a measure of competence, in the eyes of both the individual child and his peers. Children put considerable energy into becoming proficient at team and individual sports. Children with poor gross motor skills are often teased and suffer social rejection.

Fine motor skills are also perfected during this period. Eye–hand coordination necessary for writing and drawing improves during the early years of middle childhood, and by third or fourth grade children are often skilled at writing rapidly. Children with delayed or awkward fine motor skills may have academic problems during the early elementary years, as they struggle to write or copy mathematics problems.

Since new levels of cognitive functioning, including reasoning ability, develop in middle childhood, it is important to note that brain development undergoes significant changes during the early part of this period. Some areas of the brain are growing more nerve pathways, while others are eliminating unused synapses and increasing the number of others in the interest of developing more specialized functions (Kagan, 1984). The frontal lobe of the cerebral cortex develops more rapidly between 5 and 8 years of age. This is the area of the brain associated with consciousness and thinking processes involving language (T. Shapiro & Perry, 1976; Janowsky & Carper, 1996). By about age 8, the brain has reached 90% of its growth. Since brain growth and the development of higher cognitive functions occur at roughly the same time, it is assumed that brain maturation plays a significant role in the child's new mental abilities.

THE TRANSITION FROM PRESCHOOL TO MIDDLE CHILDHOOD

Although most theories of development regard the years of middle childhood as a distinct period, it is useful to think of the years from 5 to 7 or 8 as a *transitional phase* during which the abilities of the middle years are developing rapidly but may not be consistently present (White, 1996). The first- or second-grade child often seems to straddle the preschool period and middle childhood, at times advancing in cognitive skills and real-world abilities, at other times relying on egocentric thinking and imagination. It is therefore important to describe this transitional period in order to appreciate the tasks and stresses that 6- and 7-year-olds encounter.

The period from years 5 to 7 or 8 historically has been defined as a turning point in development across cultures, as a time when the child becomes capable of reasoning, learning, and perceiving reality accurately. During this period cognitive and emotional maturation allow the child to function autonomously and to learn new skills that prepare her for adulthood. Familial and social expectations of the child also change. Formal schooling begins at age 5 or 6 in many societies; in cultures without formal education, apprenticeship for adult work skills and social roles begins at this age (Rogoff, 1990; Sameroff & Haith, 1996).

When the child enters school she experiences separations from parents in a more structured environment than preschool. She must adapt to elementary school routines and learning activities that place demands on her cognitive abilities, and adapt to new people in authority. The transition is also psychological. The child knows she will have to function more autonomously. She may be intuitively aware of the demands school places on her to marshal new cognitive abilities, which during this phase are on the way, but perhaps not fully developed. From the perspective of the 5- or 6-year-old, entry into school may seem like an awesome task. Beginning school is a developmental transition for parents as well, symbolizing for many parents their child's capacity for being on her own and creating for some parents a sense of loss of the close relationship of early childhood. Parents' attitudes and circumstances can have a strong impact on the child's transition into school. If a parent is encouraging and positive, the child is likely to enter school more confidently. If a parent is anxious or stressed, the child may pick up these feelings and become anxious about school.

Once in school the child intuitively realizes that fantasy and play are not adequate vehicles for mastering the developmental tasks of middle childhood. Although school-age children continue to enjoy fantasy and fantasy play, they become aware that they will be evaluated by the skills they develop. They realize they must learn to read and write and become proficient at organized games and sports. For the 5- to 7-year-old, meeting these demands of reality, however defined by his culture, often seems daunting. He is becoming aware of the abilities he is expected to develop but is also aware that he does not yet have them. He observes the superior skills of adults and older children and wonders how he will be able to learn them. Most children use this concern as a source of motivation and work hard at learning academic skills. First graders often appear serious and absorbed when they are trying to learn a mathematics concept or sound out a passage in reading. On the other hand, the strain of stretching their cognitive abilities and adapting to the requirements of learning helps explain their high level of activity on the playground and the emotional volatility at home that is common in 6-year-olds.

THE STRESS OF STARTING SCHOOL: A BRIEF CASE EXAMPLE

Tanisha, a 6-year-old I saw in play therapy, expressed her anxiety about starting first grade by reversing roles with me. During several sessions before school began I became the student and she was my teacher who carefully looked over my writing of the alphabet. She corrected my "mistakes" and was stern and bossy. She sent me to the principal's office so that he could examine my papers. In play she was presenting her apprehensions that she would not be successful and that her teacher would not think her work was good. However, within a month of starting school Tanisha began playing a kind, supportive teacher—a reflection of her first-grade teacher—who gave stars on many of my papers and allowed me "extra time" to finish my work. This new content suggested she was realizing that the demands of school would not be beyond her ability and that she could succeed. As therapy proceeded, I always knew when this bright and conscientious child was struggling to master an academic task, because the role play involving the stern teacher and the student who made many mistakes would resurface. Parenthetically, adjustment to school was not Tanisha's primary issue. Her mother, whom she had not lived with for much of her life, was dying of AIDS, and treatment focused on her reactions to loss and her anger and disappointment that her mother had been largely absent from her life. This example, however, suggests that practitioners need to be alert to the developmental hurdles a child is coping with and be ready to tailor interventions to help the child master current developmental tasks.

Other children may temporarily shrink back from the reality expectations of early middle childhood by trying to hold onto the wishful and omnipotent orientation of the preschooler. This can mean different things. For some children, it may reflect temporary anxiety about performance. One 6-year-old who was anxious about learning to read insisted, "I already know how to read, even grown-up books!" For other children, apparent holding on to a younger child's orientation may be a sign of lags in developmental progress.

Signs of Developmental Lag: A Brief Case Example

Jason, age 6, refused to do schoolwork in first grade and constantly tried to get other children to play with him while class was going on. He also reverted to toddler-like behavior at times, grabbing or hugging other children without warning and, a few times, biting. This child was developmentally somewhat immature. His fine motor coordination was not well developed, and he resisted trying to write letters because their shaky appearance made him feel inferior. He was a bit behind in cognitive development. In play sessions, he created elaborate scenarios of teams of dinosaurs fighting on another planet. When I attempted to inject a reality orientation into this play by asking if the dinosaurs went to school (a foolish question), he said, "We don't have schools on this planet!" Jason's behavioral regression and attempt to hold onto a fantasy orientation reflected his intuitive awareness that he was less ready for school than other children in his class. When clear limits, in the form of a behavioral plan, were put in place, his behavior gradually conformed more to classroom expectations. Over the course of the year, his reality orientation and cognitive skills seemed to mature and he mastered the academic expectations of first grade. The spurt in cognitive maturity that many children show at age 6 did not occur for Jason until he was nearly 7.

This example underlines *the importance of recognizing individual differences in the rate of development.* During the transition from preschool to middle childhood, it is also common to see unevenness in the acquisition of cognitive skills. A child who is behind in learning to read may have more advanced ability in mathematics.

During this transitional phase, children also struggle with the implications of having a superego. An internal conscience requires the child to monitor and set limits on her own behavior. It also punishes the child with negative feelings—guilt, shame, anxiety—when she violates her own internalized sanctions. In part, internalizing a conscience requires giving up a sense of omnipotence, and accepting the rules and values that parents have presented to the child during the early years. The task of coming to terms with the presence of rules on the inside is frustrating and anxiety producing for 6- and 7-year-olds. They still have strong volatile impulses, yet an internal voice warns and corrects them. Berta Bornstein (1951) described the superego of the young school age child as "not only harsh and rigid but still a foreign body" (p. 280). When the superego is newly internalized, children can be particularly hard on themselves and reactive to feelings of guilt and self-blame. They are especially sensitive to being scolded because the adult's reprimand awakens the internal voice of conscience and makes them feel doubly punished. Because young school-age children are working hard to establish internal rules, they are quite sensitive to violations of rules by others. They may point out that other children, especially younger siblings, are behaving badly. They may also monitor parent's behavior. At times they may act impulsively, as if trying to deny the existence of the conscience, only to be painfully reminded of its presence when they feel guilty afterward. A 6-year-old girl captured the dilemma of feeling controlled by a internal "foreign body" when she screamed to her mother, "I hate my conscience!"

ATTACHMENT

During the middle years, the child's reliance on attachment to parents continues to decrease. The school-age child has many more strategies for emotional regulation than does the younger child. Consequently, he handles on his own many situations that would have elicited attachment behavior when he was younger. School-age children are more capable of autonomously coping with novel situations, separations, and mild circumstances of threat or danger. Attachment needs are also increasingly transferred to peer relationships, as friends begin to provide some of the emotional security and satisfaction that have been present in the parent–child relationship.

Children still show attachment behavior, in terms of wanting physical closeness, toward parents in many situations. Although 9-year-olds, for example, are capable of putting themselves to bed, most prefer to have a bedtime ritual with parents that affirms their ongoing attachment. In situations of stress, such as serious illness or injury, traumatic experience, or loss of a loved one, school-age children register their need for protection and security by activating attachment behavior. Moreover, attachment behavior increases during the transition to middle childhood, particularly in response to entry into school.

ATTACHMENT BEHAVIOR IN RESPONSE TO STRESS: A BRIEF CASE EXAMPLE

Six-year-old Abby was referred by her single mother midway through her kindergarten year. Although Abby had a history of solid development, she began to show symptoms of separation anxiety when she began kindergarten. This coincided with her mother's taking a job requiring an hour's commute each way, which meant that Abby spent about 11 hours each day in school and child care. Abby's reactions to this new schedule and the emotional demands of formal schooling included anger at her mother when she was picked up at the end of the day, shadowing of her mom and clinginess at home, and coming into her mother's bed each night. She also had retrieved her transitional object—a tattered blanket—and would wrap herself in it when she got home every day. Abby's mother said that prior to entering school, these symptoms had not been in evidence. Abby's teacher said she was doing very well in school.

In a play session Abby chose big and small opossum puppets. (I had bought these to help children express concerns about attachment and separation: the baby opossum could be Velcro-attached to the parent's back.) Abby played out a repeated scenario. The mother and child opossums would be together with their tails entwined hanging from the door knob. Then the mother would leave and a skunk puppet would come and try to eat the baby, but the mother would come back and rescue her. Similarly a baby turtle would swim away from her mother and be eaten by a shark. The mother turtle would come and punch the shark in the stomach, and the shark would burp the baby up and they would be reunited. Abby got a lot of pleasure out this play, and I pointed out that the babies liked to be with their mothers and they even worried about bad things happening when their mothers were gone. I said also, "Even girls can worry when their moms are gone for a long time." Abby agreed this was true.

Abby was a resilient child who was stressed by the new cognitive demands of school tasks, by the intensity of her schedule, and by long daily separations from her mom. She had to function at a high level during a long day with several changes of environment. She seemed to hold things together at school and child care, but when her mom picked her up she showed intense attachment behavior and regressive behavior, including dependence on her security blanket and coming into her mom's bed.

In a short-term intervention I framed Abby's difficulties as reflecting anxiety about separation. Her mother and I came up with a plan that emphasized her attachment to her mother: Abby's mother designated a special time for them to play together three times each week; she made an album of photos of herself with Abby for Abby to take to child care, with the instruction that Abby could look at the pictures if she got lonely; she began putting Abby's feelings about missing her into words. Additionally, we held some joint sessions with Abby and her mom to talk directly about her separation reactions. In these sessions Abby's mom told her that she knew it had been harder this year because the days were longer and they were apart for much longer times. As we talked about these issues, Abby would not say much but would cuddle up on the couch next to her mom. In one of these sessions, her mother commented that Abby had enjoyed swimming lessons last year but this year had complained almost every time she went to swimming class. She said, "I think it's because she was in a small, heated pool last year, and now she's graduated to a big unheated one." We asked Abby about this, and she said it was true. I was struck by the aptness of this change as a metaphor for the transition to middle childhood. I said that maybe that was the way this whole year had felt—that starting kindergarten and being away from her mom all day was like jumping into a big cold pool and it made her upset and worried. I said that now that her mom understood what worried Abby, she could help her feel better.

Attachment History and School-Age Development

Attachment history in infancy and toddlerhood continues to be a predictor of adjustment in middle childhood. The child's internalized working models of self, others and relationships are carried forward, affecting self-confidence, independence and peer relationships (Rubin & Rose-Krasnor, 1992). The longitudinal studies of Sroufe and his colleagues, which have been described in previous chapters, show that school age children with histories of secure attachment are "less dependent, less often isolated and less often the passive recipient of aggression," than children judged insecurely attached in the early years (Sroufe & Jacobvitz, 1989, p. 197). They are also more self-confident in meeting the tasks of middle childhood, which require increasing ability to function independently. Sroufe notes, "The roots of independence were in the . . . effective meeting of needs in infancy . . . " whereas "anxious attachment in infancy predicts dependency problems in preschool, middle childhood and preadolescence" (Sroufe, 1990, p. 341). Sroufe acknowledges that as childhood proceeds, many influences on the individual child's developmental pathways present themselves. Nevertheless, quality of attachment during the first 2 years continues to differentiate between children up to age 11.

SOCIAL DEVELOPMENT

The tasks of social development are more complex for school-age children compared with younger children. The school-age child enters the larger world, symbolized by elementary school, and must learn its values, rules, and routines. He must learn "appropriate" behavior in this larger context, through interactions with adult authorities as well as with peers. In middle childhood, even though parents remain central, other adults and peers take on increasing importance. Through relationships with peers, the school-age child continues to learn about sharing, negotiation, handling conflict, and social comparison. He also develops a clearer sense of himself as an autonomous person. In contrast to his relationships with adults, which involve feelings of dependency, with peers he feels more like an equal among equals (Liederman, 1989). The child's sense of self is increasingly determined by how he evaluates himself in relation to peers.

Social Perspective Taking

During the school-age years, children become increasingly sophisticated in understanding the perspectives of others. The preschool child tends to see the situations of others egocentrically and tries to assimilate another person's viewpoint into her own viewpoint. Beginning at age 6, the child becomes more able to see and acknowledge another person's different point of view. Over the next several years the child gradually realizes that there can be multiple ways of viewing a situation and can imagine how her own ideas appear to another person.

However, the fact that a 10-year-old has well-developed abilities in social perspective taking does not mean she always uses them. Ten-year-olds continue to show egocentric thinking, especially when they are feeling needy or under stress.

By age 10–12, a child can hold opposing or different viewpoints in mind at the same time (Gurucharri & Selman, 1982). For example, an 11-year-old girl in a divorce adjustment group described her feelings about her mother's upcoming remarriage: "Sometimes I wish she wasn't getting married again. He is nice and everything, but it's going to feel strange with him living with us. I asked my dad and he said he didn't care if she got remarried. I think he doesn't like it. But maybe it will be a good thing, because I see that my mom's a lot happier now. I want her to be happy." This child understood the perspectives of others as she reflected on her own. She also demonstrated a related capacity that also develops during late middle childhood—the ability to tolerate emotional ambivalence. The capacity to acknowledge having two feelings simultaneously has a developmental progression. Preschool children take an all-or-nothing perspective: they say that a person cannot feel happy and sad at the same time. Similarly they cannot yet take a balanced perspective on others in terms of seeing another person's "good" and "bad" qualities. The ability to understand ambivalence and to see others as a mix of characteristics develops during the school-age years and is clearly present at about age 10 (Harter, 1983b).

Because of their perspective-taking skills and repeated exposure to social cues and rules, school-age children are more adept than younger children at sizing up the feelings, wishes, and expectations of others and the social demands of a situation. For example, an 8-year-old is more likely than a 4-year-old to be attuned to when it is appropriate to be quiet. An 8-year-old at a religious service may be restless or bored, but he knows he cannot express these feelings except in a whisper. Further, he knows he must wait until the service is over before he can be active. By contrast, a 4-year-old may say in a normal voice during the service, "Daddy, when is it going to be over?" The 4-year-old has trouble containing her restlessness. As her own needs become imperative, she has less ability to behave in socially appropriate ways.

As perspective taking improves, so does the child's ability to see below the surface of behavior and to attribute psychological qualities and motives to others. Up to age 8, children tend to describe others in terms of their behavior and physical characteristics. After 8, because of improving ability to analyze and synthesize information, they begin to describe others in terms of internal, psychological characteristics (Barenboim, 1981). A 7-year-old may say, for example, "Andy runs around too much and yells too much," whereas a 10-

year-old describing the same child might say, "Andy is really hyper and silly, and is always trying to get you to pay attention to him." This ability has analogs in perception of social situations. Children become more able to assess other people's intentions and the psychological resonances of communication. For example, a preschool child may be confused by an adult's sarcastic remark because she cannot understand its psychological intent, whereas an older school age child has a strong emotional response because she understands the hostile intent of the statement.

Prosocial Behavior

The capacity for prosocial and altruistic behavior is not firmly present until middle childhood. Prosocial behavior requires the ability to take the other person's point of view, to be able to deduce the feelings of others, and to temporarily set aside one's own needs and desires. Prosocial behavior is supported by the internalization of moral standards, by the cognitive changes that create increased objectivity and decreased egocentrism, and by exposure during the preschool years to situations requiring the development of social skills (Zahn-Waxler & Smith, 1992). Prosocial and altruistic behavior increase with age, particularly when children are exposed to adult models of altruism. However, in a culture that emphasizes competition, children who at 9 or 10 are more sensitive to others' needs than they were at 4 or 5 may not behave any more altruistically because they have been socialized to be concerned about getting ahead of others and therefore restrain helpful impulses (Rushton, 1976; Elkind & Weiner, 1978). Prosocial behavior is encouraged in a competitive society, however, by participation in sports requiring teamwork and communication and in organizations like the Girl Scouts and Boy Scouts that attempt to foster individual skill development and social responsiveness.

Gender and Prosocial Behavior

Numerous studies have shown that girls show more prosocial behavior and empathy for others than do boys (Zahn-Waxler & Smith, 1992). Across middle childhood, compared with boys, girls' behavior becomes increasingly prosocial and their moral reasoning demonstrates more capacity for role taking and empathy (Gilligan, 1982; Eisenberg et al., 1987). These findings have been explained in several ways:

• *Identification.* Mothers and female child care providers are the primary caregivers of children. Because of same-sex identification, girls are likely to value prosocial acts of helping and caregiving.

• *Socialization.* Girls are more likely to be expected to care for younger siblings; in general, they are more likely to be rewarded for caretaking or conflict-resolving behavior. Aggressive behavior is discouraged in girls and is permitted and in some situations encouraged in boys.

• *Attunement to emotions.* Girls are more sensitive than boys to their own feelings and are more adept at reading the emotions of others (Brody, 1985). This has been interpreted as an effect of socialization.

• *Culture.* Children identify with and assimilate female and male gender stereotypes that are presented by their culture: "Many cultures . . . emphasize the value for males of behavior that may be incompatible with empathy (e.g., competition, aggression, assertion, achievement, and independence). In contrast, for females, appropriate gender-role-related patterns such as empathy, compassion, caregiving, emotional connection, commitment, and relationship may be emphasized" (Zahn-Waxler & Smith, 1992, p. 240).

Friendships

School-age children's close friendships are based on mutual liking, sharing of interests, and gender. Same-sex friendships become the norm as gender identification becomes more firmly established and children take in culturally based gender expectations (Thorne, 1986). The same tendency toward choosing as friends people who are similar to oneself leads to increasing same-race friendships as children get older (Hartup, 1992). Across middle childhood, children's friendships deepen and their ideas about what a friend is evolve. For a 6- to 8-year-old, the idea of a friend is organized around concrete activities: "Jenna is my friend because we like to play with our dolls together." Older children begin to think of friendships as relationships that involve commitment, loyalty, mutual support, and responsibility (Damon, 1983). An 11-year-old boy said, "James is my best friend. He treats me nice and he helps me. Like my mama said I couldn't go out of the house without picking up my stuff, and James helped me so we could go soon. I help him too if he needs it."

Friends serve a number of functions. Since friendships are more egalitarian than are relationships with adults they provide the child with a sense of identification with another person who is like themselves. Rather than comparing themselves with adults, whose abilities are generally far beyond the school-age child's, they can more comfortably compare themselves with friends. They also may gain some relief from the superego by seeing that their friends are not always successful at living up to the dictates of conscience. By observing their friends, they are relieved from the need to be perfect and can become more self-accepting (Gemelli, 1996). Children who have friends in their classrooms make better adjustment to school. Stable friendships during the early years of school provide support for the transition into middle childhood (Ladd, 1990). Attachments to friends serve some of the same functions of attachment to parents by helping the child feel safe and secure (Howes, 1988). Friendships provide opportunities for learning to behave cooperatively, preparing children for the more intimate emotional sharing of adolescence (Hartup, 1992).

Working things out with friends also provides practice in resolving conflicts. Although children who are good friends have frequent conflicts, they are also motivated to resolve conflicts in order to preserve the friendship (Hartup, 1992). Consequently, friends are more likely to disengage from a conflict than to attempt to win through coercion (Newcomb & Bagwell, 1995). By contrast, children who are extremely shy, aggressive, or coercive of others tend to have fewer friends and more unstable friendships, which deprives them of some of the "developmental advantages" of learning social skills through relationships with friends (Hartup, 1992). Children who are rejected by peers make poorer adjustment to school. Without the social support provided by friends, they are less motivated to succeed and develop more negative attitudes toward school (Ladd, 1990). When antisocial school-age children do have friends, they mutually reinforce antisocial behavior, supporting each other in defining themselves against social norms. The choice of antisocial friends has been linked to histories of coercive parent–child relations during the early years (Dishion, Patterson, & Griesler, 1994).

Peer Group, Social Reputation, and Self-Esteem

Social reputation becomes important during the middle years, as children begin to reflect on their status in the group. School-age children are increasingly aware of how others see them. A child who is sought out by peers *knows* he is popular and gains in self-esteem from that knowledge. Another child is aware that he is less popular, and his self-esteem suffers. In contrast, a preschool child may be angry or unhappy when he is rejected by other children, but is not yet able to reflect on his social status. Because social status becomes a defining part of the sense of self during the middle years, children with lower social reputations commonly experience anxiety about themselves and suffer low self-esteem. Children who are temperamentally shy and children who are aggressive often, for different reasons, have poor reputations and have low self-esteem (Hartup, 1992).

TEMPERAMENT AND PEER RELATIONS:
A BRIEF CASE EXAMPLE

Eric, a 9-year-old, seemed, according to his parents' history, to fit Kagan's (1989) description of the temperamentally inhibited child. Children of this temperamental type are seen as shy or "slow to warm up." They show "high sensitivity to stimulation, gradual adaptation to change, and a tendency to withdraw under stress" (Lieberman, 1993, p. 120). Eric's presenting problem was school refusal. He frequently got stomachaches and headaches in the morning before school and tried to talk his parents into believing he was sick. Eric's teacher noted that he was neither a popular nor an unpopular kid but that he did not seem to know how to reach out to other kids. She said that his quiet demeanor caused him to be ignored by other boys in the class. Eric was a thoughtful and bright child, and he directly told me, "I don't want to go to school because I don't have friends there. Last year I had friends in my class, but this year none of them are in my class." He said that a lot of the boys act tough and mean and that he didn't like that. He was repelled by their aggressive behavior, even though they did not pick on him. He also said that they all hung out together and chose each other when teams were being picked. He said, "I'm not that good at football because I really don't like it, so they choose me last." I asked how that felt, and he said, "Kinda bad." He mentioned having a new friend named Mike, who had similar interests—collecting comic books and Star Wars miniatures—but said he didn't know him enough to suggest getting together outside of school. He mentioned another boy who wanted to be his friend, "But I don't really like him that much because he says disgusting things about sex, and also tells lies and brags a lot."

Eric was a self-sufficient and sensitive child who had many interests. He was not depressed. He had enough personal "dignity" to avoid the fate of many withdrawn children—being teased and bullied. But he was not assertive in trying to make friends and when a peer did something he did not like, such as talking about sex, his only strategy was to withdraw. Eric's difficulties in finding sympathetic peers were exacerbating his temperamental shyness and causing him to lose self-esteem.

"Difficult" Temperament, Impulse Control Problems, and Peer Relations

Children with histories of "difficult" temperament, ADHD (attention-deficit/hyperactivity disorder), or other problems with impulse control may also be unpopular with peers because they are too volatile and aggressive. Their cumulative history of alienating peers through negative, disagreeable behavior and their continuing impulsiveness cause them to have trouble figuring out how to act in stressful social situations: "The child who has difficulty inhibiting responses, is easily distracted and . . . is irritable may be less likely to think through his or her social dilemmas" (Rubin & Rose-Krasnor, 1992, p. 303). Consequently, he may overreact to disappointment about not being chosen first for a team or to teasing and will further alienate his peers. Aggression and antisocial behavior often derive from punitive and coercive family patterns in early childhood (Hartup, 1989). Studies of the social behavior of aggressive school-age children describe coercion, teasing, provocation, and bribing to get peers to do what they want. They are more likely to tell than to ask, less able to think of prosocial strategies to reach their goals, and more likely to become aggressive if another child refuses to cooperate (Rubin, Moller, & Emptage, 1987). Aggressive children are often described by peers as kids who spoil things. For example, a boy may run into a game of kickball, grab the ball, and run away, effectively stopping the game. He is reinforced in this behavior by the feeling of power he gains and by the intense reactions of the children whose game he has interrupted. Gradually the child who is aggressive is rejected by peers and tends to choose friends who are aggressive like himself. Then these peers mutually influence one another (Hartup, 1989).

Influence of the Group

School-age children define themselves as group members, not just as individual friends. Groups in middle childhood are organized around gender and sex roles, ethnic/racial identification, common interests, and social status. Within these groups, there are dominance hierarchies. For example, in the group of boys that plays football at recess, the best players are likely to be given the most respect by others. Children are very aware of the social groups. A bright and precociously reflective 10-year-old girl described the groups in her class as she talked about her concerns about not fitting in: "There are three groups. There are the snobby popular girls. I don't want to be with them because they're mean to the kids that aren't popular. Then there are the dweebs. They're the ones the snobby girls are mean to. Then there are some kids like me who aren't in either group. I'm not a dweeb, so they don't tease me, but sometimes I think if I have a friend who's a dweeb, the snobby girls will think I am one. I feel guilty when I stay away from a dweeb who really is nice, just because I'm afraid of being treated mean by the snobs. I don't want to be one of the snobs because all they do is talk about clothes and how much money their families have and act mean to other kids except their own group." This child's statement expresses the concern children have about being accepted in a group, as well as clearly describing the *status hierarchies that emerge in middle childhood.*

Once in a group, children are to a fair degree influenced by group norms and peer pressure becomes a strong force. However, much peer pressure reflects adult values that children have internalized (Hartup, 1992). Children with internalized prosocial values resist the ideas of other children who suggest antisocial behavior. Nor are they likely to be pulled into antisocial peer groups. By contrast, "antisocial norms are most likely to be pressed on children who are already disposed to be antisocial and aggressive" (Hartup, 1992, p. 275).

LANGUAGE AND COMMUNICATION

By age 7 the child has a basic grasp of the syntactical and grammatical structures of her native language. Compared to the preschool child who was learning basic language concepts and rules, the school-age child is learning variations of the rules and more difficult constructions such as the passive voice (Chomsky, 1969). Vocabulary continues to increase, though not as rapidly as during the preschool years. Although there is a range of language ability across individual children, school age children generally possess sufficient facility with language to express what they are thinking and to tell coherent narratives having a beginning, middle, and end. However, these gains do not mean that it becomes easy for school-age children to talk about emotionally charged topics. It it one thing to describe the ordinary events of the day, and another to reveal distressing or conflictual *feelings.* Consequently, play and other types of symbolic representation continue to be essential forms of communication in intervention with school-age children (Webb, 1991b).

Language Difficulties and the Academic Tasks of Middle Childhood

Even though most children demonstrate adequate oral language skills in middle childhood, more subtle difficulties, such as problems in reading and writing, come to light as the child must apply language skills to academic tasks in school. Children with a history of a language disorder during the preschool years often develop reading and writing disorders in the middle years (Arnold, 1990). In particular, children with problems in receptive language are likely to have learning disorders in the area of reading, because they have difficulties in comprehension. Delayed speech is a strong predictor of later reading and spelling problems. It is likely that many reading/writing disorders are an extension of the mechanisms underlying expressive and receptive language problems. Children with difficulties in auditory processing, which is the basis of their receptive language problems, later have trouble learning to read phonetically because this approach to reading requires them to differentiate between sounds and to remember sequences of sounds that make up words (Hooper & Willis, 1989). Children with visual deficits have trouble matching sounds with symbols. They have difficulty decoding even simple words visually. They have trouble remembering the shape of the letters as well as combinations of letters in words (Lyon, 1996). Children without learning disorders utilize both auditory and visual strategies in learning to read.

Language Issues for Immigrant Children

Immigrant children face a different type of learning challenge that is based on language knowledge rather than learning disorders. It has been estimated that by the year 2000 there will be 5 million school-age children in the United States whose first language is not English (Hakuta & Garcia, 1989). These children must learn English in order to function in school. Often they start out behind and have trouble learning English quickly enough to master the academic concepts that are presented in single-language classrooms. They are not simply learning a second language but also a second culture. They are socialized in their first culture by their parents and in the second by teachers and others. They may also be subtly or directly pressed to maintain their first language by their parents. Frequently they must function as translators for parents, and, in a role reversal that can produce anxiety and resentment, the child may become the parent's guide for navigating the new culture.

Recent research on language acquisition has rejected older ideas that bilingualism impedes cognitive development. Children are able to learn a second language without compromising their cognitive abilities (Hakuta & Garcia, 1989). However, the degree of support a child receives, on the one hand, for learning the second language and, on the other, for retaining her first language affects whether she will be competent bilingually and biculturally or conflicted about language and identity. If an "English-only" approach is taken by schools, she will feel that her native language and culture are devalued. But if her parents do not encourage biculturalism, she may feel conflicted about learning

English and the culture underlying it (Hakuta & Garcia, 1989). Immigrant children and children whose families speak languages other than English are more often referred for assessment of learning and psychiatric disorders; however, "Many of the behaviors considered problematic by teachers are, in reality, characteristics of students who are in the process of second language acquisition" (Canino & Spurlock, 1994, p. 21).

Language and Cognitive Development

Language sophistication depends on cognitive development. When children acquire the ability to reverse their thought, they are able to understand transformations in syntax. For example, in order to understand the meaning of a sentence written in the passive voice, "She was liked by her teacher," the child must be able to translate it into the active voice, "Her teacher liked her" (Elkind & Weiner, 1978). The ability to make such changes automatically depends on the capacity for reversibility, which develops between 6 and 8. In a similar way, the ability to perceive nuances and to make comparisons, which develops during this period, allows the child to understand comparative words. In contrast to preschool children, who make comparisons in absolute terms (big vs. small), school-age children understand gradations and can give descriptions using comparative terms: "My dog is bigger than yours, but his ears are a little smaller."

Between 8 and 10, children develop an appreciation for word play and jokes that depend on double meanings. They can understand the classic riddle, "What's black and white and red all over?," or the mildly dirty joke, "Hey, did you read the book called *Under the Bleachers* by Seymour Butts?" Figures of speech that would puzzle a 4-year-old can be understood by 7- or 8-year-olds. I was playing cards with a 7-year-old who said, "I might have a trick up my sleeve." Playing dumb, I said, "But you're wearing a short-sleeve shirt, so how could you?" He responded, "That's not what it means. It's not really in my sleeve. It's in my mind." School-age children can also begin to appreciate metaphor, simile, and the condensed imagery of *haiku* poetry. An 8-year-old girl, Carol Moore, wrote this *haiku*:

> "Waves slap on the shore
> And make noises like houses crumbling
> Many houses falling down." (R. Lewis, 1966, p. 114)

Language ability is also influenced by the child's language environment. Children whose parents have over time talked to them and encouraged them to put feelings and ideas into words and particularly into narratives are more likely to have good language skills. In turn, these children are more likely to share ideas with peers and improve their language skills further. Children growing up in environments emphasizing interactions using language tend to have an easier time acquiring reading and writing skills (Daiute, 1993).

The cognitive shift toward decentered perspective taking means that school-age children can use language to communicate in new ways. While a preschool child has trouble identifying another's perspective, the school-age child knows that others see things differently than she does. The young school-age child may still be quite egocentric in her thinking, but she is a better communicator because she now can listen to another child and respond in terms of what she has said, as opposed to responding strictly from an egocentric point of view (Piaget, 1952a). The practice she has had negotiating with peers during the preschool period, combined with cognitive advances and increasing peer orientation, has prepared her for communication that takes another child's ideas into account. Older school-age children are more sophisticated in perspective taking and can shape what they say to fit their perception of the other's viewpoint. For example, a 10-year-old boy who collects superhero comic books communicates in a specialized language when talking to another collector. When he talks to an adult who does not know much about these comics, he can realize this and provide more explanation. It may take the 10-year-old a few moments to realize that the adult does not have the same knowledge he does, but when he does understand this he can communicate in ways that lead to consensual meaning (Selman, 1980; Hoffman, 1977).

The maturing of language and cognitive abilities during middle childhood has important implications for self-regulation. As the school-age child becomes increasingly adept at putting internal states into words—worry, frustration, anger, and other feelings—he becomes more able to delay acting on his feelings. He learns that speaking his mind can be an effective way of gaining perspective on private thoughts, both through his own self-reflection and through the feedback he gets from others. When parents encourage verbal expression they convey that words can be used to understand the world or resolve conflict. This promotes the use of verbalization as a means of regulating affect and impulse. By contrast, in families where verbal interaction is discouraged, interpersonal empathy is devalued, or secrecy is enforced, the school-age child does not feel permitted to put private thoughts into words. In dysfunctional families where sexual abuse occurs, for example, the child is compelled to be silent and often has no outlet except private fantasy for coping with the trauma of abuse.

PLAY AND FANTASY

As the middle years proceed, the fantasy play so prominent during the preschool period declines. It is often said that play is the work of the preschooler. For the school-age child, a work orientation emphasizing intellectual mastery and physical competence gradually supplants play as a compelling interest (Erikson, 1963). Children who continue to insist that play is their reason for being are increasingly seen as immature. In part this shift in orientation is forced on the child by external reality: she must learn to work in order to master school tasks, which require her increasingly to be organized, logical, and unplayful. But new cognitive capabilities increase her internal motivation to learn new skills. These rapid cognitive advances offer the child the possibility of understanding the world through systematic, logical thinking, replacing the preschooler's tendency to try to understand through imaginative thinking. Play remains important to the school-age child, but fantasy play is gradually supplanted by the organized and ritualized play of games and sports. At the same time, children may continue fantasy play by themselves and with best friends.

Games with Rules

By age 4, preschool children can learn how to play simple board games. They can count, take turns, and understand that winning depends on reaching the last square first. However, preschool children do not enjoy structured games as much as fantasy play. Games with rules constrain their egocentric imagination, and they have not yet developed far enough cognitively to be intellectually interested in the structure and logic of a game. They often cannot accept losing and may quit or cheat to avoid losing or react with intense disappointment if they lose. By 6 or 7, however, children can learn somewhat more complicated games, play by the rules more gracefully, take some pleasure in following the twists and turns of the game, and enjoy exercising their skills. They still may be intensely competitive, intent on winning, and disappointed in losing. However, even though games are competitive, they are explicitly social and cooperative, since the players must follow a set of rules for the game to go on. Young school-age children often have difficulty learning their roles in complex games like baseball, and mistakes based on excitement and impulsiveness are common. A few years ago I went to my 7-year-old niece's T-ball game. When a ball was hit to the center of the infield, *all* four infielders ran toward it. The shortstop picked up the ball and threw it to first base, but the first baseman was not on the base to catch it because he had run toward the ball. As children reach 10–12 years of age, they begin to enjoy games that involve strategy rather than chance (Baumeister & Senders, 1988). Games also symbolize the child's developing peer orientation and become one of the important vehicles he uses to assess his status among peers (Ruble, 1983). Skillful children are respected by peers. Children who frequently ignore rules, blow up in the middle of a game, or otherwise "spoil the game" risk rejection by peers.

The structure of the games of middle childhood mirrors many of the general developmental tasks of this period. Organized playground games such as kickball, soccer, basketball, hopscotch, and jump rope implicitly socialize children to take turns, improve their skills, focus on planning and goals, exert sufficient control over emotions to allow the game to proceed, and follow the rules (Piaget & Inhelder, 1969). Psychoanalytic theory emphasizes that structured games represent displacements of aggression. They allow the child to exert power and to feel dominant without being aggressive in a way that will hurt the other person (Peller, 1954). The ability to play structured games indicates that the child has learned to tolerate frustration and delay gratification (A. Freud, 1965). Learning to play games with complicated scenarios and rules requires self-discipline and concentration.

Even the spontaneous fantasy play of school-age children frequently becomes ritualized and rule governed. For example, 10-year-old boys in play with miniature army men or action figures often devise elaborate systems of rules for combat. School-age children often create structure around physical activities, turning rough-and-tumble play into games with rules (Pellegrini, 1987). For example, at a family picnic a group of cousins, girls and boys, ranging from 8 to 12, were taking turns swinging out on a rope and dropping into a river. Gradually, they began suggesting specific ways of doing this and a competition evolved, with more and more elaborate tasks being proposed. They had to turn around on the rope and face the bank before dropping into the water; or skim the water with their feet before letting go; or grasp their knees after letting go to cannonball into the water. Implicitly, they seemed impelled to introduce structure, competition, and consensually defined skills into what had begun as spontaneous play.

Hobbies as Play

Typical school-age activities such as hobbies and collecting depict the evolution of play. Children collect dolls, comic books, sports cards, action figures, rocks, soda cans, or colored glass beads, to name a few. Commercial interests appeal to and exploit school-age children's passion for collecting by continuously creating new collectible objects, often as spin-offs from popular children's movies. Sometimes children assemble collections of disparate objects that have personal meaning and keep them in a special box. Other hobbies involve craft projects, plastic models, or making things out of scrap materials. Anna Freud (1965, p. 84) suggested that hobbies are "halfway between work and play" because they involve mental skills of organizing and categorizing objects or the ability to build or assemble things, yet also are vehicles for the expression of fantasy. The connection between work and play is most obvious in objects like dolls and action figures, which are both collected and used in fantasy play.

Fantasy

The movement from social dramatic play to organized games tells only part of the story of the evolution of play. In middle childhood, a kind of mental play, internal fantasy, increases as play with peers becomes more ritualized. Fantasy continues to fulfill the functions that dramatic play did for the preschooler: pleasure, imagined fulfillment of wishes, exploration of reality, imagining oneself in more advanced roles, and rehearsal of actions and plans. In psychoanalytic theory, internal fantasy is seen as a substitute for action and is therefore associated with the capacity for controlling behavior. Fantasy provides the school-age child with an outlet for expressing wishes that are not possible to achieve in reality, as well as negative or unacceptable thoughts and feelings that would invite punishment or criticism if expressed in action.

School-age children often keep their fantasies private from adults. Their involvement with fantasy is most often registered by their interest in movies and TV programs, and by the kinds of play they do alone or with best friends. Two 10-year-old boys had seen the film *Desperado*, a story of revenge featuring extreme violence. When they were playing together they sometimes acted out scenes from the film and sometimes drew elaborate pictures of the main character mowing down 20 adversaries. The appeal of such play is that it supports the school-age child's wish to be competent and powerful, even in the face of extreme odds. These two boys were not aggressive in their behavior toward each other or other children. Their wishes to be powerful and dominating were contained in fantasy. In general, however, the content of children's fantasy becomes more realistic and social as they move through middle childhood (Sarnoff, 1976). Instead of daydreaming about being a superhero, like a 6-year-old, a 9-year-old imagines himself being a hero or success in his peer group.

COGNITIVE DEVELOPMENT

By age 7 the child is moving away from egocentric thinking and is using logic. The child becomes aware that intuition based on an awareness of surface appearances is not always correct (Smith & Cowie, 1991). Piaget's famous experiments with mass and volume illustrate this shift in thinking. Piaget and Inhelder (1969) described middle childhood, specifically 7–12 years of age, as the phase of *concrete operations*. Unlike toddlers and preschoolers, who solve problems by manipulating objects physically, the school-age child learns about reality by manipulating the objects of his perception *mentally*. The essence of the move from Piaget's sensorimotor stage to the stage of concrete operations, then, is *a shift from action to thought*. During the preschool period, the child has slowly developed the ability to represent experience mentally, a process that goes hand in hand with the development of language. Mastery of language, which proceeds rapidly across the preschool period, provides the school-age child with a vehicle for organizing experience mentally.

Concrete operations involve basic reasoning processes but are distinguished from formal operations—abstract, hypothetical thinking—that develop in adolescence by the fact that the child can only use them to think about objects that are visible in front of her, rather than purely mental phenomena. In the conservation experiment with water in different containers, for example, the school-age child looks at concrete reality and thinks about what she observes, reasoning that since no water was added the amount of water is the same (Kagan, 1984). She realizes that the shape of the containers makes the amount of water look different, and she is aware that if the steps in the procedure were reversed, the amount of water would be the same. Her thinking involves *reversibility*, which Piaget posits as a hallmark of concrete operations. Instead of being tied to her immediate impressions, a child can systematically think back over what she has perceived. For example, by age 8, she can learn a reverse procedure to check a math problem: if $10 - 6 = 4$, then I can check my answer by adding, $4 + 6 = 10$. In the conservation experiment an 8-year-old is likely to explain that the water could be poured back into the first container where it would look exactly as it did at first, using reversible thinking to prove that the amount is the same (Piaget & Inhelder, 1969).

The ability to perform mental operations based on logic and reasoning, however, requires another developmental advance—"decentration." To think logically, the child must be able to distinguish between the subjective and the objective. Piaget argued that the shift from egocentric to decentered thought between the ages of 6 and 7 heralds and makes possible the development of higher-level cognitive functions. When the child begins to see reality from the decentered as opposed to the egocentric perspective, he is freer to view the world from the more analytical and logical perspective implied in concrete mental operations (Piaget, 1952b). The ability to decenter also allows for a clearer understanding of causality. Unlike the more egocentric preschooler, the school-age child can separate his fantasies from the actual causes of events. A 9-year-old, for example, may be sad and angry about his parents' separation, but he is less likely than a preschooler to believe something he did caused the separation. In middle childhood impressionistic, intuitive thinking remains important, but thinking characterized by reasoning and analysis now is also available.

Cognitive Advances in the Transition to Middle Childhood

Although brain maturation proceeds steadily throughout childhood, there appears to be a spurt between 6 and 7, which correlates with a number of changes in perceptual and cognitive abilities that appear at about age 7 (Case, 1985; Janowsky & Carper, 1996). Along with the more general shift toward decentration and improved perspective taking, the abilities listed below provide the foundation for concrete mental operations:

Spatial Orientation

The child knows her own right from left at age 6 but has difficulty saying which is the right or left side of a person sitting opposite her. By age 7–8, she is able to do this (T. Shapiro & Perry, 1976).

Time Orientation

Older preschool children know the days of the week, but children are not able to learn to tell time or understand how the calendar is organized until about 7 (T. Shapiro & Perry, 1976). This clearer sense of how time is organized allows school-age children to think ahead and to plan their actions more efficiently than a preschooler can.

Seriation

In one of Piaget's tasks, children were asked to arrange 10 sticks of uneven lengths in an order from shortest to longest. Preschool children typically could not accomplish this. They might get a few of the sticks in the correct order, but then seemed to get mixed up and arrange the rest in a random order. By contrast, 7-year-olds grasp the concept of a series and are able to arrange the sticks correctly. This ability to apply a concept of size, weight, length, or some other quantifiable character- istic to a group of objects is one of the building blocks of mathematical understanding (Piaget & Inhelder, 1969).

Visual Organizational Ability

The child becomes "less and less bound by the organization or lack of organization of visual materials he looks at. Increasingly, he is able mentally to reorganize materials into patterns that are more interesting or satisfying" (Elkind, 1994, p. 123). The school-age child can look beyond surface perceptions to imagine new patterns, whereas the pre- schooler has difficulty doing this. Elkind and Weiss (1967) demon- strated this change in the ability organize visual materials by asking children to name pictures of objects that were pasted on a page in a "disordered array." The objects were placed at odd angles and showed no organized pattern of alignment in relation to each other. When pre- school children were asked to name the 15 objects, they seemed to become confused by the lack of organization of the objects. They named some objects twice and did not name others. Younger school- age children, age 6–8, had no trouble naming all the objects, because they mentally organized the disarrayed objects, using a systematic strategy of scanning the objects from right to left or up to down.

A more homely real-life example of the child's visual organiza- tional ability is demonstrated by the child's job of cleaning up her room. While many children do not like to pick up their rooms, an 8- year-old can generally do it without assistance because she can bring order out of chaos mentally, thinking about where things go. By con- trast, a 5-year-old is likely to feel overwhelmed by toys strewn across the floor because she is not yet able to construct an image of the room with everything in its place. Consequently, the younger child will need an adult to help her organize the task.

Part–Whole Discrimination, Ability to Move between Details and Overall Perceptions and to Perceive Multiple Variables

Preschool children may focus on specific aspects of a picture or on the whole picture but have trouble moving back and forth between the two levels of perception. For example, Elkind (1994) summarizes one of his own studies: "When young children are asked to compare com- plex figures, such as two houses that are alike except for the number of windows, they say the two are the same if they find only one similarity, without any further exploration for possible discrepancies. Children of seven or eight explore both houses systematically before deciding whether the two are alike or different" (p. 123). The child is now able to perceive two or more aspects of a problem at once. By contrast, the child under 6 tends to see only one dimension of a problem (Siegler, 1996). The ability to move back and forth between parts and wholes, between details and larger organizing ideas, is the basis of categorization and classification. As they move through middle childhood, children's ability to view reality in categories with multiple variables increases.

Auditory Processing

School-age children, compared with preschoolers, are more able to process information given orally. They are more adept at using verbal cues to understand a problem. This ability is based on their more sophisticated grasp of language and their improving capacity for strictly mental representation. It has clear implications for school performance, since teachers frequently give directions and define problems using words alone.

These changes in cognition and perception which emerge during the early part of middle childhood are of critical importance because they are needed for the learning tasks children confront in elementary school. The elementary-school curriculum assumes by second and third grade that children possess these abilities. Those children who do not, for whatever reason, are at a tremendous disadvantage, and are at risk socially and emotionally. A third-grade boy who had average overall intelligence but serious learning disorders that put him far behind his peers told me, "I'm the dumbest kid in my class." As is typical of younger school-age children, this boy was not able to take a balanced view of his weaknesses and strengths. His evaluation of himself in absolutist terms, characteristic of his level of development, contributed further to his low self-esteem.

Memory

Memory improves with cognitive development. During the preschool years memory grows with language development. Memories that are encoded verbally are more firmly registered (Kagan, 1984). During the school-age years, improving memory is related to the child's more sophisticated strategies for processing information. *By the end of the middle years, the child's ability to categorize memories and deliberately recall information is nearly as efficient as an adult's* (Kail, 1990). School-age children remember more than preschoolers do because they intuitively apply rules for recalling information. They have learned to sort information by time, place, category, and other cues, all of which serve to organize memories and thus facilitate recall. As the ability to think in categories improves, so does memory, because categories allow for more effective storage of information (Neimark, Slotnick, & Ulrich, 1971; Kagan, 1984). Improved memory ability allows the child to keep a sequence of steps in mind, which means he can follow stepwise instructions common in academic tasks (Case, 1985).

These developing cognitive abilities are reinforced by formal instruction as well as by the value placed on memory in the elementary-school classroom. School tasks encourage children to intentionally remember information. The capacity for retrieval of information stored in memory improves in middle childhood, but this ability is also reinforced by the stress on being able to retrieve information to answer questions in class. Motivated by school tasks, older school-age children create strategies for remembering—repeating information to themselves, or creating mental cues, categories, or images that help them remember (Flavell, 1985; Bjorklund, 1990). For example, an 8-year-old girl who was learning the multiplication tables told me, "I kept having trouble with the nines, but then my aunt told me a trick—you can always tell what the next one is going to be by adding 10 and subtracting 1, like 6 times 9 is 54, so you know that 7 times 9 is going to be 63."

The Executive Processes

Kagan (1984) contrasts the differences in cognitive abilities of preschool and school-age children by pointing out that school-age children make more use of "executive processes," by which he means *skills in approaching and thinking about problems.* These cognitive skills enhance ability to solve problems. Table 10.1 summarizes Kagan's discussion of the executive processes.

SELF-REGULATION

Cognitive processes increase self-regulation as middle childhood proceeds. The ability to think about experience logically and coherently reduces the child's anxiety. The school-age child understands the world and himself better than the preschooler does. He can more precisely appraise stressful situations and take coping actions that are appropriate (Lazarus & Folkman, 1983). Because his reality testing is more accurate, he is less vulnerable than the preschooler to fears of the unknown. The school-age child's improving capacities for sustained attention and goal-directedness implicitly permit him to maintain self-control. At the same time, psychological defense mechanisms become more sophisticated as means of protecting the child from anxiety. As the repertoire of defenses expands, the defenses themselves become more efficient.

TABLE 10.1. Executive Processes and Problem Solving in Middle Childhood

- *Ability to articulate a problem and generate ideas about what actions can be taken to solve it.*

- *Knowing cognitive strategies that will help in problem solving.* For example, a school-age child who is told to remember a set of pictures will spend time studying them because she knows the extra attention will help her remember them; by contrast, a 4-year-old will not look at the pictures for as long as the school-age child does, apparently because she does not yet understand that a longer study will improve memory.

- *Knowing when to activate cognitive rules and strategies to solve problems.* Essentially, school-age children ask themselves, "What do I need to think about to figure out this problem?"

- *A more flexible approach to problem solving.* A preschool child is more likely to persist in solving a problem in the same way, even if he is not succeeding, while a 9- or 10-year-old is more likely "to discard inefficient solutions that are not working and to search systematically for better alternatives" (Kagan, 1984, p. 231).

- *Longer attention span, ability to resist distractions, and better control of anxiety.* More solid self-regulation allows school-age children to keep focused on problem solving even when the problem is hard to solve.

- *Ability to continuously monitor performance.* The child can pay attention to how he is working on a task and evaluate whether he is on the right track.

- *Faith in her ability to think about problems.* A younger child stops trying if she cannot figure out a problem, whereas a school-age child knows from experience that thinking can work.

- *Awareness of shortcomings in thinking.* Older school-age children are usually aware when a solution they have arrived at is inadequate. Unlike preschoolers, who are less concerned about mistakes or ideals of performance, school-age children have internalized standards of performance that cause them to search for the best solution to a problem.

Note. Data abstracted from Kagan (1984).

Anxiety during Middle Childhood

School-age children respond with anxiety to some of the same situations that were troublesome in early childhood: separation, worry about losing control, fear of body damage, and confusion about reality. However, for children who have histories of secure attachment, live in safe circumstances, and have not been traumatized, these earlier sources of anxiety are not so pressing as for the younger child. They also have more ability to handle these sources of anxiety. Their cognitive abilities make it easier for them to sort out whether a situation is really dangerous. They have had enough experience in the world to appraise situations more accurately. For example, a 3-year-old who is threatened by another child may become terribly anxious because he cannot separate the threatening words from the actuality of being hurt. By contrast, a 10-year-old has learned that threats and the actions described in threats are frequently two different things. So when a peer casually says, "I'm going to kick your butt," he can appraise the threat by evaluating the context in which it occurs. He may conclude, without much conscious thought, "This is my friend. He likes to push people around with words, but he doesn't get in fights. What he really meant was that he didn't like it that I took the rebound away from him. I don't have to worry about this." On the other hand, if the other child's tone is angry or if he is known to act with physical aggression, the child will appraise the threat differently and get ready to protect himself.

The anxieties of the school-age child match the developmental tasks of middle childhood. She is particularly concerned about being rejected or excluded or seen as inadequate by peers. Consequently she is very aware of her performance—in academics, social relations, or athletics—compared with that of peers. The school-age child has a firm self-representation and can look at herself from an outside perspective. When her performance falls short of her self-representation, she may become anxious. This anxiety may be increased by the superego's moral judgments and criticisms.

Strategies for Self-Regulation and Coping

Several components of self-regulation come together in middle childhood. These emerging self-regulatory abilities contribute to the evident calmness, self-control, and ability to sustain attention that we see in normal school-age children. When school-age children are faced with external or internal stressors, they are likely to take an active coping stance, drawing on their own self-regulatory strategies or seeking help from others. They are motivated to exert control over stressors and avoid passive acceptance (Band & Weisz, 1988).

Representational Competence

The cognitive and linguistic advances during middle childhood promote an increasing ability to mentally organize and make sense of experience. The capacity to think about stressful experiences reduces anxiety. Representational competence also has an interpersonal, communicative dimension in the middle years. The child can tell the story of his experience with clarity. Unlike a preschooler, who may not be able to find all the words he needs or whose emotions during a stressful experience may overwhelm his cognitive grasp of it, the school-age child can gain relief from anxiety because he is able to describe what happened. For example, an 8-year-old boy who got lost in the woods near his house came home and told his father, "I went to a new part of the woods, not where the path goes and I got lost. I looked around, and I couldn't see any houses. There was a hill, a little one, and I went up to the top of it, but I still couldn't see where I was. I was really scared. Then I saw this old barbed wire. It was just on the ground. I followed along it, and after a little while I could see the townhouses near the other parking lot. Then I knew where I was, and I ran home." This boy was agitated when he came home, but he visibly calmed down after he told his story and his father listened to it. He was able to reduce his fear by communicating what happened to him.

Cognitive Control of Emotional Arousal

The school-age child is less at the mercy of strong emotions than the preschooler because he can use mental strategies to control his feelings (Zahn-Waxler & Smith, 1992). He can rationalize distress saying, for example, "This isn't so bad. I'll get over it." He can also combine rationalization with denial: "It's not that important to be the captain of the team as long as I get to play."

Use of Emotions as "Internal Monitoring and Guidance Systems" (Cummings & Davies, 1996, p. 125)

Emotions themselves are the indicators of how a person is feeling and therefore contribute to self-regulation. Like attachment, "emotional security" is a set goal in humans—we strive to maintain felt security or psychic equilibrium (Cummings & Davies, 1996). A range of emotional responses, not simply anxiety, can signal the need to make efforts to restore a feeling of security. The school-age child differentiates among her emotions and knows more clearly than the preschooler what they mean. She is therefore less likely to be overwhelmed by strong emotions in a stressful situation. Just as she is better able to cognitively appraise external situations, she has more skill in appraising her emotions and responding to them with an aim of maintaining or restoring a sense of security. In normally developing children, the use of discrete emotions as signals combines with cognitive appraisal strategies to support self-regulation (Cicchetti, Ackerman, & Izard, 1995).

Ability to Remain Focused on Goal-Directed Actions Even When External Support Is Not Being Provided (Karoly, 1982)

While preschool children are distracted by both external stimuli and their own thoughts, school-age children can resist distraction and sustain their attention. This ability is in part the result of the moral learning that one should finish what one starts, but it is primarily based on the cognitive skill of being able to imagine the sequence of steps needed to achieve a goal and on the sense of oneself as autonomous. Preschoolers, by contrast, often need the support of others to maintain goal-directed behavior.

Increasing Self-Control

Social learning theorists define self-control as a special aspect of self-regulation that involves the ability to remain focused on a goal in the face of stress or interference (Patterson, 1982b). Increasingly, school-age children make this a conscious process and use cognitive strategies to maintain a focus. For example, an 8-year-old who is up to bat maintains his concentration on the pitcher in spite of being razzed by the opposing players, who are yelling, "Hey batter, you can't hit, you'll miss it by a mile." This child hears the heckling and understands its intent is to ruin his concentration. He controls his affective responses and also may use internal talk ("Just watch the pitcher. Be ready to swing if it's a good one.") in order to stay ready to hit the ball.

Ability to Delay Gratification Based on Cognitive Evaluation

Harter (1983b), summarizing studies where children were offered a bigger reward if they were able to wait and a smaller one if they were not, states, "A steady decrease in the choice of the less desirable reward was obtained across kindergarten through sixth grade, indicating that children were increasingly able to delay gratification in anticipation of the more desirable reward" (p. 348). As children proceed through middle childhood, they become less impulsive and more thoughtful in their decision making.

Ability to Understand the Concept of Planning and to Make Conscious Plans

By age 8, children can think through several steps in a plan of action. Conscious planning helps the school-age child remain focused on a goal and allows her to resist distractions and frustration when things do not go according to plan (Harter, 1983b).

Use of Social Comparison

In middle childhood, children assess their performance by comparing themselves with peers. This is different from the comparisons preschoolers make. The comparisons of preschoolers are more concerned with making sure they are being treated fairly or getting the same privileges as are given to peers. School-age children compare themselves with peers in order to assess how they stack up. The desire to compare favorably with their peers serves to inhibit school-age children from acting in ways defined as "deviant" by the peer group, thus stimulating self-regulatory actions.

Influence of Internalized Feelings of Self-Pride and Self-Shame on Behavior

The school-age child realizes he may feel badly afterwards if he does something that deviates from his internalized values. He is also aware that he will feel good about himself if he accomplishes a goal he approves of (Bandura, 1978; Harter, 1983b).

Capacity to Tolerate Conflicting Feelings

This ability corresponds with the cognitive capacity to see alternative interpretations to a problem. At age 9 or 10, children acknowledge that they can feel more than one emotion at the same time. The child can accept that there may be negative and positive aspects to a situation. This ability to tolerate ambivalence allows the child to contain her feelings, rather than acting in response to them.

Increasingly Effective Defense Mechanisms

A greater range of psychological defenses becomes available. These "higher level" defenses are more effective in helping the child cope with anxiety and, compared to the more "primitive" defenses, they interfere less with the child's overall functioning. It should be noted that there is reason to be concerned if a child seems to be relying on unconscious defenses to cope with stress to the exclusion of more conscious and adaptive coping mechanisms.

Nevertheless, the defenses that develop during middle childhood are a useful part of the child's repertoire of self-regulatory strategies. Table 10.2 defines the defenses that develop during middle childhood.

Automatic use of defenses, as well as conscious suppression and self-distraction, helps account for the school-age child's ability to avoid distressing feelings. Parents sometimes worry that a school-age child is not showing the emotions she "should" feel. For example, the school-age child whose parent has recently died may appear to be unaffected, because she is using the defense of isolation. She may also immerse herself in action to avoid thoughts about the loss, or resist and avoid talking about the parent's death in order to avoid painful feelings. School-age children can only tolerate the pain of grieving for brief periods, and these defenses help them manage and reduce the intensity of painful feelings (Webb, 1993b; E. R. Shapiro, 1994). (This is not to say that school-age children do not grieve, but rather that they may grieve in spurts over time or express their grief behaviorally through increased attachment behavior or sleep disturbances.) Such defenses parallel the school-age child's general tendencies to be present oriented rather than thinking much about the past and to focus attention on concrete experience at hand. The child's ability to focus on the present following a parent's death has both adaptive and defensive functions, as we see in the following case example:

> Several months into the treatment of a 9-year-old girl whose father had died, I asked her when she thought about her dad. She said, "I think about him sometimes at night, but I don't think about him now in school, so I'm getting my work done." I mentioned that a few months before it had been hard to get her work done because she'd been thinking about her dad a lot, and she agreed. This kind of compartmentalization is typical and was helping this child focus on normal developmental tasks. This example points to a difference between child and adult grieving. Often, for adults, grieving pervades nearly every waking moment (E. R. Shapiro, 1994). Consequently, it is important to discuss the child's tendency toward compartmentalization with parents, who may be concerned or upset

that their child is not sad. They need to know it is a normal aspect of childhood grieving, reflecting a developmentally appropriate use of defenses.

Self-Regulation and Culture

Different cultures and subcultures have contrasting values regarding display of emotions. Children learn these display rules during the toddler and preschool years, and by school-age implicitly know what kinds of emotional expression are expected or permitted in particular situations and relationships (Saarni, 1979). Self-regulation must be understood in this context. For example, Harris (1985) points out that Nepalese children appear shy and hesitant before speaking to adults, even those they know well, because they are expected to show defer-

---

**TABLE 10.2. Defenses in Middle Childhood
(A. Freud, 1966; Berman, 1979)**

- *Repression.* Involves the elimination, or "forgetting," of unacceptable feelings, impulses, or thoughts from conscious awareness.

- *Sublimation.* Avoiding direct awareness of aggressive impulses and sexual curiosity through "neutralized" activities, such as games, collecting, projects, creativity, and (in general) interest in things outside the self.

- *Reaction formation.* Turning an impulse or wish into its opposite. An example is the transformation of the preschooler's intense interest and curiosity about sex differences to the school-age child's tendency toward sex segregation—"Boys are stupid. We're not letting any of them in our club."

- *Displacement in fantasy.* Impulses that would be negative, aggressive, intrusive, or antisocial if acted out are experienced "at a distance" through fantasy. Displacement in fantasy can involve either the child's own fantasizing, or her enjoyment of TV shows and movies where impulsive, aggressive behavior is depicted.

- *Isolation.* Involves repressing the affect connected with a thought so that the thought has a "neutral" quality. Very frequently school-age children can describe a stressful event in a matter-of-fact tone but have trouble answering when asked how they *felt* about it. This is isolation at work.

- *Doing and undoing.* Expression of a negative impulse, followed immediately by its opposite. A child who is angry with her parent—either directly or privately—undoes the impulse by being oversolicitous, apologetic, or spontaneously saying, "I love you, Mom."

- *Turning against the self.* Involves punishing the self for having a forbidden impulse. In response to anger toward a parent, for example, the child feels guilty and "beats himself up" by condemning himself.

---

ence and respect. In that culture "impulsiveness," or poor self-regulation, might be defined as being boisterous in the presence of adults. American culture, by contrast, does not require as much deference, and children know that many adults accept expressions of excitement.

Within American culture, however, different groups have contrasting rules for emotional display, which in a climate of racism may be misinterpreted. For example, school-age African-American children may talk more loudly and excitedly when in a group than white children do. This is consistent with the rules of emotional display many African-American children have learned. However, their behavior may be equated with a lack of control or impulsiveness by a white teacher or clinician who has been socialized to be more restrained in displays of emotion. This misinterpretation of a cultural difference, perhaps intensified by prejudice, may turn into a judgment about mental health (Canino & Spurlock, 1994).

Self-Regulation and Coping in Dangerous Environments

The school-age child, more than younger children, comes into direct contact with his community. He may ride the bus or walk to school. On the streets in poor urban neighborhoods he may be exposed to threats and danger, and in consequence may develop coping strategies that would not be appropriate in safer neighborhoods. It is important to assess whether a child's fears and anxiety are realistic in order to understand whether his self-regulatory strategies are adaptive. If a child lives in a dangerous neighborhood where he is threatened or exposed to violence and where people he knows have been victimized by crime, it is appropriate to be afraid. A child in this situation, rather than having a separation anxiety disorder, is, from an attachment perspective, behaving appropriately when she insists on staying near her parent. Alternatively, a school-age child who has been exposed to violence in his neighborhood may adopt an alert, aggressive stance as a means of self-protection. Canino and Spurlock (1994) suggest that clinicians may mistake coping responses elicited by living in a dangerous environment as psychopathology; however, "a high degree of isolation of affect, denial, displacement and hyperalertness may be necessary for these children to survive their environment. They often present as distractible and unmotivated, and school performance frequently becomes their lowest priority" (p. 57).

MORAL DEVELOPMENT

During middle childhood moral abilities expand and are refined. The decline of egocentric thinking supports moral development. By age 7–8, the ability to take a decentered perspective allows the child to balance self-interest with the social norm of following the rules. Rather than thinking only about herself, the school-age child recognizes, on principle, that the needs of others must be recognized. As the child's ability to think in logically consistent ways develops, she comes to expect consistency between beliefs and actions, both her own and those of others (Kagan, 1984). A 9-year-old may resist a friend's suggestion that they shoplift some candy because she knows that action would not be in accord with her belief that stealing is wrong. This child refuses her friend's dare not just out of fear of punishment or internal anxiety and guilt but also because it is inconsistent with what she believes.

Because school-age children can think in logical terms, they more easily understand the rationales for correct behavior that adults provide. For example, a parent tells an 8-year-old, "You wouldn't want one of your friends to borrow your bike without asking, so you shouldn't do that to someone else." The 8-year-old can understand the logic of this statement, in part because he can now think in terms of logical propositions and in part because he can appreciate the feelings of others (Harter, 1983b). However, parental modeling continues to be the most powerful determinant of the morality children internalize. The child who has observed a parent borrow things without asking is likely to be more confused than impressed by the parent's moral directive.

Compared with adolescents, school-age children tend to accept rules and authority. They assume that if a rule exists, it must be there for a reason. This is a very different stance from that of a young adolescent, who analyzes adult rules and dictates for evidence of inconsistency. School-age children's general acceptance of authority makes them teachable and coachable. At the same time, since they tend to believe that authority is valid, they are often very uncomfortable with peers who openly defy authority.

School-age children are very aware of social norms. They are motivated to fit into their peer group and are very attuned to adult standards. They are particularly aware of rules and try to follow the rules of their teacher and school, at least in public. Older school-age children fit Kohlberg's (1984) level of moral development called the "Authority and Social Order Orientation." They tend to be conformistic, going along with rules because their peers do. Although children may know the principle contained in a rule, they often follow rules unthinkingly because "that's what you're supposed to do."

Given this conformistic moral orientation, school-age children do not like to be seen as "deviant." When a school-age child consistently ignores or violates school rules, his peers often stigmatize him and try to avoid him, because they do not want to be associated with wrongdoing. Children with untreated ADHD and behavioral disorders are often stigmatized by their peers. By early elementary age, for example, normal children notice that children with impulsive behavior problems are different—off the wall, annoying, or aggressive. As a result they are frequently rejected. The reasons for rejection include their intrusiveness, impulsiveness, frequent violation of personal and social boundaries, failure to follow rules, and apparent obliviousness to situational and social cues. Peers worry that associating with the child with ADHD will cause them to get in trouble (Whalen & Henker, 1992).

SENSE OF SELF

The school-age child's sense of self is based on comparisons with others. Whereas the preschool child wishfully tries to imbue the self with power through fantasy expressed in play about adult roles or superheroes, the school-age child begins to evaluate herself in more realistic ways, particularly by comparing herself with her peers. By age 7 the child measures her abilities by ranking herself within her peer group. During middle childhood, "children become progressively more accurate in assessing their own competence in relation to their peers" (Harter, 1983b, p. 336). They know who is "the best" and "the worst," as well as gradations in between. What children evaluate about each other differs across cultures. In the United States, children's rankings of one another reflect the ethos of a competitive society. In contrasting cultures, where fitting into the group is important, peers may judge each other based on whether they are cooperative and show respect for authority (Damon & Hart, 1988).

The school-age child is much more sensitive than the preschooler to the feedback she gets from peers. She thinks about her actions in the light of other's responses and mentally rehearses what she is going to do with an eye to how her peers are likely to respond. Her feelings about herself are socially influenced. If her friends admire her ability at jump rope, she feels pride; if peers make fun of her mistakes, she is vulnerable to negative feelings—

anxiety, embarrassment, self-doubt. Compared to the preschooler, then, her self-esteem depends more on her awareness of how she is perceived by others. However, the school-age child's self-esteem is only relatively dependent on her social status. The development of self-esteem in middle childhood is strongly related to a history of being accepted and supported by parents (Harter, 1983b). Children with high self-esteem in earlier periods of development are likely to be more resilient in the face of teasing or rejection by peers than are children whose self-esteem has been damaged by insecure attachments or maltreatment.

Identification

School-age children, in contrast to preschoolers, take real people as heroes and role models. It is common for children to admire their parents, particularly the same-sex parent, with whom they identify. Since most elementary school teachers are women, girls frequently identify with teachers they admire. Children also attempt to imitate public figures such as sports stars. For example, a boy shooting baskets alone began to speak in a sportscaster's voice, describing himself as Michael Jordan: "Jordan takes the pass. He goes up, he's airborne! He scores!" This 10-year-old's identification with a great sports hero has much in common with the preschooler's identification with superhero characters. The difference is that the school-age child chooses real-life models and uses the identification to support the development of real-world skills.

The school-age child's increasing peer orientation also means that she takes older same-sex peers as role models and objects of identification. Often older siblings fill this role as well. Younger school-age children admire the accomplishments and abilities of older peers. At the same time, an older child's skill in basketball seems more attainable to a younger child than becoming like Michael Jordan. Younger children watch older children to learn how to improve their skills and how to behave in new situations. Older children sometimes take pleasure in acting as mentors for younger ones. They enjoy being admired and like to demonstrate their skills. Often a younger child will risk doing something that makes him anxious if he knows an admired older peer has done it. Recently, the parent of a 10-year-old boy who was being referred to me said, "He didn't want to see you until we told him that Chris [a 14-year-old he looked up to] had seen you. He asked Chris, and Chris told him you were a cool guy. Then he had no problem coming."

The Relationship between Self-Control and Self-Concept

School-age children put a strong emphasis on feeling and acting in control. By age 8 or 9 the child tries to control his behavior in order to live up to his internal standards, not simply to please others. Feeling in control of one's emotions and behavior fosters self-esteem (Harter, 1983b). A 9-year-old who breaks down and cries in response to losing a game later feels disturbed and embarrassed by his loss of control. The link between self-control and self-esteem is most evident in children who frequently "lose control" because of ADHD or other impulsive behavior. Children who blurt things out, move impulsively, invade other children's personal space, or constantly interrupt what others are saying are often stigmatized as "hyper" by their peers. As these negative responses and the child's own awareness of difficulties with impulse control become part of his self-concept, self-esteem suffers.

Similarly, a school-age child with learning disabilities becomes aware that she cannot control the way her brain works. She is aware of a required goal—to read a passage—and also realizes that she cannot do it. As she realizes what she cannot do and compares her own performance with peers who read with ease, her self-esteem declines.

SELF-ESTEEM ISSUES OF A CHILD WITH LEARNING DISORDERS: A BRIEF CASE EXAMPLE

Jill was an 8-year-old girl I saw in supportive psychotherapy to help her cope with serious learning disorders in reading, writing, and auditory processing. In sessions, Jill worked dilligently on school-like tasks. She would laboriously write stories and bring in books to read to me. Her performance was slow, labored, and full of errors, yet her choice of academic tasks demonstrated her strong motivation to succeed, her need to call attention to the problem, and her frustration over not being successful. Jill was aware of her learning problems and spoke about her frustration and desire to do better. Jill presented a vivid image of her struggle with learning disorders. As we talked about how she felt when she couldn't understand what the teacher was asking, I said that kids with a learning problem often blamed themselves and felt dumb. Jill said, "I don't blame myself. I blame my imaginary friend. What I do is when I don't know the answer I take a gun and shoot my imaginary friend." I said, "So you blame her for not knowing the answer?" "Yeah, if she can't tell the answer, I blast her." Jill was attempting to externalize the problem by blaming her imaginary companion. She knew very well that *she* didn't know the answer, but was using a typical school-age defense of displacing negative feelings about the self into fantasy.

Jill also tried to compensate for feelings of inadequacy caused by her learning disorders by identifying with boys. She made fun of the "wimpy," feminine girls in her class and claimed that she was the toughest girl. She said that boys were more fun to play with because they played "rough and tough." She was trying to disassociate herself from a gender stereotype of middle childhood—that girls are "good" in school—because she fell short of the academic skills girls are supposed to have; in compensation, she tried to fit herself into one of the male gender stereotypes—that boys are more physical and tough.

Capacity for Self-Observation

School-age children have much more capacity for self-observation than do younger children. They usually are at ease answering the question "What are you good at?" because they can take an outside perspective on themselves. They have an image of what they are like and are aware of their strengths and weaknesses. By contrast, a preschool child has trouble answering the same question, because she cannot take an outside perspective on herself. School-age children can also give concrete self-descriptions: "I'm pretty friendly. I'm getting better at basketball. I used to write scratchy, but my handwriting is good now." They can see themselves across time, both as the same person and as developing in skill (Damon & Hart, 1988). For example, a 9-year-old girl showed me a number of gymnastics moves. I asked how she got good at cartwheels and headstands. She said, "I practiced a lot. When I was 6, I couldn't do a headstand and my legs would get all lopsided if I did a cartwheel, but now I've learned how to do it so my legs are straight."

School-age children are not yet able to reflect on psychological reasons for their strengths or problems. They are oriented toward the external and concrete. Questions about motivations underlying their behavior are likely to be met with "I don't know." But school-age children can at least identify a problem or concern. This has implications for intervention. A school-age child can participate in setting goals. He can say, for example, "I wish I had more friends. Sometimes other kids tease me." This can open the way to conversations, either directly or in displacement, about the skills needed to get along with peers.

In middle childhood, the self-image is based not simply on immediate ideas about the self but also on comparisons of present and past representations of the self. New cognitive abilities allow children to understand their earlier experiences in new ways. The ability to decenter in middle childhood allows the child to differentiate between past and present self-images, contributing to new views of the self (Gemelli, 1996). A child may say, "When I was 4, I used to think about robbers and monsters and I'd be scared to go down to the basement. Now [at age 10], I still get that feeling when I go down there, but I know it's not real. I'm not a scaredy-cat like I was when I was 4." The ability to differentiate between past and present viewpoints has important implications for intervention with school-age children. In Chapter 3, I described an 8-year-old, Alex, whose continuing fears were rooted in experiences of abuse by his father when he was 3 and 4. The cognitive aspect of Alex's treatment involved helping him understand that he was responding to certain anxiety-producing situations from the perspective of a 3-year-old, and pointing out that, now, as an 8-year-old he knew much better how to appraise situations and get help.

Gender and Sense of Self

At the beginning of middle childhood, at age 6 or 7, the child increasingly adopts gender-specific behavior and avoids behavior associated with the opposite gender. This development coincides with the awareness of *gender constancy*, the understanding that gender cannot be changed. The child's implicit awareness that "I am a girl and I will always be a girl" leads to an insistence on behaving "like a girl, not like a boy," in terms of culturally defined characteristics (Slaby & Frey, 1975). Gender identity now includes more specific information than the fact of being a girl or boy. Particularly through observing older peers, the child learns, for example, what girls are like, what girls like to do, what they do in certain situations. Identification with same-sex peers, relatives, and other adults, including media celebrities, furthers gender socialization.

As the school-age years proceed, children continue to elaborate gender roles. In general, girls' value relationships and nurturance, whereas boys emphasize personal autonomy and competition (Maccoby, 1988). O'Brien (1992) describes a study of boys' and girls' interactional styles in middle childhood that illustrates these gender contrasts: "Girls' conversations are marked by expressions of acknowledgment and agreement and the regular exchange of speaking turns; boys interrupt each other, make demands and refuse to comply with others' demands, tell jokes or stories, and generally compete with each other for attention" (p. 339). Gilligan (1982) has argued that these contrasting styles of relating and defining the self lead to somewhat different views of moral questions in girls and boys: girls are more oriented to take relationships into account in making moral judgments—to be concerned, for example, about whether feelings will be hurt or relationships will be damaged; boys, she argues, tend to invoke rules as the basis for deciding moral questions.

While these broad constructions of male emphasis on autonomy and female emphasis of relatedness are useful metaphors for understanding gender differences, empirical studies show many more similarities than differences in the development of girls and boys. (Damon, 1983; O'Brien, 1992). O'Brien (1992) points out that older school-age children tend to recognize their similarities and the ways feminine and masculine behavior overlap, even while they maintain sex segregation in play. Rather than thinking of boys and girls as rigidly polarized in the development of the self, it is helpful to think of a "relational self" and an "autonomous self," as coexisting within each individual. Gender socialization influences how girls and boys balance these two competing self-orientations (Atwood & Safyer, 1993).

Racial and Ethnic Awareness in Middle Childhood

Although children take in information about ethnicity during early childhood, they become more aware of their racial and ethnic identity during the elementary-school years (P. A. Katz, 1987). At about the same time children attain gender constancy, they realize that ethnicity is also not changeable (Aboud, 1984). This is in part a function of general cognitive tendencies toward identifying and classifying differences. Implicit and explicit socialization experiences and exposure to different groups at school also increase ethnic awareness. Race, ethnicity, and gender strongly influence peer relationships. Just as boys and girls form separate groups, younger school-age children tend to choose as friends peers with whom they identify. This trend continues throughout the middle years (Rotherham & Phinney, 1987). In schools with multicultural populations, children's awareness of their own ethnic identity is greater because they interact with peers who look different from them and speak different dialects or languages. By contrast, children living in homogeneous communities have less awareness of ethnic differences.

In general, minority children show greater awareness of race and ethnicity than do children who identify with the majority white group (Spencer, 1987). Minority children learn about their minority status and majority values through personal experiences, mass media, and exposure to institutions such as schools where majority norms dominate. Cross (1987) has shown that African-American children with good self-esteem nevertheless may show strong interest in white cultural symbols and attitudes because they correctly perceive the status and power associated with them. This interest in the majority culture also indicates the tendency of minority families to socialize their children to develop "bicultural competence" so that they can function in both majority and minority cultures (Cross, 1987).

Spencer (1987) has argued that children in "castelike minorities," whose group faces discrimination and devaluation based on racist views in the majority society, may devalue their own ethnicity as they become aware of the majority culture's negative views. This awareness frequently occurs during the middle years, when new cognitive abilities and exposure to the wider world allow the child to realize that others can perceive her negatively because of categorical attributes that identify her has a member of a particular group. Many minority group members recall the first incidents of prejudice toward them as occurring in elementary school, as in the following case example:

> A biracial child of a single white mother had lived in an ethnically mixed urban neighborhood during her early years. Although she identified with her mother's ethnicity at that time, she often saw her paternal grandparents, who were African-American, and realized vaguely that she was a mix of black and white. When she was 9 her family moved to a small town where she was the only "nonwhite" child in her school. She was shocked when other children called her racial epithets and rejected her. To defend herself, she denied the black part of her identity and made up a new one, telling other children, "I'm Spanish!"

Although this example is about a biracial child, it reflects the realization that comes to most minority children—that they can be subject to social rejection on a categorical rather than a personal basis. During the school-age years, when self-esteem is strongly influenced by the child's sense of how well she is accepted by peers, the risk of devaluing her minority identity may be greater. In view of this risk, Spencer (1987) argues that it is important for minority parents and other significant adults to stress the strengths and values of their ethnicity, so that the child can react to racism and discrimination from the perspective of a positive ethnic identity, essentially realizing, "That's the way they feel about us. But that's their problem. I feel good about who I am." This perspective has implications for intervention. School-age minority children who present with low self-esteem should be assessed for conflicts about their racial identity and offered positive messages about their ethnicity by their parents and social worker. Positive ethnic socialization is likely to be most powerful when the practitioner represents the same group as the child (Greene, 1992).

OVERVIEW OF DEVELOPMENTAL PROGRESS
IN MIDDLE CHILDHOOD

Since the period of middle childhood covers a long period (from 6 to 11 or 12), it may be useful to step back from the description of domains of development and to present a brief summary of the child's progress during this period. Near the end of this period, the child of 10 or 11 who has a history of successful mastery of developmental tasks and who has not yet entered puberty is likely to appear confident, competent, reasonable, and calm. He is capable of logical thought, can look at situations from multiple perspectives, and has many adaptive strategies of self-regulation. He has developed skills through concentration on learning and practice. Several years ago when I told a colleague who had grown children that my son was 10 years old, she exclaimed, "Ten-year-olds should be bronzed like baby shoes!" She went on to say that 10 is a "perfect age" because children are mature, self-controlled, relatively independent, and self-possessed. If they were "preserved" at 10, she said, they—and their parents—would not have to go through the struggles of adolescence.

Although middle childhood is generally seen as continuing up to age 11 or 12, during the last year or so of the period there are signs of the disequilibrium that characterizes early adolescence. The onset of puberty and the adolescent growth spurt begin for many children between 10 and 12, with girls, on average, being a year ahead of boys. While 11- and 12-year-olds retain the cognitive abilities they have developed over the course of middle childhood, the internal stresses of rapid physical growth, hormonal changes, sexual maturation, and sexual interest challenge the school-age child's capacity to maintain calm and self-control. Consequently, many 11-year-olds, compared with just a year earlier, are more active, defiant of authority, self-centered, and emotionally labile. The child's self-regulatory capacities, while still functioning well most of the time, cannot always withstand the new pressures of growth toward adolescence (Sarnoff, 1976; Pipher, 1994). The child of 11 or 12 has consolidated the developmental accomplishments of middle childhood but is moving into the transformations of self in adolescence.

APPENDIX: SUMMARY OF MIDDLE CHILDHOOD DEVELOPMENT, 6 TO 11 OR 12 YEARS OF AGE

Overall Tasks

• To develop and utilize a sense of calm, educability, and self-control
• To develop a real-world skills and a sense of competence
• To establish oneself in the world of peers

Attachment

• Child uses autonomous coping rather than attachment seeking in situations of mild stress (6 years +)
• Rituals symbolizing attachment persist—bedtime routines, gestures of affection (6 years +)
• Proximity seeking may be activated in situations of severe stress or during transitions, such as entry into school (6 years +)
• Attachment needs are increasingly expressed in friendships with peers (6 years +)

Social Development

• Increasing orientation toward peers, development of friendships (6 years +)
• Social skills (sharing, negotiation, etc.) develop through peer interaction (6 years +)
• Development of peer group norms and status hierarchies (6 years +)
• Elaboration of gender roles and behavior (6 years +)
• Prosocial behavior, based on internalization of values and improved perspective taking (6 years +)
• Social perspective taking: increasingly clear understanding of others' viewpoints, social expectations, and social cues (6 years +)
• Awareness of the psychological intent of others (8–10 years)
• Holds two opposing viewpoints in mind at the same time (10–12 years)

Language and Communication

• Basic facility in syntax and grammar established (6–7 years)
• Gradually increasing understanding of nuances of meaning and more difficult grammatical features such as the passive voice (6–7 years +)
• Gradually increasing ability to put thoughts and feelings into words (6 years +)
• Narrative ability—child can tell an organized story (7 years +)
• Understanding of wordplay, jokes, figures of speech, metaphor (8–10 years)

Play and Fantasy

- Play is increasingly sublimated into a work orientation, emphasizing physical skills and intellectual competence (6–7 years +)
- Play continues to be an important source of pleasure and discharge, but now is increasingly ritualized into games (6 years +)
- Fantasy play is increasingly ritualized and rule governed (6 years +)
- Uses of fantasy include displacement of feelings and wishes into imaginary scenarios and imagining the self in more competent or grown-up roles (6 years +)
- Interest in collections and hobbies (7–8 years +)
- Interest in games involving planning and strategy (10–12 years)

Cognitive Development

- Increasingly accurate perception of reality (reality testing) (6 years +)
- Reversibility—systematic ability to analyze perceptions by thinking back over them (6–7 years)
- Improving understanding of cause and effect; decline in magical thinking (6–7 years)
- Decentration: decline in egocentrism and increase in decentered thought allows child to distinguish between subjective and objective reality (6–7 years +)
- Concrete operations: processes of logic and reasoning can be applied to understand immediate reality (6–7 years +)
- Developmental spurt in cognitive functions at about age 7: spatial organization; visual organizational ability; time orientation; distinctions between parts and wholes; seriation; auditory processing (6–8 years)
- Memory: improved registration and categorization of memory contributes to mastery of academic tasks (6 years +)
- Executive processes: new skills in thinking about problem solving, sustaining attention to intellectual tasks (7–8 years +)

Self-Regulation

- Application of cognitive strategies to self-regulation: logical thinking; representational competence; conscious control of arousal and anxiety; using thinking to delay acting on impulses; conscious intent to stay focused on attainment of goals (6 years +)
- Internalization of values, expectations, rules, and social norms fosters self-control (6 years +)

- Psychological defense mechanisms become more effective in limiting anxiety (6 years +)
- Desire to receive approval of peers sets limits on impulsive behavior (6–7 years +)
- Capacity to see conflicting views and tolerate ambivalence improves self-control (10 years)

Moral Development

- Decentered thinking and perspective taking enable child to better understand and empathize with the needs of others (6 years +)
- Development of the conscience (superego) as an internal force controlling behavior (5–7 years)
- Cognitive understanding of rationales, rules, and norms of correct behavior (6–7 years +)
- Social conformity and acceptance of authority supports adherence to rules and expectations (6 years +)

Sense of Self

- Self-esteem based on awareness of competence, status in peer group (6–7 years +)
- Identification with parents, other adults, and peers as role models (6–7 years +)
- Capacity for self-control influences self-esteem and self-concept (6–7 years +)
- Increasing awareness of identity—personal characteristics, gender expectations, racial and ethnic identity (7 years +)
- Awareness of racism, negative stereotypes applied to the self (7–8 years +)
- Increasing capacity for self-observation (8 years +)
- Ability to make comparisons between past and present characteristics of the self (7–8 years +)
- Internalized values create need to gain self-esteem by pleasing oneself, not just others (8 years)

❖ CHAPTER 11 ❖

Practice with
School-Age Children

School-age children are usually referred because of problems that show up at school. Examples of typical presenting symptoms include the following:

- Behavioral and academic problems at school
- Attention/concentration problems
- Restlessness/hyperactivity
- Impulsive, aggressive, oppositional, or defiant behavior
- Poor peer relationships
- Social withdrawal/social immaturity/rejection by peers
- Generalized anxiety and separation anxiety

From a developmental perspective, these problems can be understood as difficulties in mastering the tasks of middle childhood. Often these symptoms represent problems in self-regulation, particularly overreliance on the defenses of early childhood rather than more mature and adaptive regulatory strategies. The child may be unable to consistently maintain the self-control, calmness, flexibility, and educability associated with middle childhood. Since the same symptoms can represent different problems, a careful assessment is necessary. Attention to the child's progress in different developmental domains helps specify areas of strength and areas requiring intervention.

The assessment process for school-age children should recognize the increasing complexity of the interaction between the child's developmental progress and the multiple and complex environments he experiences. Assessment should draw on multiple sources of information, including parents, other caregivers, and teachers as observers of the child, as well as on multiple observations. Only rarely can evaluation findings based on one session be considered reliable and complete. The child should be observed in multiple contexts, ideally both individually and in a family session, and also at home and at school. Scales of developmental level and symptomatology assess child behavior and specific problems. These include comprehensive instruments, such as the Child Behavior Checklist (Achenbach & Edelbrock, 1983), and more specialized questionnaires on problems such as ADHD (attention-deficit/hyperactivity disorder), depression, and anxiety disorders. Self-report instruments that ask the child to assess himself should be viewed with caution. They often do not produce accurate information, because the school-age child tends to deny problems and frequently can figure out which answers will make him appear "normal" (Folman, 1995).

ASSESSMENT

Evaluation of a school-age child should involve the following areas of assessment:

Developmental Level

Sarnoff (1976) defines psychopathology in the middle years as resulting from "the inability of the child to produce at appropriate times the pliability, calm and educability expected in a latency age child" (p. 186). If we observe this inability, then questions about the child's functioning in several developmental domains must be considered. Is she relying on omnipotent fantasies? Are her coping strategies and defenses more like those of a younger child? Does she remain more egocentric than expected? Does she withdraw from peers or show an inability to get along with them? Does she have difficulty regulating impulses? Are there cognitive or language deficits or academic difficulties that are suggestive of learning or language disorders?

Identification of cognitive difficulties that contribute to poor academic performance is particularly important. The developmental tasks of middle childhood are intertwined with the growth of academic skills, and academic difficulties often interfere with development in other domains.

History of Developmental Interferences

In taking the child's developmental and interactional history, possible developmental interferences, such as exposure to violence, chronic parental fighting, divorce, losses, abuse, and trauma, should be noted. Very often, the child's inability to proceed with normal development in middle childhood is tied to defenses and coping mechanisms established in response to anxiety-provoking experiences during early childhood. For example, a history of physical or sexual abuse may result in a child's using withdrawal into fantasy and dissociation as preferred defenses. Such children may appear quiet and shy but seem "normal" in that they do not have behavioral problems. However, when they begin school, their reliance on daydreaming and dissociation makes it hard for them to concentrate on learning. As with all emergency-based coping strategies, dissociation helped the child survive the abuse, but if it persists as a defense it will interfere with developmental tasks in middle childhood.

Reality Orientation

Assessment of orientation to reality helps determine the child's developmental level. Middle childhood is characterized by increasing appreciation of the demands of following rules, doing well in school, and being perceived as similar to one's peers. The school-age child is motivated to succeed and willing to practice to develop skills. It is useful to analyze whether she is giving priority to the demands of external reality (parents, school, peer relationships) or whether she is drawn toward magical thinking as a defense against feelings of inadequacy or vulnerability in the real world.

INTERVENTION

Some of the typical goals of therapy with school-age children are the following:

- To remove emotional barriers that prevent them from feeling competent in work and with peers
- To help them move from action-based modes of expression to modes involving language, thought, and fantasy
- To help them move away from the compensations of magical thinking and toward a more reality-oriented stance

• To help them develop coping strategies that permit them to maintain a capacity to learn

The developmental advances of middle childhood permit a broad array of intervention approaches and techniques, including the following:

Cognitive-Behavioral Interventions

School-age children's new cognitive skills—decentration, perspective taking, logical thinking, improved understanding of cause and effect—make possible interventions that help them make sense of stressful experiences. For example, in sexual abuse treatment a 9-year-old girl can cognitively grasp the accuracy of a statement that differentiates the abuser's motives and behavior from her own: "He is responsible for what he did to you. You did not cause it to happen, and it is not your fault." Further, the school-age child's capacity for decentered thinking can be drawn on to help her differentiate between herself in the abuse situation and her overall self (Zimrin, 1986). This opens the way to cognitive interventions that aim to strengthen the child's self-image and separate the abuse from her sense of self.

The older school-age child's ability to analyze cause-and-effect sequences and use reversible thought implies that he can sometimes understand the connections between thoughts and impulses and behavior, and can realize that a feeling may have caused him to act, as demonstrated in the following case example:

> Mark, a 10-year-old with many fears and inadequate defenses and coping skills, was provoking fights at school. His foster mother called me before his session and told me that he had been sent to the office for fighting the previous day. I asked Mark what had happened, and he said, "Two guys jumped on me. They held me down and punched me." I began working backward, asking him how the fight got started. He said, "They told me 2 weeks ago that they were going to get me. So I saw them out in front waiting for the bus, and I knew they were waiting for me." I asked if they'd said anything to him, and he said, "No, maybe they didn't see me." When I said I was still not sure how the fight started, he said, "Well I kicked one of them in the stomach." My approach was to go over this situation in detail, clarifying that his provocative aggression was based on his fear of being beaten up. This made him attack even though he hadn't been attacked. Because he was afraid, he had put himself into the exact situation he feared. I expressed my concern that he'd put himself into a dangerous situation when he didn't need to. I said, "I

don't like you to get hurt, and it makes me feel bad for you when you do something that makes other people want to hurt you." We also discussed alternative ways of responding. I asked, "What else could you do if you're worried about those guys?" We explored several possibilities: stay away from those kids; tell the teacher; stick with your friends so you feel safer; stay back until the bus comes and get on after they do, and don't sit by them. I also tried to help him appraise the severity of the threat in retrospect: "It's good to be careful and be ready to do something if they really do come after you, but if they threatened you 2 weeks ago and still hadn't done anything by yesterday, maybe they were just talking big." This approach models thinking through fears and gaining some control over them through the use of reasoning. It does not require autonomous self-reflection or insight by the child, abilities which are still beyond those of the school-age child. The therapist functions as an "auxiliary ego," helping the child utilize reasoning abilities and making suggestions of more adaptive ways to deal with anxiety (Harter, 1983a; Chethik, 1989). This cognitive approach also aims to facilitate development by calling attention to and exercising the school-age child's new ability to think things through. The therapist helps the child practice age appropriate cognitive skills whose development has been impeded by reliance on appraisal styles and coping mechanisms formed by early experiences of trauma or neglect (Reinecke, Dattilio, & Freeman, 1996).

School-age children can also be engaged in behavioral treatment more easily than younger children. The school-age child's understanding of cause and effect enables him to conceptualize how rewards can be contingent on appropriate behavior. This understanding enables him to see the possible benefits of controlling defiant or aggressive behavior (Barkley, 1997). In behavior management programs involving token economies, the child's participation can be enlisted because he sees that he will be rewarded for changing his behavior. Such programs depend on the child's developing cognitive skills, including thinking logically, using cognitive strategies to control behavior, and self-monitoring. Further the child's active and externalizing orientation in middle childhood is likely to make him interested in a treatment program that emphasizes control over behavior rather than understanding of feelings.

Group Treatment

Group intervention is particularly appropriate for school-age children because of their compelling interest in peer relationships. School-age children think groups are "normal," in the sense that they spend a lot of time in groups at school. Most children's groups focus around scripts and structured tasks, which from the child's perspective makes them seem similar to familiar classroom activities. Dealing with issues in a group has several advantages that derive from the developmental characteristics of middle childhood (Kalter, 1988):

- Children get support from one another. Especially when groups are composed of children at about the same level of development, they can identify with each other.
- The group provides "safety in numbers." Children do not feel singled out or stigmatized as they often do initially in individual or family treatment.
- Being with peers who have similar situations or symptoms reduces conscience-driven anxiety about self-revelation.
- By becoming aware of other children's experiences, the individual child's experience is normalized.
- By observing how other group members have coped with or solved problems, children can expand their own range of coping devices.

Individual Play Therapy

Individual treatment that combines play, structured activities, and talk is an effective approach in middle childhood. However, practitioners beginning to work with school-age children often feel that the child is "resistant," or "lacks insight," or "doesn't seem to know he has problems." Such observations are largely accurate, and, from a developmental perspective, they are normative. School-age children usually do not talk about their problems in a sustained way. In the individual treatment situation, many children actively avoid talking about worries, painful experiences, and problems. This is consistent with the following characteristics of children in this developmental stage:

- *External orientation.* In middle childhood, children are more oriented to the outer world than to their internal consciousness, and they tend more toward doing than toward feeling.
- *Defenses.* Their defense mechanisms are more adequate to prevent painful, forbidden, or anxious thoughts from coming into consciousness; they are also more adept at conscious suppression.
- *Conscience.* School-age children tend to resist talking about symptoms and problems—such as getting into fights, being disruptive in class, or defying a parent—because they are associated in the child's mind with being bad. Because the superego is now internalized, bad-

ness is felt inside. Consequently, the child resists talking about problems in order to avoid feeling guilty.

• *Social awareness.* School-age children are very aware of what is appropriate socially and highly invested in being like everyone else—in being "normal." They often worry that their friends will find out they are in therapy. To have a problem is to feel abnormal, defective, or crazy.

> One day, I was waiting for an 8-year-old boy to come for his first appointment. I looked out of my office window and saw his mother pulling him bodily out of the car. He was crying and resisting. He had gotten himself together by the time they got into my office, I think because he didn't want to embarrass himself by crying. Part way through the hour, we were playing with puppets. He hid behind a chair and stuck his puppet up and said, "I'm not crazy." This gave me a chance to address his fear. I said, "Sometimes kids think I'll prove they're crazy, but that's a mistake—that's not why kids come to see me. They come because they have some worries, and I know how to help with worries."

Displacement

The school-age child tries to avoid difficult feelings and worries through conscious suppression, unconscious defenses, or displacement into play and fantasy. Through displacement, forbidden impulses, strong feelings, and conflicts can be experienced as if not connected to the self. Children can unconsciously use the displacement of symbolic play and action to describe their emotional dilemmas. When we enter the child's fantasy world through the medium of play or other displacement activities such as drawing, storytelling, or therapeutic games, we can learn about the child's inner experience of his difficulties without requiring the child to talk directly about them. The practitioner must also learn to respond to the play and fantasy with displaced interpretations, so that the child's defenses are not challenged too strongly. An example of a displaced interpretation would be speak in universal terms about "how girls feel," instead of "how you feel"; or to talk about "another boy I knew who had some worries" and then tailor the story to fit the child's problems. In many cases the eventual goal will be to make connections between the play and the child's actual problems, including talking directly about the problems and helping the child understand how they began.

In this chapter I will present two examples to illustrate the use of displacement and other developmentally relevant approaches in work with school-age children. The first case presents a 7-year-old whose early history of chronic trauma threatened to interfere with the transition to middle childhood. The second demonstrates the ability of a child with previous adequate development to use the cognitive skills of middle childhood in coping with family stressors during two periods of treatment at 8 and 11 years of age.

WORKING TO MASTER THE TRAUMA
OF REPEATED ABUSE: A CASE EXAMPLE

Michael was a 7-year-old boy in foster care who presented with manifest sadness, statements that he wished he was dead, and aggression and sexual behavior toward his younger biological sister, who lived in the same foster home. He was working at grade level in school and did not show behavior problems there. He was in an excellent foster care placement and had made a strong attachment to his foster mother.

Michael's early experience up to age 4 was chaotic. His father was physically and sexually abusive to him and his two sisters. He took nude pictures of them and prostituted his older sister, which Michael sometimes witnessed. The children also witnessed frequent violence between their mother and father. Both parents abused alcohol and cocaine. The children often were left alone while the parents were away at bars or procuring drugs. All three children were removed for neglect and abuse when Michael was 4. They were returned to their mother, but were removed again 4 months later when it was discovered that the father was living with the family and continuing to abuse the children. Michael's older sister was assessed as severely disturbed secondary to trauma and was placed in a residential setting. Michael and his younger sister returned to the same foster home and were eventually adopted by that family after parental rights were terminated.

A sexual abuse treatment agency referred Michael to the clinic where I was on staff because he was showing symptoms of depression and had threatened to hurt himself. Michael had been in sexual abuse treatment for 1 year. During this treatment, Michael had described a number of incidents of sexual abuse, primarily involving fondling of his genitals by his father. He revealed that his mother did nothing to protect him. Treatment had focused on direct educational interventions regarding sexual abuse. Michael was told that his father's behavior was wrong and that no adult had the right to sexually abuse a child. Additionally, the therapist worked with his foster parents to structure the home environment so that Michael and his sister would not be able to act sexually toward each other. The therapist and foster parents repeatedly defined appropriate boundaries and behavior for Michael and his sister.

This intervention had been very helpful to Michael. However, as he gained some control over impulses to act out sexually and aggressively, he became more anxious and depressed. The switch in emphasis from behavioral to emotional symptoms was an effect of intervention as well as development. He had been helped to remember and describe in words a number of traumatic experiences of sexual abuse, at a time when increasing cognitive capacities permitted better verbal encoding of memories. He had gained a perspective that emphasized the wrongness of the abuse and the responsibility of the perpetrators of abuse, at a time when internalization of moral values is proceeding. He had been helped to limit his sexualized behavior, at a time when the ability to exert self-control becomes an important component of the conscience and the sense of self.

Formulation of Presenting Symptoms

From a psychodynamic point of view, Michael had begun to rely less on "acting out" as a defense against anxiety. Acting out serves the defensive function of relieving unconscious tension through action. Acting out is very common response to trauma-based anxiety and environmental reminders of traumatic events. Michael's sexual abuse treatment had helped him gain some control over tendencies to act out. At the time of referral to me, his foster mother noted a significant decline in sexualized behavior. However, it appeared that chronic trauma in his experience had not been fully addressed. Consequently, even though Michael relied less on acting out as means of discharging trauma-based anxiety, the anxiety remained internalized as depressive symptoms. Recent studies of PTSD (posttraumatic stress disorder) in children indicate that trauma is a risk factor in the development of depression (Pynoos et al., 1996). When the affective and cognitive symptoms of trauma persist, the child may become increasingly distressed and depressed because of his inability to control the symptoms (McFarlane, 1995). I hypothesized that for Michael the restriction of acting out as a means of discharge intensified the internalization of emotional symptoms, resulting in increased anxiety and depression.

Approaches to the Treatment
of Trauma in Middle Childhood

My approach to Michael's treatment was to see if he could use the emerging developmental abilities of middle childhood to reduce his depression, increase self-control, and master the traumas of his early years by creating a *trauma story* that would contain and reduce the affective power of the memories of trauma. In working with traumatized children we try to help them develop representational competence retrospectively. The experience of trauma overpowers coping capacities, supplanting thinking and words with raw and overwhelming affect. The sense of personal continuity and narrative memory are also severely disrupted, so that the child's representation of traumatic events is imagistic and distorted rather than an organized narrative. This is particularly likely, as was true for Michael, when trauma has been chronic (Terr, 1991).

Helping the client put his story into words is a well-accepted principle in the treatment of traumatized adults. This principle holds for children too. We want to help traumatized children (1) develop an understanding of what happened; (2) create a narrative of the traumatic events that is coherent and as accurate as possible; (3) name the affects that accompanied the trauma; (4) label the traumatic events as *past* rather than current events, so that the trauma is thought of as an incident or series of incidents in the narrative of the child's past life, not a fearful lens for viewing the world; and (5) process the trauma from his current more advanced cognitive perspective, taking advantage of the fact that representational competence improves as cognitive development proceeds (this is particularly important for the child who was very young when the traumatic events occurred).

However, technique with children needs to be adapted to the child's primary representational modes, including play, reenactment, and other types of symbolic expression. Very often, the play of traumatized children is disorganized and lacking in narrative, simply repeating over and over an image of the traumatic events. It becomes the therapist's job to help the child structure this seemingly chaotic play into a narrative that clarifies what happened, establishes sequences of cause and effect, and describes the child's affective reactions (Gil, 1991). Michael's case presents the process of helping young school-age child move from play expression of concerns about trauma to describing traumatic events in words and creating a verbal narrative. I will not present the entire case narrative, but rather will use sessions from the early months of treatment to illustrate the use of displacement techniques in the creation of a trauma story.

Posttraumatic Play in Michael's Early Sessions

In order to learn how Michael was remembering and constructing his traumatic experiences during the first 4 years of his life, I took a less directive approach than that taken by the therapist at the sexual abuse treatment agency. I encouraged Michael to play and hoped that by observing his play I would begin to learn how his traumatic experiences continued to influence his affects and view of the world. During the early sessions, Michael played while I watched. His play had many of the characteristics of posttraumatic play. It was driven, repetitive, and restricted in content. As he played with dinosaurs, the biting, roaring, and killing was unremitting in an amoral universe where everyone fought everyone else and there was no protection for anyone.

Michael's play symbolically demonstrated how adaptations to trauma can interfere with emerging developmental tasks. In early middle childhood, children learn that there is a social order that sets standards for behavior and a "social contract" that provides rewards for appropriate behavior. When a child has suffered gross violations of the social contract, as Michael had when his parents abused him, he experiences "a disruption of a belief in a socially modulated world" (Pynoos et al., 1996, p. 340). Michael's pessimism about this issue was reflected in his early play in treatment. There was no evident order in the play world he created, only repetitious violence. This play also reflected difficulties in creating a coherent narrative, an accomplishment that preschool children practice and school-age children achieve. As is typical of posttraumatic play, there was no developing story in Michael's play, but rather a single repetetive scenario involving a violent "bad guy" who never died.

Creating a Safe Therapeutic Environment

Unlike many children his age, Michael did not invite me to join the play. This was consistent with the self-reliant and mistrustful attitude he had developed in response to betrayal and abuse by his parents. A few times during the first few sessions I asked Michael to tell me about the dinosaurs—what made them so angry, why they were fighting each other. In response to these mild questions, Michael looked startled. This told me that he might be experiencing my questions as intrusive and perhaps that my simply noticing what he was doing made him anxious. Abused children frequently adopt a watchful, unobtrusive style, remaining quiet and self-contained in order to keep the abuser's attention away from them. It appeared that Michael was generalizing this style. Michael had adapted to the abusive situation by becoming hypervigilant and by overregulating affects. His need to feel in control, both of his environment and his feelings, had to be respected. In response, I tried to be friendly but undemanding. I realized that I would need to pace my interventions carefully and respond first to Michael's strengths before beginning to address his anxiety (Pearce & Pezzot-Pearce, 1997).

During these sessions Michael also spent time drawing. His drawings showed artistic talent. In contrast to his reactions to my questions about his play, he was at ease talking about the content of his drawings. Discussion of his artwork seemed a safe vehicle for building our relationship. His early drawings were about more neutral subjects than his play. He drew planet earth with green land masses and blue oceans. Then he drew other planets. Over the first month of treatment, a routine developed in which Michael would begin the session by drawing several pictures, then play chaotically with dinosaurs or action figures. I suggested another element to this routine—a return to drawing at the end of the session. I did this because I wanted Michael to experience a sense of structure and control in our sessions. I did not want him to associate his therapy primarily with the posttraumatic play that heightened his anxiety, and I did not want him to leave sessions filled with anxiety. Traumatized children who are not helped to seal off traumatic material during a session are more likely to act out after the session. They may learn to view therapy as a time when they are flooded with affective arousal and resist coming to sessions.

Michael's Drawings: Identifying Developmental Strengths

In assessing any child, it is important to identify areas of strength and developmental adequacy. When Michael drew and talked about his drawings, he demonstrated many of the normal characteristics of a younger school-age child. He was calm and thoughtful. He would take a moment to look at what he had drawn, then comment on it. For example, after he had drawn the head of a bird, he pointed to the eye, which he had drawn as an outer circle of black, an inner area of yellow, and a black dot in the middle, and said, "That's the way a bird's eye looks." Then he said, "I couldn't get the beak right." Drawing seemed to symbolize the forces of progressive development in Michael, in contrast to his compulsive play, which symbolized an internal preoccupation with trauma. Drawing was a more neutral activity that was completely under his control. Consequently, he had more ability to defend against anxiety and posttraumatic reminders while drawing. His drawings covered many different subjects that interested him and reflected some of the cognitive abilities and interests of school-age children. He applied internal standards of accuracy to his work, as when he commented that he had not gotten the bird's beak right. He explained the content of his drawings in a coherent way and implicitly used them to create a sense of organization to his world. For example, he drew a careful picture of his room at home, showing the placement of his bed, chest of drawers, the location of the door and windows, and many other details. The discussion of this picture led Michael to tell me that he didn't like to sleep in his room by himself and that he was glad his foster brother shared the room with him. I asked him what he was afraid of, and he was evasive. Nevertheless, his drawing had opened the way to his first verbalization of the anxiety that was registered nonverbally in his play.

Drawing as a Displacement of Posttraumatic Anxiety

Another picture allowed us to expand the discussion of Michael's fears a bit. He drew an ocean scene. At one end there was a large wave and nearby a shark's fin sticking out of the water. Near the other end a boy was riding a surfboard in the direction of the big wave. Before completing the picture Michael made a revision. He changed the boy into a heavily armored dinosaur. This seemed a response to the dangers in the picture: he had given the boy on the surfboard some protection, perhaps making him invulnerable. In response to my questions, Michael explained that the dinosaur was not in danger from the wave because he could jump right over it. He explained that the sharks would not be able to hurt the dinosaur. When I told him that it looked like he had changed the picture in the middle, he laughed and agreed. I asked why he had decided to change it. He pointed to the big wave and said, "At first this was going to be just plain water and he was going to be a person. And then the fish was going to bite him." I said, "So maybe it was looking like this person could get hurt out here by the sharks or the wave, but if you turn him into a dinosaur, he can keep himself safe because he's so strong and protected by his armor." In this drawing, he was able to peek at his feelings of vulnerability and then compensate for them. This picture suggested Michael's strong motivation to master his fears, which could more easily be expressed because of his complete control of what he drew.

Displaced Interpretations of Posttraumatic Play

After Michael began to feel comfortable talking about fearful themes in his pictures, it became possible for him to tolerate some commentary on his play. During the second month of treatment, he brought a collection of plastic action figures that included superheroes and villains from cartoon shows as well as the Teenage Mutant Ninja Turtles. I was pleased because I felt that his decision to bring these toys from home reflected his growing investment in our relationship. First we looked over the figures together. Then Michael launched into his usual play, with figures killing each other. After watching for several minutes, I noticed that one superhero figure was defeating all challengers. I asked who he was, and Michael said, "He's a bad guy." This figure was eaten by sharks and blown up by bombs, yet he continued to defeat the other figures. I said, "It seems like this bad guy can't be stopped or killed. He keeps coming back." The play continued with this theme. A few minutes later I told Michael I wanted to tell him a story that his play made me think of: "Sometimes if a kid has had bad things done to him by a grown-up and it keeps happening over and over again, the kid feels like the bad guy keeps coming back. Even when the kid is taken away from the person who was hurting him and begins to live with a family that takes care of him, sometimes a kid can still worry about getting hurt, even though he's safe now." Michael's response was to tell me a story about a kid he knew who had "a bad guy coming back." He said, "Now the bad guy doesn't know where he lives. I think his name was Michael."

Since his story mirrored mine, I decided to expand it. I told him that I had known a kid whose dad had hit him and touched his privates. Since he was living with his dad, he couldn't get away, so he always felt like his dad was like a bad guy who would always come back. Even when he was safe with a new family, he remembered the bad things his dad had done and felt scared. After this story, Michael's play changed. The bad guy figure was punished for his misdeeds. He was forced to swallow bombs, which blew up inside him. Then a Ninja Turtle figure killed him. Although the play was still violent, it had changed from hopeless posttraumatic play, in which the bad guy dominated, to the defeat of the bad guy. The triumph of a good guy—a Ninja Turtle who might be considered a self-representation—suggested that Michael could imagine a different outcome to the experience of being abused.

This theme continued in the next session, when for the first time he divided the dinosaurs into good guy and bad guy teams and then had the good guys repeatedly defeat the bad guys. There was more order in this play. The good and bad dinosaurs faced each other individually. After each fight, two more dinosaurs were brought forward. Compared with the chaotic play during the first few months of treatment, this play resembled a game with rituals and rules, and thus was more typical of a younger school-age boy's play. I asked Michael to take a break from play and told him a story about a kid who had played in a similar way. I said, "This kid always beat on the bad guys, and we figured out that he played that way because he was mad at someone who had hurt him. He wanted to punish that person, and his play was a way of imagining that." I told Michael that the therapist at the previous agency had told me that his father had hurt him. Michael agreed. I asked him to tell me about it, and he recounted some instances of his father's sexual abuse. He made clear that he had hated what had happened to him and that he thought his father had been wrong. Since Michael was able to talk about being sexually abused, I asked him to tell me other things that happened when he lived with his mom and dad. My aim was to expand the scope of our discussion in order to help develop a trauma story that would include more than sexual abuse.

Expanding the Trauma Story

Sometimes directive educational treatment for sexual abuse can be too narrow in scope. Sexually abused children often have been traumatized in other ways. It is important to observe for other traumatic events, even though the manifest problem is sexual abuse. Effective treatment gives the child a chance to fully represent his difficult experiences. Michael described many instances of his father's violent behavior. He had witnessed his father beat his mother and sisters many times. He said, "My dad chased my mom with a knife. One time he threw a glass at her and it broke on the wall." I asked how he had felt at these times. He said, "Sad. Scared too. I was afraid my mom would get killed. Sometimes he would bust down the door."

I asked if he still worried about getting hurt by his dad now, even though he was living with his foster family. He said that he wasn't worried because he dad didn't know where he lived. However, he indicated that he *was* afraid by immediately telling about a dream in which a man broke into his house, chased him and found him in every place he hid, and finally shot him. I said, "That was a very scary dream. It reminds me of how kids feel when grown-ups are doing bad things to them. The grown ups are so strong that the kid can't really stop them, so all he can do is try to hide. But that's the reason you're not living with your dad anymore, because he did all those mean things." Michael agreed and then talked about times his father had slapped his face and spanked him with a belt. I empathized with his fear and said that his father was wrong to have hurt him, his sisters, and his mom.

At the end of this session, I said, "I'm really glad you could tell me about all this. Now I know what it was like for you. Now you're probably feeling a lot safer. I would like to keep talking about what you remember." My impression was that Michael gained some relief by talking about these memories of his father's violence and his fears.

The emphasis of Michael's trauma story changed. Although his sexual abuse experiences had probably been traumatic, the more profound sources of his posttraumatic stress were his memories of being physically abused and witnessing his father's violence. He had been presenting his anxiety about violence and damage in his play since the very first session. As we continued to piece together his story over many sessions, I constantly tried to help him integrate his memories with the affects he had experienced. I made frequent comparisons between his past and present experiences, aiming to help him differentiate his fears from his present reality of living in a caring and protective family. In this work I was constantly aided by Michael's emerging developmental capacities to understand cause and effect, to take a decentered view of past events, and to think in more logical and organized ways about his experience.

USING DEVELOPMENTAL STRENGTHS: A CASE EXAMPLE

Stacey, age 8½, was referred to me by her mother, Ms. Kline, within a few weeks after she decided to separate from Stacey's stepfather. Ms. Kline and her husband had been married for 2 years. Stacey's biological father had died in an auto accident when she was only 3 months old. Ms. Kline had raised Stacey and her older sister as a single parent until she married when Stacey was 6 years old. Ms. Kline reported that Stacey had developed an affectionate relationship with her stepfather, Bill, and that she seemed depressed. Ms. Kline said Stacey and her sister had felt betrayed when they overheard their stepfather angrily say he was glad to be leaving the family. She was worried about the impact of Bill's angry statement, even though she had told the girls that the divorce was not their fault. Over the next month, Stacey frequently called him, but he often did not respond to her messages. Within 4 months he moved to another state and contacted her even less often.

Stacey demonstrated many of the qualities we expect in a school-age child who is developing adequately. She was thoughtful, calm, articulate, and self-possessed. She immediately showed a capacity to use displacement to represent her concerns, which seemed to center on anger about the divorce and feelings of abandonment. She drew two pictures: one was of an angry man whose head appeared to be exploding; the other was an idealized image of her family, including her stepfather, having a good time on the roller-coaster at an amusement park. These pictures conveyed the reality of an angry divorce, followed by a denial in fantasy that expressed her wish that the family would be reunited and happy again. The choice of a roller-coaster may also have expressed Stacey's anxious sense of the precariousness of her parents' relationship. Her work on these drawings was careful, demonstrating the motivation to do a good job that is typical of well-developing 8-year-olds. She was calm as she drew and as she explained the pictures, suggesting that she was expressing conflictual issues without consciously relating them directly to herself. This was a sign of adequate development in the area of self-regulation (Sarnoff, 1987). Although the picture of the angry man surely represented her stepfather and perhaps her own anger about the divorce, she simply explained, "This is a guy who's blowing his top." When I asked what had made him mad, she said, "Who knows?"

When I asked Stacey about the arguments her mother and stepfather were having, she looked very somber and explained calmly, "They're getting a divorce." When I suggested that many kids were upset about parents fighting and deciding to divorce, she denied being upset but admitted that her sister was. When I suggested that her second picture showed a time her family was happier and that now she and her sister might be sad, she ignored this comment and told me a story that she said she'd read in a book: "A prince wasn't getting along with his wife, so he ran away. A wizard turned him into a frog and put him in a pond, and his wife was in the pond and she was a frog too, so they got back together." I said that maybe she wished her mother and stepfather would get back together, and she responded in a rational tone, "My mom told me they're not," essentially stating the facts while avoiding acknowledgment of the reunion fantasy in her story.

Stacey showed the school-age child's ability to repress and compartmentalize painful affects. She was much more disturbed by the loss of her stepfather and her sense of an intact family than she let on. Her defenses and capacities for conscious suppression and self-distraction kept her sad and angry feelings at a distance. Her mother had explained the reasons for the divorce to her, and Stacey had a good cognitive understanding that her parents had been arguing frequently for over a year. At age 8½, she did not seem to blame herself for the divorce as egocentric preschool children tend to do. Her ability to observe the conflict from a relatively decentered perspective lessened fantasies of self-blame. Because of her strong identification with her mother, she did not, at least immediately after the separation, struggle with questions about which parent to be loyal to, which is a very common reaction of younger school-age children (Wallerstein & Kelly, 1980). Stacey's primary reactions to the divorce focused first on an overall sense of deprivation and disruption and then increasingly on her anger and confusion regarding her sense of being betrayed by her stepfather. These became the main themes of a therapy lasting 6 months.

Displacement Activities in Intervention

During the first month of therapy, which coincided with exposure to several arguments between her mother and stepfather over the division of property, Stacey produced a "book" of drawings that she added to each week. The pictures symbolized Stacey's primary concerns about her parents' divorce. The first several pages showed sharks swimming in the ocean foraging for food. I commented that the sharks looked upset and possibly angry. Stacey said that they were very angry because there was not enough food. I offered a displaced interpretation, suggesting that when parents divorce and are fighting about who gets the house and furniture and money, kids sometimes worry that they won't have a place to live or money to buy food. In a subsequent session, a picture showed people living in houses near the ocean. Some of the people foolishly swam in the ocean and were attacked by the hungry sharks. In a later picture, the houses turned out to be sitting on earthquake faults and were destroyed. These images condensed Stacey's feelings of anger, deprivation, and fear. Even though she was consistently calm as she drew, the content of the pictures showed her internal sense that a disaster had befallen her and her family. In a parent session with Ms. Kline, I asked her to assure the children that she would be able to support them however the property settlement turned out. In a family session Ms. Kline empathized with their distress, saying that she was able to take care of them and that the conflicts she and her husband were having would diminish as the divorce was settled. I also attempted to discuss these issues with Stacey's stepfather, but he was unwilling to talk with me.

After her mother and I put her feelings of anger and disruption into words, Stacey stopped drawing and we began play to Connect Four, a paper-and-pencil game that involves joining lines to form squares. We also played cards. In these games, she controlled everything. She shuffled the cards, dealt them, and acted as the authority on the rules. She was a good player who frequently beat me because of her skill; however, if she began to lose, she would look me in the eye with a defiant smile and openly cheat. I commented that she wanted to be in control, even to the point of cheating. She laughed and agreed. I asked if she would cheat if she were playing with a friend. She looked surprised and said, "No way." I had expected this answer, because it appeared that Stacey's game play in therapy had some special functions and that it was not subject to the same standards of fairness that would be used in play with a peer. This type of play continued over several sessions, with Stacey keeping running score sheets of her victories. I understood Stacey's pleasure in controlling the games as a reversal of her recent real experiences. I told her, "When I can't do anything to win it reminds me of how kids feel when something happens that they can't stop from happening. Like if their parents decide to get a divorce. Maybe the kids don't want that to happen, but they can't stop the grown-ups from doing it. Or, like what's happened to you with your stepdad—I think you'd like to see him more, but he's so wrapped up in his own worries that he doesn't call you. I've known other kids this has happened to, and it made them really angry and sad." Stacey listened carefully and said, "I don't care that much." At this point she was unable to tolerate sad feelings. However, my comment about her stepfather's inconsistent behavior seemed to give permission for Stacey to express angry feelings more directly.

Displacement Play and Transference

Reid (1993) notes that school-age children often use game playing in therapy to express strong emotions and transferences in activity that is displaced from the real situation of conflict: "Strong feelings of anger, resentment, frustration, and jealousy can be discharged within the safe confines of the game. In particular, negative feelings a child may have about his parents or other adult figures will be more easily expressed in a game situation" (p. 332). Just as the game is used as a safe vehicle for expressing negative feelings, the adult opponent in the game, the therapist, becomes a stand-in for significant adults. Since the context is "play," the child can displace toward the therapist feelings and impulses that she might be too anxious to express directly toward parents. Stacey was very angry at her stepfather. She felt frustrated by her inability to control when she could see him. These feelings were presented in our games through making fun of my inability to win and her insistence on controlling the game. At the same time, she was friendly toward me and looked forward to our sessions.

Therapy created for Stacey both a safe place to express anger and disappointment and a consistent relationship that symbolically took the place of her damaged relationship with her stepfather. These themes came through clearly in a note she wrote after a game:

> Stacey RULES at Connect Four against Douglas Davies! Cause he isn't too good! But don't tell him I said that. I think he would get mad, knowing his temper.
> Love, Stacey

Stacey's note simultaneously put me down and expressed affection for me. A few weeks later she expressed her love and anger toward her stepfather in transference to me even more directly when she made me a Christmas card. She spent 10 minutes carefully coloring it. On the front she had written, "Merry Christmas. Love, Stacey. Please turn over." On the other side she had written, "You are so stupid!" She laughed uproariously when I turned it over. I laughed with her and said she had played a good trick. I said I was reminded of how kids do not like to be tricked by grown-ups and sometimes want to pay them back. I said, "I think you have felt tricked by Bill. When he and your mom were together, he was nice to you and had fun doing things with you. Now he almost never sees you. I think that's felt like a terrible trick."

Working Through Reactions to Parental Divorce

In the next session Stacey returned to her book of drawings. This time she drew a family living in a house that was in a safe place. The family—a mother and two daughters—seemed to represent her family in its new configuration, without a father. She said, "Before they were in a spot where an earthquake shook down their house, but this time they read about earthquakes in *National Geographic* and found a place where there weren't any quakes. Also they built a better house." I asked if they were still near the ocean with the sharks. She said, "Yeah, but they don't swim in the ocean now. Now they're smart. They learned not to swim there because the dad did and he was eaten by sharks." I said, "The dad?" In response she quickly undid the implied aggression toward her stepfather by saying, "Really, it was a very old man who had a heart attack in the water and they ate him after he was dead." Compared to her first drawings, this depiction of a family showed some acceptance of the new composition of her family. Ms. Kline had told me that she and her husband had settled the divorce issues and were not arguing now. The image of the family as safe suggested Stacey was aware that the conflict had diminished. Her anger toward her stepfather was still strong, as represented in the father who was eaten by sharks; however, her anger was still not acceptable to her on a conscious level, so she denied it by modifying the story of who had been eaten by sharks. Nevertheless, her angry feelings were quite intense, as indicated by the next picture she drew, a river full of piranhas. Moving back into the displacement of transference, she threatened to draw me in the water with the piranhas. When I expressed mock alarm, she laughed and said, "All right, I won't put you in there. Let's play Connect Four."

During the first 3 of months treatment, Stacey used displacement through drawing and games to symbolically approach her feelings about the loss of her stepfather. Through a combination of displaced and direct interpretation I helped her acknowledge her feelings in their real context. Gradually, she was able to talk about her disappointment and anger directly. She began to complain about her stepfather's failure to see her regularly. She was critical of him for making promises and failing to keep them. When he told her he would be moving away to attend a distant university, she continued to describe her mixed feelings in sessions. She said she wished he would stay but accepted his explanation that he needed to complete his education. She continued to be angry at him, and I felt that her anger was in part a defense against sad feelings. However, Stacey denied this when I suggested it. In fact, talking directly about her feelings about the divorce and her stepfather's move over several sessions seemed to accomplish some working through of the disruption of her life. This was evident in her mother's reports that she was happier. Her affect in sessions was more buoyant and the controlling play declined. During the termination process, I asked Stacey what advice she might give other kids whose parents were divorcing. Her answer implicitly expressed the school-age child's tendency to use cognitive strategies to regulate affect: "Tell them to think that it happened for a good reason."

Work with an Older School-Age Child: Stacey's Second Treatment

Two and a half years later, Ms. Kline called to ask me to see Stacey, who was now 11. Ms. Kline told me that she was planning to marry again within a few months and that Stacey seemed angry and anxious. She was often rude and sarcastic toward her mother and sometimes toward her mother's fiancé. She was arguing constantly with her older sister. It appeared that Stacey was worried about her mother's upcoming marriage, and that her previous experience of divorce and loss formed the context of her anxiety. When her mother made plans to marry again, Stacey felt threatened by the possible repetition of making an attachment to a father and then losing him.

Because of their advanced cognitive abilities, older school-age children are capable of analyzing problems within their families and realistically worrying or being angry about them. Since these concerns are conscious, though kept private, it is often possible to move fairly quickly from displacement to direct discussion of the problems, especially when, as was true for Stacey, the child has had a previous relationship with the therapist. Even though many school-age children are unwilling to initiate a discussion of problems, they are often responsive when a therapist puts the problem into words accurately.

In the second round of therapy, occurring 2 years after the first, Stacey's way of presenting and working on her concerns showed similarities and differences from the first treatment. She still utilized the displacement of a transference relationship, alternating between seeking my interest and approval and playfully acting rude and rejecting me. This transference revealed both sides of her ambivalence about her mother's remarriage—she wanted a father but resisted that wish because of her anxiety about loss. She still chose to play Connect Four and card games with me. This seemed to be Stacey's way of reestablishing our relationship and affirming its continuity.

Despite these similarities in presentation, there were also important differences that reflected her gains in development during the intervening 2 years. Stacey was more consciously aware of what was bothering her than she had been 2 years previously. With some help, she could discuss her worries, as opposed to expressing them in displacement. When we played games, she always played fairly. She might playfully make fun of me when I lost, but she did not cheat or change the rules. Because she was able to think about what was bothering her and to tolerate ambivalent feelings more easily, she had less need to hide her concerns from herself via displacement. This did not mean that she could talk with ease about her worries. But she responded more readily when I commented on transference behavior or directly brought up concerns about her mother's remarriage.

Although older school-age children often resist talking directly about problems, they frequently agree with direct interpretations that are phrased in concrete terms and presented with empathy for the child's feelings. Once the therapist has established a solid relationship with a school-age child, direct interpretation can be used to help the child organize and understand emotionally painful experiences and memories. For example, early in the second period of treatment, I tried to help Stacey connect her anxiety about her mother's new relationship with her memories of the divorce. I said, "Other kids I've known have been mad and worried when their mom decides to get married again. That's because they start thinking about the divorce and they don't want to go through that again. I think it was sad and upsetting for you when Bill and your mom divorced. You never knew your real dad, and Bill was the closest to a dad you ever had. But he didn't see you much after he moved out and then he moved away. That really hurt your feelings." Stacey listened thoughtfully and said, "You're right." When I said directly that I thought she and her sister were worried the new marriage would also end in divorce and they would have to go through the same painful feelings all over again, Stacey said, "I bet he'll be gone in 3 months." This comment confirmed my impression that Stacey was consciously thinking about the possibility of another loss.

Stacey brought up other related concerns. She described her mother's fiancé, Andy, as "nice" but said she didn't really know him very well. She described the pressure she felt from her mother to become close to him. I said, "It takes a long time to get to know someone well. Just because your mom is excited about marrying Andy doesn't mean you have to feel the same way right away. It seems like you like him, but you want to get to know him better." Stacey looked thoughtful and agreed. I also suggested that since she was worried that the relationship might not endure, it was normal for her to be cautious about getting close to Andy. Stacey was also alert to changes in her mother. For example, she complained that her mother wanted Stacey and her sister to be on their best behavior when Andy was around. I commented that since her mom's relationship with Andy was still new, maybe she was extra sensitive to anything that might cause a problem. I also said, however, that if they were going to be a family she and her sister should feel free to be themselves with Andy.

Developmental Guidance

In a parent guidance session, Ms. Kline expressed concern that Stacey and her sister were speaking rudely and sarcastically to both herself and Andy. I suggested that Stacey was showing her anxiety about the remarriage. I also pointed out that her anxiety intersected with developmentally normal behavior common in 11-year-olds: as school-age children begin the transition to adolescence, they frequently become more contentious and critical of their parents. This reflects the child's unconscious awareness that her coming developmental tasks involve differentiating the self from parents and learning to function more autonomously (Blos, 1979). In describing this process to Ms. Kline, I pointed out that a normal aspect of development in preadolescents was being intensified by the stress of Stacey's fears that her mother's new marriage would fail.

Utilizing the Older Child's Cognitive Abilities

When I told Stacey that her mother had said she was saying rude things particularly to Andy, Stacey immediately agreed and said, "Yeah, my sister and I are trying to drive him away." I asked how she thought they could do that. She said, "Maybe he'll be disgusted by us bad kids and give up." This gave me a chance to revisit issues from the first treatment. I told her that perhaps she and her sister had *felt* they had driven Bill, their first stepfather, away, even though that was not the reason for the divorce. If a kid feels that, I said, she might think it's better to show how bad she can be *before* the marriage. Stacey said that she liked Andy, but that she really did not want to go through another divorce.

This second treatment particularly made use of Stacey's cognitive abilities. At age 11, she could assess similar and different aspects of a situation that seemed the same. She became anxious when her mother decided to remarry because she was afraid of a repetition of divorce. But she also was able to compare the differing personalities of her previous stepfather and her new stepfather. Her new stepfather, she gradually realized, was more emotionally attuned to her and more interested in her school and sports activities. As Stacey differentiated Andy from Bill, she became less anxious about their relationship. After her mother and Andy were married, I continued to see Stacey periodically, each time reviewing her reactions to her mother's new marriage.

In the second short-term treatment when Stacey was 11, it was easier to move from displacement activities to direct discussion of problems than had been true during the first treatment. In part this was because there were differences in the presenting problems. Stacey's anxiety over her mother's remarriage was not as acute and painful as her distress over the divorce. However, Stacey's ability to approach problems cognitively, control the intensity of her feelings, and tolerate ambivalence had increased as a result of ongoing development between ages 8 and 11. Consequently, she had less need to disguise her thoughts and feelings through displacement.

A Developmental Perspective on Intervention

Stacey's case is a good illustration of "intermittent therapy," a model in which the therapist provides intervention when difficulties occur, terminates when the problems are resolved, and remains available for future therapy (Hoyt, 1995). The intermittent treatment model is appropriate for children because they are developing rapidly and may need help at different points in development. After a child and parents have been helped to master a particular developmental hurdle, then therapy can cease, with the understanding that it may resume when a new hurdle presents itself.

I saw Stacey in the first intervention for about 6 months, until she had begun to cope with the divorce and loss of her stepfather. When her anxiety about loss resurfaced 2 years later in reaction to her mother's plans to remarry, I saw her again for about 6 months. In this model, the therapist works to establish a positive attachment relationship with the parent and child in order to support their relationship and the child's development. The therapeutic relationship then becomes used in the same way a child uses the attachment relationship: at times of stress, confusion, or anxiety, the parent and child can draw on the attachment relationship with the therapist for "refueling," guidance or clarification. Intermittent treatment is especially likely to be needed when a child has experienced trauma or loss, because at each new level child may need to reprocess the trauma or loss from the perspective of her new level of development (Shapiro, 1994; Webb, 1993b). The practitioner who thinks developmentally can create treatment plans and interventions that respond to the child's emerging developmental tasks and skills.

OBSERVATION EXERCISES

1. Spend 2–3 hours observing a group of elementary-school children. Preferably observe in three contexts: the regular classroom, the playground at recess, and a special class such as gym or music.

   a. Choose one child and observe her or his behavior in class and interaction with peers at recess. In class, look for attentional capacities and interest in work. On the playground, look for social abilities, place in status hierarchies, and general level of involvement with peers.

   b. Observe for gender-based behavior. Do girls and boys play in segregated groups as the developmental literature of middle childhood suggests? Do you see instances of sustained interactions between boys and girls? Do you observe differences in the themes of boys' versus girls' play and interactions?

   c. Observe for behavior that reflects the social and moral values of school-age children. For example, do you see evidence of social rejection or stigmatization? Instances of prosocial behavior? Reactions to children who show difficulties controlling impulses? Controversies over rules or "correct" behavior? Negotiation of controversies?

2. Observe for developmental progress across middle childhood by spending 1 hour observing first graders (age 6–7) and 1 hour observing fourth graders (age 9–10). What differences do you see in the areas of social skills, peer orientation, physical abilities and self-regulation?

❖ CHAPTER 12 ❖

Conclusion: Developmental Knowledge and Practice

For a concluding review of the implications of developmentally based practice, I will return to the case of Jared, the toddler who struggled with ongoing fearful reactions to witnessing his father's abuse of his mother (see Chapters 6 and 7). Like many traumatized young children who experience frequent hyperarousal, Jared had begun to adopt the defense of aggression as a means of warding off danger when he felt anxious. He was aggressive both at home and at child care. His development was at risk because he was beginning to rely on aggression as a means of coping with anxiety, and also because others were already reacting negatively to his aggression. From a transactional perspective, the angry and distressed responses of child care providers and peers to his aggression fueled his anxiety and insecurity, reinforcing his sense that he needed to be aggressive to feel safe. The influence of anxiety on his perceptions and the negative feedback he was receiving created a risk that he would adopt an impulsive and aggressive style that would severely limit his possibilities for adaptive development.

Although Jared's mother was very invested in him, unwittingly she was also reinforcing his aggressive behavior. When he would hit her at home, she would become sad but would not stop him. She felt unable to set limits on him. Her sense of helplessness based on her own traumatic abuse prevented her from giving Jared the protection (in this case from his own impulses) he needed in order to feel secure. Their individual experiences of trauma were being carried into their relationship. The pattern of domestic violence was be repeated, this time with Jared in the abusive role. I was concerned that if she did not set limits on his aggression, he would continue to use it to cope with anxious or angry feelings and even would be at risk to become an abuser himself.

APPLYING PRACTICE KNOWLEDGE AND SKILLS

What resources and strengths can we find in the child and parent or parents to help a child like Jared cope with trauma? How does developmental knowledge that integrates maturational, transactional, and ecological perspectives inform intervention planning? What skills do practitioners need to translate this knowledge into intervention strategies? My work with Jared was informed by a knowledge of the developmental capabilities of older toddlers, by an analysis of how Jared's posttraumatic defenses and symptoms were interfering with the development of self-regulation, by an understanding of the crucial importance of attachment in supporting developmental progress, by an awareness that Jared's interactions in the world outside his family—in this case, the child care center—would also influence his development, and by my training in play therapy and child–parent intervention.

Assessment of Strengths

In Jared's case, two sources of strength were present. The first was his mother's investment in him, including her capacity for empathy, and the presence of some attachment strategies that they could use to relieve his distress. Mrs. Taylor was capable of carrying out one of the new functions of attachment that emerge during the toddler period—helping the child construct an understanding of the world through explanation, clarification, and reassurance. The second resource was Jared's developmental capabilities in the areas of symbolic play and language. In the first two sessions, Mrs. Taylor told the story of her husband's breaking the door, sending shattered glass cascading over herself and Jared. Jared's play in response to this story (having a dinosaur break down a door and bite a baby) demonstrated that he had age-expected resources for understanding and communicating about his experience. His receptive language ability permitted him to take in his mother's words, and his capacity for symbolic play allowed him to represent what the experience had meant to him.

Developmental Knowledge and Intervention Planning

Developmental understanding informed the intervention approach and goals in the following ways:

• *Attachment perspective.* Understanding of the continuing salience of attachment for toddlers led to a choice of parent–child treatment. Especially when a young child has been traumatized, the security provided by the attachment relationship is the most critical resource. But precisely because toddlers rely much more heavily on the attachment relationship than on themselves to maintain a sense of security, trauma creates a challenge to the attachment relationship. The traumatized toddler implicitly has this feeling: the fact that this frightening and overwhelming event could happen to me must mean that my parent cannot keep me safe and secure. This distressing awareness often leads to behavior that shows the child is questioning the viability of the attachment relationship. With these issues in mind, I established strengthening the child–parent attachment as a primary goal of intervention.

• *Maturational perspective.* Jared's capacity to represent his fears and memories in play made it possible for his mother and me to learn specifically how he had constructed the experiences of witnessing his father's violence. His emerging language ability made it possible for him to process his traumatic experiences through verbal understanding. A second goal of intervention was to use these developmental capacities to help him gain some mastery of trauma by interpreting his play as representing frightening memories, by putting them into words, by locating them in the past rather than in the present, and by offering verbal reassurance. This goal implicitly aimed to take advantage of areas of strength—play and language—in order to undo the maladaptive rigidity of a developmental function—regulation of affect and impulse—that had been compromised by trauma. I hoped that if Jared could be helped to think about his experiences and fears at a higher cognitive level in language and if his sense of security in the attachment could increase, then he would be able to move beyond a reliance on his aggressive defenses, which had great potential to interfere with his later development.

• *Ecological perspective.* It is necessary to be aware of all of the child's environments—home, child care, school—and to be ready to intervene when a setting outside the home has the potential to interfere with a child's development. There was a real risk that Jared's aggression would cause him to be identified as a mean or uncontrollable child by his child care providers. At the time of referral, they were already considering expelling him from the program. A third intervention goal was to help his caregivers understand his aggressive behavior in the context of his traumatic exposure to violence and to ask them to give the treatment some time to work before dismissing him from the program. With Mrs. Taylor's permission, I met with his teachers and explained that his aggression was based in trauma and that his mother and I would be working to help him master the trauma. This intervention was helpful to his teachers because it enabled them to see his previously unexplained behavior in a new context. I also suggested some ways that Jared could be helped to feel more secure in the day care setting. For example, I asked them to assign one regular teacher to be Jared's particular attachment figure at the center, and also suggested that they be ready to move in quickly when they saw signs that Jared was looking anxious or was in a situation that might spike his anxiety, so that they could intervene before his aggression escalated.

Skills Needed in Practice with Children

This case, like all work with children and their families, required a range of skills in the practitioner. These practice skills can be gained in a number of ways, including the following:

• *Observing children in their natural settings, in order to gain practice in assessing developmental level.* New practitioners sometimes feel uncertain about the relevance of developmental thinking when they are confronted with serious presenting problems and symptoms. It may feel tempting to set developmental assessment aside and plunge into intervention. But until one has skill in making quick assessments based on a practical knowledge of development, such interventions will often be misguided. It is helpful to balance our observations of development made while we feel under pressure to intervene with observational situations where we do not have to do anything but watch and think. Observations made in natural settings—child care centers, playgrounds, schools, homes, malls—can contribute to the confidence with which we make developmental assessments in practice.

• *Attending special training programs on topics relevant to work with children,* such as play therapy techniques, using art in intervention, specialized interventions for issues such as sexual abuse and behavioral problems, and parent/family work. Training in play therapy is essential for practitioners who work with children. To become a skilled child practitioner, one must learn how to understand children's play, how to play with children in a therapeutic manner, how and when to intervene using displacement techniques, and how to modify play approaches to match the developmental level of the child.

• *Receiving regular supervision on practice issues, including ongoing case consultation.* Case-oriented supervision is particularly important during the early part of a practitioner's career, when he or she is trying to integrate diverse knowledge and skills in the context of individual cases. A skilled supervisor can contribute a great deal to a practitioner's formative experience, helping him or her find an "adaptive pathway" that supports continuing professional development.

In my work with Jared and his mother, I made particular use of skills in developmental assessment, play therapy, and parent guidance and support. I used these skills to help Mrs. Taylor understand the sources of Jared's difficulties and to provide information about the meaning of his play and his need for secure attachment, so that Mrs. Taylor could function as a cotherapist. Helping her establish herself in this role was essential to realizing the goals of intervention, because Jared, as a toddler who relied on his attachment relationship with his mother, was much more influenced by her interventions than by mine. Mrs. Taylor became adept at understanding Jared's symbolic play and verbalizing empathy for his fears. She and I responded to his post-traumatic play by saying that he was just remembering what happened when daddy broke the door, that it was not happening now, and that she intended to keep him safe.

EVER-PRESENT COMPLICATIONS IN PRACTICE

While it is useful to articulate practice guidelines in the abstract, it is also important to realize that each child and each family must be approached with a respect for the unique ways they express their distress, the unique barriers that prevent them from resolving problems, and the unique resources they can use to move to a more adaptive pathway of development. I have tried to convey this idea throughout the book by presenting many case examples that demonstrate individualized applications of developmental practice principles.

Often these barriers and resources become evident when intervention reaches a plateau or sticking point. Then the practitioner must look for new ways to intervene. In the case of Jared, Mrs. Taylor had been very successful at verbalizing the meaning of Jared's play and reassuring him. But an impasse developed as it became evident that Mrs. Taylor was unable to set limits on his aggression toward her. She had trouble understanding that her inability to stop Jared from hitting her was contradicting her verbal assurances that violence would not occur in their family again. I believed that Jared would not feel confident in the attachment relationship until his mother could show him that she could keep herself safe.

Fortunately, Jared's play in sessions became a vehicle for helping Mrs. Taylor understand his need for limits. Jared pretended to have a party and served his mother and me coffee and cake. But when his mother asked for another cup, he pretended to pour "burning hot" coffee onto her leg. When she pretended to cry, Jared moved out of pretend and began hitting her hard on the leg with a Lincoln log. He was hurting her, but she did not stop him. I intervened by taking the Lincoln log from Jared, telling him that I did not allow hurting. I would not let him hurt his mother, and I would not let him be hurt. Jared struggled with me for a moment and looked frightened. His mother took him on her lap and comforted him.

This incident allowed Mrs. Taylor to examine her own responses to Jared's aggression. She realized that she was making things worse by taking his aggression and pretending to cry. I pointed out that when I restrained him he had shown us that beneath the aggressive tough guy was a frightened 2-year-old who needed to feel safe and protected on his mother's lap.

Her reflections on her sense of helplessness in the face of Jared's aggression ushered in a period of work lasting several months on her own traumatization. Gradually, as part of this work, she recognized that she had projected aspects of her relationship with her husband onto her relationship with Jared. As Mrs. Taylor consciously separated the two relationships, she saw more clearly that Jared's aggression needed to be handled with firm limits. Her new firmness, combined with her ongoing empathic responsiveness, allowed Jared to relax his hyperalert, aggressive defense. Her firmness signaled to him that he did not have to constantly test her ability to be protective. His aggressive behavior gradually diminished.

INTERVENTION AND DEVELOPMENTAL OUTCOME

Intervention that is timely and effective can have an important positive impact on a child's subsequent development. Although the child's relationships with his or her parents, the balance of risk and protective factors, and experiences in school and with peers will have much more cumulative influence on a child's development than will intervention, timely intervention can be an important turning point. It can help a child move away from a maladaptive pathway and onto a more adaptive one that has long-term implications for development.

I worked with Jared and his mother early in my social work career. I ran into Mrs. Taylor a few times over the years and was able to learn how Jared's development had proceeded. It had not been without problems. He struggled to learn to read in the early grades and began to develop low self-esteem about his school performance. Both his academic abilities and self-esteem improved after he was diagnosed with a learning disorder and appropriate special education was provided. However, in the areas of most concern during the treatment—regulation of affect and impulse and adaptive use of relationships—Jared had done well. A few years ago, Mrs. Taylor sent me a note, and it was a shock to learn that Jared had just turned 21. She described him as a caring, calm, and humorous person who has a good relationship with his girlfriend. She wrote that this driven aggression had stopped during our treatment when he was 3 and had never resurfaced.

References

Aber, J. L., & Allen, J. P. (1987). Effects of maltreatment on young children's socioemotional development: An attachment theory perspective. *Developmental Psychology, 23,* 406–414.

Aboud, F. E. (1984). Social and cognitive bases of ethnic identity constancy. *Journal of Genetic Psychology, 145,* 227–229.

Achenbach, T. M., & Edelbrock, C. S. (1983). *Manual for the child behavior profile and child behavior checklist.* Burlington, VT: Author.

Ahrons, C. R., & Rodgers, R. H. (1987). *Divorced families.* New York: Norton.

Ainsworth, M. D. S. (1967). *Infancy in Uganda: Infant care and the growth of love.* Baltimore: Johns Hopkins University Press.

Ainsworth, M. D. S. (1982). Attachment: Retrospect and prospect. In C. M. Parkes & J. Stevenson-Hinde (Eds.), *The place of attachment in human behavior* (pp. 3–30). New York: Basic Books.

Ainsworth, M. D. S., Blehar, M. C., Waters, E., & Wall, S. (1978). *Patterns of attachment: A psychological study of the Strange Situation.* Hillsdale, NJ: Erlbaum.

Alexander, P. C. (1992). Application of attachment theory to the study of sexual abuse. *Journal of Consulting and Clinical Psychology, 60,* 185–195.

Amato, P. R. (1993). Children's adjustment to divorce: Theories, hypotheses and empirical support. *Journal of Marriage and the Family, 55,* 23–28.

American Psychiatric Association. (1994). *Diagnostic and statistical manual of mental disorders* (4th ed.). Washington, DC: Author.

Anderson, D. J., Williams, S., McGee, R., & Silva, P. A. (1987). DSM-III disorders in preadolescent children: Prevalence in a large sample from the general population. *Archives of General Psychiatry, 44,* 69–76.

Anthony, E. J. (1974). The syndrome of the psychologically invulnerable child. In E. J. Anthony & C. Koupernik (Eds.), *The child in his family: Children at psychiatric risk* (pp. 529–545). New York: Wiley.

Anthony, E. J. (1986). Terrorizing attacks on children by psychotic parents. *Journal of the American Academy of Child Psychiatry, 25,* 326–335.

Anthony, E. J., & Cohler, B. J. (Eds.). (1987). *The invulnerable child.* New York: Guilford Press.

Arnold, L. E. (1990). Learning disorders. In B. D. Garfinkel, G. A. Carlson, & E. B. Weller (Eds.), *Psychiatric disorders in children and adolescents* (pp. 237–256). Philadelphia: Saunders.

Atwood, R., & Safyer, A. W. (1993). The autonomous self vs. the relational self: Implications of clinical assessment and treatment in child psychotherapy. *Journal of Analytic Social Work, 1,* 39–54.

Baldwin, A. L., Baldwin, C. P., Kasser, R., Zax, M., Sameroff, A., & Seifer, R. (1993). Contextual risk and resiliency during late adolescence. *Development and Psychopathology, 5,* 741–761.

Baldwin, D. A. (1995). Understanding the link between joint attention and language. In C. Moore & P. J. Dunham (Eds.), *Joint attention: Its origins and role in development* (pp. 131–158). Hillsdale, NJ: Erlbaum.

Baldwin, D. A., & Markman, E. M. (1989). Mapping out word–object relations: A first step. *Child Development, 60,* 381–398.

Band, E. B., & Weisz, J. (1988). How to feel better when it feels bad: Children's perspectives on coping with everyday stress. *Developmental Psychology, 24,* 247–257.

Bandura, A. (1978). The self system in reciprocal determinism. *American Psychologist, 33,* 344–358.

Barenboim, C. (1981). The development of person perception in childhood and adolescence: From behavioral comparisons to psychological constructs to psychological comparisons. *Child Development, 52,* 129–144.

Barkley, R. A. (1997). *Defiant children* (2nd ed.): *A clinician's manual for assessment and parent training.* New York: Guilford Press.

Barnard, K. E., Magyary, D., Sumner, G. A., Booth, C. L., Mitchell, S. K., & Spieker, S. (1988). Prevention of parenting alterations for women with low social support. *Psychiatry, 51,* 248–253.

Bartholomew, K., & Horowitz, L. M. (1991). Attachment styles among young adults: A test of a four category model. *Journal of Personality and Social Psychology, 61,* 226–244.

Bates, E., Camaioni, L., & Volterra, V. (1975). The acquisition of performatives prior to speech. *Merrill–Palmer Quarterly, 21,* 205–226.

Bates, E., O'Connell, B., & Shore, C. (1987). Language and communication in infancy. In J. D. Osofsky (Ed.), *Handbook of infant development* (2nd ed., pp. 149–203). New York: Wiley.

Bates, J. E. (1983). Issues in the assessment of difficult temperament. *Merrill–Palmer Quarterly, 26,* 299–319.

Bates, J. E. (1987). Temperament in infancy. In J. D. Osofsky (Ed.), *Handbook of infant development* (2nd ed., pp. 1101–1149). New York: Wiley.

Bates, J., & Bayles, K. (1988). Attachment and the development of behavior problems. In J. Belsky & T. Nezworski (Eds.), *Clinical applications of attachment* (pp. 253–299). Hillsdale, NJ: Erlbaum.

Baumeister, R. F., & Senders, P. S. (1988). Identity development and the role structure of children's games. *Journal of Genetic Psychology, 52,* 163–176.

Baumrind, D. (1993). The average expectable environment is not good enough: A response to Scarr. *Child Development, 64,* 1299–1317.

Beardslee, W. (1989). The role of self-understanding in resilient individuals: The development of a perspective. *American Journal of Orthopsychiatry, 59,* 266–278.

Beeghly, M., & Cicchetti, D. (1994). Child maltreatment, attachment and the self system: Emergence of an internal state lexicon in toddlers at high social risk. *Development and Psychopathology, 6,* 5–30.

Bell, C. C., & Jenkins, E. J. (1993). Community violence and children on Chicago's southside. *Psychiatry, 56,* 46–54.

Bell, S. M., & Ainsworth, M. D. S. (1972). Infant crying and maternal responsiveness. *Child Development, 43,* 1171–1190.

Belsky, J., & Rovine, M. J. (1988). Nonmaternal care in the first year of life and security of infant–parent attachment. *Child Development, 59,* 157–167.

Benjamin, L. S. (1993). Every psychopathology is a gift of love. *Psychotherapy Research, 4,* 1–24.

Bennett, J. W., Jr., & Davies, D. (1981). Intervention and adaptation in the third year: The mother–child dialogue. *Journal of Child Psychotherapy, 7,* 19–32.

Benoit, D., & Parker, K. (1994). Stability and transmission of attachment across three generations. *Child Development, 65,* 1444–1456.

Bergmann, T., & Freud, A. (1965). *Children in the hospital.* New York: International Universities Press.

Berk, L. E. (1992). Children's private speech: An overview of theory and the status of research. In R. M. Diaz & L. E. Berk (Eds.), *Private speech: From social interaction to self-regulation* (pp. 17–53). Hillsdale, NJ: Erlbaum.

Berman, S. (1979). The psychodynamic aspects of behavior. In J. Noshpitz (Ed.), *Handbook of child psychiatry: Vol. 2. Disturbances in development* (pp. 3–28). New York: Basic Books.

Bernstein, V. J., Hans, S. L., & Percansky, C. (1991). Advocating for the young child in need through strengthening the parent–child relationship. *Journal of Clinical Child Psychology, 20,* 28–41.

Besharov, D. J. (1990). Crack children in foster care: Re-examining the delicate balance between children's rights and parents' rights. *Children Today, 19,* 21–25.

Bevin, T. (1993). Violent deaths of both parents: Case of Marty, age 2½. In N. B. Webb (Ed.), *Helping bereaved children: A handbook for practitioners* (pp. 156–168). New York: Guilford Press.

Bibace, R., & Walsh, M. E. (1980). Development of children's concepts of illness. *Pediatrics, 66,* 912–917.

Bjorklund, D. F. (1990). *Children's strategies: Contemporary views of cognitive development.* Hillsdale, NJ: Erlbaum.

Black, M., Nair, P., Schuler, M., Keane, V., Snow, L., & Rigney, B. (1997). Risk factors for disruption in primary caregiving among infants of substance abusing women. *Child Abuse and Neglect, 21,* 1039–1051.

Blos, P. (1979). *The adolescent passage.* New York: International Universities Press.

Blos, P., Jr., & Davies, D. (1993). Extending the intervention process: Report of a distressed family with a damaged newborn and a vulnerable preschooler. In E. Fenichel & S. Provence (Eds.), *Development in jeopardy: Clinical responses to infants and families* (pp. 51–92). Madison, CT: International Universities Press.

Blount, R. L., Davis, N., Powers, S.W., & Roberts, M. C. (1991). The influence of environmental factors and coping style on children's coping and distress. *Clinical Psychology Review, 2,* 193–116.

Bolger, K. E., Patterson, C. J., Thompson, W. W., & Kupersmidt (1995). Psychosocial adjustment among children experiencing persistent and intermittent family economic hardship. *Child Development, 66,* 1107–1129.

Bornstein, B. (1951). On latency. *Psychoanalytic Study of the Child, 6,* 279–285.

Bowlby, J. (1969). *Attachment and loss: Vol. I. Attachment.* New York: Basic Books.

Bowlby, J. (1973). *Attachment and loss: Vol. II. Separation.* New York: Basic Books.

Bowlby, J. (1978). Attachment theory and its therapeutic implications. *Adolescent Psychiatry, 6,* 5–33.

Bowlby, J. (1980). *Attachment and loss: Vol. III. Loss.* New York: Basic Books.

Bowlby, J. (1988). *A secure base: Parent–child attachment and healthy human development.* New York: Basic Books.

Brazelton, T. B. (1990). Saving the bathwater. *Child Development, 61,* 1661–1671.

Brazelton, T. B. (1992). *Touchpoints: Your child's emotional and behavioral development.* Reading, MA: Addison-Wesley.

Brazelton, T. B. (1996). A window on the newborn's world: More than two decades of experience with the Neonatal Behavioral Assessment Scale. In S. J. Meisels & E. Fenichel (Eds.), *New visions for the developmental assessment of infants and young children* (pp. 127–146). Washington, DC: Zero to Three.

Brazelton, T. B., Nugent, J. K., & Lester, B. M. (1987). Neonatal Behavioral Assessment Scale. In J. D. Osofsky (Ed.), *Handbook of infant development* (2nd ed., pp. 780–817). New York: Wiley.

Brazelton, T. B., & Yogman, M. Y. (1986). Introduction: Reciprocity, attachment and effectance: Anlage in early infancy. In T. B. Brazelton & M. Y. Yogman (Eds.), *Affective development in infancy* (pp. 1–9). Norwood, NJ: Ablex.

Bretherton, I. (1986). Representing the world in symbolic play: Reality and fantasy. In A. W. Gottfried (Ed.), *Play interactions: The contribution of play materials and parental involvement to children's development* (pp. 119–148). Lexington, MA: Lexington Books.

Bretherton, I. (1987). New perspectives on attachment relations: Security, communication and internal working models. In J. D. Osofsky (Ed.), *Handbook of infant development* (2nd ed., pp. 1061–1100). New York: Wiley.

Bretherton, I., McNew, S., & Beeghly-Smith, M. (1981). Early person knowledge as expressed in gestural and verbal communications. In M. E. Lamb & L. R. Sherrod (Eds.), *Infant social cognition* (pp. 333–377). Hillsdale, NJ: Erlbaum.

Briere, J. (1992). *Child abuse trauma: Theory and treatment of the lasting effects.* Newbury Park, CA: Sage.

Brody, R. L. (1985). Gender differences in emotional development: A review of theories and research. *Journal of Personality, 53,* 102–149.

Bronfenbrenner, U. (1979). *The ecology of human development: Experiments by nature and design.* Cambridge, MA: Harvard University Press.

Brownell, C. A., & Brown, E. (1992). Peers and play in infants and toddlers. In V. B. Van Hasselt & M. Hersen (Eds.), *Handbook of social development: A life-span perspective* (pp. 183–200). New York: Plenum.

Brownell, C. A., & Carringer, M. (1990). Changes in cooperation and self–other differentiation during the second year. *Child Development, 61,* 838–848.

Bruner, J. S. (1983). *Child's talk.* New York: Norton.

Bruner, J. S. (1985). Vygotsky: A historical and conceptual perspective. In J. V. Wertsch (Ed.), *Culture, cognition and communication: Vygotskian perspectives* (pp. 21–34). New York: Cambridge University Press.

Bruner, J. S., & Lucariello, J. (1989). Monologue as narrative recreation of the world. In K. Nelson (Ed.), *Narratives from the crib* (pp. 73–97). Cambridge, MA: Harvard University Press.

Brunnquell, D., & Hall, M. D. (1982). Issues in the psychological care of pediatric oncology patients. *American Journal of Orthopsychiatry, 53,* 32–44.

Budwig, N., & Wiley, A. (1995). What language reveals about children's categories of personhood. In L. L. Sperry & P. A. Smiley (Eds.), *New directions in child development: No. 65. Exploring young children's concepts of self and other through conversation* (pp. 21–32). San Francisco: Jossey-Bass.

Camara, K. A., & Resnick, G. (1988). Interparental conflict and cooperation: Factors moderating children's postdivorce adjustment. In E. M. Hetherington & J. D. Arasteh (Eds.), *Impact of divorce, single-parenting and stepparenting on children* (pp. 169–195). Hillsdale, NJ: Erlbaum.

Camara, K. A., & Resnick, G. (1989). Styles of conflict resolution and cooperation between divorced parents: Effects on child behavior and adjustment. *American Journal of Orthopsychiatry, 59,* 560–575.

Campbell, S. B. (1990). *Behavior problems in preschool children.* New York: Guilford Press.

Campo, A. T., & Rohner, R. P. (1992). Relationships between perceived parental acceptance–rejection, psychological adjustment, and substance abuse among young adults. *Child Abuse and Neglect, 16,* 429–440.

Canino, I. A., & Spurlock, J. (1994). *Culturally diverse children and adolescents: Assessment, diagnosis and treatment,* New York: Guilford Press.

Carlson, B. E. (1990). Adolescent observers of marital violence. *Journal of Family Violence, 5,* 285–299.

Carlson, V., Barnett, D., Cicchetti, D., & Braunwald, K. (1989). Disorganized/disoriented attachment relationships in maltreated infants. *Developmental Psychology, 25*(4), 525–531.

Case, R. (1985). *Intellectual development: From birth to adulthood.* Orlando, FL: Academic Press.

Cassidy, J. (1986). The ability to negotiate the environment: An aspect of infant competence as related to quality of attachment. *Child Development, 57,* 331–337.

Chang, P. (1990). Psychosocial needs of long-term cancer survivors: A review of the literature. *Pediatrician, 18,* 20–24.

Chess, S., & Thomas, A. (1986). *Temperament in clinical practice.* New York: Guilford Press.

Children's Defense Fund (1995). *The state of America's children yearbook 1995.* Washington, DC: Author.

Children's Defense Fund (1998). *The state of America's children yearbook 1998.* Washington, DC: Author.

Chethik, M. (1989). *Techniques of child therapy: Psychodynamic approaches.* New York: Guilford Press.

Chomsky, C. (1969). *The acquisition of syntax in children from 5 to 10.* Cambridge, MA: MIT Press.

Cicchetti, D., Ackerman, B. P., & Izard, C. E. (1995). Emotions and emotional regulation in developmental psychology. *Development and Psychopathology, 7,* 1–10.

Cicchetti, D., & Beeghly, M. (1987). Symbolic development in maltreated toddlers. In D. Cicchetti & M. Beeghly (Eds.), *New directions in child development: No. 36. Symbolic development in atypical children* (pp. 5–29). San Francisco: Jossey-Bass.

Cicchetti, D., Rogosch, F. A., Lynch, M., & Holt, K. D. (1993). Resilience in maltreated children: Processes leading to adaptive outcome. *Development and Psychopathology, 5,* 629–647.

Cicchetti, D., Toth, S., & Bush, M. (1988). Developmental psychopathology and incompetence in childhood: Suggestions for intervention. In B. B. Lahey & A. E. Kazdin (Eds.), *Advances in clinical child psychology* (Vol. 11, pp. 1–77). New York: Plenum Press.

Clark, K. (1955). *Prejudice and your child.* Boston: Beacon Press.

Clark, R., Paulson, A., & Conlin, S. (1993). Assessment of developmental status and parent–infant relationships: The therapeutic process of evaluation. In C. H. Zeanah, Jr. (Ed.), *Handbook of infant mental health* (pp. 191–209). New York: Guilford Press.

Clary, E. G., & Miller, J. (1986). Socialization and situational influences on sustained altruism. *Child Development, 57,* 1358–1369.

Cole, M., & Cole, S. R. (1989). *The development of children.* New York: Scientific American Books.

Comer, J. P., & Poussaint, A. F. (1992). *Raising black children.* New York: Plume.

Connolly, J. A., & Doyle, A. (1984). Relation of social fantasy to social competence in preschoolers. *Developmental Psychology, 20,* 797–807.

Coons, S., & Guilleminault, C. (1982). Development of sleep–wake patterns and non–rapid eye movement sleep stages during the first six months of life in normal infants. *Pediatrics, 69,* 793–798.

Cramer, B. (1986). Assessment of parent–infant relationships. In T. B. Brazelton & M. Y. Yogman (Eds.), *Affective development in infancy* (pp. 27–38). Norwood, NJ: Ablex.

Crittenden, P. M. (1992a). Children's strategies for coping with adverse environments: An interpretation using attachment theory. *Child Abuse and Neglect, 16,* 329–343.

Crittenden, P. M. (1992b). Quality of attachment in the preschool years. *Development and Psychopathology, 4,* 209–241.

Crittenden, P. M. (1992c). Treatment of anxious attachment in infancy and early childhood. *Development and Psychopathology, 4,* 575–602.

Crockenberg, S. (1988). Social support and parenting. In H. Fitzgerald, B. Lester, & M. Yogman (Eds.), *Theory and research in behavioral pediatrics* (pp. 141–174). New York: Plenum.

Cross, W. E., Jr. (1987). A two-factor theory of black identity: Implications for the study of identity development in minority children. In J. S. Phinney & M. J. Rotherham (Eds.), *Children's ethnic socialization: Pluralism and development* (pp. 117–133). Newbury Park, CA: Sage.

Cummings, E. M., & Davies, P. (1996). Emotional security as a regulatory process in normal development and the development of psychopathology. *Development and Psychopathology, 8,* 123–139.

Cummings, E. M., Iannotti, R. J., & Zahn-Waxler, C. (1985). The influences of conflict between adults on the emotions and aggression of young children. *Developmental Psychology, 21,* 495–505.

Daiute, C. (1993). Synthesis. In C. Daiute (Ed.), *New directions in child development: No. 61. The development of literacy through social interaction* (pp. 121–124). San Francisco: Jossey-Bass.

Damon, W. (1983). *Social and personality development.* New York: Norton.

Damon, W., & Hart, D. (1988). *Self-understanding in childhood and adolescence.* Cambridge, UK: Cambridge University Press.

Davies, D. (1991). Intervention with male toddlers who have witnessed parental violence. *Families in Society, 72,* 515–524.

Davies, D. (1992). Psychotherapy of a preschool cancer survivor: Promoting mastery and understanding. *Child and Adolescent Social Work, 9,* 289–305.

Davis, L. V., & Carlson, B. E. (1987). Observation of spouse abuse: What happens to the children. *Journal of Interpersonal Violence, 2,* 278–291.

Deasy-Spinetta, P. (1981). The school and the child with cancer. In J. J. Spinetta & P. Deasy-Spinetta (Eds.), *Living With childhood cancer* (pp. 153–168). St. Louis, MO: Mosby.

DeCasper, A. J., & Fifer, W. P. (1980). Of human bonding: Newborns prefer their mother's voices. *Science, 208,* 1172–1176.

Demos, V. (1986). Crying in early infancy: An illustration of the motivational function of affect. In T. B. Brazelton & M. Y. Yogman (Eds.), *Affective development in infancy* (pp. 39–73). Norwood, NJ: Ablex.

Diamond, A. (1991). Environmental influences on the young brain. In K. R. Gibson & A. C. Peterson (Eds.), *Brain maturation and cognitive development* (pp. 107–126). New York: Aldine de Gruyter.

Dishion, T. J., Patterson, G. R., & Griesler, P. C. (1994). Peer adaptations in the development of antisocial behavior: A confluence model. In L. R. Huesmann (Ed.), *Current perspectives on aggressive behavior* (pp. 61–95). New York: Plenum.

Dishion, T. J., Patterson, G. R., & Kavanagh, K. A. (1992). An experimental test of the coercion model: Linking theory, measurement and intervention. In J.

McCord & R. E. Tremblay (Eds.), *Preventing antisocial behavior: Interventions from birth through adolescence* (pp. 253–282). New York: Guilford Press.

Dodge, K. A. (1983). Behavioral antecedents of peer social status. *Child Development, 54,* 1386–1399.

Dodge, K. A., Pettit, G. S., & Bates, J. E. (1994). Effects of physical maltreatment on the development of peer relations. *Development and Psychopathology, 6,* 43–55.

Drell, M. J., Siegel, C. H., & Gaensbauer, T. J. (1993). Post-traumatic stress disorder. In C. H. Zeanah, Jr. (Ed.), *Handbook of infant mental health* (pp. 291–304). New York: Guilford Press.

Dubow, E. F., & Ippolito, M. F. (1994). Effects of poverty and quality of home environment on changes in the academic and behavioral adjustment of elementary school-age children. *Journal of Clinical Child Psychology, 23,* 401–412.

Duncan, G., Brooks-Gunn, J., & Klebanov, P. (1994). Economic deprivation and early development. *Child Development, 65,* 296–318.

Dunn, B. (1993). Growing up with a psychotic mother: A retrospective study. *American Journal of Orthopsychiatry, 63*(2), 177–189.

Dunn, J. (1987). The beginnings of moral understanding: Development in the second year. In J. Kagan & S. Lamb (Eds.), *The emergence of morality in young children* (pp. 91–111). Chicago: University of Chicago Press.

Dunst, C. J. (1993). Implications of risk and opportunity factors for assessment and intervention practices. *Topics in Early Childhood Special Education, 13,* 143–153.

Easterbrooks, M. A., & Goldberg, W. A. (1984). Toddler development in the family: Impact of father involvement and parenting characteristics. *Developmental Psychology, 55,* 740–752.

Easterbrooks, M. A., & Goldberg, W. A. (1990). Security of toddler–parent attachment: Relation to children's sociopersonality functioning during kindergarten. In M. T. Greenberg, D. Cicchetti, & E. M. Cummings (Eds.), *Attachment in the preschool years: Theory, research and intervention* (pp. 221–224). Chicago: University of Chicago Press.

Eckenrode, J., Laird, M., & Doris, J. (1993). School performance and disciplinary problems among abused and neglected children. *Developmental Psychology, 29,* 53–62.

Edelman, P. (1997). The worst thing Bill Clinton has done. *Atlantic Monthly, 253,* 43–58.

Egeland, B., Carlson, E., & Sroufe, L. A. (1993). Resilience as process. *Development and Psychopathology, 5,* 517–528.

Egeland, B., & Farber, E. A. (1987). Invulnerability among abused and neglected children. In E. J. Anthony & B. J. Cohler (Eds.), *The invulnerable child* (pp. 253–258). New York: Guilford.

Egeland, B., Sroufe, L. A., & Erickson, M. (1983). The developmental consequences of different patterns of maltreatment. *Child Abuse and Neglect, 7,* 459–469.

Eisenberg, N., Shell, R., Pasternack, J., Lennon, R., Belber, R., & Matty, R. M.

(1987). Prosocial development in middle childhood: A longitudinal study. *Developmental Psychology, 23,* 712–718.

Elkind, D. (1994). *A sympathetic understanding of the child* (3rd ed.). Boston: Allyn & Bacon.

Elkind, D., & Weiner, I. B. (1978). *Development of the child.* New York: Wiley.

Elkind, D., & Weiss, J. (1967). Studies in perceptual development: III. Perceptual exploration. *Child Development, 38,* 1153–1161.

Emde, R. N. (1989). The infant's relationship experience: Developmental and affective aspects. In A. J. Sameroff & R. N. Emde (Eds.), *Relationship disturbances in early childhood: A developmental approach* (pp. 33–51). New York: Basic Books.

Emde, R. N. (1992). Social referencing research: Uncertainty, self and the search for meaning. In S. Feinman (Ed.), *Social referencing and the social construction of reality* (pp. 79–94). New York: Plenum.

Emde, R. N., & Buchsbaum, H. K. (1990). "Didn't you hear my mommy?": Autonomy *with* connectedness in moral self emergence. In D. Cicchetti & M. Beeghly (Eds.), *The self in transition: Infancy to childhood* (pp. 35–60). Chicago: University of Chicago Press.

Emde, R. N., Gaensbauer, T. J., & Harmon, R. J. (1976). *Emotional expression in infancy.* New York: International Universities Press.

Emde, R. N., Johnson, W. F., & Easterbrooks, M. A. (1987). The do's and don'ts of early moral development: Psychoanalytic tradition and current research. In J. Kagan & S. Lamb (Eds.), *The emergence of morality in young children* (pp. 245–276). Chicago: University of Chicago Press.

Emde, R. N., & Sameroff, A. J. (1989). Understanding early relationship disturbances. In A. J. Sameroff & R. N. Emde (Eds.), *Relationship disturbances in early childhood: A developmental approach* (pp. 3–16). New York: Basic Books.

Engel, S. (1995). *The stories children tell: Making sense of the narratives of childhood.* New York: Freeman.

Engel, S. (1996). The guy who went up the steep nicken: The emergence of storytelling during the first three years. *Zero to Three, 17,* 1–9.

Erickson, M. F., Egeland, B., & Pianta, R. (1989). The effects of maltreatment on the development of young children. In D. Cicchetti & V. Carlson (Eds.), *Child maltreatment: Theory and research on the causes and consequences of child abuse and neglect* (pp. 647–684). Cambridge, UK: Cambridge University Press.

Erickson, M. F., Korfmacher, J., & Egeland, B. R. (1992). Attachments past and present: Implications for intervention with mother–infant dyads. *Development and Psychopathology, 4,* 495–507.

Erickson, M. F., Sroufe, L. A., & Egeland, B. (1985). The relationship between quality of attachment and behavior problems in preschool in a high-risk sample. In I. Bretherton & E. Waters (Eds.), Growing points in attachment theory and research. *Monographs of the Society for Research in Child Development, 50*(1–2, Serial No. 209), 147–166.

Erickson, M. T. (1993). Rethinking Oedipus: An evolutionary perspective of incest avoidance. *American Journal of Psychiatry, 150,* 411–415.

Erikson, E. H. (1963). *Childhood and society* (2nd ed.). New York: Norton.

Estes, D., Wellman, H. M., & Wooley, J. D. (1989). Children's understanding of mental phenomena. In H. Reese (Ed.), *Advances in child development and behavior* (Vol. 22, pp. 41–86). New York: Academic Press.

Eth, S., & Pynoos, R. S. (Eds.). (1985). *Post-traumatic stress disorders in children.* Washington, DC: American Psychiatric Press.

Fanshel, D., Finch, S. J., & Grundy, J. F. (1990). *Foster children in life course perspective.* New York: Columbia University Press.

Fanshel, D., & Shinn, E. B. (1978). *Children in foster care: A longitudinal investigation.* New York: Columbia University Press.

Fantuzzo, J., & Lindquist, C. (1989). The effects of observing conjugal violence on children: A review and analysis of research methodology. *Journal of Family Violence, 4,* 77–94.

Farver, J. M., & Frosch, D. L. (1996). L. A. Stories: Aggression in preschoolers' spontaneous narrative after the riots of 1992. *Child Development, 67,* 19–32.

Fein, E. (1991). Issues in foster family care: Where do we stand? *American Journal of Orthopsychiatry, 61*(4), 578–583.

Feinstein, C., & Berger, K. (1987). The chronically ill or disabled child. In J. Noshpitz (Ed.), *Basic handbook of child psychiatry* (Vol. 5, pp. 122–131). New York: Basic Books.

Feiring, C., Lewis, M., & Starr, M. D. (1984). Indirect effects and infants' reaction to strangers. *Developmental Psychology, 20,* 485–491.

Fick, A. C., Osofsky, J. D., & Lewis, M. L. (1996). Perceptions of violence: Children, parents and police officers. In J. D. Osofsky (Ed.), *Children and youth violence: Searching for solutions.* New York: Guilford Press.

Field, T. (1989). Stressors during pregnancy and the postnatal period. In M. Lewis & J. Woroby (Eds.), *New directions in child development: No. 45. Infant stress and coping* (pp. 19–31). San Francisco: Jossey-Bass.

Field, T. (1992). Infants of depressed mothers. *Development and Psychopathology, 4,* 49–66.

Finkelhor, D. (1995). The victimization of children: A developmental perspective. *American Journal of Orthopsychiatry, 65,* 177–193.

Finkelhor, D., & Browne, A. (1985). The traumatic impact of child sexual abuse: A conceptualization. *American Journal of Orthopsychiatry, 55,* 530–41.

Fischer, K. W. (1987). Commentary: Relations between brain and cognitive development. *Child Development, 58,* 623–632.

Flavell, J. H. (1985). *Cognitive development* (2nd ed.). Englewood Cliffs, NJ: Prentice-Hall.

Foley, M. A., Harris, J. F., & Hermann, S. (1994). Developmental comparisons of the ability to discriminate between memories for symbolic play enactments. *Developmental Psychology, 30,* 206–217.

Folman, R. D. (1995). *Resiliency and vulnerability among abused and neglected children in foster care.* Unpublished dissertation, University of Michigan, Ann Arbor.

Fraiberg, S. (1974). The clinical dimension of baby games. *Journal of the American Academy of Child Psychiatry, 13,* 202–220.

Fraiberg, S. (1980). Clinical assessment of the infant and his family. In S. Fraiberg (Ed.), *Clinical studies in infant mental health: The first year of life* (pp. 23–48). New York: Basic Books.

Fraiberg, S., Adelson, E., & Shapiro, V. (1975). Ghosts in the nursery: A psychoanalytic approach to the problems of impaired mother–infant relationships. *Journal of the American Academy of Child Psychiatry, 14*, 387–421.

Fraser, M. W. (Ed.). (1997). *Risk and resilience in childhood.* Silver Spring, MD: National Association of Social Workers.

Freud, A. (1963). The concept of developmental lines. *Psychoanalytic Study of the Child, 18*, 245–266.

Freud, A. (1965). *Normality and pathology in childhood: Assessments of development.* New York: International Universities Press.

Freud, A. (1966). *The ego and the mechanisms of defense* (rev. ed.). New York: International Universities Press.

Freud, A. (1977). The role of bodily illness in the mental life of children. In R. Eissler, A. Freud, M. Kris, & A. J. Solnit (Eds.), *Physical illness and handicap in childhood* (pp. 1–12). New Haven, CT: Yale University Press.

Freud, S. (1959). Inhibitions, symptoms and anxiety. In J. Strachey (Ed. and Trans.), *Standard edition of the complete psychological works of Sigmund Freud* (Vol. 20, pp. 77–178). London: Hogarth Press. (Original work published 1926)

Freyd, J. J. (1996). *Betrayal trauma: The logic of forgetting childhood abuse.* Cambridge, MA: Harvard University Press.

Friedrich, W. N., Jaworksi, T. M., Huxsahl, J. E., & Bengston, B. S. (1997). Dissociative and sexual behaviors in children and adolescents with sexual abuse and psychiatric histories. *Journal of Interpersonal Violence, 12*, 155–171.

Frodi, A., Bridges, L., & Grolnick, W. (1985). Correlates of mastery-related behavior. *Child Development, 56*, 1291–1298.

Gaensbauer, T. (1996). Developmental and therapeutic aspects of treating infants and toddlers who have witnessed violence. In J. D. Osofsky & E. Fenichel (Eds.), *Islands of safety: Assessing and treating young victims of violence.* Washington, DC: Zero to Three.

Gaensbauer, T. J., & Mrazek, D. A. (1981). Differences in the patterning of affective expression in infants. *Journal of the American Academy of Child and Adolescent Psychiatry, 20*, 673–691.

Galdston, R. (1979). Disorders of early parenthood: Neglect, deprivation, exploitation and abuse of little children. In J. D. Noshpitz (Ed.), *Basic handbook of child psychiatry* (Vol. 2, pp. 581–593). New York: Basic Books.

Garbarino, J. (1993). Children's response to community violence: What do we know? *Infant Mental Health Journal, 14*, 103–115.

Garbarino, J. (1995). The American war zone: What children can tell us about living with violence. *Journal of Developmental and Behavioral Pediatrics, 16*, 431–435.

Garbarino, J., Dubrow, N., Kostelny, K., & Pardo, C. (1992). *Children in danger: Coping with the consequences of community violence.* San Francisco: Jossey-Bass.

Garcia-Preto, N. (1982). Puerto Rican families. In M. McGoldrick, J. K. Pearce, & J. Giordano (Eds.), *Ethnicity and family therapy* (pp. 164–186). New York: Guilford Press.

Garmezy, N. (1985). Stress-resistant children: The search for protective factors In J. E. Stevenson (Ed.), *Recent research on developmental psychopathology.* Oxford, UK: Pergamon Press.

Garmezy, N., & Masten, A. S. (1986). Stress, competence and resilience: Common frontiers for therapist and psychopathologist. *Behavior Therapy, 17,* 500–521.

Garmezy, N., & Rutter, M. (1983). *Stress, coping and development in children.* New York: McGraw-Hill.

Garrett, P., Ng'andu, N., & Ferron, A. (1994). Poverty experiences of young children and the quality of their home environments. *Child Development, 65,* 331–345.

Gauvain-Piquard, A., Rodary, C., Rezvani, A., & Lemerle, J. (1987). Pain in children aged 2–6 years: A new observational rating scale elaborated in a pediatric oncology unit: Preliminary report. *Pain, 31,* 177–188.

Gemelli, R. (1996). *Normal child and adolescent development.* Washington, DC: American Psychiatric Press.

George, C., & Main, M. (1979). Social interactions of young abused children: Approach, avoidance and aggression. *Child Development, 50,* 306–318.

Gesell, A., & Armatruda, C. S. (1947). *Developmental diagnosis.* New York: Haber.

Gil, E. (1991). *The healing power of play.* New York: Guilford Press.

Gilligan, C. (1982). *In a different voice.* Cambridge, MA: Harvard University Press.

Gleason, W. J. (1995). Children of battered women: Developmental delays and behavioral dysfunction. *Violence and Victims, 10,* 153–159.

Gondolf, E. W. (1987). Changing men who batter: A developmental model of integrated interventions. *Journal of Family Violence, 2,* 345–369.

Goodman, R. F. (1991). Diagnosis of childhood cancer: The case of Tim. In N. B. Webb (Ed.), *Play therapy with children in crisis* (pp. 310–332). New York: Guilford Press.

Greenberg, M., & Speltz, M. (1988). Attachment and the ontogeny of conduct problems. In J. Belsky & T. Nezworski (Eds.), *Clinical applications of attachment* (pp. 177–218). Hillsdale, NJ: Erlbaum.

Greene, B. A. (1992). Racial socialization as a tool in psychotherapy with African-American children. In L. A. Vargas & J. D. Koss-Chioino (Eds.), *Working with culture* (pp. 63–84). San Francisco: Jossey-Bass.

Greenspan, S. I. (1979). *Intelligence and adaptation: An integration of psychoanalytic and Piagetian developmental psychology.* New York: International Universities Press.

Greenspan, S. I. (1997). *The growth of the mind.* New York: Addison-Wesley.

Greenspan, S. I., & Greenspan, N. T. (1985). *First feelings: Milestones in the development of your baby and child.* New York: Viking.

Greenspan, S. I., & Meisels, S. J. (1996). Toward a new vision for the developmental assessment of infants and young children. In S. J. Meisels & E. Fenichel (Eds.), *New visions for the developmental assessment of infants and young children* (pp. 11–26). Washington, DC: Zero to Three.

Grizenko, N., & Pawliuk, N. (1994). Risk and protective factors for disruptive behavior disorders in children. *American Journal of Orthopsychiatry, 64*(4), 534–544.

Grossman, F. K., Eichler, L. S., & Winickoff, S. A. (1980). *Pregnancy, birth and parenthood: Adaptations of mothers, fathers and infants.* San Francisco: Jossey-Bass.

Grunbaum, L., & Gammeltoft, M. (1993). Young children of schizophrenic mothers: Difficulties of intervention. *American Journal of Orthopsychiatry, 63,* 16–27.

Grusec, J. E., & Lytton, H. (1988). *Social development: History, theory and research.* New York: Springer-Verlag.

Gurucharri, C., & Selman, R. L. (1982). The development of interpersonal understanding during childhood. *Child Development, 53,* 924–927.

Hakuta, K., & Garcia, E. F. (1989). Bilingualism and education. *American Psychologist, 44,* 374–379.

Halpern, R. (1993). Poverty and infant development. In C. H. Zeanah, Jr. (Ed.), *Handbook of infant mental health* (pp. 73–86). New York: Guilford Press.

Hammen, C. (1992). Cognitive, life stress, and interpersonal approaches to a developmental psychopathology model of depression. *Development and Psychopathology, 4,* 189–206.

Hammen, C., Burge, D., & Adrian, C. (1991). The timing of mother and child depression in a longitudinal study of children at risk. *Journal of Consulting of Clinical Psychology, 59,* 341–345.

Harris, P. L. (1985). What children know about situations that provoke emotion. In M. Lewis & C. Saarni (Eds.), *The socialization of emotions* (pp. 161–185). New York: Plenum.

Harter, S. (1978). Effectance motivation reconsidered. *Human Development, 21,* 34–64.

Harter, S. (1983a). Cognitive-developmental considerations in the conduct of play therapy. In C. E. Schaefer & K. J. O'Connor (Eds.), *Handbook of play therapy* (pp. 95–127). New York: Wiley.

Harter, S. (1983b). Developmental perspectives on the self-system. In E. M. Hetherington (Ed.), *Handbook of child psychology* (4th ed.): Vol. IV. Socialization, personality and social development (pp. 275–385). New York: Wiley.

Hartup, W. W. (1989). Social relationships and their developmental significance. *American Psychologist, 44*(2), 120–126.

Hartup, W. W. (1992). Peer relations in early and middle childhood. In V. B. Van Hasselt & M. Hersen (Eds.), *Handbook of social development: A lifespan perspective* (pp. 257–281). New York: Plenum.

Hartup, W. W. (1996). The company they keep: Friendships and their developmental significance. *Child Development, 67,* 1–13.

Haviland, J. M., & Lelwica, M. (1987). The induced affect response: 10-week-old infants' responses to three emotional expressions. *Developmental Psychology, 23,* 97–104.

Hawley, T. L., Halle, T. G., Drasin, R. E., & Thomas, N. G. (1995). Children of addicted mothers: Effects of the "crack epidemic" on the caregiving environment and the development of preschoolers. *American Journal of Orthopsychiatry, 65,* 364–379.

Henning, K., Leitenberg, Coffey, P., Turner, T., & Bennett, R. (1996). Long-term psychological and social impact of witnessing violent physical conflict between parents. *Journal of Interpersonal Violence, 11*(1), 35–51.

Herman, J. L. (1992). *Trauma and recovery.* New York: Basic Books.

Hernandez, D. J. (1988). Demographic trends and the living arrangements of children. In E. M. Hetherington & J. D. Arasteh (Eds.), *Impact of divorce, single-parenting and step-parenting on children* (pp. 3–22). Hillsdale, NJ: Erlbaum.

Herrenkohl, R., Herrenkohl, E., & Egolf, B. (1983). Circumstances surrounding the occurrence of child maltreatment. *Journal of Consulting and Clinical Psychology, 51,* 424–431.

Hetherington, E. M., Stanley-Hagan, M., & Anderson, E. R. (1989). Marital transitions: A child's perspective. *American Psychologist, 44*(2), 303–312.

Hirschfeld, L. A. (1996). Seeing race. *Michigan Today, 28,* 2–3.

Hirshfeld, D. R., Rosenbaum, J. F., Biederman, J., Bolduc, E. A. Faranone, S. V., Snidman, N., Reznick, J. S., & Kagan, J. (1992). Stable behavioral inhibition and its association with anxiety disorder. *Journal of the American Academy of Child and Adolescent Psychiatry, 31,* 103–111.

Hoffman, M. L. (1977). Personality and social development. *Annual Review of Psychology, 28,* 259–331.

Hooper, S. R., & Willis, W. G. (1989). *Learning disability subtyping: Neuropsychological foundations, conceptual modes, and issues in clinical differentiation.* New York: Springer-Verlag.

Hornik, R., & Gunnar, M. R. (1988). A descriptive analysis of infant social referencing. *Child Development, 59,* 626–634.

Horowitz, M. J. (1986). *Stress response syndromes* (2nd ed.). Northvale, NJ: Aronson.

Howes, C. (1988). Peer interaction of young children. *Monographs of the Society for Research in Child Development, 53*(1, Serial No. 217).

Hoyt, M. F. (1995). *Brief therapy and managed care.* San Francisco: Jossey-Bass.

Hubert, N. C., Wachs, T. D., Peters-Martin, P., & Gandour, M. J. (1982). The study of early temperament. *Child Development, 53,* 571–600.

Ilg, F. L., & Ames, L. B. (1958). *Child behavior.* New York: Harper & Row.

Institute of Medicine. (1996). *Fetal alcohol syndrome.* Washington, DC: National Academy Press.

Izard, C. E., & Malatesta, C. Z. (1987). Perspectives on emotional development: I. Differential emotions theory of early emotional development. In J. D. Osofsky (Ed.), *Handbook of infant development* (2nd ed., pp. 494–554). New York: Wiley.

Jaenicke, C., Hammen, C., Zupan, B., Hiroto, D., Gordon, D., Adrian, C., & Burge, D. (1987). Cognitive vulnerability in children at risk for depression. *Journal of Abnormal Child Psychology, 15,* 559–572.

Jaffe, P., Wolfe, D., Wilson, S., & Zak, L. (1986). Similarities in behavioral and social maladjustment among child victims and witnesses to family violence. *American Journal of Orthopsychiatry, 56,* 142–146.

Janowsky, J. S., & Carper, R. (1996). Is there a neural basis for cognitive transitions in school age children? In A. J. Sameroff & M. M. Haith (Eds.), *The five to seven year shift: The age of reason and responsibility* (pp. 33–62). Chicago: University of Chicago Press.

Jay, S. M. (1988). Invasive medical procedures: Psychological intervention and assessment. In D. K. Routh (Ed.), *Handbook of pediatric psychology* (pp. 401–425). New York: Guilford Press.

Johnson, M. H. (1997). *Developmental cognitive neuroscience.* Cambridge, MA: Blackwell.

Johnston, J. R., Kline, M., & Tschann, J. T. (1989). Ongoing postdivorce conflict: Effects on children of joint custody and frequent access. *American Journal of Orthopsychiatry, 59,* 576–592.

Kagan, J. (1981). *The second year: The emergence of self-awareness.* Cambridge, MA: Harvard University Press.

Kagan, J. (1983). Stress and coping in early development. In N. Garmezy & M. Rutter (Eds.), *Stress, coping and development in children* (pp. 191–216). New York: McGraw-Hill.

Kagan, J. (1984). *The nature of the child.* New York: Basic Books.

Kagan, J. (1989). Temperamental contributions to social behavior. *American Psychologist, 44,* 668–674.

Kagan, J., Kearsley, R. B., & Solano, P. R. (1978). *Infancy: Its place in human development.* Cambridge, MA: Harvard University Press.

Kagan, J., Resnick, J. S., Clark, C., Snidman, N., & Garcia Coll, C. (1984). Behavioral inhibition to the unfamiliar. *Child Development, 55,* 2212–2225.

Kail, R. (1990). *The development of memory in children.* New York: Freeman.

Kalter, N. (1987). Long term effects of divorce on children: A developmental vulnerability model. *American Journal of Orthopsychiatry, 57,* 587–599.

Kalter, N. (1988). *Time-limited developmental facilitation groups for children of divorce: Early elementary school manual.* Ann Arbor, MI: Author.

Kalter, N., Kloner, A., Schreier, S., & Okla, K. (1989). Predictors of children's postdivorce adjustment. *American Journal of Orthopsychiatry, 59,* 605–618.

Karls, J., & Wandrei, K. E. (1994). *Person-in-environment: A system for describing, classifying and coding problems of social functioning.* Silver Spring, MD: National Association of Social Workers.

Karoly, P. (1982). Self-management problems in children. In E. J. Mash & L. G. Terdal (Eds.), *Behavioral assessment of childhood disorders.* New York: Guilford Press.

Kates, W. G., Johnson, R. L., Rader, M. W., & Strieder, F. H. (1991). Whose child is this? Assessment and treatment of children in foster care. *American Journal of Orthopsychiatry, 61,* 584–591.

Katz, E. R. (1980). Illness impact and reintegration. In J. Kellerman (Ed.), *Psychological aspects of childhood cancer* (pp. 14–46). Springfield, IL: Thomas.

Katz, I. (1996). *The construction of racial identity in children of mixed parentage: Mixed metaphors.* London: Kingsley.

Katz, P. A. (1987). Developmental and social processes in ethnic attitudes and self-identification. In J. S. Phinney & M. J. Rotherham (Eds.), *Children's ethnic socialization: Pluralism and development* (pp. 92–100). Newbury Park, CA: Sage.

Kaye, K. (1982). *The mental and social life of babies: How parents create persons.* Chicago: University of Chicago Press.

Kaye, K., & Fogel, A. (1980). The temporal structure of face-to-face communication between mothers and infants. *Developmental Psychology, 16,* 454–464.

Kilpatrick, K., Litt, M., & Williams, L. (1997). Post-traumatic stress disorder in child witnesses to domestic violence. *American Journal of Orthopsychiatry, 67,* 639–643.

Klee, L., Kronstadt, D., & Zlotnick, C. (1997). Foster care's youngest: A preliminary report. *American Journal of Orthopsychiatry, 67,* 290–298.

Knitzer, J., & Aber, J. L. (1995). Young children in poverty: Facing the facts. *American Journal of Orthopsychiatry, 65,* 174–176.

Kochanska, G., Aksan, N., & Koenig, A. (1995). A longitudinal study of the roots of preschoolers' conscience: Committed compliance and emerging internalization. *Child Development, 66,* 1752–1769.

Kohlberg, L. (1984). *Essays on moral development: Vol. II. The psychology of moral development.* New York: Harper & Row.

Kopp, C. B. (1982). Antecedents of self-regulation: A developmental perspective. *Developmental Psychology, 18,* 199–214.

Kopp, C. B., & Kaler, S. R. (1989). Risk in infancy: Origins and implications. *American Psychologist, 44*(2), 224–230.

Kozol, J. (1991). *Savage inequalities: Children in America's schools.* New York: Crown.

Kurtz, P. D., Gaudin, J. M., Wodarski, J. S., & Howing, P. T. (1993). Maltreatment and the school aged child: School performance consequences. *Child Abuse and Neglect, 17,* 581–589.

Ladd, G. W. (1990). Having friends, keeping friends, making friends, and being liked by peers in the classroom: Predictors of children's early school adjustment? *Child Development, 61,* 1081–1100.

La Freniere, P., & Sroufe, L. A. (1985). Profiles of peer competence in the preschool: Interrelations between measures, influence of social ecology and relation to attachment history. *Developmental Psychology, 21,* 58–68.

Lamb, M. E., & Roopnarine, J. L. (1979). Peer influences on sex-role development in preschoolers. *Child Development, 50,* 1219–1222.

Landry, S. H., Chapieski, M. L., Richardson, M. A., Palmer, J., & Hall, S. (1990). The social competence of children born prematurely: Effects of medical complications and parent behaviors. *Child Development, 61,* 1605–1616.

Lansky, L. L., List, M. A., Lansky, S. B., Cohen, M. E., & Sinks, L. F. (1985). Toward the development of a play performance scale for children (PPSC). *Cancer, 56,* 1837–1840.

Lazarus, R. S., & Folkman, S. (1983). *Stress, appraisal and coping.* New York: Springer-Verlag.

Leach, P. (1978). *Your baby and child.* New York: Knopf.

Lehmann, P. (1997). Post-traumatic stress disorder (PTSD) in a sample of child witnesses to mother assault. *Journal of Family Violence, 12,* 241–253.

LeVine, R. A., & Miller, P. M. (1990). Commentary. *Human Development, 33,* 73–80.

Lewis, M. L., & Brooks-Gunn, J. (1979). *Social cognition and the acquisition of self.* New York: Plenum.

Lewis, R. (1966). *Miracles: Poems by children of the English-speaking world.* New York: Simon & Schuster.

Li, J., & Bennett, N. (1994). *Young children in poverty: A statistical update.* New York: National Center for Children in Poverty, Columbia University School of Public Health.

Lieberman, A. F. (1992). Infant–parent psychotherapy with toddlers. *Development and Psychopathology, 4,* 559–574.

Lieberman, A. F. (1993). *The emotional life of the toddler.* New York: Free Press.

Lieberman, A. F., & Pawl, J. H. (1990). Disorders of attachment and secure base behavior in the second year of life: Conceptual issues and clinical interventions. In M. T. Greenberg, D. Cicchetti, & E. M. Cummings (Eds.), *Attachment in the preschool years: Theory, research and intervention* (pp. 375–397). Chicago: University of Chicago Press.

Lieberman, A. F., & Pawl, J. H. (1993). Infant–parent psychotherapy. In C. H. Zeanah, Jr. (Ed.), *Handbook of infant mental health* (pp. 427–442). New York: Guilford Press.

Liederman, P. H. (1989). Relationship disturbances and development through the life cycle. In A. J. Sameroff & R. N. Emde (Eds.), *Relationship disturbances in early childhood* (pp. 161–192). New York: Basic Books.

Littner, N. (1960). The child's need to repeat his past: Some implications for placement. *Social Services Review, 34,* 128–148.

Locke, J. L. (1993). *The child's path to spoken language.* Cambridge, MA: Harvard University Press.

Londerville, S., & Main, M. (1981). Security of attachment, compliance, and maternal training methods in the second year of life. *Developmental Psychology, 17,* 289–299.

Long, N., & Forehand, R. (1987). The effects of divorce and marital conflict on children's personality development: An overview. *Journal of Developmental and Behavioral Pediatrics, 8,* 292–296.

Luthar, S. S., & Zigler, E. (1991). Vulnerability and competence: A review of research on resilience in childhood. *American Journal of Orthopsychiatry, 61,* 6–22.

Lyon, G. R. (1996). Learning disabilities. In E. J. Mash & R. A. Barkley (Eds.), *Child psychopathology* (pp. 390–435). New York: Guilford Press.

Lyons-Ruth, K. (1996). Attachment relationships among children with aggressive behavior problems: The role of disorganized early attachment patterns. *Journal of Clinical and Consulting Psychology, 64,* 64–73.

Lyons-Ruth, K., Connell, D., Zoll, D., & Stahl, J. (1987). Infants at social risk: Relations among maltreatment, maternal behavior and infant attachment behavior. *Developmental Psychology, 23,* 223–232.

Lyons-Ruth, K., Repacholi, B., McLeod, S., & Silva, E. (1991). Disorganized attachment behavior in infancy: Short-term stability, maternal and infant correlates and risk-related subtypes. *Development and Psychopathology, 3,* 377–396.

Lyons-Ruth, K., & Zeanah, C. H., Jr. (1993). The family context of infant mental health: I, Affective development in the primary caregiving relationship. In C. H. Zeanah, Jr. (Ed.), *Handbook of infant mental health* (pp. 14–37). New York: Guilford Press.

Lyons-Ruth, K., Zeanah, C. H., & Benoit, D. (1996). Disorder and risk for disorder during infancy and toddlerhood. In E. J. Mash & R. A. Barkley (Eds.), *Child psychopathology* (pp. 457–491). New York: Guilford Press.

Maccoby, E. E. (1983). Social-emotional development and response to stressors. In N. Garmezy & M. Rutter (Eds.), *Stress, coping and development in children* (pp. 217–234). New York: McGraw-Hill.

Maccoby, E. E. (1988). Gender as a social category. *Developmental Psychology, 24,* 755–765.

MacFarlane, J. (1975). Olfaction in the development of social preferences in the human neonate. In M. Hoffer (Ed.), *Parent–infant interaction*. Amsterdam: Elsevier.

Mahler, M. S., Pine, F., & Bergman, A. (1975). *The psychological birth of the human infant*. New York: Basic Books.

Main, M., & Cassidy, J. (1988). Categories of response to reunion with the parent at age six: Predictable from infant attachment classifications and stable over a one-month period. *Developmental Psychology, 24,* 415–426.

Main, M., & Hesse, E. (1990). Parents' unresolved traumatic experiences are related to infant disorganized attachment status: Is frightened and or/ frightening parental behavior the linking mechanism? In M. T. Greenberg, D. Cicchetti, & E. M. Cummings (Eds.), *Attachment in the preschool years: Theory, research and intervention* (pp. 161–184). Chicago: U. of Chicago Press.

Main, M., Kaplan, N., & Cassidy, J. (1985). Security in infancy, childhood and adulthood: A move to the level of respresentation. In I. Bretherton & E. Waters (Eds.), Growing points of attachment theory and research. *Monographs of the Society for Research in Child Development, 50*(1–2, Serial No. 209), 66–106.

Main, M., & Solomon, J. (1990). Procedures for identifying infants as disorganized/disoriented during the Ainsworth Strange Situation. In M. T. Greenberg, D. Cicchetti, & E. M. Cummings (Eds.). *Attachment in the preschool years: Theory, research and intervention* (pp. 121–160). Chicago: University of Chicago Press.

Malatesta, C. Z., & Haviland, J. M. (1985). Signals, symbols and socialization: The modification of emotional expression in human development. In M. Lewis & C. Saarni (Eds.), *The socialization of emotions* (pp. 89–116). New York: Plenum.

Malmquist, C. P. (1986). Children who witness parental murder: Post-traumatic aspects. *Journal of the American Academy of Child Psychiatry, 25*(3), 320–325.

Maluccio, A. N., & Fein, E. (1985). Growing up in foster care. *Children and Youth Services Review, 7,* 123–134.

Marcus, D. E., & Overton, W. F. (1978). The development of gender constancy and sex role preferences. *Child Development, 49,* 434–444.

Martin, C. L., & Halverson, C. E. (1981). A schematic processing model of sex typing and stereotyping in children. *Child Development, 52,* 1119–1134.

Marvin, R. S. (1977). An ethological-cognitive model for the attenuation of mother–child attachment behavior. In T. Alloway, L. Kramer, & P. Pilner (Eds.), *Advances in the study of communication and affect: Vol. 3. Attachment behavior* (pp. 25–60). New York: Plenum.

Marvin, R. S., & Stewart, R. B. (1990). A family systems framework for the study of attachment. In M. T. Greenberg, D. Cicchetti, & E. M. Cummings (Eds.), *Attachment in the preschool years: Theory, research and intervention* (pp. 51–86). Chicago: University of Chicago Press.

Maslin-Cole, C., & Spieker, S. J. (1990). Attachment as a basis for independent motivation: A view from risk and nonrisk samples. In M. T. Greenberg, D. Cicchetti, & E. M. Cummings (Eds.), *Attachment in the preschool years: Theory, research and intervention* (pp. 245–272). Chicago: University of Chicago Press.

Masten, A. S., Best, K. M., & Garmezy, N. (1990). Resilience and development: Contributions from the study of children who overcome adversity. *Development and Psychopathology, 2,* 425–444.

Matas, L., Arend, R., & Sroufe, L. A. (1978). Continuity of adaptation in the second year: The relationship between quality of attachment and later competent functioning. *Child Development, 49,* 547–555.

Mayes, S. D. (1991). Play assessment of preschool hyperactivity. In C. E. Schaefer, K. Gitlin, & A. Sandgrund (Eds.), *Play diagnosis and assessment* (pp. 249–282). New York: Wiley.

McClosky, L., Figueredo, A., & Koss, M. (1995). The effects of systemic family violence on children's mental health. *Child Development, 66,* 1239–1261.

McDonough, S. C. (1993). Interaction guidance: Understanding and treating early infant–caregiver relationship disturbances. In C. H. Zeanah, Jr. (Ed.), *Handbook of infant mental health* (pp. 414–426). New York: Guilford Press.

McFadyen, A. (1994). *Special care babies and their developing relationships.* New York: Routledge.

McFarlane, A. C. (1995). Stress and disaster. In S. E. Hobfoll & M. deVries (Eds.), *Extreme stress and communities: Impact and intervention* (pp. 247–265). Dordrecht, The Netherlands: Kluwer.

McGee, R., & Wolfe, D. A. (1991). Psychological maltreatment: Towards an operational definition. *Development and Psychopathology, 3,* 3–18.

McLoyd, V. C. (1989). Socialization and development in a changing economy: The effects of paternal job and income loss on children. *American Psychologist, 44,* 293–302.

McLoyd, V. C. (1990). The impact of economic hardship on black families: Psychological distress, parenting and socioemotional development. *Child Development, 61,* 311–346.

McLoyd, V. C., & Wilson, L. (1991). The strain of living poor: Parenting, social support and parent mental health. In A. C. Huston (Ed.), *Children in poverty: Child development and public policy.* New York: Cambridge University Press.

Meisels, S. J. (1996). Charting the continuum of assessment and intervention. In S. J. Meisels & E. Fenichel (Eds.), *New visions for the developmental assessment of infants and young children* (pp. 27–52). Washington, DC: Zero to Three.

Meltzoff, A. N. (1988). Infant imitation after a 1-week delay: Long term memory for novel acts and multiple stimuli. *Developmental Psychology, 24,* 470–476.

Meltzoff, A. N., & Borton, R. W. (1979). Intermodal matching by human neonates. *Nature, 282,* 403–404.

Messer, S. C., & Beidel, D. C. (1994). Psychosocial correlates of childhood anxiety disorders. *Journal of the American Academy of Child and Adolescent Psychiatry, 33,* 975–983.

Meyer, C. H. (1993). *Assessment in social work practice.* New York: Columbia University Press.

Michaelson, L., & Lewis, M. (1985). What do children know about emotions and when do they know it? In M. Lewis & C. Saarni (Eds.), *The socialization of emotions* (pp. 117–140). New York: Plenum.

Minde, K. (1993). Prematurity and serious medical illness in infancy: Implications for development and intervention. In C. H. Zeanah, Jr. (Ed.), *Handbook of infant mental health* (pp. 87–105). New York: Guilford Press.

Minde, K., & Stewart, D. (1988). Psychiatric services in the neonatal intensive care unit. In R. Cohen (Ed.), *Psychiatric consultation in childbirth settings* (pp. 151–164). New York: Plenum Press.

Mindel, C. H. (1980). Extended families among urban Mexican Americans, Anglos and blacks. *Hispanic Journal of Behavioral Sciences, 2,* 21–34.

Molin, R. (1988). Treatment of children in foster care: Issues of collaboration. *Child Abuse and Neglect, 12,* 241–250.

Mossler, D. G., Marvin, R. S., & Greenberg, M. T. (1976). Conceptual perspective taking in 2- to 6-year-old children. *Developmental Psychology, 12,* 85–86.

Mueller, N., & Silverman, N. (1989). Peer relations in maltreated children. In D. Cicchetti & V. Carlson (Eds.), *Child maltreatment: Theory and research on the causes and consequences of child abuse and neglect* (pp. 569–578). Cambridge, UK: Cambridge University Press.

Mulhern, R. K., Wasserman, A. L., Friedman, A. G., & Fairclough, D. (1989). Social competence and behavioral adjustment of children who are long-term survivors of cancer. *Pediatrics, 83,* 18–25.

National Research Council (1993). *Understanding child abuse and neglect.* Washington, DC: National Academy Press.

Neimark, E. D., Slotnick, N. S., & Ulrich, T. (1971). Development of memorization strategies. *Developmental Psychology, 5,* 427–432.

Nelson, K. (1989). Monologue as representation of real-life experience. In K.

Nelson (Ed.), *Narratives from the crib* (pp. 27–72). Cambridge, MA: Harvard University Press.

Newcomb, A. F., & Bagwell, C. (1995). Children's friendship relations: A meta-analytic review. *Psychological Bulletin, 117,* 306–347.

O'Brien, M. (1992). Gender identity and sex roles. In V. B. Van Hasselt & M. Hersen (Eds.), *Handbook of social development: A lifespan perspective* (pp. 325–345). New York: Plenum.

Ornitz, E. M., & Pynoos, R. S. (1989). Startle modulation in children with posttraumatic stress disorder. *American Journal of Psychiatry, 146,* 866–870.

Osofsky, J. D. (1996a). Introduction. In J. D. Osofsky & E. Fenichel (Eds.), *Islands of safety: Assessing and treating young victims of violence* (pp. 5–8). Washington, DC: Zero to Three.

Osofsky, J. D. (Ed.). (1996b). *Children and youth violence: Searching for solutions.* New York: Guilford Press.

Osofsky, J. D., & Eberhart-Wright, A. (1988). Affective exchanges between high risk mothers and infants. *International Journal of Psycho-Analysis, 69,* 221–231.

Paley, V. G. (1981). *Wally's stories: Conversations in the kindergarten.* Cambridge, MA: Harvard University Press.

Paley, V. G. (1986). *Mollie is three: Growing up in school.* Chicago: University of Chicago Press.

Paley, V. G. (1988). *Bad guys don't have birthdays: Fantasy play at four.* Chicago: University of Chicago Press.

Parker, J. G., & Asher, S. R. (1987). Peer relations and later personal adjustment: Are low-accepted children at risk? *Psychological Bulletin, 102,* 357–359.

Parker, S. J., & Zuckerman, B. S. (1990). Therapeutic aspects of the assessment process. In S. J. Meisels & J. P. Shonkoff (Eds.), *Handbook of early intervention* (pp. 370–369). New York: Cambridge University Press.

Patterson, G. R. (1982). *A social learning approach: 3. Coercive family process.* Eugene, OR: Castalia.

Patterson, G. R., DeBaryshe, B. D., & Ramsey, E. (1989). A developmental perspective on antisocial behavior. *American Psychologist, 44,* 329–335.

Pearce, J. W., & Pezzot-Pearce, T. D. (1997). *Psychotherapy of abused and neglected children.* New York: Guilford Press.

Pellegrini, A. (1987). Rough-and-tumble play: Developmental and educational significance. *Educational Psychologist, 22,* 23–43.

Pellegrini, A. D., & Jones, I. (1993). Play, toys and language. In J. H. Goldstein (Ed.), *Toys, play and child development* (pp. 27–44). Cambridge, UK: Cambridge University Press.

Peller, L. E. (1954). Libidinal development as reflected in play. *Psychoanalysis, 3,* 3–11.

Perry, B. D. (1994). Neurobiological sequelae of childhood trauma: Posttraumatic stress disorders in children. In M. Murberg (Ed.), *Catecholamine function in post-traumatic stress disorder: Emerging concepts* (pp. 233–255). Washington, DC: American Psychiatric Press.

Piaget, J. (1948). *The moral judgment of the child.* Glencoe, IL: Free Press.

Piaget, J. (1951). *Judgment and reasoning in the child.* London: Routledge & Kegan Paul.

Piaget, J. (1952a). *The language and thought of the child.* London: Routledge & Kegan Paul.

Piaget, J. (1952b). *The origins of intelligence in children.* New York: International Universities Press.

Piaget, J. (1962). *Play, dreams and imitation in childhood.* New York: Norton.

Piaget, J., & Inhelder, B. (1969). *The psychology of the child.* New York: Basic Books.

Pipher, M. (1994). *Reviving Ophelia: Saving the selves of adolescent girls.* New York: Ballantine Books.

Powell, G. J. (1985). Self-concepts among Afro-American students in racially isolated minority schools: Some regional differences. *Journal of the American Academy of Child Psychiatry, 24,* 142–149.

Proch, K., & Taber, M. A. (1985). Placement disruption: A review of the research. *Children and Youth Services Review, 7,* 309–320.

Pynoos, R. S., Steinberg, A. M., & Goenjian, A. (1996). Traumatic stress in childhood and adolescence: Recent developments and current controversies. In B. van der Kolk, A. C. McFarlane, & L. Weisaeth (Eds.), *Traumatic stress: The effects of overwhelming experience on mind, body, and society.* (pp. 331–358). New York: Guilford Press.

Radke-Yarrow, M., McCann, K., DeMulder, E., Belmont, B., Martinez, P., & Richardson, D. T. (1995). Attachment in the context of high-risk conditions. *Development and Psychopathology, 7,* 247–265.

Radke-Yarrow, M., & Sherman, T. (1990). Hard growing: Children who survive. In J. Rolf, A. S. Masten, D. Cicchetti, K. H. Neuchterlin, & S. Weintraub (Eds.), *Risk and protective factors in the development of psychopathology* (pp. 87–119). New York: Cambridge University Press.

Radke-Yarrow, M., & Zahn-Waxler, C. (1984). Roots, motives and patterning in children's prosocial behavior. In E. Staub, D. Bar-Tal, J. Karylowski, & J. Reykowski (Eds.), *The development and maintenance of prosocial behavior: International perspectives on positive morality* (pp. 81–99). New York: Plenum.

Reed, E. S. (1995). Becoming a self. In P. Rochat (Ed.), *The self in infancy: Theory and research* (pp. 431–448). Amsterdam: Elsevier.

Reese, M. F. (1982). Growing up: The impact of loss and change. In D. Belle (Ed.), *Lives in stress: Women and depression* (pp. 65–88). Beverly Hills, CA: Sage.

Reid, S. (1993). Game play. In C. E. Schaefer (Ed.), *The therapeutic powers of play.* Northvale, NJ: Aronson.

Reinecke, M. A., Dattilio, F. M., & Freeman, A. (1996). General issues. In M. A. Reinecke, F. M. Dattilio, & A. Freeman (Eds.), *Cognitive therapy with children and adolescents* (pp. 1–9). New York: Guilford Press.

Reiss, D. (1989). The represented and practicing family: Contrasting visions of family continuity. In A. J. Sameroff & R. N. Emde (Eds.), *Relationship disturbances in early childhood* (pp. 191–220). New York: Basic Books.

Rende, R., & Plomin, R. (1993). Families at risk for psychopathology: Who becomes affected and why? *Development and Psychopathology, 5,* 529–540.

Renken, B., Egeland, B., Marvinney, D., Mangelsdorf, S., & Sroufe, L. A. (1989). Early childhood antecedents of aggression and passive-withdrawal in early elementary school. *Journal of Personality, 57,* 257–281.

Rice, M. L. (1989). Children's language acquisition. *American Psychologist, 42,* 149–156.

Richters, J. E., & Martinez, P. E. (1993). Violent communities, family choices, and children's chances: An algorithm for improving the odds. *Development and Psychopathology, 5,* 609–627.

Rieder, C., & Cicchetti, D. (1989). Organizational perspective on cognitive control functioning and cognitive–affective balance in maltreated children. *Developmental Psychology, 25,* 382–393.

Rogoff, B. (1990). *Apprenticeship in thinking: Cognitive development in social context.* New York: Oxford University Press.

Rose, S. A., & Ruff, H. A. (1987). Cross-modal abilities in human infants. In J. D. Osofsky (Ed.), *Handbook of infant development* (2nd ed., pp. 318–362). New York: Wiley.

Rosenthal, J., Motz, J., Edmonson, D., & Groze, V. (1991). A descriptive study of abuse and neglect in out-of-home placement. *Child Abuse and Neglect, 15,* 249–260.

Rosser, R. (1994). *Cognitive development: Psychological and biological perspectives.* Needham Heights, MA: Allyn & Bacon.

Rotherham, M. J., & Phinney, J. S. (1987). Introduction: Definitions and perspectives in the study of children's ethnic socialization. In J. S. Phinney & M. J. Rotherham (Eds.), *Children's ethnic socialization: Pluralism and development* (pp. 10–28). Newbury Park, CA: Sage.

Rovee-Collier, C. K. (1990). The "memory system" of prelinguistic infants. In A. Diamond (Ed.), *The development and neural bases of higher cognitive functions.* New York: New York Academy of Sciences.

Rowland, J. H. (1989). Developmental stage and adaptation: Child and adolescent model. In J. C. Holland & J. H. Rowland (Eds.), *Handbook of psychooncology* (pp. 519–543). New York: Oxford University Press.

Rubin, K. H., Bream, L., & Rose-Krasnor, L. (1991). Social problem solving and aggression in childhood. In D. J. Pepler & K. H. Rubin (Eds.), *The development and treatment of childhood aggression* (pp. 219–248). Hillsdale, NJ: Erlbaum.

Rubin, K. H., Coplan, R. J., Fox, N. A., & Calkins, S. D. (1995). Emotionality, emotion regulation, and preschoolers' social adaptation. *Development and Psychopathology, 7,* 49–62.

Rubin, K. H., Moller, L., & Emptage, A. (1987). The Preschool Behavior Questionaire: A useful index of behavior problems in elementary school–age children? *Canadian Journal of the Behavioural Sciences, 19,* 86–100.

Rubin, K. H., & Rose-Krasnor, L. (1992). Interpersonal problem solving and social competence in children. In V. B. Van Hasselt & M. Hersen (Eds.), *Handbook of social development: A lifespan perspective* (pp. 229–256). New York: Plenum.

Ruble, D. (1983). The development of social comparison processes and their role achievement-related self-socialization. In E. T. Higgins, D. Ruble, & W. Hartup (Eds.), *Social cognition and social behavior: Developmental perspectives* (pp. 162–188). New York: Cambridge University Press.

Rushton, J. P. (1976). Socialization and the altruistic behavior of children. *Psychological Bulletin, 83,* 898–913.

Rutter, M. (1981). Stress, coping and development: Some issues and some questions. *Journal of Child Psychology and Psychiatry, 22,* 326–356.

Rutter, M. (1985). Resilience in the face of adversity: Protective factors and resistance to psychiatric disorder. *British Journal of Psychiatry, 147,* 598–611.

Rutter, M. (1987). Psychosocial resilience and protective mechanisms. *American Journal of Orthopsychiatry, 57,* 316–331.

Rutter, M. (1989). Psychological sequelae of brain damage in children. *American Journal of Psychiatry, 138,* 1533–1544.

Rutter, M. (1990). Psychosocial resilience and protective mechanisms. In J. Rolf, A. S. Masten, D. Cicchetti, K. H. Neuchterlin, & S. Weintraub (Eds.), *Risk and protective factors in the development of psychopathology* (pp. 181–214). New York: Cambridge University Press.

Rutter, M., & Garmezy, N. (1983). Developmental psychopathology. In E. M. Hetherington (Ed.), *Handbook of child psychology: Vol. 4. Socialization, personality and social development* (pp. 775–911). New York: Wiley.

Rutter, M., & Quinton, D. (1984). Parental psychiatric disorder: Effects on children. *Psychological Medicine, 14,* 853–880.

Saarni, C. (1979). Children's understanding of display rules for expressive behavior. *Developmental Psychology, 15,* 424–429.

Salzinger, S., Feldman, R. S., Hammer, M., & Rosario, M. (1993). The effects of physical abuse on children's social relationships. *Child Development, 64,* 169–187.

Sameroff, A. J. (1993). Models of development and developmental risk. In C. H. Zeanah, Jr. (Ed.), *Handbook of infant mental health* (pp. 3–13). New York: Guilford Press.

Sameroff, A. J., & Chandler, M. J. (1975). Reproductive risk and the continuum of caretaking casualty. In F. D. Horowitz, E. M. Hetherington, S. Scarr-Salapatek, & G. Siegel (Eds.), *Review of child development research* (Vol. 4, pp. 187–244). Chicago: University of Chicago Press.

Sameroff, A. J., & Emde, R. N. (Eds.). (1989). *Relationship disturbances in early childhood.* New York: Basic Books.

Sameroff, A. J., & Haith, M. M. (1996). Interpreting developmental transitions. In A. J. Sameroff & M. M. Haith (Eds.), *The five to seven year shift: The age of reason and responsibility* (pp. 3–15). Chicago: University of Chicago Press.

Sameroff, A. J., Seifer, R., Baldwin, C. P., & Baldwin, A. (1993). Stability of intelligence from preschool to adolescence: The influence of social and family risk factors. *Child Development, 64,* 96–105.

Samuels, A., & Taylor, M. (1994). Children's ability to distinguish fantasy events from real life events. *British Journal of Developmental Psychology, 12,* 417–427.

Sander, L. (1975). Infant and caretaking environment: Investigation and conceptualization of adaptive behavior in a system of increasing complexity. In E. J. Anthony (Ed.), *Explorations in child psychiatry* (pp. 129–166). New York: Plenum.

Sarnoff, C. A. (1976). *Latency.* Northvale, NJ: Aronson.

Sarnoff, C. A. (1987). *Psychotherapeutic strategies in the latency years.* Northvale, NJ: Aronson.

Scaife, M., & Bruner, J. (1975). The capacity for joint visual attention in the infant. *Nature, 253,* 265–266.

Schaefer, C. E., & Reid, S. E. (Eds.). (1986). *Game play.* New York: Wiley.

Schafer, W. (1979). Expressive symbolism in spontaneous play before two years of age. In D. Wolf (Ed.), *New directions in child development: No. 3. Early symbolization.* San Francisco: Jossey-Bass.

Schneider-Rosen, K. (1990). The developmental reorganization of attachment relationships: Guidelines for classification beyond infancy. In M. T. Greenberg, D. Cicchetti, & E. M. Cummings (Eds.), *Attachment in the preschool years: Theory, research and intervention* (pp. 185–220). Chicago: University of Chicago Press.

Seifer, R., & Sameroff, A. J. (1986). The concept, measurement and interpretation of temperament in young children. *Advances in Developmental and Behavioral Pediatrics, 7,* 1–43.

Seligman, M. E. (1975). *Helplessness: On depression, development and death.* San Francisco: Freeman.

Seligman, M. E., Kaslow, N., Alloy, N. B., Peterson, C., Tanenbaum, R. L., & Abramson, L. Y. (1984). Attributional style and depressive symptoms among children. *Journal of Abnormal Psychology, 93*(2), 235–238.

Selman, R. L. (1980). *The growth of interpersonal understanding.* New York: Academic Press.

Shantz, C. U. (1987). Conflicts between children. *Child Development, 58,* 282–305.

Shapiro, E. R. (1994). *Grief as a family process.* New York: Guilford Press.

Shapiro, T., & Perry, R. (1976). Latency revisited: The age 7 plus or minus 1. *Psychoanalytic Study of the Child, 31,* 79–105.

Share, D., Givens, C., Davies, D., Eley, E., & Chesler, J. (1992). "A star is born" in Ypsilanti. *American Journal of Public Health, 82,* 611–612.

Shatz, K. (1992). Dividing up the neocortex. *Science, 258,* 237–238.

Sher, K. J., Walitzer, K. S., Wood, P. K., & Brent, E. E. (1991). Characteristics of children of alcoholics: Putative risk factors, substance use and abuse, and psychopathology. *Journal of Abnormal Psychology, 100,* 427–448.

Sheridan, M. J. (1994). A proposed model of substance abuse, family functioning and abuse/neglect. *Child Abuse and Neglect, 19,* 519–530.

Siegler, R. S. (1996). Unidimensional thinking, multidimensional thinking and characteristic tendencies of thought. In A. J. Sameroff & M. M. Haith (Eds.), *The five to seven year shift: The age of reason and responsibility* (pp. 63–84). Chicago: University of Chicago Press.

Silverman, P. R., & Worden, J. W. (1992). Children's reactions in the early months after the death of a parent. *American Journal of Orthopsychiatry, 62,* 93–104.

Silverman, P. R., Nickman, S., & Worden, J. W. (1992). Detachment revisited: The child's reconstruction of a dead parent. *American Journal of Orthopsychiatry, 62*, 494–503.

Singer, D. G., & Singer, J. L. (1990). *The house of make-believe: Play and the developing imagination.* Cambridge, MA: Harvard University Press.

Singer, J. L. (1993). Imaginative play and adaptive development. In J. H. Goldstein (Ed.), *Toys, play and child development* (pp. 6–26). Cambridge, UK: Cambridge University Press.

Slaby, R. G., & Frey, K. S. (1975). Gender constancy and selective attention to same sex models. *Child Development, 46*, 849–856.

Smith, P. K., & Cowie, H. (1991). *Understanding children's development* (2nd ed.). Cambridge, MA: Blackwell.

Sorce, J. F., Emde, R. N., Campos, J. J., & Klinnert, M. D. (1985). Maternal emotional signaling: Its effect on visual cliff behavior of one-year-olds. *Developmental Psychology, 21*, 195–200.

Spangler, G., & Grossman, K. E. (1993). Biobehavioral organization in securely and insecurely attached infants. *Child Development, 64*, 1439–1450.

Speltz, M. L. (1990). The treatment of preschool conduct problems: An integration of behavioral and attachment concepts. In M. T. Greenberg, D. Cicchetti, & E. M. Cummings (Eds.), *Attachment in the preschool years: Theory, research and intervention* (pp. 399–426). Chicago: University of Chicago Press.

Spencer, M. B. (1985). Cultural cognition and social cognition as identity factors in black children's personal–social growth. In M. B. Spencer, G. K. Brookins, & W. R. Allen (Eds.), *Beginnings: The social and affective development of black children* (pp. 215–230). Hillsdale, NJ: Erlbaum.

Spencer, M. B. (1987). Black children's identity formation: Risk and resilience of castelike minorities. In J. S. Phinney & M. J. Rotherham (Eds.), *Children's ethnic socialization: Pluralism and development* (pp. 103–116). Newbury Park, CA: Sage.

Spencer, M. B. (1990). Development of minority children: An introduction. *Child Development, 61*, 267–269.

Spencer, M. B., & Horowitz, F. D. (1973). Racial attitudes and color concept. Attitude modification in black and Caucasian preschool children. *Developmental Psychology, 9*, 246–254.

Spencer, M. B., & Markstrom-Adams, C. (1990). Identity processes among racial and ethnic minority children in America. *Child Development, 61*, 290–310.

Sroufe, L. A. (1983). Infant–caregiver attachment and patterns of adaptation in preschool: The roots of adaptation and competence. In M. Pelmutter (Ed.), *Minnesota Symposium on Child Psychology* (Vol. 16, pp. 41–83). Hillsdale, NJ: Erlbaum.

Sroufe, L. A. (1989). Relationships, self and individual adaptation. In A. J. Sameroff & R. N. Emde (Eds.), *Relationship disturbances in early childhood* (pp. 70–94). New York: Basic Books.

Sroufe, L. A. (1990). Considering normal and abnormal together: The essence of developmental psychopathology. *Development and Psychopathology, 2,* 335–347.

Sroufe, L. A., Egeland, B., & Kreutzer, T. (1990). The fate of early experience following developmental change: Longitudinal approaches to individual adaptation. *Child Development, 61,* 1363–1373.

Sroufe, L. A., & Fleeson, J. (1986). Attachment and the construction of relationships. In W. W. Hartup & Z. Rubin (Eds.), *Relationships and development* (pp. 51–72). Hillsdale, NJ: Erlbaum.

Sroufe, L. A., & Jacobvitz, D. (1989). Diverging pathways, developmental transformations, multiple etiologies and the problem of continuity in development. *Human Development, 32,* 196–203.

Sroufe, L. A., & Waters, E. (1977). Attachment as an organizational construct. *Child Development, 48,* 1184–1199.

Steinglass, P. (1987). *The alcoholic family.* New York: Basic Books.

Steinman, S. (1981). The experience of children in a joint-custody arrangement. *American Journal of Orthopsychiatry, 51,* 403–414.

Stern, D. N. (1974). The goal and structure of mother–infant play. *Journal of the American Academy of Child Psychiatry, 13,* 402–421.

Stern, D. N. (1977). *The first relationship: Mother and infant.* Cambridge, MA: Harvard University Press.

Stern, D. N. (1983). The early development of schemas of self, other and "self with other." In J. D. Lichtenberg & S. Kaplan (Eds.), *Reflections on self psychology.* Hillsdale, NJ: Erlbaum.

Stern, D. N. (1985). *The interpersonal world of the infant.* New York: Basic Books.

Stern, D. N. (1995). Self/other differentiation in the domain of intimate socioaffective interactions: Some considerations. In P. Rochat (Ed.), *The self in infancy: Theory and research* (pp. 419–430). Amsterdam: Elsevier.

Straus, M. (1983). Ordinary violence, child abuse and wife-beating: What do they have in common? In D. Finkelhor, R. J. Gelles, G. T. Hotaling, & M. A. Straus (Eds.), *The dark side of families: Current family violence research* (pp. 213–234). Beverly Hills, CA: Sage.

Susman, E. J., Hollenbeck, A. R., Nannis, E. D., & Strope, B. E. (1980). A developmental perspective on psychosocial aspects of childhood cancer. In J. L. Schulman & M. J. Kupst (Eds.), *The child with cancer* (pp. 129–142). Springfield, IL: Thomas.

Takahashi, K. (1990). Are the key assumptions of the "Strange Situation" procedure universal? *Human Development, 33,* 23–30.

Taylor, R. D., & Roberts, D. (1995). Kinship support and maternal and adolescent well-being in economically disadvantaged African-American families. *Child Development, 66,* 1585–1597.

Terr, L. (1990). *Too scared to cry: Psychic trauma in childhood.* New York: Harper & Row.

Terr, L. (1991). Childhood traumas: An outline and an overview. *American Journal of Psychiatry, 148,* 10–20.

Teti, D. M., Gelfand, D. M., Messinger, D. S., & Isabella, R. (1995). Maternal depression and the quality of early attachment: An examination of infants, preschoolers and their mothers. *Developmental Psychology, 31,* 364–376.

Thomas, A., & Chess, S. (1977). *Temperament and development.* New York: Brunner-Mazel.

Thomas, A., Chess, S., & Birch, H. G. (1968). *Temperament and behavior disorders in children.* New York: New York University Press.

Thompson, S. K. (1975). Gender labels and early sex role development. *Child Development, 46,* 339–347.

Thorne, B. (1986). Boys and girls together—but mostly apart: Gender arrangements in elementary school. In W. Hartup & Z. Rubin (Eds.), *Relationships and development* (pp. 167–184). Hillsdale, NJ: Erlbaum.

Tomasello, M. (1995). Understanding the self as social agent. In P. Rochat (Ed.), *The self in infancy: Theory and research* (pp. 449–460). Amsterdam: Elsevier.

Trad, P. V., & Greenblatt, E. (1990). Psychological aspects of child stress: Development and the spectrum of coping responses. In L. E. Arnold (Ed.), *Childhood stress* (pp. 23–50). New York: Wiley.

Trevarthen, C., Murray, L., & Hubley, P. (1981). Psychology of infants. In J. A. Davis & J. Dobbing (Eds.), *Scientific foundations of pediatrics* (2nd ed., pp. 211–274). London: Heinemann.

Tronick, E. Z., Als, H., Adamson, L., Wise, S., & Brazelton, T. B. (1978). The infant's response to entrapment between contradictory messages in face-to-face interaction. *Journal of Child Psychiatry, 17,* 1–13.

Tronick, E. Z., Cohn, J. E., & Shea, E. (1986). The transfer of affect between infants and mothers. In T. B. Brazelton & M. Y. Yogman (Eds.), *Affective development in infancy* (pp. 11–26). Norwood, NJ: Ablex.

Tronick, E. Z., & Gianino, A. F., Jr. (1986a). The transmission of maternal disturbance to the infant. In E. Z. Tronick & T. Field (Eds.), *Maternal depression and infant disturbance* (pp. 5–13). San Franciso: Jossey-Bass.

Tronick, E. Z., & Gianino, A. F., Jr. (1986b). Interactive mismatch and repair: Challenges to the coping infant. *Zero to Three, 6,* 1–6.

Troy, M., & Sroufe, L. A. (1987). Victimization among preschoolers: The role of attachment relationship history. *Journal of the American Academy of Child and Adolescent Psychiatry, 26,* 166–172.

Tyson, P., & Tyson, R. (1991). *Psychoanalytic theories of development.* New Haven, CT: Yale University Press.

van der Kolk, B. (1987). *Psychological trauma.* Washington, DC: American Psychiatric Press.

van der Kolk, B., & Fisher, R. (1994). Childhood abuse and neglect and loss of self-regulation. *Bulletin of the Menninger Clinic, 58*(2), 145–168.

Van Dongen-Melman, J. E. W. M., & Sanders-Woudstra, J. A. R. (1986). Psychosocial aspects of childhood cancer: A review of the literature. *Journal of Child Psychology and Psychiatry, 27,* 145–180.

van IJzendoorn, M. (1995). Adult attachment representations, parental responsiveness, and infant attachment: A meta-analysis on the predictive validity of the Adult Attachment Interview. *Psychological Bulletin, 117,* 387–403.

Vaughn, B., Egeland, B., Sroufe, L. A., & Waters, E. (1979). Individual differences in mother–infant attachment at twelve and eighteen months: Stability and change in families under stress. *Child Development, 50,* 971–975.

Volterra, V. (1984). Waiting for the birth of a sibling: The verbal fantasies of a 2-year-old boy. In I. Bretherton (Ed.), *Symbolic play: The development of social understanding* (pp. 219–248). Orlando, FL: Academic Press.

Vondra, J. A., Barnett, D., & Cicchetti, D. (1989). Perceived and actual competence among maltreated and comparison school children. *Development and Psychopathology, 1,* 237–255.

Vondra, J. A., Barnett, D., & Cicchetti, D. (1990). Self-concept, motivation, and competence among preschoolers from maltreating and comparison families. *Child Abuse and Neglect, 14,* 525–540.

Vuchinich, S., Bank, L., & Patterson, G. R. (1992). Parenting, peers and the stability of antisocial behavior in preadolescent boys. *Developmental Psychology, 28,* 510–521.

Wachtel, E. F., & Wachtel, P. L. (1986). *Family dynamics in individual psychotherapy: A guide to clinical strategies.* New York: Guilford Press.

Wallerstein, J. S. (1985). Children of divorce: Preliminary Report of a ten-year follow-up of older children and adolescents. *American Journal of Orthopsychiatry, 55,* 545–553.

Wallerstein, J. S., & Kelly, J. B. (1980). *Surviving the breakup: How children and parents cope with divorce.* New York: Basic Books.

Ward, M. J., & Carlson, E. A. (1995). Associations among adult attachment representations, maternal sensitivity and infant–mother attachment in a sample of adolescent mothers. *Child Development, 66,* 69–79.

Webb, N. B. (1991a). Observation of parental violence: Case of Michael, age 4. In N. B. Webb (Ed.), *Play therapy with children in crisis* (pp. 26–44). New York: Guilford Press.

Webb, N. B. (1991b). Play therapy crisis intervention with children. In N. B. Webb (Ed.), *Play therapy with children in crisis* (pp. 26–44). New York: Guilford Press.

Webb, N. B. (1993a). Assessment of the bereaved child. In N. B. Webb (Ed.), *Helping bereaved children* (pp. 19–42). New York: Guilford Press.

Webb, N. B. (1993b). Counseling and therapy for the bereaved child. In N. B. Webb (Ed.), *Helping bereaved children* (pp. 43–61). New York: Guilford Press.

Webb, N. B. (1996). *Social work practice with children.* New York: Guilford Press.

Weiss, B., Dodge, K. A., Bates, J. E., & Pettit, G. S. (1992). Some consequences of early harsh discipline: Child aggression and a maladaptive social information processing style. *Child Development, 63,* 1321–1335.

Wellman, H. M. (1990). *The child's theory of mind.* Cambridge, MA: MIT Press.

Werner, E. E. (1990). Protective factors and individual resilience. In S. J. Meisels

& J. P. Shonkoff (Eds.), *Handbook of early intervention* (pp. 97–116). New York: Cambridge University Press.

Werner, E. E. (1993). Risk, resilience and recovery: Perspectives from the Kauai Longitudinal Study. *Development and Psychopathology, 5,* 503–515.

Werner, E. E., & Smith, R. S. (1992). *Overcoming the odds: High risk children from birth to adulthood.* Ithaca, NY: Cornell University Press.

Whalen, C. K., & Henker, B. (1992). The social profile of attention-deficit/hyperactivity disorder: Five fundamental facets. In G. Weiss (Ed.), *Child and adolescent psychiatric clinics of North America: Attention-deficit/hyperactivity disorder* (pp. 395–410). Philadelphia: Saunders.

White, M., & Epston, D. (1990). *Narrative means to therapeutic ends.* New York: Norton.

White, S. H. (1996). The child's entry into the "age of reason." In A. J. Sameroff & M. M. Haith (Eds.), *The five to seven year shift: The age of reason and responsibility* (pp. 17–32). Chicago: University of Chicago Press.

Williams, J. S., Singh, B. K., & Singh, B. B. (1994). Urban youth, fear of crime, and resulting defensive actions. *Adolescence, 29,* 323–330.

Wilson, M. N. (1989). Child development in the context of the black extended family. *American Psychologist, 44,,* 380–385.

Winnicott, D. W. (1958). *Collected papers: Through paediatrics to psychoanalysis.* London: Tavistock.

Winnicott, D. W. (1965). *The maturational processes and the facilitating environment.* London: Hogarth Press & Institute for Psychoanalysis.

Winnicott, D. W. (1971). *Playing and reality.* London: Routledge.

Wolfe, D. A. (1987). *Child abuse: Implications for child development and psychopathology.* Newbury Park, CA: Sage.

Wooley, J. D. (1995). The fictional mind: Young children's understanding of imagination, pretense and dreams. *Developmental Review, 15,* 172–211.

Worden, J. W. (1996). *Children and grief: When a parent dies.* New York: Guilford Press.

Yogman, M. W. (1982). Development of the father–infant relationship. In H. Fitzgerald, B. Lester, & M. W. Yogman (Eds.), *Theory and research in behavioral pediatrics* (Vol. I, pp. 221–279). New York: Plenum.

Zahn-Waxler, C., & Kochanska, G. (1990). The development of guilt. In R. Thompson (Ed.), *Nebraska Symposium on Motivation: Vol. 36. Socioemotional development* (pp. 109–137). Lincoln: University of Nebraska Press.

Zahn-Waxler, C., & Smith, K. D. (1992). The development of prosocial behavior. In V. B. Van Hasselt & M. Hersen (Eds.), *Handbook of social development: A lifespan perspective* (pp. 229–256). New York: Plenum.

Zeanah, C. H., Jr., Anders, T. F., Seifer, R., & Stern, D. N. (1989). Implications of research on infant development for psychodynamic theory and practice. *Journal of the American Academy of Child and Adolescent Psychiatry, 28,* 657–668.

Zeltzer, L. K., & LeBaron, S. (1986). Fantasy in children and adolescents with chronic illness. *Developmental and Behavioral Pediatrics, 7,* 195–198.

Zimrin, H. (1986). A profile of survival. *Child Abuse and Neglect, 10,* 339–349.

Zuckerman, B., & Bresnahan, K. (1991). Developmental and behavioral consequences of prenatal drug and alcohol exposure. *Pediatric Clinics of North America, 83,* 1387–1407.

Zuckerman, B., & Brown, E. R. (1993). Maternal substance abuse and infant development. In C. H. Zeanah, Jr. (Ed.), *Handbook of infant mental health* (pp. 143–158). New York: Guilford Press.

Index

transactional approach, 150
understanding child perspective, 111–112
videotaped, 163–164

K

Kagan, Jerome, 3, 52, 114, 120, 122, 139, 140, 177, 191, 192, 193, 194, 196, 200, 260, 265, 278, 296, 307, 316, 319, 320, 329

L

Language development, 3–4
child maltreatment effects, 61
cognitive development and, 311–312
construction of meaning, 179–181
immigrant children, 310–311
infant, 130, 143–144
middle childhood, 309–312, 323, 338
preschool, 238–240, 271
preschooler assessment/treatment, 276–277
self-regulation and, 181, 312
toddler, 174–175, 178–182, 191
word play, 311
Learned helplessness, 78–79

M

Magical thinking, 247–248
Mahler, Margaret, 197–198
Mastery motivation, 146–147
Maturation, 3–4, 114
implications for treatment, 368
infant development, 117–118
Medical treatment, 278–280
Memory
infant development, 139–141
middle childhood development, 319–320
preschool development, 230, 249
toddler development, 177–178
Middle childhood. *See* School-age children
Minority populations, 74–76, 335–336
Mirror recognition, 197
Moral development
internalization of moral controls, 262–263
logical thinking and, 329
middle childhood, 294, 329–330, 340
preschool-age, 227–228, 259–264
toddler, 192–197, 204–205

Motor skills development
infant, 139
preschool-age, 228
school-age, 295–296
toddler, 171

N

Neonate development, 120–123
drug exposure effects, 71

O

Oedipus complex, 267–268

P

Parenting
capacity for fostering attachment, 26
effects on preschooler self-image, 264–265
function, 54
harsh/coercive, 57–59
parental conflict, 55–57
parental psychopathology, 68–70
protective factors, 47–48, 78
risk factors, 54–71
social risk factors, 71–76
in transactional model of development, 4–5
See also Child–caregiver interaction; Family functioning
Patterson, G. R., 58
Peer relationships, 233–236
antisocial school-age children, 306
impulsive behavior in middle childhood, 307–308
preschooler development, 254, 263
school-age development, 295, 305–309
sense of self in middle childhood, 330–331
status hierarchies in middle childhood, 308–309
Personality characteristics
difficult temperament in infants, 125–126, 158–159
parent–child interaction, 53
resilience-associated, 46–47
temperament and school-age peer relations, 307–308
temperament as transactional process, 53–54
temperamental risk factors, 52–53
Pharmacotherapy, 224